Soldiers, Spies, and Statesmen

Soldiers, Spies, and Statesmen
Egypt's Road to Revolt

Hazem Kandil

VERSO
London • New York

First published by Verso 2012
© Hazem Kandil 2012

All rights reserved

The moral rights of the author have been asserted

1 3 5 7 9 10 8 6 4 2

Verso
UK: 6 Meard Street, London W1F 0EG
US: 20 Jay Street, Suite 1010, Brooklyn, NY 11201

www.versobooks.com

Verso is the imprint of New Left Books

ISBN-13: 978-1-84467-961-4

British Library Cataloguing in Publication Data
A catalogue record for this book is available from the British Library

Library of Congress Cataloging-in-Publication Data
Kandil, Hazem.
Soldiers, spies, and statesmen : Egypt's road to revolt / Hazem Kandil.
p. cm.
Includes bibliographical references and index.
ISBN 978-1-84467-961-4 (hardback : alk. paper) — ISBN 978-1-84467-962-1
(ebook)
1. Egypt—Armed Forces—Political activity. 2. Civil-military relations—Egypt.
3. Egypt—Politics and government—1952–1970. 4. Egypt—Politics and government—
1970–1981. 5. Egypt—Politics and government—1981– 6. Revolutions—Egypt—
History—20th century. 7. Revolutions—Egypt—History—21st century. 8. Police
power—Egypt. I. Title.
DT107.827.K36 2012
322.50962—dc23
2012027535

Typeset in Bembo by MJ Gavan, Cornwall
Printed and bound in the US by Maple Vail

To the heroes of Tahrir Square for demonstrating that Egyptians can be everything they thought they were

We would see the defenders of the homeland sooner or later become its enemies, constantly holding a dagger over their fellow citizens, and there would come a time when we would hear them say to the oppressor of their country: "If you order me to plunge my sword into my brother's breast or my father's throat, and into my pregnant wife's entrails, I will do so, even though my right hand is unwilling."

Rousseau, *Discourse on the Origin of Inequality*, 1755

Contents

Introduction   I

Prelude: Countdown to the July 1952 Coup   7

1. The Dark Side of Militarism: The March 1954 Crisis   15

2. Two States Within a State: The Road to June 1967   43

3. Eradicating the Centers of Power: The Corrective
   Revolution of May 1971   99

4. Twilight of the Generals: October 1973 and Its Discontents   113

5. The Long Lull Before the Perfect Storm: Revolt in
   January 2011   175

6. On the Threshold of Power: The Military After the Revolt   221

Acknowledgments   245

Notes   247

Bibliography   273

Index   293

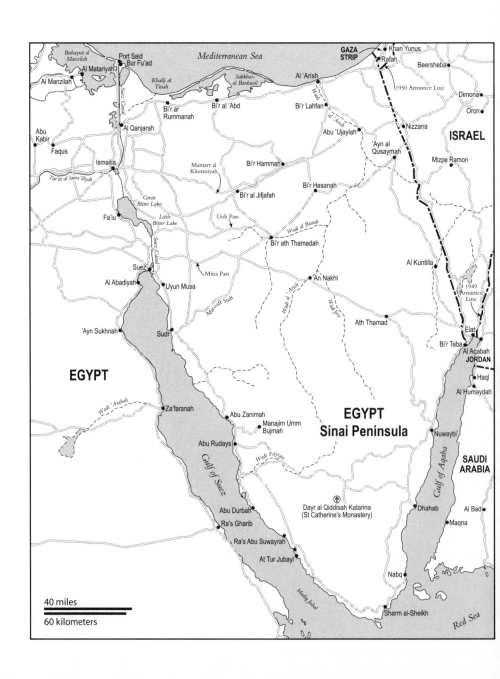

Introduction

Revolutions break our heart whether they fail or succeed. To study revolution is to study how the masses awaken from their slumber and thrust themselves onto the center stage of their own history only to watch their aspirations either usurped or repressed. In the very best of cases, outcomes fall way below expectations. But as disheartening as studying revolutions may be, these rare and enigmatic episodes draw scholars like a magnet. The heroism of everyday life is simply too hard to resist.

Personally, I have been thinking and writing about the prospects of revolution in Egypt for as long as I can remember. Five years ago, I resolved to publish a book about it. But shortly before the manuscript was complete, words jumped right off the page and materialized before my eyes: Egyptians finally revolted. And between a tranquil university campus in Los Angeles and the barricades around Tahrir Square, the manuscript assumed its final form. This time the Angel of History was facing forward; this time the Owl of Minerva took flight at dawn. This was a book about history caught unexpectedly in real time.

The root causes of the January 25 Revolt in Egypt are as impossible to disentangle and rank as those inspiring any other revolution. At the very least one must admit that it is too early to determine why the millions who have been repressed for so long took to the streets on that particular day and vowed not to return home. Political failure, economic crises, ideological agitation, and new forms of organization all appear to have been hopelessly intertwined during these last fatal moments in the life of the regime. Likewise, predicting the outcome of this massive upheaval can only be a matter of speculation at this point; if a new regime did in fact emerge, it would take years to crystallize. So steering away from these formidable—and probably futile—tasks, this book aims at a much more modest and concrete goal, which is to understand what made the revolt possible once its preconditions had arrived. Instead of asking what triggered the uprising, I try to explain how its path was cleared. How was it possible for the people to defy their seemingly invincible dictatorship and get away with it? The answer in this case, as well as in countless others, is the position of the military and security forces. The fact that no revolt triumphs as long as the old regime's coercive organs are willing and capable of suppressing it is one of the few truisms in the field of revolution theory. One might even claim that revolution scholars agree on little else. It is such a commonsense assumption that many—mistakenly—take it for granted.

But why did the agents of coercion fail to protect their political masters in Egypt, even though they had not been worn out by war (like in 1917 Russia) or civil strife (like in 2011 Libya)? The initial success of the revolt in Egypt challenges the simplistic assumption that the military and security forces are essentially the "iron fists" or "heavy hands" of authority, or other such metaphors that portray them as mere appendages rather than independent institutions with distinct corporate interests. The armed forces and the security establishment are full partners in any country's ruling bloc. They work *with* rather than *for* the political apparatus—no matter what the constitution says. And while the interests of the three partners usually coincide (projecting an image of unity), they are never identical.

Machiavelli wrote: "Between the armed and unarmed man no proportion holds, and it is contrary to reason to expect that the armed man should voluntarily submit to him who is unarmed, or that the unarmed man should stand secure among armed retainers."[1] This quintessential axiom rings true today as much as it did in the sixteenth century. Yet the conventional approach to analyzing the relationship between politicians and the custodians of violence is to assume that the military and security act just like other pressure groups, bargaining with civilians to promote their interests. But these powerful institutions have more at stake than other pressure groups—their corporate interests are entwined in the mind of their members with the nation's security (maybe even its existence), and they are therefore determined to compel politicians to assign absolute priority to questions of war against foreign and domestic enemies. And because force is their *ultima ratio*, unlike other social organizations, politicians cannot simply check their influence through legal and administrative means, or even by increasing their popular legitimacy.

So how can civilian leaders subordinate their mighty partners? They usually negotiate a power arrangement demarcating spheres of influence. And the relative weight of each of the three institutions is what renders one regime democratic, another military-dominated, and a third an authoritarian police state. Hence, analyzing any regime must begin by clarifying (or demystifying) the relationship within this "power triangle."* This is the essence of *institutional realism*, which highlights the

---

* What about economic and ideological power? I believe in general that there are three "sources" of social power: coercive, economic, and ideological. Yet in terms of

unrelenting power struggle between self-interested institutions within the state. It conceives the state not as a reified or monolithic body, but as an amalgam of institutions, each with its own power-maximizing agendas. Sometimes they are in conflict (no matter how muted), and at other times they are in alliance, but their aim is always to further their interests. Naturally, this competition results in power configurations that privilege some interests while repressing others, but even slight changes in domestic or geopolitical circumstances can disrupt the existing balance, precipitating a new round of struggle that finally results in new power formations. In this way, we can see that regime type reflects the prevailing balance of power at any given time, not an official hierarchy or ingrained practices.

A good point to start the analysis of the struggle within Egypt's power triangle is the July 1952 coup, when leaders of the Free Officers Movement (just like other coup makers) effected an immediate division of labor among those who ran the government, those who handled security, and those who controlled the officer corps. The components of this internally differentiated regime oscillated between cooperation and competition over the six decades that followed the coup. This is because their interests, while sometimes overlapping, remained essentially separate. The political leadership needed military and/or security support to preserve its power should the masses refuse to obey, but played them off against each other to increase its autonomy and avoid falling hostage to any of them. The security establishment understood that its influence was contingent on the persistence of autocracy, that transition to democracy would spell its downfall from power. As for those who remained in the military, the adverse effects of politicization on the combat readiness and public image of the corps was unsettling. Their preference was to return to the barracks after implementing the needed reforms, and reintervene only if necessary. Driven by varying interests, the three institutions were inevitably drawn into a fervent competition over regime domination, a competition that unfolded within a turbulent domestic and geopolitical environment. The goal was surely not for one institution to eliminate the rest, but rather for one partner in the ruling bloc to subordinate the other two. For years, the shifting alliances among the components of this triangular ruling complex, as well as between them and the intervening forces within and outside the country, continually altered the balance of power

---

"institutions of rule," the modern world knows only three: political, military, and security. Economic and ideological powers are loosely organized in networks and agencies of varying sizes and functions and are mostly located in civil society; their influence over the state must pass through one of the three ruling institutions. This is why economics and ideology are accounted for in this book through their relationship with the three partners in the ruling coalition.

between them. Yet the overall trajectory was one where the political and security components of the regime gradually coalesced to sideline their third partner. The military-dominated order of the 1950s began to founder by the 1970s. The day Hosni Mubarak took office, Egypt had already metamorphosed from a military to a police state. And the day he was deposed was brought forth by a military that saw in the popular uprising an opportunity for retribution.

The work at hand is a revisionist history of the subtle configurations of Egypt's July 1952 regime from start to finish based on primary sources (memoirs, interviews, declassified documents, news clips) and a rereading of a massive amount of secondary literature. The realist historian E. H. Carr said: "The real job of the historian is never simply to ask questions and look up the answers in the book, but to find answers which aren't in the book; and that requires understanding and imagination quite as much as access to facts."[2] In line with his valuable advice, this book essentially reconstructs the critical junctures of the six-decade power struggle that consumed Egypt—a reconstruction centered on institutions as the primary players in a social drama governed by the logic of power. As problematic as this reconstruction might appear to some, it is a necessary first step on the road to clear understanding of the Egyptian question. The political scientist and veteran Egyptian diplomat Boutros Boutros-Ghali began his memoirs by explaining:

> Whoever intends to write about the past must be aware that ... important events rarely unfold in a coherent narrative and sequence; they are scattered through time ... but once the different aspects of a single subject are collected, they appear much more connected than they did in reality. The thoughts and actions that [seem to have] occurred in a random and segregated manner appear in the form of a lucid and flowing sequence. That is why reality as it occurred is truly difficult to grasp ... Historians ... ultimately pass judgments on the [sequence of] events in its full constructed form.[3]

After a brief overview of the military grievances underlying the 1952 coup, the first five chapters of the book examine in great detail the climactic episodes that locked Egypt on its destined pathway: the March 1954 crisis; the June 1967 defeat; the May 1971 "corrective revolution"; the October 1973 war; and the January 2011 revolt. Each chapter outlines the balance of forces, the issues at stake, the constituting events, and the outcome that set the stage for the next encounter. The concluding chapter presents the January 25 Revolt as one of several episodes of struggle, an episode that simply reshuffled the players and reconstituted the field of forces to pave the way for yet another round.

To my knowledge, no other work has yet integrated the whole string of episodes that occurred in the period between 1952 and 2012 in a single analytical narrative, whose unfolding is examined systematically through a distinct theoretical model. In fact, the 2011 revolt has taken many by surprise because of the misguided belief that the Egyptian regime has maintained its military character throughout. In other words, observers unanimously treated army support as a constant, not a variable. Even the earthquake that shook Egypt to the core left this unshakable consensus intact, with writers insisting that the high command had no qualms with the existing order and only reluctantly deserted Mubarak and his cronies because they became liabilities. This is clearly because very few took the military seriously as an institution with distinctive interests, depicting it instead as a supplement to the regime, and conflating the officer corps with any political actor with a military background (whether he be president, intelligence chief, or prime minister).

The key to explaining the initial triumph of the 2011 uprising is therefore to understand that the ruling bloc has not been as well integrated as many assumed. The day the people resolved to overthrow their rulers, the military was no longer invested in the regime; it has become the least privileged member of the ruling coalition that emerged out of the 1952 coup. After a series of wars, conspiracies, coup plots, and socioeconomic transformations, the balance within Egypt's tripartite alliance tilted heavily toward the security apparatus, with the political leadership living contentedly in its shadow, and the military subordinated, if not totally marginalized. The economic niche that the military controlled began to diminish with the aggressive privatization policy of the capitalists who colonized the ruling party; its social privileges were dwarfed by those of the security and political elite; the quality of its manpower deteriorated significantly as a result of the social and educational collapse of the Mubarak years; its exclusive reliance on the United States might have made it impressive on paper, but in reality has crippled its capacity to project regional power. Unfortunately for the political rulers, the effort to isolate the army ultimately backfired because passing the responsibility of domestic repression from the military to the police weakened its coercive power, and the substitution of officers with crony capitalists in leading government posts imposed unbearable austerity measures on the population. The conjunction of these two processes provoked the uprising that was welcomed, rather than repressed, by the armed forces. Once the people took to the streets, it was only natural for officers to rally to their side. The revolt was not a bullet they had to dodge, but rather a golden opportunity to finally outflank their unruly partners and get back on top.

Prelude: Countdown to the July 1952 Coup

The outcome of revolution rarely corresponds with the intentions of those who carry it out, and both the 1952 coup and the 2011 uprising in Egypt are ample proof. Still, exploring the background and intentions of those who attempted to overthrow their rulers helps unlock the logic of the regimes they unintentionally produced. So what exactly inspired the July 23, 1952 coup, which was carried out by a secret cabal of junior officers, calling themselves the Free Officers Movement, and set the stage for Egypt's new regime?

Egypt had been occupied by the British since 1882, under the pretext of protecting the Egyptian sovereign from his own army. In other words, when their predecessors in the military intervened in politics to demand greater rights for officers and citizens, they brought nothing but disaster. For decades, Egypt lay at the mercy of a stifling colonial mandate that not only exploited its resources, and dismissed monarchs and cabinets that defied its will, but also kept the army understaffed, unequipped, and trained for little more than parade ground marches—even when Egyptians won nominal independence and a constitution in 1923, it was through a massive revolt that civilians (spearheaded by the liberal al-Wafd Party) ignited four years earlier, without any military participation. Worse, three decades after this glorious upheaval, the British still had the upper hand. The young and promising King Farouk, who ascended the throne in 1936 (at the age of sixteen), could scarcely rule freely with the British army stationed a few miles away from his capital, and his frustration was redirected toward the country's shaky parliamentary system. To assert royal prerogative in the face of the Wafd majority party, he developed the habit of fabricating reasons (sometimes in agreement with the British) to dissolve parliament, dismiss elected cabinets and place royalists on the political saddle. He even went so far as to form a secret assassination squad, known as the Iron Guards, to dispose of his political enemies. Al-Wafd, in turn, felt morally justified to ally with anyone (including the British) to guarantee their democratic right to lead parliament and the executive. This cat-and-mouse game between the crown and the majority party not only poisoned domestic politics, it empowered the British even further. Exasperation with formal politics diverted popular energy toward a rising religious movement that claimed that national independence could only be achieved through moral reform and strict adherence to Islam. The Muslim Brotherhood, a movement established in the port city of Ismailia on the Suez Canal in 1928, was gaining new followers by the day. Its ranks had swelled by the late 1940s to an alleged 2 million supporters, which represented 10 percent of the population.

This was the Egypt under which the Free Officers (most of them in their thirties at the time of the coup) had come of age. But politics was not the only thing on the mind of those patriotic members of the Free Officers; social disparities and stagnation were equally alarming at the time. Although over half of Egypt's 21 million inhabitants were employed in agriculture, 12,000 large and middling landowners (crowned by 147 elite families) controlled a third of arable land, while close to 11 million peasants remained landless. Observers at the time hoped that the budding capitalist class, emboldened by a sudden influx of wealth, would level the social field by breaking the economic monopoly of this archaic landed class. Egyptian merchants had amassed great fortunes by selling cotton, the country's main export product, at prices inflated by the American Civil War in the 1860s, and again by making the best out of the demand created by the two world wars. However, merchants were slow in making the transition to industrialism. In the 1950s, manufacturing contributed a mere 8 percent to the national income, and most of Egypt's 1.3 million workers were little more than glorified artisans.[1] More importantly, the country's nascent industrialists did not seem determined to transform the regime politically. In other developing countries, especially those laboring under the colonial yoke like Egypt, capitalists usually encouraged coups. Failing to dismantle (or share power with) the landed elite, fearful of radical popular forces, and eager to industrialize the country as rapidly as possible, capitalists elect to hand over political power to a strong executive capable of protecting and furthering their economic interests. That is to say: the bourgeoisie surrendered the sword to the military dictatorship to save the purse.

Egypt had all the ingredients that favored such a scenario during the period preceding the coup. The mostly absentee landed class remained set in its ways, refusing calls for land reform and resisting commercialization and capitalization of agriculture, preferring to squander its wealth on the conspicuous consumption of imported luxuries. More dangerously, it undercut local demand in the countryside by reducing wages and increasing rents. To top it off, capitalists felt politically helpless next to this landed class, occupying only a humble 14 percent of seats in the last parliament before the coup (elected in 1950), compared with the landowners' 63 percent.[2] At the same time, the British occupation and the perceived corruption of political life fueled radical and fascist tendencies among students, professionals, and workers. The demonstrations, strikes, and political assassinations of the postwar years were hardly conducive to business.

Meanwhile, the officer corps itself was becoming larger and middle class in composition. Although the British had for long made sure the army remained limited in size and staffed by meek aristocrats, the gathering storm of Nazism forced it to revise its position and prepare a somewhat reliable force for the dark days ahead—hence their infusion of the military with middle-class members (the sons of middling landowners, professionals, and merchants), those who could actually fight. As part of the preparation for a possible war, the 1936 Anglo-Egyptian Treaty reallocated British officers to the strategic Suez Canal Zone and sanctioned an enlarged Egyptian military to defend the cities and provide logistical support. Over the following decade, the army expanded from 3,000 to 100,000 men, and while its size was reduced after it had served its purpose in the Second World War, it remained relatively large at 36,000 men. The founders of the Free Officers Movement belonged to the first batch of middle-class youth that joined the Military Academy in the late 1930s (eight of the eleven ringleaders came from landless families), and they naturally resented the privileges of the landed elite.[3] It is also conceivable that, by virtue of their links with the British army, Egyptian officers learned to appreciate the importance of modern democratic statehood, and realized that their control over the means of violence put them in the best position to transform their own society accordingly.

Nonetheless, Egyptian capitalists remained wedded to the old aristocracy until the very end. Despite their eagerness to do away with this spendthrift and thoughtless class, they favored compromise over revolution. Egypt's still limited industrialization meant that its proletariat was too small and dispersed to make a bid for power. Increasing radicalization in the cities was perhaps unsettling, but it was certainly far from threatening. Capitalists believed there was still time for reform. Also, massive peasant revolts were equally unlikely because the Egyptian state (comparable to Russia in 1905, and unlike France in 1789) had strong control mechanisms in place in the countryside. Like their Russian counterparts in 1917, Egyptian capitalists worried that spearheading a revolt against the landowning class might ultimately work against them: that the ensuing turmoil might sweep away *all* economic elites, landlords and industrialists alike.

While the bourgeoisie was still weighing its options, the 1952 coup seemed to present a reasonable way out: it promised to undermine large landowners, encourage industry, and keep social unrest in check.

Capitalists, therefore, welcomed the coup at first, though they certainly played no role in initiating it, nor did they manage to control the forces it unleashed. Nor were the Free Officers committed liberals seeking to modernize Egypt in the interests of capitalism. If anything, the movement was notorious for its ideological eclecticism: a few of its members were Islamists; some were socialists, Communists, or fascists; many were pragmatists; and the majority did not think beyond removing the corrupt political elite and returning to the barracks.

So if the coup was neither designed to save a distressed capitalist class nor to modernize and democratize Egypt, what really motivated it? A brief survey of the decade leading to the coup reveals three factors that impinged directly on the military's image and corporate interests: first, humiliation at home and abroad; second, the increased reliance on the military for domestic repression; and third, transferring control over military affairs from elected government to the monarch.

Most historians have noted the demoralizing effect of the so-called February 4, 1942, incident, when officers stationed around the royal palace stood powerless as British tanks surrounded them and forced King Farouk, almost at gunpoint, to replace the existing government (suspected of Nazi sympathies) with one led by the liberal al-Wafd. Although the king did not call on the army to interfere, the officers' pride was irrevocably bruised as they watched their sovereign humiliated by the British ambassador, Sir Miles Lampson (Lord Killearn), while they stood by impotent. Four hundred officers, including the founder and leader of the Free Officers Movement, infantry lieutenant colonel Gamal Abd al-Nasser, met three days later at the Officers Club and decided to organize resistance against British troops. They sent a delegation led by another Free Officer, artillery major Salah Salem, to inform the monarch of their decision, only to be warned by his chamberlain that such a provocation could only push Britain to further escalate.[4] The whole incident left the officers bitter toward the whole political elite: the cowardly king who obeyed foreign dictates, the opportunist majority party that formed a government under foreign tutelage, and of course, the British bullies. In a letter to a school friend, a devastated Nasser bemoaned: "I am ashamed of our army's powerlessness."[5] Major General Muhammad Naguib of the Border Guards, who Nasser later enlisted as a figurehead for the movement (believing that his seniority would lend credibility to the coup), tendered his resignation after the army failed to uphold the country's honor, and described the incident in his memoirs as the turning point that convinced him that a regime change was needed.[6] This distressing episode was also highlighted in the memoirs of other leading Free Officers, such as cavalry lieutenant colonel Khaled Muhi al-Din, who together with Nasser devoured piles of history and philosophy books and explored various political movements in search of a way out for Egypt, as well as signal corps major Anwar al-Sadat, who was imprisoned by the British during the war because of his pro-German activities and was only readmitted to the ranks after secretly joining the king's Iron Guards (while doubling as member of the anti-royalist Free Officers).

But as disheartening as this episode was, the real military disaster took place six years later, in Palestine. The establishment of the State of Israel on Egypt's eastern border prompted an impromptu intervention by the Egyptian military against this new, unwelcome entity. The operation was framed as a defense of Palestinian rights, but it was also an attempt by the crown to play a leading role in the Arab world and thereby regain some of its lost prestige. Dozens of Egyptian officers volunteered to help prevent the wholesale dispossession of their Palestinian neighbors, but they were worried about embroiling the military in a formal war—after all, the last time it had seen combat was 1882, when it tried, fruitlessly, to prevent the British invasion of Egypt. The Palestine War of 1948 would therefore be the first military engagement in over half a century. Furthermore, the army was utterly unprepared in terms of training and equipment, for even though the British employed other colonial armies in their war effort (notably, the Indian), they reserved the Egyptian forces for logistical support. The military's reluctance to fight was voiced by the general staff, and supported by the elected government. King Farouk, however, vetoed both generals and ministers and sent his men to their doom. Defeat inevitably followed. Morale was so low within the military that from September–December 1948, 28 officers and 2,100 soldiers were arrested on the battlefield and deported to Egypt for mutiny.[7] The tragedy turned to scandal when Egyptian Senate hearings in 1949 revealed that European governments, eager to get rid of their defunct weapons from both world wars, offered the king's courtiers substantial commissions to help them unload their stockpiles.[8] To add insult to injury, Nasser was included in the delegation sent to the Greek island of Rhodes in February 1949 to negotiate the first Arab-Israeli truce, a political defeat no less humiliating than the military one.

These devastating defeats were unquestionably what politicized the officer corps. It is no coincidence that the first leaflet distributed by the Free Officers, in November 1949, was devoted to condemning those responsible for the Palestine catastrophe, and the first communiqué they issued after the coup denounced the treacherous politicians responsible for the army's defeat in 1948.[9] In another letter to his school friend, Nasser, the leader of the Free Officers, invoked the image of their soldiers "dashed against fortifications... using defective arms which had been purchased by the king's cronies, a collection of petty crooks who profited from the war by realizing huge commissions from arms deals."[10]

He also described how his battalion had no maps or tents, how he and his men were left without logistic support, subject to contradictory orders from incompetent palace officers. Nasser had spent weeks under siege in the Palestinian village of Fallujah, where he and fellow officers came to see that the civilian leadership was utterly responsible for their current ordeal. Naguib, who was injured twice during the war, reached the same conclusion: the real enemy was in Cairo.[11]

Yet the situation worsened: infuriated soldiers returned home only to find thousands of their countrymen locked up in detention centers, because the king saw the Palestine War as a good opportunity to declare martial law and silence the opposition. The monarch expected the army to finish the job and repress civilian demonstrators, especially after the police proved unreliable—in October 1947 seven thousand police officers organized anti-government strikes, which continued intermittingly until 1952.[12] Things became still more complicated when Britain retracted its promise to evacuate Egypt after the war, and in October 1951, the Egyptian government unilaterally abrogated the 1936 Anglo-Egyptian Treaty in protest. The Egyptian military was caught in an awkward position. The treaty had legitimatized British presence in the Suez Canal Zone, but now Britain officially became an occupying force once more. In its rhetoric, the government encouraged citizens to carry out armed attacks against British installations, but then required the army to prevent them. The situation exploded two months later when British forces began scourging villages for sheltering Egyptian "terrorists." Following a particularly nasty incident, when the British demolished the village of Kafr Abdu, officers sent a petition to the king and government asking permission to defend Egyptian sovereignty, but the petition was ignored. A month later, seven thousand British troops occupied the Suez Canal city of Ismailia. The government ordered the police to resist. In the bloody battle, 50 police officers were killed and 80 injured. The occasion was marked as Police Day, and henceforth, January 25 was celebrated annually in honor of the police martyrs (the revolt of 2011 started on that day to underline the disparity between the heroic police of yesterday and the brutal one of today). The following morning, rioters set fire to downtown Cairo. The army was ordered in to restore calm, but officers now felt they were becoming the henchmen of a regime that had lost all legitimacy—as evidenced by the fact that four cabinets ruled in quick succession from January–July 1952[13]. It became clear that there was a power vacuum in Egypt and that none of the political forces were ready to capture the moment, simply because they only thought of power in terms of "the force of numbers, the force of the masses, and never the force of arms."[14]

A final, though less spectacular factor, which had an enormous impact on officers, was the expansion of the monarch's jurisdiction over military affairs. Throughout his reign, the king strove to wrest effective control of the army from elected governments. As a mark of symbolic power, he changed the army emblem in October 1944 from "God, Country and King" to "God, King and Country." King Farouk not only refused to be held accountable for his ill-fated decision to send the military to the Palestine War, he now demanded the right to appoint the war minister and the chief of staff, and to create the new position of commander-in-chief of the armed forces—to be occupied by someone beholden to him alone and responsible for all military appointments and promotions. In order to appease the king, the Wafd government agreed in 1950 to relinquish its constitutional right to control the military. Immediately, the king set to work. The list of incompetents he appointed to leading army positions included his diplomat brother-in-law and his corrupt prison warden, who forced prisoners to till the king's land for free. His intention to install a malicious border patrol officer (who had barely survived assassination at the hands of Nasser) to the top military post days before the coup was one of its immediate causes. Naguib reflected the general dismay within the ranks when he complained to confidants that the army could not obey a high command composed of arms dealers, land speculators, and other criminal elements.[15] When the old general was elected chairman of the Officers Club against the royalist candidate in January 1952, it became clear that the palace was losing the loyalty of the corps.

Institutional grievances of this magnitude certainly explain why the coup was endorsed (or at least allowed) by the armed forces as a whole. Regardless of the social, political, or ideological motives of the ringleaders, the coup succeeded because it was perceived by scores of officers and soldiers as strictly for the benefit of their esteemed institution. In their view, the coup was not a matter of disrupting military discipline, but rather of reestablishing it. Their aim was to liberate Egypt from foreign occupation and install a reformed civilian regime that would enhance military power and restore its credibility. They were neither set on assuming political power nor on administering a transformative socioeconomic modernization program, while the quick turnover of military governments in Iraq (between 1936 and 1941) and Syria (between 1949 and 1951) alerted them to the inherent instability of military rule. Nasser and his close allies in the movement, however, thought otherwise. Captivated by the Turkish officer-turned-revolutionary-turned-stateman Mostafa Kemal Atatürk's reforms in the 1920s and 1930s, they saw the coup as only a first step in the long-term and far-reaching "revolution from above" that would build a strong centralized state with a modern industrial economy. Herein lies the root of the struggle that would consume the country for the next six decades.

The Dark Side of Militarism:
The March 1954 Crisis

In a single stroke, on the night of July 23, 1952, eighty middle-ranking officers seized the leadership of the armed forces, arrested all generals (except for the two who endorsed the coup), and cashiered all brigadiers and lieutenant colonels that did not participate. The king facilitated their job in two ways: despite the fact that military discontent pointed toward an impending coup, he left the capital for the summer palace in Alexandria as usual; and once he received news about irregular army movements, he ordered an emergency meeting of the high command at the army headquarters in Cairo, making it easier for the Free Officers to capture the entire top brass and therefore paralyze the military hierarchy. Without his army, King Farouk was powerless. He pleaded for U.S. support, considering that his relations with the British had been strained after their 1942 showdown. But the Americans had decided it was high time for a modernizing coup in Egypt to put an end to political chaos and economic stagnation lest the country drift to communism (the same policy they adopted in Latin America). Besides, the Free Officers had shared their intentions with the U.S. embassy shortly before the coup and pledged to protect American interests. The United States in turn weighed in on the British not to intervene on behalf of a king they already disliked. The king was forced to abdicate and, on August 2, 1952, departed Egypt for the last time.

The ringleaders then organized themselves in a fourteen-member Revolutionary Command Council (RCC) to assume executive authority until a new government was elected. These were roughly the same members of the executive committee of the Free Officers Movement. Demand for secrecy had forced the movement to assume a cellular shape with no hierarchy, branches, or committees. A freshly recruited Free Officer (usually through Nasser's recommendation, and always with his approval) would only know those in his own cell and a couple of names on the executive committee. Only Nasser had the full list of members. To ensure the military's loyalty, both the executive committee and the RCC, which replaced it right after the coup, included all service branches: four from the infantry; three from the cavalry (armored corps); three from the air force; two representatives from the artillery; and one from the signal corps (military communications) and the border guards. In fact, real power lay with the infantry. On the council, the three men who would later control Egypt's political, military, and security institutions belonged to this service. The future president Gamal Abd al-Nasser was the effective leader of the Free Officers; Abd al-Hakim Amer, soon-to-be general commander of the armed forces, had been Nasser's kindhearted and overgenerous "soul mate" since the day he joined the army; and Zakaria Muhi al-Din, the architect of Egypt's new security apparatus, was the cousin of Nasser's intellectual companion Khaled Muhi al-Din (who represented the cavalry on the RCC), but was distinguished from both by his solid, practical, and cool-minded temperament, as well as by his piercing glance and long silences. It was the meticulous and security-oriented Zakaria (referred to usually by his first name to separate him from his cousin and because it rhymed with Beria, Stalin's security henchman) who was in charge of planning the coup and leading the units that surrounded the king in Alexandria, and it was the second-tier Free Officer Captain Salah Nasr of the 13th Infantry Battalion (later to become Egypt's intelligence czar) who played a key role in protecting the new regime during its first days in power. The infantryman Youssef Sediq, who did not belong to this troika, was pressured to resign and leave the country in March 1953. RCC members who did not have troops on the ground to fall back on, such as Anwar al-Sadat of the signal corps and the two air force representatives, gave carte blanche to Nasser, who had recruited them to the movement. In effect, therefore, Nasser always had the majority of the RCC vote in his pocket, and was challenged only by the figurehead he had handpicked, Major General Muhammad Naguib of the border guards, and the free-spirited and increasingly left-leaning Khaled.

Once the RCC was established, Nasser directed his infantry aide Salah Nasr to prepare two lists: a list of independent-thinking officers who might compromise the security of the emerging regime, and another of those who belonged to the Free Officers Movement and might therefore harbor political ambitions. According to Nasr's memoirs, out of the 3,500 officers on the first list, 800 were asked to retire, 2,300 were reassigned to administrative duties within the army, and the rest were appointed to civilian positions. The 329 officers on the second list were placed under strict surveillance before almost all of them were let go in a couple of years. Curiously, another 71 officers were killed in "random accidents" between March and December 1953. In order to preserve their loyalty, the purged officers were told that their role as "leadership representatives" to civilian posts was necessary to revolutionize the bureaucracy.[1] These sugarcoated purges killed two birds with one stone: they destroyed the Free Officers power base in the army, while creating a loyal network of commissars within the state bureaucracy. The RCC then created the Republican Guard in June 1953, which in the words of its first chief, Abd al-Muhsen Abu al-Nur, was meant to defend the new regime against the rest of the military, and in October of the same year, the National Guard, to train citizens loyal to the revolution.[2] Finally, Law 505 of 1955 introduced mandatory conscription and expanded the promotion of NCOs to officers, since big armies are more difficult to enlist in a coup. The now secure military was used to neutralize political threats from monarchists and landlords, as well as intransigent workers and peasants. Firmly in control, the coup makers began to debate the future.

As in most cases, the success of the coup caused an immediate split within the ranks between those who wanted to return to barracks and resume their professional duty, and those who aspired to create a military regime to revolutionize society from above. The division ran from the RCC downward. Those in favor of withdrawing found support in Naguib, the council's nominal leader, and Khaled Muhi al-Din, the most intellectually mature member of the group, in addition to the critical mass within the artillery and cavalry, the army's democratic-leaning and professional-minded elite services. Advocates of revolution from above organized around Nasser, the RCC's effective leader, and those second-tier Free Officers (lieutenants and captains who had no significant role before the coup) whose loyalty he shrewdly cultivated in his own service (the infantry) and in small branches, such as the air force, and the still minuscule military police and intelligence. The confrontation between the two camps thrust the country onto a turbulent path between 1952 and 1954, and its outcome shaped the new regime—an outcome determined largely by their very different strategies.

NASSER'S POWER BLOC

The position of officers adamant to stay in power was well articulated in a speech that Nasser delivered to weavers in the Shubra al-Khima factory, on December 20, 1953, in which he warned that the military "did not carry out this revolution to govern or lead ... one of our first goals was to restore genuine representative life ... but we were appalled by the bargains, demands, maneuvers, and deceit ... we decided that this country should not be ruled by a class of political mercenaries."[3] Or as he later wrote in his *Philosophy of the Revolution*, that the Free Officers had considered themselves the vanguard of the nation, that they needed only to take the first step to encourage the masses to follow. Instead, those who flocked to benefit from the coup were none other than the petty stranglers of the old elite.[4]

It is true that it was Nasser who invited Naguib to join the coup at the last moment because he thought that a popular and highly decorated general would add credibility to a movement led by colonels and majors in their early thirties, and guarantee the support of many politically unaffiliated officers, but he kept a close eye on the old general from the beginning because he knew that figureheads usually develop an appetite for command once they get a taste of it. That is why he surrounded Naguib with members of his own entourage. When Naguib became the first president of the new republic, Nasser acted as his *chef de cabinet*, and appointed his good friend Captain Abd al-Muhsen Abu al-Nur head of the Republican Guard, the elite unit charged with protecting the president. Nasser also held (informal) weekly meetings with RCC members to coordinate their stances before convening under Naguib, who chaired the council.[5] These containment tactics, however, represented a modest part of Nasser's overall plan to consolidate power. His grand strategy stood on three pillars: building an entrenched security force; replacing the existing power centers with a new political apparatus; and garnering geopolitical support.

(i) The Security Community

In most authoritarian regimes, the multiplication of offices is believed to provide an extra security measure. It keeps the central decision maker more informed than any single actor, and allows him to divide and conquer when necessary. Instinctively paranoid, Nasser adopted this doctrine faithfully. He assigned similar tasks to civilian and military security organs, and created within each sector several competing bodies. What emerged was a hydra-headed security community, which was quite successful in terms of domestic repression.

Nasser's first official post after the coup was that of interior minister. There he found an adequate infrastructure to build on. For seven decades, the British had been improving on the secret police apparatus they found in Egypt in 1882. They created the Ministry of Interior in March 1895, followed by the Special Section in 1911 for domestic surveillance. They also sent officers for training in London, Paris, and St. Petersburg.[6] Although the Free Officers promised to abolish the notorious secret police, it soon became clear that Nasser intended to expand the agency and bend it to his purposes.

Already in the 1940s, political detention had become a standard practice against dissidents, especially after political crimes were redefined in a 1937 stature to include any expression of contempt of government. The wide use of detention was not only a result of increased British intolerance in the years leading up to the Second World War, but also a product of the enhanced state capacity for coercion. Prisons, for example, were expanded in the late 1930s to include detention camps built either in the desert (such as Huckstepp, al-Tur, and al-Wahat), or on the outskirts of cities (such as Tura, Abu-Za'bal, and al-Qanater). During the war years, these camps held a total of 4,000 political detainees, and by the early 1950s, the number swelled to 25,000, and it is estimated that during Nasser's tenure some 100,000 citizens passed through them.[7] Another example of enhanced state capacity was surveillance. Nasser inherited the system the British called the City Eye—a modern version of the *basaseen* (onlookers) structure, which had existed in Egypt for centuries. This was basically an expansive network of informers, or more accurately, common folk reporting any suspicious activities in return for modest rewards; these included beggars, porters, vendors, cabdrivers, telephone operators, and scores of other people.

Increased detention and surveillance capabilities notwithstanding, the system was evidently inefficient—or else how did the Free Officers manage to circumvent it? Nasser's initial concern therefore was how to close the gaps. After investigating the system for four months, Nasser passed his ministerial responsibilities in October 1953 to his security wizard, fellow RCC member Zakaria Muhi al-Din. The methodical Zakaria was a man of few words and remarkable deeds—the Egyptian journalist Mohamed Hassanein Heikal recounts being struck during his first meeting with Zakaria, in October 1951, by the fact that he was voluntarily submitting counterintelligence reports to the political leadership, despite only being an infantry officer[8]—and now he was in charge of restructuring Egypt's entire security apparatus. Unlike almost all other Free Officers, this vault of a man died in May 2012 at the age of ninety-four years without having made a single public revelation about his founding role in the regime.

Although police officers took no part in the coup, the Free Officers Movement had directed Zakaria beforehand to cultivate relations with the few who resented the regime. We do not have a list of his police contacts, but we know that relying on a handful of policemen, supplemented by several of his own military lieutenants, Zakaria refashioned the police corps, after purging 400 of its 3,000 officers.[9] Next, the old Special Section, under the supervision of military intelligence officers, was transformed into a new intelligence organ with expanded capabilities and jurisdiction: the General Investigations Directorate (GID)—renamed in 1971 as the State Security Investigations Sector (SSIS). Combining his ministerial position with that of director of the Military Intelligence Department (MID), Zakaria reoriented this agency as well toward internal political security, i.e., monitoring Egyptian dissidents rather than spying on the armies of other countries, as it was supposed to.[10] He then selected a handful of MID officers to help him create Egypt's first civilian intelligence agency, the General Intelligence Service (GIS), in December 1953, which he headed for a couple of years. Zakaria was also asked to recruit a group of loyal military captains, train them as security agents, and assign them to Nasser's home-run intelligence unit—soon to be known as the President's Bureau of Information (PBI). So in a few short years, Zakaria had built a "veritable pyramid of intelligence and security services ... [whose] labyrinthine complexity and venality" became the mainstay of Egypt's new political order.*[11] And although he later assumed several nonsecurity posts (including the premiership and vice presidency), Zakaria maintained his hegemony over the country's sprawling and intrusive security apparatus throughout—an apparatus directed solely to the protection of the regime.

But apart from the ingenious founder, foreign expertise was crucial to the construction of this security community—after all, it was foreign powers that had originally designed modern security systems within the colonies. The American embassy provided a million dollars' worth of surveillance and antiriot equipment immediately following the coup. Americans also helped Zakaria reinforce the unobtrusive City Eye system through a whole range of electronic equipment and techniques for installing bugs and hidden cameras in hotel rooms, army mess halls, private residences, and automobiles.[12] Even in terms of how to prepare timely intelligence estimates, Egypt turned to an American: Charles Cremeans, future head of the CIA's Office of National Intelligence Estimates. But Nasser expected more. In October 1952, he requested CIA assistance in overhauling the entire security system, and Kermit Roosevelt, director of CIA operations in the Middle East, was more than willing. A few months later, a troika of intelligence operatives set up camp in Cairo; James Eichelberger, Miles Copeland, and Frank Kearn had all served in the U.S. Army Counterintelligence Corps, and later witnessed the transformation of the Office of Strategic Services (OSS) into the CIA. In other words, they combined civilian and military intelligence expertise. Their designated contact in Egypt was another Nasser loyalist, Captain Hassan al-Tuhami, who administered an intensive training program that involved inviting several CIA experts for short visits, as well as sending Egyptian operatives for instruction

---

* It is important to note here that although all these agencies dealt with security, they cannot be considered similar. Amy Zegart, who studies the evolution of security agencies, reminds us: "Reality is not nearly so neat. National security agencies vary. They do not look alike at birth. Nor do they develop along the same path" (Amy B Zegart, *Flawed by Design: The Evolution of the CIA, JSC, and NSC*, Stanford, CA: Stanford University Press, 1999: 40). This was certainly the case in Egypt, as we will see in the following chapters.

abroad.[13] Captain Abd al-Fattah Abu al-Fadl, who was a vital part of that program, recalls how former German intelligence officers provided another important source of expertise; and it was the CIA that initiated this Nazi connection, putting Nasser in contact with prominent SS and Gestapo officers in hiding.* Later, in April 1958, Egypt signed a training and intelligence-sharing agreement with the KGB, which provided the latest surveillance technologies and interrogation techniques. A similar agreement was signed a decade later with Eastern German intelligence, the Stasi.[14]

If Zakaria did Nasser's bidding in the domestic security sector, he expected the same of his delegate in the army: Abd al-Hakim Amer. When the republic was declared on June 18, 1953, Nasser insisted that Naguib's first presidential decree would be to promote Amer from major to major general, and appoint him commander-in-chief of the armed forces. This meteoric rise in rank (perhaps the most meteoric in history) placed Amer officially on the top of the military chain of command. This is because Nasser did not believe in the Communist measure (adopted in Russia and China) of attaching political commissars to army units to report on officers; he preferred direct control from above. Amer was, of course, a perfect candidate. He was not only Nasser's most intimate friend since college and his right-hand man in the Free Officers Movement, but he was also the only RCC member that Naguib trusted, since he had served as his chief of staff during the 1948 war in Palestine, and because his amiable, cheerful, and appeasing personality made him seem harmless. The president's press secretary, Riyad Samy, says Naguib would not have surrendered control of the army to anyone else.[15]

Amer's main task was to coup-proof the military. This he accomplished through an office that Nasser had created while serving as Naguib's *chef de cabinet*, the conspicuously named Office of the Commander-in-Chief for Political Guidance (OCC), which was nominally responsible for issuing political directives to the corps, while in reality charged with monitoring suspicious activities. To staff the office, Amer turned to "Zakaria's boys," the second-tier Free Officers selected and trained by Zakaria to serve as the country's new security stratum. Salah Nasr served as the first OCC head in June 1953, followed by Abbas Radwan

---

* These included Lieutenant General Wilhelm Farmbacher of the German Wehrmacht; two SS operatives, Otto Skorzeny (SS Mussolini contact) and Oskar Direwanger (of the SS Warsaw branch); and four Gestapo officers, Leopold Gleim (head of the Gestapo in Warsaw), Franz Buensch, Joachim Deumling, and Alois Anton Brunner (Miles Copeland, *The Game of Nations: The Amorality of Power Politics*, London: Weidenfeld and Nicolson, 1970: 87; Owen L. Sirrs, *A History of the Egyptian Intelligence Service: A History of the Mukhabarat, 1910–2009*, New York: Routledge, 2010: 33).

in 1956, and Shams Badran from 1958 until the office was abolished in 1967. OCC functioned as a political watchdog, ferreting out trouble-making officers and ensuring the loyalty of the rest through dispensing patronage. It accomplished this through three main mechanisms: severing relations between RCC members (except for Nasser) and the rest of the military under the pretext of allowing Amer to perform his duties without outside interference; isolating the officer corps from all political and ideological forces; and, most important, creating a secret network of politically ambitious officers who did not participate in the coup itself but were eager to prove their worth by helping secure the revolution. Nasser, the first OCC chief, began to organize this cell-based network immediately after the coup. By 1967, its members exceeded 65,000 officers.[16] It is through this embedded organization that the OCC monitored political views and activities within the army, administered political indoctrination, and decided on promotions and assignments. This new security community would come to play a significant role in Egypt's political fortunes; its dramatis personae would tip the balance in Nasser's favor in 1954; create the *mukhabarat* (intelligence) state of the 1960s; constitute the formidable "centers of power" between 1967 and 1971; and ultimately pave the ground for Egypt's ostentatious police state by the end of 1970s.

(ii) The Political Apparatus

While Naguib rested confidently on his popularity on "the street," Nasser was busy building concrete political organizations to mobilize popular support. This was certainly a more effective strategy. As an avid reader of Machiavelli, Nasser certainly knew that "People are by nature inconstant. It is easy to persuade them of something, but it is difficult to stop them from changing their minds. So you have to be prepared for the moment when they no longer believe. Then you have to force them to believe."[17] To start with, he created the new Ministry for National Guidance for censorship and propaganda in November 1952. The minister, RCC member Salah Salem, did his best to keep Naguib away from the limelight, and later to tarnish his reputation and boost Nasser's image instead. Here, too, Nasser relied on foreign expertise, notably the OSS operative Paul Linebarger, America's leading black propagandist; Leopold von Mildenstein, Joseph Goebbels's Middle East information director; and the SS black propaganda expert Johannes von Leers.[18]

To further cultivate his popular base, Nasser dissolved all existing political parties (via Law 179 of 1953) and replaced them with the loosely organized, mass-based Liberation Rally in January 1953, which was basically a platform for arranging pro-regime rallies and public lectures. It had no clear hierarchy, and its work depended on 1,200 district offices open for all those willing to offer their support to the new regime. These were mostly corrupt officers and political opportunists eager to get on the bandwagon, as well as rural notables and capitalists, willing to send their peasants and workers to demonstrate under Nasser's banner, to protect their financial interests in these uncertain times. Nasser appointed himself secretary-general of this new organization, though he delegated its everyday management to two junior associates, majors Ibrahim al-Tahawi and Ahmed Te'ima, whose job was primarily to monitor the public mood and political trends, and foil mobilization efforts by other political forces (particularly Islamists and Communists) through organizing counterrallies. In addition, as recounted by Suleiman Hafez, who served briefly as interior minister in 1953, the two majors submitted regular reports to the ministry against suspect activists.[19]

(iii) Geopolitical Support

The final component of Nasser's strategy was to secure geopolitical support for his faction. At this point, the only candidate was the United States. America's Middle East policy in the 1950s was to encourage national independence movements to curtail British and French hegemony, and then draw the newly independent nations to its orbit through strategic alliances and economic aid. After two world wars convinced the Americans to cast aside their isolationism and engage with the "old world" across the Atlantic, they figured that although they lacked the experience of Europeans in dealing with Africa and Asia, their comparative advantage lay in the fact that they had never acted as an imperialist power (outside Latin America and the Pacific). The key to promoting U.S. influence therefore was to lend a helping hand to those eager to liberate themselves from European imperialism, and to pose as a true partner in helping develop the postcolonial world. Toward the end of 1951, Secretary of State Dean Acheson formed a special committee on the Arab world under the chairmanship of Kermit Roosevelt, from the newly established CIA. The committee suggested the need for "an Arab leader who would have more power in his hands than any other Arab leader ever had before, 'power to make an unpopular decision' ... one who deeply desires to have power, and who desires to have it primarily for the mere sake of power."[20] This recommendation was made more explicit in a British Foreign Office minute on December 3, 1951, which described the joint American-British view as follows: "the only sort of Government with which we can hope to get an accommodation is a frankly authoritarian government ... both ruthless and efficient ... We need another Mustafa Kemal [the Turkish officer who led a modernizing coup in 1921, and assumed the title Atatürk, the father of the Turks], to secularize and Westernize his country … Even though Egyptians are not Turks, and men like Mustafa Kemal cannot be ordered *à la carte!*"[21]

In February 1952, Kermit Roosevelt traveled to Cairo to find an Egyptian Atatürk. He had been to Egypt twice before: first in 1944 to help establish the Cairo branch of the OSS (the CIA's predecessor), and then in 1950 to instruct the Egyptian Interior Ministry on how to counter communism. During both visits, he developed a list of contacts in the military, and set up a CIA-run military training program for young Egyptian officers. Curiously, six among the fifty officers that received American intelligence and military training played a crucial role in the 1952 coup, and two actually became members of the RCC. The air force officer Aly Sabri, the first official liaison between the RCC and the United States, admitted—without much elaboration—that "the attendance of many Egyptian officers at US service schools during the past two years had a very definite influence on the coup d'état in Egypt."[22] Apparently, Roosevelt's mission was to set the stage for a peaceful replacement of Egypt's archaic and corrupt monarchy before the increasing radicalization of Egyptian workers and peasants drove the country into the arms of communism. Only the military, thought Roosevelt, could modernize the state along lines agreeable to the West without causing too much turmoil. Through Ambassador Jefferson Caffery's good offices, the CIA representative held three meetings in March 1952 with members of the Free Officers, including Nasser.[23] According to one participant in those early meetings (Hussein Hammudah), discussions focused on how the Americans could convince their Anglo-Saxon partners not to resist the coup, to prevent a repeat of 1882, when the British aborted a similar move by the army, in return for guarantees from the Free Officers to implement the needed reforms to modernize the Egyptian economy and keep the Communists in check.[24] Three nights before the Free Officers seized power, on July 19, 1952, Nasser asked Sabri to inform the U.S. assistant military attaché (David Evans) that the coup was now impending, and to stress once more that it would not harm American interests. The United States carried out its part of the deal, refusing to extend support to a pleading king, and advising him instead to submit to the officers' demands. President Franklin D. Roosevelt immediately welcomed the coup, warned the British not to intervene, and directed his ambassador in Cairo—who infamously referred to the Free Officers as "my boys"—to support the new rulers.[25]

The day following the coup, Nasser relayed an even more important message to the Americans, this time asking for CIA help in reorganizing Egypt's internal security apparatus. To add a sense of urgency to his demand, Nasser warned of Communist-led disturbances throughout the country. The message resonated with a hastily prepared report by the agency, "The Expected Consequences of a Reoccupation of Cairo and Alexandria by British Forces," which concluded that violent confrontations would pave the road to a Communist takeover. This is why, according to the Cairo CIA station chief, Colonel William Lakeland, the agency responded favorably. Kermit Roosevelt met Nasser's delegates shortly after the coup to draw the general guidelines for future cooperation. This was followed by a series of private meetings between CIA representatives James Eichelberger and Miles Copeland with Nasser and his associates at Lakeland's apartment.[26]

Parallel to this security track, other meetings were held between Nasser and the Americans to discuss political and socioeconomic reform. The RCC member Khaled Muhi al-Din, who attended a couple of those meetings at the house of Abd al-Moun'em Amin (another officer Nasser charged with contacting the United States), noted that the Americans adamantly requested the quick adoption of land reform.[27] At the beginning of 1952, a U.S. advisory committee, convinced that the Bolshevik and Chinese revolutions relied mainly on deprived peasants, suggested that land redistribution was an indispensable buffer to communism. This was reinforced, in February 1952, by a State Department brochure entitled "Land Reform: A World Challenge," calling for swift action in that direction to channel agrarian capital toward rapid industrialization. On August 20, 1952, Washington sent a telegram to its ambassador in Cairo stating, "The Government of the United States will give encouragement and assistance to land reform ... to lessen the causes of agrarian unrest and political instability," and then went on to detail what this law should include.[28] Barely three weeks later, on September 9, the RCC issued a hastily prepared agricultural reform law.

In return, Nasser sought the U.S. president's support to convince the British to evacuate the country. Dwight Eisenhower first sent Steve Meade from the U.S. military to evaluate the power balance within the RCC. Meade reported back in May 1953 that Nasser held a tight grip over the council and that the new regime was fairly stable. Secretary of State John Foster Dulles, the first high-ranking official to visit the new republic, seconded the report the following month.[29] Afterward, the United States exerted so much pressure on the British to negotiate their way out of Egypt that Churchill protested in a lengthy letter to Eisenhower, on June 12, 1953, that America's bias toward Nasser "in spite of the numerous far-reaching concessions which we made" was surprising and frustrating—concluding, dramatically, "we should not think we had been treated fairly by our great Ally."[30]

But while the United States understood from day one that Naguib was merely a front man and acted accordingly, there were other reasons why the CIA in particular was enthusiastic about supporting Nasser. True to its Cold War conviction that military strongmen are more reliable than erratic civilians, the agency was worried about Naguib's promise to reinstate civilian democratic rule. As early as July 30, 1952, Dean Acheson had noted in a cable to the U.S. ambassador in Cairo that a return to democracy would have unexpected consequences, and that a small group of officers would be easier to handle than a multiparty system.[31] The historian, and special assistant to President Kennedy, Arthur Schlesinger explains the logic behind this doctrine, citing support for Nasser as one its prominent instances:

> [Premature civilianization of coup-installed regimes] would only alien-
> ate those who held the real power—the military—and open the door
> to incompetent liberals who would bring about inflation, disinvestment,
> capital flight, and social indiscipline and would finally be shoved aside by
> the communists … the process of development was so inherently disrup-
> tive that the first requirement had to be the maintenance of order. The
> basic issue is not whether the government is dictatorial or is representa-
> tive and constitutional. The issue is whether the government, whatever
> its character, can hold the society together … civilian government tended
> to be unstable and soft; military governments were comparably stable and
> could provide the security necessary for economic growth.[32]

But what sealed the deal for the Americans was Nasser's demonstra-
tion that Naguib was soft on communism. Nasser had brandished his anti-Communist credentials in clamping down on the Kafr al-Dawar strike. Kafr al-Dawar was a small textile industrial city on the outskirts of Alexandria. The labor activist Helmi Yassin, who helped organize the strike, explains that workers heard the revolutionary communi-
qués promising to restore the people's rights, and so decided the time was perfect to press forward their right to control the organization of production instead of the antirevolutionary factory owners. None of them suspected that on the morning of August 13, 1952, Nasser would dispatch five hundred troops to shoot them, and execute two of the ringleaders after a summary trial five days later. For the workers, the military's shocking behavior was totally unjustified, especially considering they were demonstrating in support of the revolution.[33] In his meetings with CIA officials, Nasser exposed how Naguib was reluctant to sign the execution orders of the agitators; that he openly criticized the land-reform law; and that he nominated a constitutional lawyer with leftist sympathies (Abd al-Razeq al-Sanhouri) to the premiership. Naguib tried to explain to the Americans that executing workers would fuel further radicalism; that progressive taxation on agricul-
tural land was better for the economy than its random parceling; and

that Sanhouri was not a Communist. But his justifications fell on deaf ears. The communication channels that Nasser established with the Americans before and after the coup secured their trust and gave him more access to Washington.[34] At the end, not only the United States, but the capitalist West in general, leaned toward the strong leader they all believed would be tough on communism: Nasser.

NAGUIB'S NOT-SO-POWERFUL BLOC

While Nasser set himself the task of creating a new order, Naguib continued to invest in the old; while the former was pushing forward, the latter insisted on swimming against the current. Naguib still believed in the binding power of the law, the legitimacy of the old political groups, the need for democracy, and the importance of popularity in general. Instead of the security coterie with which Nasser surrounded himself, Naguib attracted constitutional lawyers who carried great weight in the old regime, notably Abd al-Razeq al-Sanhouri, head of the State Council (Egypt's highest administrative court), who was charged with issuing a new constitution following the coup, and Suleiman Hafez, another legal heavyweight, who had drafted the monarch's abdication letter. But while Egypt's first president busied himself with the process of drafting a new constitution, his rival promoted the view that revolutionary legitimacy trumps any constitution. Perhaps more important, Naguib's fatal mistake of appointing the lawyer Suleiman Hafez as interior minister in September 1952, to signal his respect for the law, made it easy for Nasser to take over the ministry in June 1953 with the reasonable argument that the country needed a firmer grip than that of a constitutional lawyer at this critical juncture.

Naguib also tried to make himself popular with the old political elites, portraying himself in speeches and personal interviews as pro-democracy and free enterprise, and distancing himself from RCC decrees against political parties and large landowners.[35] The problem was, of course, that Egypt's sociopolitical structure was designed to weaken the hand of those elites vis-à-vis the state. Muhammad Ali, the founder of the modern Egyptian state in the first half of the nineteenth century—following the example of Hohenzollern Prussia, tsarist Russia, and Japan's soon-to-come Meiji Restoration—had dismantled the Mamluks' military aristocracy, established in the thirteenth century, and tied the landed class to his expansive state. So instead of dividing sovereignty over the land among loyal warlords, each autonomously managing his own plot, governing the population that lived on it, collecting taxes, and raising militias in time of war, Muhammad Ali declared himself the sole proprietor of the land and treated Egyptian landlords as his subjects. He also established a central tax-collecting authority, a modern judicial system, and a standing army with a professional officer corps and nationally recruited conscripts. Egypt's mostly absentee landlords had remained in this position ever since; they had no independent source of power to confront whoever controlled the state—as Nasser diligently strove to.

Another mistake: Naguib rested too confidently on the fact that he had become an immediate sensation following the coup, and tried to preserve his folk-hero image by spending most of the period between 1952 and 1954 traveling around the country in a train (Truman style), galvanizing the masses through inspirational speeches. In that, he was enormously successful: "People lost control when they saw him, applauding, chanting, and throwing themselves on his car."[36] Considering popularity his main asset, the president wasted the efforts of his closest military associates on a trivial popularity-boosting campaign instead of planting them in the emerging security sector: Riyad Samy was hired as press secretary, and Muhammad Riyad was put in charge of protocol. He also flirted with the leaders of the Muslim Brothers, beginning from 1954, with the hope that garnering the support of the most popular force on the street would eventually help him send the officers back to the barracks and remain president under a liberal constitution.[37] What the president failed to understand, in contrast to his sober rival, was that popularity was a mercurial asset that could evaporate as easily as it could be gained.

One of Naguib's worst flaws, however, related to how he went about securing foreign support. As opposed to Nasser's direct and aggressive campaign to build a security alliance with the United States, Naguib—too worried about tarnishing his reputation—preferred a more roundabout approach. Instead of relying on loyal officers, he encouraged the Muslim Brotherhood to endorse him in their discussions with the British and the Americans. Between May 1953 and January 1954, the Muslim Brotherhood representatives Munir Delah and Saleh Abu-Raqiq conducted two rounds of talks with Mr. Evans and Mr. Creswell of the British embassy, in which they mentioned that Naguib would be a better guardian of democracy.[38] Those talks overlapped with another seven rounds with the Americans, between May and August 1953, in which the Brotherhood's general guide, Hassan al-Hudaybi himself, participated. In one meeting, on June 4, the Brotherhood envoy Mahmoud Makhlouf tried to promote the president by claiming: "Naguib would be willing to sign a secret understanding with the US. The Moslem Brotherhood would support such a move. [But] Opposition might be encountered from Abdel Nasser." On their July 17 meeting, the general guide relayed that he and Naguib supported the "withdrawal of the military from the government and their replacement by a coalition of 'good men' from the various political parties."[39]

There were several problems with this approach. For one thing, the Western powers, as we have seen, were not particularity enthusiastic about democracy. The fact that Naguib was negotiating through an Islamist movement was an additional turn-off. But the biggest problem was that the president was quite reserved with his own representatives. Naguib recounted several unsolved difficulties during his secret talks with the Muslim Brotherhood between December 1953 and March 1954 through his secretaries Samy and Riyad and the Brotherhood dignitaries Hassan Ashmawi and Munir Delah. While he wanted to reestablish democracy, they wanted a package deal in which Naguib would remain president, provided he appointed a pro-Brotherhood chief of staff, Major General Rashad Mehanna from the artillery. Naguib confessed to his press secretary Samy that he was noncommittal because he never imagined the Brotherhood would turn against him; he neglected the fact that a return to democracy would mostly benefit the liberal al-Wafd Party, not Islamists.[40]

Naguib's main shortcoming, though, was that he developed no organization within the army, let alone the new security regime being assembled under his nose. It is true that his pro-democratic stance had the support of the bulk of the officer corps, but he did not try to coordinate their actions, preferring to pass down orders through official channels rather than create a network of loyal officers. Even when artillery and cavalry officers begged him in August 1952 to do just that, he turned them down, fearing that fractures within the military would push the country to the brink of civil war. Naguib's viewpoint, as he later confided to the head of the Republican Guard, Abd al-Muhsin Abu al-Nur, was that he had no need to weave conspiracies; he was the highest-ranking officer in the realm, let alone president of the republic and chair of the RCC; he thus expected officers to obey him unconditionally.[41] Despite Samy's repeated pleas that his boss build a political power base within the corps, a Naguib dazzled with the aura of authority insisted that it was beneath him as a major general to reach out to junior officers; he also held that it would serve him better to professionalize rather than further politicize the corps.[42] He also underestimated his rival's influence among officers, refusing to acknowledge that a colonel with an "undistinguished public presence"—as he referred to Nasser in his memoirs—could threaten him.[43] In his heart, Naguib counted on the support of the people, rather than the military. But even that was difficult to preserve despite the energy he devoted to building his popular charisma, simply because Egyptians were tired of the old system and wanted a strong leader to reform the country. As Naguib himself later confessed, the people wanted "an Egyptian Ataturk," a role he was unwilling to play.[44] Nasser, on the other hand, did not waver.

BETWEEN TWO MUTINIES

One is tempted after comparing Nasser's and Naguib's power strate-
gies to conclude that the latter was clearly outmaneuvered from the
start, that the result of their power struggle was decided before it had
even begun. Not only was Nasser in control of the new security organs
and the country's only mass party, but he also succeeded at winning
the favor of a major world power, the United States. Nasser's problem,
however, was time: he had scarcely enough of it to bring the military
in line and subdue the old political forces. Thus, mutiny spread among
officers, first in the artillery (in January 1953) and then in the cavalry
(in March 1954). Army dissidents cared little about Nasser or Naguib as
such; their aim was to establish democratic rule, and they rallied around
Naguib because he sympathized with their position. Nasser's victory
seemed impossible considering that by virtue of their equipment and
firepower the artillery and cavalry were the most formidable services
in the Egyptian army. Also, the second mutiny was backed up by vast
popular demonstrations orchestrated by the Muslim Brotherhood, and
including scores of liberals and Communists. How could the budding
security establishment keep such a massive force in check?

(i) The Artillery Mutiny

The first episode in this rapidly unfolding power struggle began with
the artillery mutiny. A major bloc within the artillery corps longed for
the resumption of parliamentary life, which required withdrawing the
military to barracks and handing over power to an elected civilian government. They believed that the coup was meant only to purge political
parties of corrupt elements, remove the obstinate king, and force the
British to evacuate Egypt. Once these tasks were established, full-
fledged democracy should ensue. Also, as a privileged service working
with advanced equipment, artillery officers (like their counterparts
in the cavalry, and unlike those of the most rudimentary service, the
infantry) were professional-minded and eager to turn their attention
back to military duties. The ongoing purges and the undermining of
military discipline in the name of political loyalty doubtlessly offended
their professional temperament. They also held a grudge against Nasser
after discovering that his appointment of the admired artillery colonel
Rashad Mehanna to the three-member Regency Council, established
after the king's exile to run the country until the crown prince reached
the proper age, was meant to sidetrack rather than promote him. In
June 1953, Egypt became a republic and all the vestiges of monarchism,
including the Regency Council, were abolished. To add insult to injury,
Mehanna was discharged that October and placed under house arrest

for allegedly conspiring with the Muslim Brotherhood. Nasr admits that Nasser feared the charismatic Mehanna, the first officer to form secret cells within the army back in the 1940s, and plotted his removal from power.[45]

On December 14, 1952, the artillery captains Muhsen Abd al-Khaleq and Fathallah Ref'at submitted a petition to Nasser on behalf of their colleagues demanding that the RCC be reconstituted to allow each service equal representation, and that each branch should elect its own representatives to the council. The petitioners added, threateningly, that they could not accept overthrowing one king only to be ruled by fourteen (alluding to the RCC members). To explore the depth of their dissent, Nasser asked them to sketch a blueprint of the political system they envisaged, advising them to print it at Military Intelligence headquarters for discretion. The artillery officers did not swallow the bait. Instead, these suspicious requests convinced them that Nasser and his collaborators were beyond reform and must be removed at once. Between December 30 and January 7, they held four secret meetings with fifteen other colleagues from the artillery, in addition to a handful of cavalry officers, to plan a countercoup. They also met the Muslim Brotherhood's general guide twice to assure his organization's support. Their plan was to arrest all RCC members (except Naguib) during one of their weekly meetings, using units from the 1st Artillery Brigade, which was stationed a couple of blocks away from RCC headquarters, then seize control of the capital using the 2nd Artillery Division and Artillery School companies, before declaring a short transitional period, under Naguib, to draft a new constitution and prepare for elections.

Samy Sharaf, an artillery lieutenant whose brother was one of the participants, tipped the Military Intelligence Department, and was rewarded with membership of the agency. On January 16, Zakaria Muhi al-Din apprehended thirty-five culprits, tried them summarily, and sentenced twelve of them to prison, including Mehanna, by March 19.[46] As soon as the ringleaders were detained, five hundred artillery officers met at their service headquarters and threatened to use force to free their colleagues. To deescalate the situation, Zakaria promised to release them after they had spent a mere three years in prison. In a letter from prison, Captain Abd al-Khaleq maintained that the failure of the artillery's countercoup paved the way for dictatorship under Nasser and his "Beria," referring to Zakaria.[47] This might have been true for the moment, but the army still had not lost its resolve; a much bigger mutiny was in the works.

(ii) The Cavalry Mutiny

After subduing the artillery, the stage was set for an even greater challenge to Nasser's plan to stay in power. For one thing, tensions began rising between an increasingly distrustful Naguib and Nasser's faction. After complaining, during an RCC meeting on December 20, that the media was deliberately ignoring his speeches, council members hurled insults at Naguib, accusing him of trying to hijack the revolution. Then, on February 23, 1954, RCC members decided to hold their weekly meeting at Nasser's office without inviting the president. When Naguib, who was actually present in the building, objected, he was asked to go home. The aim was to convince him to accept his figurehead role. But the attempt backfired two days later when Naguib raised the stakes and resigned, declaring that his military honor forbade him from presiding over "a state of informants" run by a security coterie trained by CIA and ex-Gestapo operatives.[48] Naguib confessed to his legal counselor that his resignation was aimed at arousing the people and the soldiers, which it eventually did.[49] Feeling threatened, the security branch began to roll. Acting on their own initiative, Nasr, director of the OCC, and the head of the Republican Guard, Abu al-Nur, replaced the guard unit stationed outside the president's house with soldiers from Nasr's 13th Infantry Battalion, and detained guard officers loyal to Naguib. With Naguib unarmed, Nasser called his bluff, not only accepting his resignation on February 26 but also placing him under house arrest after claiming to the press that he was becoming unbearably dictatorial and corrupt.[50]

What Nasser did not expect, however, was that Naguib's resignation would trigger a cavalry mutiny, followed by a vast popular revolt. Like their colleagues in the artillery, cavalry officers felt that the RCC was driving the country toward dictatorship rather than reformed democracy, and was going to entangle the military in politics irrevocably. When Naguib announced his intention leave, cavalrymen formed an eight-member delegation, led by captains Ahmed al-Masri and Farouk al-Ansari, to negotiate a peaceful settlement with the RCC on February 26 before the president's resignation was declared, whereby Naguib would head an interim civilian government that would write a new constitution and supervise elections before the end of the year. Nasser and his associates expressed their concern that implementing democracy prematurely would bring back reactionary forces. At which point, the delegation withdrew from the talks and called for a sit-in at the cavalry mess hall, the so-called Green Mess Hall. Three hundred officers heeded the call, and units from the 4th Armored Division, the army's strategic reserve force, began surrounding the military general headquarters (GHQ), which was right across from the Green Mess Hall.

The dissidents demanded Naguib's reinstatement, Amer's dismissal, the dissolution of the RCC, and the immediate transition to democracy. Nasser rushed to the hall to convince the officers to call off the strike. He was accompanied by Hassan al-Tuhami and his security men to secretly record the names of the agitators. But his attempt was foiled when the strikers refused to admit any of the operatives to the hall, and asked that Nasser come alone. Following a heated debate during which the mutinous officers accused RCC and security officers of corruption and abuse of power, the encircled Nasser exclaimed: "Who gave you the right to speak for the people?" to which one of the cavalrymen responded: "We are the parliament of the people until a parliament is formed." Thoroughly intimidated, especially after hearing tank movements outside the hall, Nasser pledged to fulfill all their demands, including the dissolution of the RCC and the creation of a new government under Naguib and the cavalry's RCC representative, Khaled Muhi al-Din. He then headed back to RCC headquarters, informed the council of his decisions, and dispatched Khaled to Naguib's house in the early hours of February 27 so that the pair could take charge.[51] Nasser was so disturbed that he asked his family to evacuate the house immediately. His wife, Tahiya, remembered how he frantically told her that cavalry units might be on their way to bomb the house.[52]

It seemed for a moment that it was all over, that the power struggle had ended with Nasser's defeat. But the tide soon turned. "It took only one hour," as Khaled bitterly reported, "for the situation to reverse completely. It was during the sixty minutes that passed between my trip to Naguib's house and back that everything turned upside down."[53] Scholars who examined this critical juncture usually interpreted what followed as a Nasser-orchestrated maneuver, but a close examination of the memoirs of some of those involved reveals that it was the nascent security group that took the lead, and Nasser simply went along. In fact, we know from a future conversation between Nasser and Khaled that the former's thinking at that stage was set on the impractical plan of returning to the army, lying low for a while, and then plotting another coup.[54] It was the security men, who realized that democracy would cut their promising new careers short, who pulled the strings that night and tilted the balance in Nasser's favor. The infantry officer Gamal Hammad, who drafted the Free Officers' first communiqué after coming to power, was present at GHQ as the events unfolded and described how Nasser was a mere spectator during that bold counter-attack.[55] This was also the view of the three officers who were at the receiving end of this security-coordinated strike: Naguib, Khaled, and the cavalry mutiny leader Ahmed al-Ansari. Naguib noted how the press was already documenting human rights violations and asking for reprisal. It was only natural for security officers, he said, to understand that the resumption of democratic life "would mean their end, that they will be held accountable for what they did."[56] Khaled recalled warning Nasser that an intramilitary confrontation could escalate into a blood-bath, but the latter responded submissively: "I no longer understand what is going on."[57] Ansari, in a letter from prison to Hammad, blamed himself for taking Nasser's word instead of arresting him and his associates. Nasser's integrity, Ansari continued, was beyond reproach, but cavalrymen underestimated the ferocity of the new security elite who stood to lose from democracy; they were the ones who paved the road to authoritarianism; they were the real conspirators.[58] This last sentence acquires greater significance in light of Sadat's claim that Nasser had initially defended democracy during the first RCC meeting on July 27, 1952, but it was the power-hungry security coterie he thought would protect the revolution that ended up controlling it.[59]

So if it was not Nasser who called the shots, then who did, and how? Emphasizing how desperate times call for desperate measures, two of these officers-turned-security-men, Shams Badran and Abbas Radwan, convinced a reluctant Nasser to allow them to offer the imprisoned artillery officers their freedom in return for helping to put down the cavalry uprising. The two then quickly sealed the deal and informed their boss, Salah Nasr, that the artillery was at his service. Nasr, who got wind of the impending cavalry mutiny from one of his inform-ers hours before it took place, wasted no time: he advised Nasser to meet with the dissidents at the Green Mess Hall to try to defuse the situation; meanwhile, he sent out agitators to other services to portray the cavalry's call for democracy as a ploy aimed at delivering the country to Khaled's Communists.[60] As soon as Khaled left GHQ, Nasr made his move:

I ordered my old 13th Infantry Battalion to surround cavalry headquar-ters, and the freshly released artillery officers to block tank outlets. I then asked [Aly] Sabri [the air force captain who joined the new security elite] to send jets roaring at low altitudes over the besieged officers for intimidation. Meanwhile, I dispatched Tuhami and five intelligence offic-ers to detain Naguib at artillery headquarters. When Amer discovered I had ordered troop movements without his approval, he called me into his office, grabbed my shirt, and screamed hysterically, with his gun pointed at me: "I will kill you! I will not allow the country to descend to chaos! I am the commander-in-chief, not you!" But as soon as I assured him that eve-rything was under control, and that the revolution was now safe, he calmed down. At this point, Khaled dashed into the office, asking who ordered the siege against the cavalry. I asked him to warn his colleagues that if they did not disperse they would be bombed to the last man. Finally, I ordered the Military Police to storm in and detain the leaders of the mutiny. By the end of the day, the situation was resolved. I ordered Radwan, my assistant, to keep an eye out and went home to get some sleep.[61]

To everyone's surprise, however, the pendulum swung back in the other direction. Few people were aware of the overnight confrontation that was taking place around cavalry headquarters, but what everyone woke up to on the morning of February 27 was a communiqué by the minister of national guidance, RCC member Salah Salem, declaring Naguib's removal. The minister claimed that the former president was never part of the Free Officers Movement, but was placed in charge out of respect for his age, and that lately, driven by a clear inferiority complex, he had demanded dictatorial powers. Immediately, hundreds of thousands of demonstrators took to the streets of Cairo chanting: "To prison with Nasser! No revolution without Naguib!" The size of the uprising was so overwhelming that even Nasser's security associates admitted that repressing it might result in a bloodbath. Salah Salem rushed back to GHQ, screaming that the mob almost turned his car upside down and that they must be appeased before they set the country on fire. The Muslim Brotherhood, Naguib's allies, were the main force behind the demonstrations, as the Brotherhood member, and one of the junior organizers of the uprising, Mahmoud Game' confessed.[62] A cornered Nasser was forced to reinstate Naguib to the presidency as well as the chairmanship of the RCC. But the situation was not exactly back to square one: empowered by the people's revolt, the cavalry called for another meeting, on March 4, 1954, insisting that the military withdrew from politics. Naguib's triumphant return to office on the crest of popular support and with the backing of the army's strongest service provided him with a golden opportunity to strike against his rivals. Yet he preferred reconciliation, and to demonstrate his goodwill, he appointed Nasser as prime minister. This proved to be his undoing.

THE NEW REGIME CONSOLIDATES POWER

Nasser's spies immediately set to work. In three days, the security organs rounded up thousands of those who participated in the uprising. Before the week was over, the RCC carried out its greatest bluff in the form of the March 5 Decrees, which called for the election of a constitutive assembly in three months to draft a new democratic constitution, and lifted the ban on political activity and ended censorship of the press. Naturally, the RCC's sudden change of heart aroused Naguib's suspicions, but he had no choice but to go along, otherwise the council would have accused him of opposing democracy. By way of securing himself against a possible plot, though, he demanded on March 8 the right to appoint senior officers down to brigade commanders (to undercut Amer); the right to veto cabinet decisions (to keep Nasser in check); and a popular referendum on his presidency (to legitimize his post). When the RCC accepted without discussion, Naguib became even more disconcerted. But again he did nothing, giving Nasser the benefit of the doubt and convincing himself that maybe the latter believed his Liberation Rally could be quickly reorganized into a political party capable of winning the coming elections.[63] Soon, however, the subsequent March 25 Decrees made it clear that a plot was simmering. The new decrees revoked all restrictions on old-regime parties, and prohibited Free Officers from partaking in elections. Formally, the decrees spelled the end of the revolution. In reality they were a veiled call to action by all those who stood to lose by the restoration of the old order: officers who participated in the coup and feared punishment; peasants who benefited from land redistribution; workers who preferred dictatorship to the domination of liberal capitalist parties; the petty bourgeois that had barely begun to enjoy the breakdown of the rigid social hierarchy; and the Muslim Brothers who feared the return of the powerful al-Wafd Party. Again, the most vulnerable stratum was the security elite, for as soon as censorship was lifted, the press launched a concerted campaign against their abuse of power and demanded their trial. According to one artillery officer, these decisions were widely understood within the corps as an invitation to carry out another coup.[64] Pro-democracy officers and popular forces felt outmaneuvered: their goal was to move forward, not backward; they aspired for a new and reformed democracy, but the March decrees promised the return of the old corrupt one. Forced to choose, they found themselves unwittingly coalescing against the return to democracy.

We know from Nasr's memoirs that he was the mastermind behind the March decrees. His aim was to provoke "a revolution against the [pro-democracy] revolution."[65] To neutralize popular opposition, he advised Nasser to cut a deal with the Muslim Brotherhood. After a short negotiation with the imprisoned general guide, the organization agreed to abandon Naguib in return for releasing its detainees and renewing its precoup alliance with Nasser. On March 26, Nasser followed the release of five hundred Brotherhood detainees with a highly publicized visit to the general guide to show respect. Four days later, the guide denounced in a press conference the old party system, and thereafter ignored Naguib's pleas for support, refusing to return his calls or receive his envoys. Naguib bitterly complained that for days, every time he called the guide, the latter was in the bathroom.[66] The movement was clearly led to believe that Nasser was finally ready to give it its due.

In believing so, the Islamist movement was not entirely naïve. Nasser, who had joined several political groups in the 1940s to explore them from within, became a member of the Brotherhood shortly before the

1948 war—out of political expediency rather than ideological affinity. We know that the first five-member cell of the Free Officers, formed in September 1949, was entirely composed of Brotherhood members (Nasser, Khaled, Abd al-Mon'iem Abd al-Ra'ouf, Kamal al-Din Hussein, Hassan Ibrahim), and that those who joined later were Brotherhood collaborators (notably, Amer, Sadat, and 'Abd al-Latif al-Baghdadi). We also know that Nasser and Khaled went even further and joined the Brotherhood's Special Order—the movement's secret militant arm.[67] In addition, Nasser's involvement in training Brotherhood militants was well documented by the famous incident on May 25, 1949, when he was interrogated for seven hours by Prime Minister Ibrahim 'Abd al-Hady, Chief of Staff Osman al-Mahdy, and Director of the Political Police Ahmed Tal'at regarding an army training manual that was found with the Brotherhood militia in Palestine with his name on it. Nasser got off the hook with great difficulty by alleging that he lent it to an officer who was later killed in action and maybe they found it on him. The Brothers adhere to an even more enticing story, which traces their relationship with Nasser back to 1941 when Major Mahmoud Labib was charged with creating an Islamist base in the army. On his deathbed, Labib entrusted the list of members of the Brotherhood's Committee of Free Soldiers in the Army to Nasser. After he passed away in December 1951, Nasser ran the committee for his own purposes.[68] This was confirmed by Naguib's claim that the Brothers helped Nasser directly in creating the Free Officers.[69] This story was also corroborated by the Free Officer Hussein Hammudah, who participated with Nasser and five others in weekly Brotherhood meetings between 1944 and 1948, before being suspended because of the Palestine War. Nasser then asked Hammudah in November 1950 to form a new organization within the army based on the members of the old Brotherhood organization in the military. Hammudah added that during this period Nasser was solely responsible for the military training of the movement's youth.[70] Nasser's wife, Tahiya, wrote in her memoirs that around those years her husband used to receive guests at the house and introduce them to firearms.[71] Clearly, these were not military cadets.

On the eve of the coup, Nasser realized that in light of the movement's vast organizational resources and manpower, it was prudent to enlist its support. During a meeting on July 18, 1952, he asked the Brotherhood cadres Hassan Ashmawi, Saleh Abu-Raqiq, and Salah Shadi to order movement sympathizers in the army and police not to resist the coup; to use their militant organ if needed to help the army intercept any British attempt to reoccupy Cairo; and to organize demonstrations in support of the new regime. In fact, the coup did not proceed before the general guide gave the green light on July 21.[72] To confirm the story, the young Brotherhood member Mahmoud

Game' says he was instructed by his leadership the night before the coup to secure key installations.[73] The honeymoon between Nasser and the Muslim Brotherhood continued during the first months following the coup. In 1953, he instructed Interior Minister Suleiman Hafez to exclude the Brotherhood from the ban on political parties, referring to them as "our greatest supporters."[74] When movement leaders sought to control the government and name its ministers, and when Nasser learned that they supported the artillery mutiny to put him under pressure, the two sides inevitably clashed. But even after the ruthless Nasser disbanded the movement and detained 540 of its members (including the general guide) on January 14, 1954, he continued to appeal to its popular base by, for example, attending the annual ceremony commemorating the birth of the movement's founder on February 12, 1954 (while preventing Naguib from coming along), and declaring on that occasion: "I am struggling to fulfill the principles he died for and God is my witness."[75] This long and convoluted relationship made the Muslim Brothers assume they could trust Nasser—as it turned out, they were wrong.

Following his fake rapprochement with the Brotherhood, Nasser received a visit from Ibrahim al-Tahawi and Ahmed Te'ima, his security lieutenants, at the Liberation Rally. They offered to organize a general strike, spearheaded by public transport workers, to bring the country to a standstill, and asked for Nasser's permission to bribe Sawi Ahmed Sawi, head of the transport union. On March 27, one million workers went on strike in support of Nasser. That same day, the Liberation Rally, with the help of the military police, brought truckloads of peasants to Cairo, chanting antidemocracy slogans: "No parties! No parliament! No elections!" The strike and accompanying demonstrations lasted for three days.[76]

Meanwhile, the security trio of Nasr, Badran, and Radwan launched a petition-signing campaign within the armed services, demanding Naguib's resignation and the retraction of the March decrees. Officers were reminded that they might lose their jobs, possibly their lives, should the old regime be reinstated. Those who objected were bullied by their colleagues in order to sign, and those who persisted were either relieved from their duties (thirty-four officers) or detained (twenty-six officers). The content of this military petition was broadcast by public radio, followed by similar petitions from the police and labor unions. This was followed by a comprehensive military and police strike, organized by security agents within both. People were made to understand that the state's coercive organs now stood united behind Nasser, and that pro-Naguib demonstrations would be mercilessly quelled—as exemplified by the brutal clampdown against the Shubra al-Khima workers on March 26. On March 29, Nasser announced that—having heard the "impulse of the street"—the March decrees would be revoked, but to maintain order all strikes and demonstrations were now banned.[77] It was yet another of those Napoleonic moments when a revolution initially espousing democracy gives way to a military dictatorship by mobilizing the support of its peasant and urban poor beneficiaries, then dismissing them.

Naguib tried to fight back. He called the interior minister and asked him to crack down on the antidemocracy demonstrations, but Zakaria said he would not do so unless Naguib sent him a signed order authorizing him to shoot unarmed civilians if necessary. Of course, Naguib refused. He then considered deploying his supporters among the cavalry, but Khaled warned him that this would lead to a massacre. He appealed to the head of the Cairo police division, the former army general Ahmed Shawky, for help. But although Shawky supported him, he was in the minority within the Interior Ministry. To make things worse, Naguib learned through French sources that the United States firmly supported Nasser, and that it had asked the British to intervene on his behalf if necessary. Naguib was left with no other option than to accept—stoically—that the coup was a mistake, and that if he was unwilling to drive the country into civil war, he must retire; "I was as exhausted as a boxer in the final round; I was not yet knocked out, but had lost too many points throughout this long game."[78]

Naguib's associates also realized they were on the losing side; some jumped ship, others were pushed over. His legal adviser (the former interior minister Suleiman Hafez) resigned on March 26; his aide-de-camp (Muhammad Riyad) escaped to Saudi Arabia on March 27—after begging him to come along; his ally at the State Council (Abd al-Razeq al-Sanhouri), who was trying to mend relations between him and the Brotherhood, was assaulted at his office on March 29 by military police officers, then spent a few days at a military hospital before being discharged from office; and his main cavalry contact (Khaled Muhi al-Din) was exiled to Switzerland. In April alone, thirty-seven pro-Naguib cavalry officers were imprisoned and dozens were purged. This was followed in June by a more systematic purge, which included another 140 officers. Nasser then followed the stick with a carrot, raising military expenditure from 17 to 25 percent, a conciliatory gesture designed to win the rank and file.[79]

The security then turned to public institutions, detaining 252 pro-democracy civil servants in what proved to be the opening act in a long series of measures designed to "cleanse" the bureaucracy and the media from "reactionary elements." On April 15, the RCC stripped anyone who held public office before the coup of all political rights, and later dissolved syndicates and student unions. Police trucks surrounded universities, and professors and students were recruited by the security apparatus to spy on their colleagues.[80] After the March 1954 crisis, the revolutionary government showed its teeth, considering all those not entirely supportive of it to be enemies of the state and agents of foreign powers. Nasser now assumed full control as prime minister, while Naguib, though still officially the president, rarely left his house, confiding to his journal: "Egypt has now entered a dark age of injustice and terror."[81] Within a few months Nasser's camp succeed in securing "total control of the armed forces ... the neutralization and eventual destruction of other existing loci of political power ... the control of education, the media, professional syndicates, trade unions, the rural structures in the countryside, the religious institutions and orders, the administration and bureaucracy, eventually, the whole society."[82]

Nasser then proceeded to tie his loose ends with the Muslim Brothers. After a highly suspicious attempt on his life, on October 26, 1954, when he was giving a speech in Alexandria and nine bullets were shot at him at close range from a lone shooter (the Brotherhood member Mahmoud Abd al-Latif) but all missed, the greatest crackdown in the history of the Brotherhood in Egypt began, with perhaps 20,000 detained in newly built concentration camps in the desert, and only 1,050 officially tried. Of those, six leaders were executed, and the rest, including the general guide, received long prison sentences. Expectedly, the movement was disbanded, its property confiscated, and the slightest expression of sympathy with it outlawed. On November 14, it was declared that security investigations had uncovered that the Brotherhood was doing Naguib's bidding, and the latter was placed under house arrest in a secluded, heavily guarded villa on the outskirts of Cairo, where he would remain for the next eighteen years. Though Naguib insisted he had nothing to do with the unimpressive assassination attempt, he expressed no sympathy for the Brothers who walked into the trap with eyes wide open. In his view, their greed—rather than gullibility—blinded them from seeing the obvious fact that Nasser was only using them to consolidate power.[83] This same greed and disposition toward backdoor deals can be observed throughout the movement's history, and has made it highly susceptible to manipulation by kings, prime ministers, or whoever was in charge; and this same tendency was in play in 2011 in the Brotherhood's relationship with the officers who held power after the popular uprising of January 25.

On June 23, 1956, a referendum approved Nasser's presidency (by 99.9 percent) and the new constitution. The RCC was dissolved, and Nasser became sole ruler. Still, Naguib's story had a postscript. During the Tripartite Attack on Egypt in 1956 (also known as the Suez Crisis), Nasser's intelligence claimed that the British were planning to drop paratroopers outside the capital to free Naguib and reinstall him. We now know, of course, that no such adventure was ever planned, but two incidents forced Nasser to take this report seriously: first, Naguib sent Nasser a letter pleading for his release to allow him to join the battle as an ordinary soldier; second, Naguib's legal adviser Hafez met General Commander of the Armed Forces Amer on November 2 to persuade him that Nasser must choose the interest of the nation over his own and reinstate Naguib to appease the British. Within days of this meeting, Hafez was detained, and Naguib reallocated by the military police to a remote desert location on the border with Sudan for two months.[84]

The March 1954 crisis was certainly a defining moment, which set the new regime on its authoritarian trajectory. How can we evaluate the triumph of Nasser's faction during this first intraregime confrontation? Naguib had greater legitimacy as the acknowledged leader of the revolution and the first president of the republic. His class supporters were key players in the old regime: the landed aristocracy and wealthy bourgeoisie. The declared aim of the coup was to build a proper democracy after driving out the occupation and purging corrupt political elements and royalists, an ideology adhered to not only by most of the educated classes, but also by a significant portion of the military itself. In short, one could consider Naguib a perfect representative of the dominant classes and ideology of the time. And if Naguib had won, Egypt would have probably followed the Turkish path, with the military overseeing the birth of a limited democracy.

Nasser, on the other hand, faced the uphill struggle that comes with trying to instate a new regime. For the founder of a new regime, as Machiavelli reminded us, "makes enemies of all those who are doing well under the old system, and has only lukewarm support from those who hope to do well under the new one."[85] So how did his faction end up on top? The answer is that Nasser immediately created a security coterie out of his most loyal lieutenants, and by 1954 it had developed far enough to realize that its interests were not the same as those of the military, and that democracy would bring their new careers to an abrupt end. It was this early division of labor that made all the difference. While the military was still dragging its feet—which is only normal in large and internally differentiated institutions—the sharp-minded security operatives moved quickly and unfalteringly, and as it turned out, quite effectively. The end result was that the military-fostered democracy option was ruled out, at least temporarily.

In Khaled Muhi al-Din's judgment, Nasser's success closed the path to democracy.[86] This is probably an exaggeration. It is true that this early battle was decisive, but it was only one among many more to come. Its outcome planted the seeds of another, grander confrontation, this time between the factions that crystallized around Nasser and Amer. Nasser did not intend to form a military dictatorship, but rather a military-backed populist regime that would allow him to rule in the name of the people. He never conceived of the military as a future partner—but Amer did. The root of the problem was that, unlike the Russian, Chinese, or even Cuban case, Nasser had no political revolutionary party to keep the military in check. His chief revolutionary organization was none other than the military itself. Now that he had consolidated power, he discovered that the only political control instrument available was the security apparatus. Over the next decade, Nasser (the chief politician) and Amer (the chief general) would scramble frantically to enlist the support of the various security agencies that would eventually arbitrate the political–military race to the top.

Two States Within a State:
The Road to June 1967

Too much ink has been spilled on the intimate relationship between Nasser and Amer. Those closest to them spoke of them as "soul brothers" until the very last day of their struggle. In fact, their special bond has been the standard explanation for why Nasser hesitated to move decisively against Amer from 1956 to 1967, despite the latter's apparent military ineptitude: he did not want to hurt his best friend's feelings. While such an explanation is obviously unsatisfactory, it rules out the possibility that what sparked the decade-long struggle between the two was personal enmity. In reality, the struggle was fueled by those who stood at the true locus of power: that is, the security elite that stood united against Naguib's faction, but was now divided into two competing camps: those who attached themselves to the political apparatus, namely, the Ministry of Interior with its General Investigations Directorate (GID), and the President's Bureau of Information (PBI), and those who attached themselves to the military, that is, the Office of the Commander-in-Chief for Political Guidance (OCC), the Military Intelligence Department (MID), and the General Intelligence Service (GIS). It was a struggle for supremacy between two sets of security institutions, masked as a personal rivalry between the president and the field marshal, a struggle that unfolded rapidly, with dizzying shifts in cleavages and alliances, only to end with disaster on the morning of June 5, 1967.

It is little wonder why, in a speech delivered after his final showdown with Amer in 1967, Nasser regretted the way security officers had transformed Egypt into a "*mukhabarat* [intelligence] state," and pledged to dismantle this state, which he partly blamed for the June defeat. The president's description was quite accurate. Many observers agree: "By any historical yardstick, what existed in Egypt was something unique, a dictatorship without a dictator."[1] That was because power was vested in the security complex, whether civilian or military, while the political apparatus had little influence. It was the security aristocracy that now ruled the country after the coup had beheaded the traditional nobility; this new aristocracy occupied the position of the old not just figuratively but in a very material sense: they inhabited royal households, married into noble families, joined exclusive social clubs, and so on. They differed from the old elite only in their draconian method of rule. The formidable security system now in place rounded up suspected dissidents on an unprecedented scale—prisons contained an average of 20,000 political detainees throughout the sixties. To live in Egypt during this period was to be constantly under the purview of a pervasive surveillance structure: phones, offices, and homes were bugged; mail was regularly checked; neighbors, colleagues, even siblings could not be trusted. Politically suspect individuals would typically be arrested at dawn, when they were too disoriented to resist, and with no one around to help. The unwelcome "dawn visitors" would then detain suspects for indefinite periods, torture them systematically, and force them to sign confessions that would land them hefty prison sentences.

How did things get so bad? After the mutinies of January and March 1954, Nasser's suspicions of the military grew. He sidelined its influential leaders, including his RCC colleagues (safe for Amer), and entrusted officers-turned-security-officials with safeguarding the regime. Yet regime stability was still threatened by the fact that security agencies were divided along a two-tiered command structure: the presidency, with Nasser at its helm, and the military leadership under Amer. Nasser, of course, controlled Interior Ministry organs, which he himself had set up and entrusted his loyal lieutenant Zakaria Muhi al-Din to run. Driven, however, by his innately conspiratorial nature, Nasser developed a veritable intelligence unit within the presidency, which was devoted, according to its director, Samy Sharaf, to gathering information about the private lives of officers and state officials through a network of informants and an elaborate tapping system.[2] In truth, this unit thrived not only on Nasser's "pathologically suspicious" character, but also on Sharaf's skill in playing "Iago to the President's paranoid Othello."[3] The PBI kept army officers and ministers under strict surveillance: recording their conversations, videotaping their private meetings, recruiting their underlings, and meticulously filing every trivial rumor regarding any of them. Through it Nasser also reached out to former officers and asked them to gather as much information as they could from colleagues still serving in the ranks. Amer, on the other hand, controlled military-based security organs (MID and military police) orchestrated by the OCC, first under Salah Nasr and Abbas Radwan, and then under the aggressive leadership of Shams Badran. Amer substantially increased his power when in 1957 his protégé Nasr took charge of the civilian GIS. More important, through dispersing benefits and promotions, Amer swayed dozens of officers to his side—only those strictly committed to professional military service resented his corruption of the corps. This alignment of forces set the stage for an epic battle for power between those competing organs, with the first round commencing in October 1956, during the Suez Crisis.

SUEZ 1956: MILITARY DEFEAT, POLITICAL TRIUMPH

The road toward the Suez War did not begin with the nationalization of the Suez Canal in July 1956, but almost two years earlier over a military-related dispute. Many officers supported the coup because of their resentment of the army's inadequacy as a fighting force, as was first demonstrated by its failure to prevent British occupation in 1882, then its powerlessness as the country's monarch was humiliated by Britain in February 1942, and finally by defeat in the 1948 Palestine war. It was thus only natural that procuring advanced weapons was at the top of Nasser's agenda. Capitalizing on his CIA links, he first turned to the United States. In October 1954, a meeting was held at the security operative Hassan al-Tuhami's apartment between Nasser and Amer, on the Egyptian side, with the CIA's Miles Copeland, and the generals Albert Gerhardt and Wilbur Eveland, representing the Americans. According to Copeland, an agreement was reached to sell Egypt $20 million worth of weapons on easy credit terms. But the following month, Washington announced only an economic aid package of $40 million; Nasser also received $3 million under the table from the U.S. president's executive budget, which was normally earmarked for CIA operations. Copeland returned to Washington in July 1955 to consult with George Allen, assistant secretary of state for the Middle East, regarding the delayed arms deal. A desperate Nasser followed this with a warning message to Kermit Roosevelt, director of the CIA's Middle East operations, in mid-September that if the deal did not go through, he might consider requesting military aid from the Eastern Bloc, but the latter did not take him seriously.[4]

Clearly, America's intention was to coax Egypt into joining the Western-oriented regional defense alliance known as the Central Treaty Organization (CENTO), or simply, the Baghdad Pact. The pact allowed U.S. and British forces to use the territories and facilities of member countries (Iraq, Iran, Turkey, Pakistan) to block Communist incursions into the region. When Egypt refused to join, the Americans, according to the future foreign minister Ismail Fahmy, encouraged Israeli raids against the Egyptian-controlled Gaza Strip between February and September 1955 under the pretext of checking the activities of Palestinian guerrillas. The raids exposed Egypt's military vulnerability even further, forcing Nasser to conclude the famous "Czech arms deal" with the Soviet Union in September 1955—a substantial deal that included 200 fighter jets and bombers, 230 tanks, 500 artillery pieces,

530 armored vehicles, 200 troop carriers, and a naval force of 3 submarines and a handful of destroyers and minesweepers.[5] Nasser made it clear that the West had only itself to blame. In a speech delivered on September 27, 1955, at a military fair, he said: "When we carried out the revolution we turned to every country ... to arm our forces, we turned to England, we turned to France, we turned to America ... [but] we only heard demands [that undermine] Egypt's dignity."[6] American strategists were stunned. They had placed too much store in Khrushchev's public pledge to the Central Committee of the Communist Party to adhere to Joseph Stalin's policy of never staking Soviet credibility on non-Communist developing countries, especially ones that were too far away and too unstable. Stalin, as is well known, was an advocate of "socialism in one country" (meaning the USSR), and intervened outside Russian borders only when success was guaranteed at the hands of a Communist party loyal to Moscow. Washington believed the Soviets eyed Third World nationalists with suspicion, if not disdain, and would never ally with them. Obviously, however, the success of the U.S. Containment Doctrine, which prevented the spread of communism outside the USSR and Eastern Europe, forced Moscow to treat postcolonial nationalists as "good enough Communists" in order to break its isolation. And before the Americans knew what hit them, Nasser strained the situation even further by recognizing Red China in May 1956. Enraged, the United States not only canceled military aid talks, but also withdrew its offer to help build the High Dam, a massive hydroelectric project that was supposed to double Egypt's industrial capacity. By doing so, Secretary of State John Foster Dulles played unwittingly into Nasser's hand. For months the president had been looking for a pretext to reclaim Egypt's rights over the Suez Canal. Now, citing the need to channel the canal's revenue toward financing the dam, a defiant Nasser nationalized the Suez Canal in front of an ecstatic crowd on July 26, 1956.

Instead of just aggravating the United States, Nasser's decision convinced three odd partners to carry out a joint military strike against Egypt, what became known as the Tripartite Aggression. Britain, France, and Israel came to this decision through very different routes, though it was the conjunction of their interests to depose Egypt's new regime that made their cooperation possible. For Britain, as Foreign Secretary Selwyn Lloyd later revealed, Nasser's obvious ambition to project power in the eastern flank of the Arab world (Jordan, Iraq, Aden, and the sheikhdoms of the Gulf) undermined its strategic allies and threatened its control of the region's oilfields. Egypt's control of the Suez Canal itself represented another problem: not only did a quarter of all British imports come through the canal, but also three-quarters of its oil needs. Of the 14,666 ships that passed through the canal in 1955, for instance, 4,358 were British. If Nasser blocked the canal, Britain might suffer "the worst industrial crisis in her history."[7]

France's grievances had to do with Nasser's actions in the North African side of the Arab world, particularly in Algeria. The French military establishment blamed Nasser for the Algerian Revolt. Hard-pressed to justify their failure to end the insurgency, French generals needed an excuse, and the most sensible one was Nasser. In the French army's propaganda, Egypt's role in Algeria was the same as the Chinese role in Vietnam, the difference being that Egypt, unlike China, could be defeated. So if France had been humbled by China in Southeast Asia, there was no need for it to suffer the same fate in the Middle East at the hands of a lesser power. If only Nasser were deposed, Algeria's Front de Liberation National (FLN) would lose its capacity to evict the French by force. As with Britain, the Suez Canal also had an influence over France's decision: "In the Gallic imagination the canal was not just a masterpiece of engineering but a tribute to the Napoleonic mission ... On a less elevated level, the Canal Company was the 'last great international stronghold of French capital.' Its board was controlled by French directors, it was staffed largely by French technicians, and it provided a modest income to tens of thousands of French shareholders."[8]

Soon after resolving to launch war against Nasser, France approached Israel. Egypt's new neighbor was alarmed by the Czech arms deal, and believed it had only a narrow window of opportunity to cripple Cairo's drive for military parity. Israel and France developed intimate military links in the 1950s as French armaments and aviation industries sought clients with long shopping lists and generous funds to help them achieve economies of scale. Transactions increased in value from a few Mirages and Mystères to a deal to help Israel establish its first atomic reactor, in Dimona. Moreover, the Mossad shared intelligence with the Service de Documentation et Centre de Espionnage (SCCE) regarding FLN activities. Now France offered Israel a full military partnership in a joint assault against a common enemy, an offer it could hardly refuse. On September 21, Shimon Peres, the man responsible for French-Israeli military cooperation, was invited to France to plan the operation.[9]

The aim of the tripartite plot, as set in the Sèvres Protocol on October 24, 1956, was simple: toppling Nasser and establishing control over the Suez Canal. However, the military plan and the logistics required to pull it off were anything but simple. Israel was assigned a diversionary role. Its forces would roll into Sinai to draw in Egypt's army. The two Western powers would then demand an immediate cease-fire and the withdrawal of each force to equal distances from the Suez Canal. Egypt would certainly refuse because such a withdrawal would mean surrendering Sinai to the Israelis. Citing the need to safeguard the international waterway, Britain and France would occupy the Suez

Canal Zone. First, Egyptian airfields would be bombed to neutralize the air force and unnerve the population; then a naval barrage would smother canal defenses to allow paratroopers to be parachuted in; and finally, a full-fledged airborne and seaborne invasion would wrest the canal cities away from Egypt and advance to Cairo to install a friendly government.

As agreed, Israel's elite strike force, the 7th Armored Brigade, stormed into Egyptian territories on October 29, 1956. Nasser issued his orders for the six battalions stationed there to block the Israeli advance until the 4th Armored Division could cross the canal to join the battle. The next day, Egypt received warnings through its ambassadors to London and Paris to withdraw ten miles from the canal within twelve hours to avert international intervention. Nasser's suspicions that a plot had been hatched were soon confirmed when Britain and France raided Egyptian airports, ravaging the country's air force. By the end of October, Egypt was confronting a force four times as big as its own, with 1,000 jets, 700 tanks, and two naval fleets with 130 warships. This was "the largest amphibious fighting force since the end of the Second World War."[10]

Naturally, Egypt's military command was startled. When Nasser got to GHQ on October 31, he was advised to surrender himself to the British to spare the country from total destruction. Amer, who was apparently suffering from a nervous breakdown, cried: "The air strikes will send the country back a thousand years. I cannot expose my countrymen to such a massacre."[11] Ahmed Hamroush, who was present at the meeting, describes how Nasser harshly responded to Amer's pleas for submission: "Nobody is going to surrender; everybody is going to fight … Your behavior is unmanly; the first shots have hardly been fired. Not only must I take direct command of the army, but I also don't want you issuing any orders … If you can't do better than mope like an old hag then you will be court-martialed."[12] Unshaken by the defeatism of his chief military commander, Nasser offered to lead the battle personally, a suggestion to which Amer quickly conceded. The president gathered that if the army was dispatched to face the Israelis in Sinai it would be caught between a rock and a hard place as soon as the Franco-British forces landed in the Canal Zone, and the road to the capital would be virtually undefended. He thus ordered all forces to pull out of Sinai in forty-eight hours (by November 2) and dig in around the banks of the canal. Despite the pressure, Nasser planned the withdrawal meticulously; his successful delaying tactics saved two-thirds of the men and equipment. He also prevented the pilots from joining the battle because he felt they were not yet equipped to take on Western aces. After effectively benching Amer, the president authorized the sinking of fifty cement tanks at the canal's northern entrance to block an invasion from the Mediterranean, even though he knew this would obstruct navigation in the entire canal. On November 2, Nasser gave a resounding speech at al-Azhar mosque, rallying Egyptians for an all-out popular resistance. He put Zakaria in charge of coordinating popular resistance throughout the country, and dispatched three former RCC colleagues to organize resistance in the canal cities, especially around Port Said, before visiting the battlefront himself days later.[13]

In a few days, the attack came to a halt. British and French troops evacuated on December 22 with no gains to speak of, followed by the Israelis in March 1957. Why did the tripartite campaign falter so soon? Nasser's swift measures certainly had some effect. In addition, the British part of the military operation faced several logistical complications. British troops had evacuated the canal in June 1956 and were already too far away; the closest detachment was in Malta, six days' sail from Egyptian shores. Assembling the troops once more proved to be one of the most "laborious, elaborate, and time-consuming" mobilization processes in military history.[14] Part of the reason for that was that Britain, as Harold McMillan confessed in his memoirs, wanted to prepare for all eventualities. This is a better way of saying that his government "lacked the imagination and initiative to move on from the Second World War ... launching a Normandy-style armada by the sure knowledge that in the time it took to cross the Mediterranean world opinion, already sympathetic to Egypt, would have moved much farther in that direction."[15] Ultimately, however, it was the actions of two countries that really mattered: the United States and the Soviet Union. The United States was not willing to accept a reverse to the retrenching of European imperialism after it had finally began to replace British and French hegemony in the Middle East, and the Soviet Union considered an assault on a country with which Moscow had just established military cooperation an unforgivable insult. It was their fierce rejection of the attack—one of the very few things they agreed on during the Cold War—that brought it to nothing.

Although the Egyptian military was officially defeated (it was forced to withdraw from Sinai, and could not prevent allied air attacks or occupation), the Suez War was hailed as a "political triumph." Of course, Nasser's calculations had turned out to be flawed: he ruled out an Israeli intervention; he thought Franco-British competition in the Middle East would preclude their cooperation; he believed France was totally consumed in Algeria and could not afford to open another front; and he estimated that the time and cost needed to assemble a substantial British force was too prohibitive.[16] Still, the president displayed great political agility in mobilizing popular resistance and securing diplomatic support out of all proportion to his country's strength. His arousing speeches and confident attitude inspired Egyptians to resist fiercely, and the stories of their heroic defiance are still part of the folklore of the citizens of the canal cities. Also, the way he presented Egypt's case to world opinion, and his willingness to compensate Britain and France for their lost shares in the Suez Canal, turned the table on the aggressors. He also proved to be a successful tactician, delaying the aggressors' success and managing to bring home two-thirds of the army intact.

But at the same time that Nasser's political leadership was being celebrated in Egypt and throughout the developing world, Amer's mediocre military abilities were exposed. Analyzing the military balance sheet, Egypt's future war minister Abd al-Ghany al-Gamasy explains:

> The political victory might have overshadowed our dismal military performance, but there was no escaping the fact that we failed to secure the country from the east or the north; that the belligerents only yielded to international pressure; and that Israel managed to secure at least one considerable gain in exchange for its withdrawal: an international peacekeeping force stationed in Sharm al-Sheikh to guarantee freedom of Israeli navigation through the Straits of Tiran into the Gulf of Aqaba in the Red Sea. Amer was supposed to reshuffle the general staff and service heads, upgrade the air force and air defenses, and establish a strong presence in Sinai to deter future Israeli aggression; none of this was done.[17]

Keen on preserving the patronage network they had established, Amer's security associates convinced him that the war was the president's fault; after all, it was his reckless decision to nationalize the canal that brought it on. They also warned him that purging his loyal subordinates under pressure from Nasser would irrevocably tarnish his reputation. Personally, Amer became apprehensive of the military prowess his friend displayed during the war. His method to win back the respect of his men was to shower them with favors, to spoil them even further than he had already done. So while Nasser demanded far-reaching changes in military leadership and organization, an embittered Amer remained unyielding, refusing during a stormy meeting on November 15 to even transfer the scandalously incompetent air force commander, Major General Sedqi Mahmoud, because he was "his man." Not only that, but Amer also lashed out at Nasser, accusing him of provoking an unnecessary war and then blaming the military for the result.[18] Amer's audacity shocked the president, who began to suspect that the military might be slipping out of his control, that his trusted lieutenant might have built his own power base in the corps. For the first time, a wedge was driven between the two longtime comrades. It could not have come at a worse time. Eisenhower expected a grateful Egypt to embrace his January 1957 offer of U.S. support for countries threatened by communism; instead, Nasser attacked the so-called Eisenhower Doctrine vehemently as an imperialist ruse that justified U.S. military intervention in the Middle

East instead of arming newly independent states to defend their own borders. On March 22, 1957, the U.S. president met with the CIA chief, Allen Dulles, and the veteran Middle East operative Kermit Roosevelt to consider means of ousting Nasser[19]—plans that would finally take shape a decade later, shaking the Egyptian regime to the core.

THE DARK YEARS

The Suez War debacle and the confrontation that followed it made the president determined to remove his friend from military command. This was easier said than done. Building on his amicable and lavish personality, Amer's security aides had placed him at the center of an elaborate patronage network within the officer corps. They talked him into promoting himself to the rank of field marshal in 1957 (a rank unknown in the Arabic lexicon), and helped him transform the army into a tribe, with him as tribal chief: allocating gifts and honors, granting personal favors, solving family disputes, inviting his men to all-night parties at his house, and making sure that the "field marshal's men" remained untouchable. During his tenure, promotions accelerated to the point where one could become a brigadier general at the age of forty (compared with colonel in the early 1950s). All officers benefited from his doubling of salaries; his raising of the retirement age; his allocation of summerhouses, automobiles, travel grants, and interest-free loans; his order to have officers' children accepted at universities regardless of their academic scores; and various other privileges.[20] For the army, the field marshal had become something of a Santa Claus. Colonel Muhammad Selim recounted one indicative incident: "A junior officer once walked up to Amer as he was about to leave GHQ and complained that he was forced to use public transportation to commute to work every day. Amer tore the top part of his cigarette packet and wrote on its back: 'Dear Fiat manager, dispense a car immediately to the bearer of this message.' The field marshal did not even ask for his name; the fact that he donned the uniform and came to him for help was enough."[21]

Amer did not want to replace the president, but aspired to having equal power. So instead of enhancing the army's fighting capacity, Amer devoted himself to transforming it into "a state within a state" through the help of his security aides. He treated the military as a personal fief, promoting officers based on their loyalty to him, rather than to Nasser or the state. To keep the president on his feet, Amer's security men provided him with a regular stream of attempted plots they claim to have foiled (such as an alleged plot in April 1957 involving British operatives and eight army officers). The aim was to make Nasser too anxious to carry out a military shake-up against their will.[22] So what had originally begun as an attempt to secure the revolution in 1954 had been gradually transformed into securing the dominance of the present military leadership. Nasser's only hope now was to persuade Amer to leave the military on his own accord, an impossible task by any measure.

The president thus turned to the next best option: acting on the advice of the PBI director, Samy Sharaf, he tried to create his own secret network within the army. Quickly realizing that the officer corps was effectively sealed off by Amer's security apparatus, Sharaf shifted his effort to the Military Academy, which was headed by a relative of his, the future war minister Muhammad Fawzy. By the end of 1956, Sharaf had recruited six cadets. Their mission was to lie low until they graduated, then actively build a network loyal to the president once they joined the service. After a few meetings, however, the field marshal's security men picked them up, and after a fiery confrontation with Nasser, the organization was disbanded. Another PBI operative, Hassan al-Tuhami, decided to bug Amer's phones on his own initiative. Again, Amer's alert security apparatus found out, and Tuhami was not only dismissed, but also exiled to Vienna for an entire decade.[23]

Exposed and increasingly on the defensive, Nasser now became entrapped in a cat-and-mouse game with his field marshal. To ease Amer's suspicions, Nasser surrendered a bit of ground by appointing the OCC director, Salah Nasr—the field marshal's right-hand security man—as head of the GIS in May 1957, and Nasr's OCC deputy Abbas Radwan as interior minister in October 1958. But in order to protect himself, Nasser employed the former GIS director Aly Sabri at the PBI to capitalize on his contacts at the agency to neutralize Nasr. The president also anticipated Nasr's official takeover in May by appointing two confidants (Amin Huwaidi and Sha'rawi Gomaa) to senior positions at the GIS in February. He then convinced Amer to appoint the second-tier Free Officer Colonel Shams Badran as the new OCC director, replacing Nasr. Badran had been acting as liaison between the presidency and the military, and Nasser hoped he would deliver the military back to him. In addition to all these tactical precautions, Nasser was ultimately reassured by the fact that Zakaria Muhi al-Din, the architect of the entire security apparatus, was unofficially supervising all civilian security agencies, regardless of who was in charge at GIS or the Interior Ministry. The president's safeguards, however, soon came to nothing. Sabri clashed with Sharaf and had to be reallocated, and the shrewd Nasr not only refused to begin his tenure unless the GIS became independent of Zakaria's hegemony, he also isolated Nasser's men, Huwaidi and Gomaa, forcing them to move to the PBI in a few months, before proceeding to ally the GIS with the military-based security group.[24] Now all military and civilian security organs (except for the president's own PBI) came under Amer's control. Worse still, the field marshal won over Badran, Nasser's supposed spy. Badran relished the fact that his new boss's laissez-faire management style, which sharply contrasted with Nasser's tight-leash supervision, would grant him virtual control of the entire military.

By 1958, Nasser's position within the security community had considerably deteriorated. That same year, however, presented Nasser with a golden opportunity to sway Amer away from command. The centerpiece of Nasserist foreign policy was Arab nationalism, a policy aimed at uniting all Arab countries under one body (like his European neighbors to the north were striving to do themselves). The first step of this long-term plan was to merge Egypt and Syria, the closest two Arab countries (in institutions and temperament) into one state: the United Arab Republic. To kill two birds with one stone, Nasser decided to combine the expansion of Egyptian influence abroad with the consolidation of his power at home, and so he kicked his friend-turned-rival upstairs by appointing him governor of Syria, now renamed the Northern Sector. The field marshal agreed, believing he would now have his own country to run. But the union lasted for only three short years. This was a disaster for Amer on many levels: first, it was his trusted Syrian aide-de-camp (Abd al-Karim al-Nahlawy) who organized the anti-Egyptian coup that dissolved the union; second, Syria's new leaders shipped Amer back to Cairo on September 28, 1961, in a humiliating fashion (rumor has it, in his undergarments); third, his military commanders again failed to fly troops to Syria fast enough to avert the coup; and finally, one of the factors that fueled the secession was that he allowed his men to run rampant all over the Syrian corps. Shaken by this spectacular blunder, Amer tendered his resignation, which Nasser accepted with great relief. Three days later, the president reappointed Zakaria as interior minister, demoting Radwan to minister without portfolio, and was preparing for a similar move against Nasr at the GIS. But in January 1962, before Nasser could catch his breath, Zakaria and Sharaf uncovered a military plot to reinstate Amer and dismiss the president if he attempted to resist.[25] It was clear that the field marshal's men were not ready to surrender their boss. Amer's ejection from the military had to wait.

This time Nasser had to improvise. In September 1962, he told Amer he intended to rule Egypt collectively through a twelve-member Presidential Council, which would include both of them, in addition to some old RCC colleagues and a few civilian ministers. To join the council, however, Amer had to resign and accept the appointment of Muhammad Fawzy, director of the Military Academy, as the new commander-in-chief. Nasser's real intention, as he later confessed to Fawzy, was to isolate his unruly field marshal with a sleight of hand from the corps.[26] Amer reluctantly agreed, not knowing exactly what he was getting into. During the council's first meeting, on September 18, Nasser announced the appointed of Aly Sabri (his close security associate) as prime minister, and reminded Amer to submit his resignation as agreed. Instead, Shams Badran, the OCC director, came to see Nasser the next day to inform him that after consulting with his men, the field marshal had decided to stay on. A furious Nasser insisted that Amer carry out his part of the deal, and all Badran managed to secure from him was an extension. After a couple of months, Badran turned up with a letter of resignation. As the president skimmed through the lines, he quickly realized it was a ploy—and a quite dangerous one. In the letter, which Badran claimed had "somehow leaked" to the officer corps and the press, Amer said he was stepping down because Nasser adamantly pursued the path of dictatorship: "What you should be working for now is democracy ... I cannot imagine that after all this time, after eradicating feudalism and manipulative capitalism, after the masses have placed their trust in you unreservedly, you still fear democracy." On that same day, before Nasser could recover from the shock, paratroopers demonstrated outside his house with their machine guns pointed toward the presidential residence. The PBI also informed him that Nasr at the GIS was plotting something big with the general staff. A few days later, Badran carried to the president a new message from the field marshal: Amer would not resign unless Nasser pledged in writing to establish democracy. The president had no choice but to negotiate with Amer. A meeting was set for December 11. The field marshal began by stressing that the political security of the armed forces depended on him personally, and that any attempt to remove him from office would lead to disaster. Amer followed his not-so-subtle threat with a list of demands that included promoting him from commander-in-chief to first vice president and deputy supreme commander of the armed forces (Nasser holding nominally the title of supreme commander), in addition to undivided control over the military's financial and administrative affairs. Realizing at this point that challenging Amer would certainly provoke a coup, the president retreated.[27]

So basically the Presidential Council gambit backfired. The field marshal not only emerged unscathed, but also his position improved considerably, in effect being promoted from the number two man to sharing the number one position. The confrontation confirmed Nasser's worst fear; he complained to Zakaria, after what he considered Amer's "silent coup," that there were now two states in Egypt, an official one, which he presided over, and a shadowy one led by Amer.[28] In a less guarded moment, he bluntly confessed to Sadat that the country was currently "run by a gang ... I am responsible as president, but it is Amer that rules."[29] The type of regime emerging in Egypt in the 1960s was therefore one of dual power, an unstable and alarming situation.

The previously lurking power struggle now came into the open. Nasser's goal was to infiltrate the military, while Amer's goal was to extend his influence over the political sphere. The president pushed Amer in March 1964 to hire Muhammad Fawzy as chief of staff, after he had refused to surrender general command to him two years earlier. The field marshal acquiesced in order to appease Nasser, but then restricted Fawzy's duties to trivial administrative tasks, and created a new position in the chain of command—the so-called Ground Forces Command (GFC)—to carry out the duties of the chief of staff.[30] Amer and his entourage, on the other hand, tightened their grip over the military and security, and began to extend their influence over civilian sectors as well, from overseeing land reform to supervising public sector companies and running sporting clubs. In truth, though, the real players in this struggle were neither Nasser nor Amer, but rather their security associates. For example, hiring Fawzy as chief of staff was proposed by his relative Samy Sharaf, the PBI director; at the same time, the OCC head, Shams Badran, had an infinitely stronger control over the military and military-based security organs than Amer himself.[31]

At this point, Nasser began to regret his disregard for political organization. If he had formed a strong ruling party, he would have kept the military in line via political commissars, as was the case in Russia and China. Instead, he resolved to control the military through secret cells loyal to his regime. Now that their loyalty had shifted to Amer, he had no way of purging them—he simply did not know who the members of these cells were.* But perhaps it was not too late. If the military had become his rival's power base, and if the security apparatuses he controlled (the PBI; the Interior Ministry's investigative organ, the GID; and the police force) were no match for Amer's ensemble (the OCC; the military and civilian intelligence agencies; and the military police), then maybe he could turn his attention to the political apparatus—maybe he could shore up his social support and transform the rudimentary organs that existed so far into an all-powerful ruling party. If he succeeded in expanding and organizing his social base, then maybe he could reduce the relative weight of the military in the ruling coalition. The idea of the Arab Socialist Union (ASU) was thus born—conceived from the beginning as a political counter to the military.

---

* It was only the trials that followed the 1967 defeat that revealed how OCC director Shams Badran had charged members of his own class (class of 1948) with managing these cells (Samy Sharaf, *'Abd al-Nasser: Keif hakam masr?* ('Abd al-Nasser: How Did He Rule Egypt?) Cairo: Madbouli al-Saghir, 1996: 359–60).

COUNTERWEIGHING THE MILITARY

Nasser deeply mistrusted political parties because they could be easily infiltrated and subverted. He preferred to mobilize support through direct appeal to the masses via speeches and state-controlled media. But by 1962, he realized how he had inadvertently cornered himself; because of his reluctance to build a powerful ruling party, the political arena became entirely dominated by the military and the security apparatus. Nasser was now determined to remedy this deficiency. He began to build on what he had. The chaotic array of political currents that constituted the Liberation Rally gave way by 1958 to a more pyramid-shaped, district-based structure called the National Union (NU). But despite its more solid structure, the NU was a nonideological control instrument open to all citizens and concerned mostly with providing crowds to welcome state dignitaries, shepherding them to root for the president during national celebrations and to vote for whatever the government ordained in referendums. Neither the Liberation Rally nor the NU had any capacity for popular mobilization. They were more like fluid social networks of all those who supported—or more accurately, sought to benefit from—the regime. They included students, workers, peasants, professionals, merchants, as well as rural notables and capitalists, coming together occasionally to express approval of whatever the regime did.

The passing of the socialist laws of 1961, which Nasser used to broaden his mass base and tighten his grip over the bureaucracy, provided the occasion to reorganize and empower the NU. Through the National Charter of 1962, Nasser announced the creation of the ASU, which was supposed to represent the will of what he called "the alliance of the people's productive forces" in achieving freedom (from imperialism), socialism (which meant a state-planned economy), and (Arab) unity. It was methodically structured along two axes: one based on profession, with committees for workers, peasants, intellectuals, soldiers, and "patriotic" capitalists, as well as the Socialist Youth Organization for students; and another on residence, with district branches in the cities and basic units in the villages (7,500 chapters in all). In theory, the ASU was supposed to provide candidates for parliament and cabinet, as well as other leadership positions, such as mayors and university deans, and "inspire" legislation and policies on all state levels. In short, it was supposed to represent the seat of political power.

The GIS deputy director and leading ASU cadre Abd al-Fattah Abu al-Fadl published an exposition of the origins and goals of this new organization in the regime's mouthpiece *Al-Tali'ah* (The Vanguard). Abu al-Fadl first explained that the ASU was a mass organization that brought together members of all social groups to allow them to resolve their conflicts and contradictions peacefully and to find common ground under the supervision of a political apparatus composed of "politically trained elements committed to the revolution's principles." Abu al-Fadl denied that the ASU was a ruling party, dismissing single-party rule as either fascist (representing the interests of the economically dominant class), or Communist (representing the dictatorship of the workers), and thus inherently prejudiced against other social groups. The ASU, in contrast, was an alliance of the people as a whole and allowed them all to express their interests and negotiate a means for coexistence. He then explained that the regime rejected political pluralism because in multiparty systems party struggles are proxies for class struggles, which the ASU aimed to eliminate; "in the absence of a basic contradiction between the interests of the people's productive forces, there is no need for each of them to form an independent political organization."[32]

All this rhetoric notwithstanding, it was clear that Nasser aspired for a Leninist-styled organization modeled on Soviet and East European (especially Yugoslavian) experiences. In a meeting with the members of the ASU's provincial executive offices, on January 12, 1966, he stressed the "vanguard" role of the party: "We cannot succeed unless we understand the masses. We must take their ideas and opinions, study them, organize them, give them back to them, and then point them in the right direction." His language then turned militaristic: "you must engage with people, recruit them, invite them ... to expand the ASU army."[33] But regardless of what Nasser desired, the ASU was not equipped to perform this vanguard role. In his enthusiasm to replicate the superb organization of Communist parties, the president seemed to have overlooked one missing ingredient: communism. Nasser was not a Communist, and did not adhere consistently to any strict ideology. He was a pragmatic man, though imbued with lofty ideas about modernity and social justice. Needless to say, without ideology there can be no ideological indoctrination.

So all the ASU was capable of was to bond key social groups to the regime through material temptations rather than ideological commitment. This was good enough to achieve Nasser's immediate goal: to revamp the political apparatus and place it on par with the military. Sharaf admitted that much: "We suffered an imbalance; the weight of the military was growing beyond control. Nasser created the ASU as a political counter to the army."[34] And because Amer was aware of this, he fought the new organization fiercely. A good example is the Alexandria summer camp incident of 1964, when the organization's youth branch (the Socialist Youth Organization) chose the following topic for its cadres to research during their stay: "How should ASU youth resist a possible coup?" When the MID reported the episode to Amer, he was naturally furious.[35]

The absence of ideology and the hidden goal of neutralizing the army condemned the ASU from the beginning to the fate of a highly centralized totalitarian body that issued directives from the top downward to keep citizens in line with regime policies and curb any opposition, rather than a mass mobilizing organ. The future ASU secretary-general Abd al-Muhsin Abu al-Nur described how he presided over nine organs, one for indoctrination, another for propaganda, a third for monitoring religious affairs, and the rest for "managing" students, workers, and peasants, and none of them tried to go beyond exerting regime control over all aspects of life.[36] The organization regulated rather than inspired society. And it did so through presenting ASU membership as a sine qua non, the fastest road to upward social mobility and the safest way to alleviate suspicions of dissent. Instead of instilling belief in the virtue and justice of the regime in the hearts and minds of its six million members, it became a magnet for opportunists from all walks of life. Those who flocked to swell its ranks did so because they realized that one no longer had to be a military or security officer to "benefit" from the revolution; another, civilian route had just opened up, and all one needed to do to join was fill out an application.

That was not the biggest problem with the ASU. Because of the deeply embedded security character of the regime, the new organization was quickly drawn into the security orbit. To begin with, the Interior Ministry screened recruits, nominated candidates for senior posts, and kept the entire body under tight surveillance through informants and bugging devices. Next, intelligence officers, such as Abu al-Fadl, were planted at the ASU to closely monitor its members and overall performance.[37] In addition, the organization itself incorporated security functions in addition to its political control duties; its members were not only expected to preach obedience to the rulers, but also to submit secret reports of any dissident views, even if expressed in the form of jokes or asides. By 1966, its secret archives held more than 30,000 files on military officers alone.[38] Nasser himself encouraged this role. During the same January 1966 meeting, he openly invited ASU members to act as informers: "You must be courageous enough that when you notice the deviation of another member to bring it to the attention of the [provincial] office, and if it is not remedied, to contact the [ASU] Secretary-General."[39] The organization became so proficient in collecting information that Salah Nasr at the GIS complained to Nasser that the ASU (aided by Sharaf's PBI) was spying on his own intelligence operatives.[40]

Obsession with security reached its zenith with the creation of the Vanguard Organization (al-Tanzim al-Tali'ie), a secret body within the ASU originally designed to help with indoctrination, but rapidly degenerating into a full-fledged intelligence organ. The idea behind the Vanguard Organization (VO), as Nasser explained during the founding meeting in June 1963, was to form secret ten-member cells of carefully selected ideological cadres to infiltrate public institutions and indoctrinate its members.[41] To help get it off the ground, the president convinced the scores of Communists that were completing their prison terms in the mid-1960s to join the new movement. In 1965, the underground Communist parties dissolved themselves and joined the new organization. Their rationale was that working with the regime would help them proliferate their ideas and—more practically—keep them out of prison. Nasser shrewdly incorporated the talented intellectual cadres and discarded the rank and file, even imprisoned many of them, so that Communist leaders would not have their own mass base within the VO. For Nasser, the VO would serve as an ideological nucleus for the regime itself, a civilian equivalent of the Free Officers cabal that he created in the military two decades before. By 1967, its membership had swelled to more than 250,000. Of course, Amer's diligent security apparatus could not have overlooked something that big. By October 1964, the field marshal had learned about the VO, and instructed Badran to keep it away from the army.

Despite its alleged indoctrinating mission, the security component of the VO was dominant from the beginning. First, its four founding members had little to do with ideology. It is true that one of the four was a socialist doctrinaire (Ahmed Fouad, who innocently thought he could influence the rest), but the other (*Al-Ahram*'s chief editor, Mohamed Hassanein Heikal) was no more than a Nasser confidant, and the last two (Samy Sharaf and Aly Sabri) were essentially security men. Second, there was the emphasis on secrecy (its existence came into the open only in August 1966) in this supposedly programmatic organization. Why would a president who openly advocated socialism need a secret body to spread his ideology? Even if Nasser wanted to model his new organization on underground Communist parties, these were underground *before*, not *after* their leaders came to power. Also, for ideological indoctrination the president had encouraged freelance socialist intellectuals, led by Lutfi al-Khuli, to issue a monthly magazine —*Al-Tali'ah* (The Vanguard)—in 1964, so again, why the need for secrecy?

This emphasis makes sense only when one considers the security role that the VO started playing, especially after 1965, when Interior Minister Sha'rawi Gomaa became its head. Instead of preaching socialism and winning new recruits, VO members were fully devoted to infiltrating social associations (universities, factories, trade unions, syndicates, the media, state bureaucracy, and the ASU itself, of which they were all members) to uncover and report on suspicious activities. As interviews with a sample of the VO's members later revealed, they were

told that their primary function was not to win people over to socialism, but rather to submit regular reports on subversive elements in their
respective institutions. This was not a simple misunderstanding; the
organization's charter explicitly mentioned: "each member is obliged
to present [security] reports ... to his superiors," which turned it, in the
words of one member, Hesham al-Salamuni, into a political Gestapo.[42]
Worse still, instead of performing the role of ideological spearhead, the
VO dragged its mother organization (the ASU) down the same road,
converting it from a potentially mass-mobilizing party to a giant security edifice centered on surveillance and political control.

But was Nasser's real aim to create a programmatic organization to
infuse political consciousness in the masses? Several reasons suggest
otherwise. To begin with, it seems that Nasser understood socialist
doctrines as means of achieving managerial control of politics and economics, rather than revolutionary purposes. Reviewing the minutes of
a secret meeting he held on March 7, 1966, at the VO's Cairo branch
provides a firsthand view of what the president aspired to. He began
by proclaiming: "We can achieve a lot ... not through punishment
and the military police ... We can change people through the [new]
political organization," but then he quickly added: "Sabri [his security
aide, VO founder, and now acting prime minister] has a point, we need
believers within the executive branches and administration ... these
can actively and effectively supervise employees ... they can also recruit
more members to help them in surveillance and oversight."[43] With this
stress on surveillance, it is hardly surprising that Nasser entrusted the
VO not to leftist intellectuals but to intelligence officers, who by disposition and training prioritized security over ideology. It would have
been very naïve of the president to believe that the VO could transform
his security associates into ideological cadres, rather than the other way
around. In the end, the gap between the intentions he professed and
the actions he carried out could be explained only by the fact that
Nasser's real goal was to create a civilian network of vested interests to
enhance his power vis-à-vis the military. This was natural considering
not only his struggle with Amer, but also the fact that there had been
eighteen attempted coups against Nasser so far. "There has been con-
tinuous intrigue over the last fourteen years and it is likely to continue,"
he said at that same meeting in March. "But I believe that it would
be impossible for the army to prepare for a coup [without political
support]."[44] In the opinion of one VO veteran, Nasser's motives were
not to create a real popular (let alone socialist) organization, but rather
to counter the power of the field marshal.[45] And the ASU, and its secret
VO, did indeed become a power to be reckoned with. But rather than
deriving their power from a broad mass base, they relied on an insular
class of political opportunists, thriving on state patronage and closely

supervised by an expanding security elite. Nasser's failure at building a mass-mobilizing party was particularly significant to the military sociologist Eric Nordlinger, who concluded quite emphatically:

> Egypt constitutes an especially telling example of the inability of praetorian rulers to build a mass party capable of monopolizing the population. For this particular failure occurred under exceptionally favorable conditions. The officers who took power in 1952 ... have had ample time to create one ... the government was headed by one of the few truly charismatic figures capable of eliciting emotion-charged support, loyalty, and energy at the mass level. Egyptian society is not divided along ethnic, racial, religious, linguistic, or regional lines that would have made the building of a nationwide party a highly problematic undertaking. And the presence of a powerful and much hated neighboring state has given rise to a nationalist fervor that could readily be used to recruit and energize a mass party ... The people needed only to be offered an organizational framework ... [Yet the ruler still assumed] that what applies within the military sphere also applies within the political realm ... [he] visualized Egypt in managerial terms, as an organization instead of a polity.[46]

To the extent that the ASU and VO had a social power base at all, it was the aspiring rural middle class and its urban offshoot in the state bureaucracy. This distinctive social composition characterized Egypt's ruling parties during the crucial decades of the 1960s and 1970s, and remained well in play until the final years of Mubarak's rule; these middling landowners and their offspring in the bureaucracy wound up constituting the backbone of the ruling party.

Recall that one of the first things the new regime did in 1952 was initiate land reform. The coup took place in a semifeudal society where 2,500 large landowners (with 147 elite families) and 9,500 middling owners controlled a third of arable land and half of the parliament's seats. There were also more than 2.5 million smallholders, and 11 million tenant farmers and landless peasants.* Aside from the rich absentee landlords, all the rest coexisted in the countryside, running their affairs with the aid of traditional social mores and hierarchy. The land reforms

---

* Around 12,000 owners controlled 2 million feddans (1 feddan = 1.038 acres), representing a third of the arable land: 9,500 of those were middling owners possessing between 50 and 200 feddans, while the rest were considered large owners, with an elite 134 families controlling between 1,000 and 5,000 feddans, then a select 12 families owning between 5,000 and 10,000 feddans; and finally, the royal family, which owned 48,000 feddans and controlled an additional 45,000 classified as religious endowments (al-Rafe'i, *Thawrat 23 yulyu 1952: Tarikhna al-qawmi fei saba' sanawat, 1952–1959*, 61–63; al-Bishri, *Al-haraka al-siyassiya fei masr, 1945–1953*: 79–80).

placed progressively lower limits on land ownership: 200 feddans in 1952, reduced to 100 in 1962, and finally 50 in 1965 (though the ceiling for family ownership was always higher). This was more than enough to run profitable agricultural projects. On the other hand, land redistribution granted each poor peasant five feddans or less—barely enough land to subsist on. While economically the peasants could not achieve independence, they were politically grateful to the revolution for providing them with a plot of land they could call their own. Therefore peasants could have offered a solid base for popular mobilization, but the insecure Nasser chose to blunt the revolutionary potential of the peasants lest they get out of control. Instead, he kept them tied down through reproducing traditional authority structures. He achieved this by allowing a prosperous rural middle class to occupy the apex of the patronage networks that were already set in place by large landlords, and thus perform the same political control function of their predecessors. So instead of redistributing all the surplus land among the peasants, or providing them with loans to buy it from the government, large owners were allowed to sell whatever exceeded their ownership limit on the open market where only financially solvent peasants could afford to buy. The relatively cheap divested land allowed small owners (controlling between 10 and 50 feddans) to become middling landowners (possessing between 50 and 200 feddans), and middling owners to become even wealthier. So the agricultural reform laws enabled the rural middle class, which had expanded modestly in number from 22,000 after the first installment of the land reform law in 1952 to 29,000 in 1965, to increase its land ownership by 29 percent, its annual income by 24 percent, and its share of state loans and subsidies by 80 percent during the same period.[47] By enhancing the economic power of the middling landowners, land reform shifted the balance of political power from large landlords to these new kulaks, who now enjoyed undisputed hegemony in the countryside. Security and stability were thus prioritized over the potential for mobilization, a potential that might have served the regime today, but could have been used against it tomorrow. Conservative village notables were considered a safer bet.

The arbitrarily passed July 1961 Socialist Laws, which crowned Nasser's drive to bring the economy under state control, further enhanced the position of the rural middle class by undermining the economic power of the wealthy urban stratum. Though one could scarcely argue that Nasser's version of state socialism was detrimental to the interests of private enterprise, capitalists and former large landlords (with a lot of cash on their hands after forcibly selling their land) were reluctant to subject themselves to the whims of what they considered a totalitarian regime and so they held back on investment, preferring to make a profit in nonproductive fields, such as real estate speculation.

Nasser tried his best to lure them back to productive investments through various tax exemptions, but this could not substitute for the lack of trust.* Following the Suez Crisis, it was estimated that out of £E45 million redirected away from agriculture, only £E6 million was invested in industry, while the rest went to real estate. In 1956 alone, real estate investment constituted 75.8 percent of all private investments. Nasser first responded in January 1957 by nationalizing foreign companies and forming the Economic Agency and the High Committee for National Planning to manage economic development. He then brought Egypt's largest banks under state control in February 1960, and formulated the first Five-Year Plan, for 1960–1965.[48]

Although the upper bourgeoisie was forced to work for the state as executive managers after the nationalization laws, it remained obstinate. In 1961 Zakaria reported that a group of thirty high-ranking officers had been meeting regularly with Egyptian capitalists, and that together they were pushing Amer to help them end the dictatorship and restore private liberties. Zakaria's report also highlighted that two-thirds of the economy was still in the hands of the private sector (that included 80 percent of commerce, and 70 percent of construction and industrial projects), and that half of Egypt's workers were employed by private businesses. A swift move against capitalists was necessary. In October 1961, Zakaria detained 40 prominent investors, and in mid-November sequestrated the financial assets of another 767. The government then took over 80 banks and insurance companies, and 367 commercial companies.[49] The Socialist Laws of 1961 were a logical next step. They eliminated the private sector in banking, insurance, international trade, heavy industry, transportation, large hotels, and the media. Even in light and medium industries and commercial companies—the last domain of private enterprise—the public sector became a partner with no less than 50 percent control. By 1967, the Supreme Council for Public Organizations supervised 48 public organizations, which in turn ran 382 affiliated companies.[50]

The bureaucracy and public sector were swelled further by state welfare laws passed during the same period. In 1962, Nasser's cabinet decided to admit all secondary school graduates to university, and to secure a job for every college graduate. As a result, state employment in the civilian sectors alone jumped from 770,000 in 1962 to about 1.1

---

* Law 306 of 1952 exempted foreign companies from taxes on commercial and industrial profits; Law 424 of 1953 exempted foreign industrial exports from income taxes; Law 430 of 1953 exempted joint stock agricultural and industrial ventures from taxes on profits; Law 277 of 1956 increased direct taxes to substitute for the lost tax revenue on commercial, agricultural, and industrial activities (Michael N. Barnet, *Confronting the Cost of War: Military Power, State, and Society in Egypt and Israel*, Princeton, NJ: Princeton University Press, 1992: 88).

million by 1967. At the same time as state employment rates were as high as 70 percent between 1962 and 1969 (employing more than 60 percent of university graduates), state salaries increased by 102 percent.[51] Needless to say, that expansion reflected neither population nor economic growth. It was part of Nasser's attempt to expand and consolidate his civilian social base.

The expansion of the urban managerial class offered the middling landowners a golden opportunity to extend their influence to the city. They now pushed their offspring to find employment in the bureaucracy and public-sector companies. That is why the bureaucratic bourgeoisie, which doubled in size between 1962 and 1965, was overwhelmingly composed of the sons of rural notables. Soon these young bureaucrats transformed the public sector into a labyrinth of commercial and financial fiefdoms, which supplemented the agricultural fiefdoms their families had established in the countryside. Strategically placed in the city and the countryside, this new elite now represented the bulwark of the ruling party, the ASU. This leads us to conclude that the guiding rational for both the land reform and socialist laws was political, not economic.* In effect, this alliance between a class of wealthy landowners and the state bourgeoisie that sprang out of it pushed the economy toward commercial and real estate investment rather than industry. Even agriculture suffered as middling landowners passed a considerable part of their returns to their urban offshoots to double it through short-term economic ventures instead of reinvesting it in the land. Land was treated as a source of prestige, not a productive asset.

But the regime had only itself to blame. The poverty of its economic policy really stemmed from the poverty of its politics. Rather than focusing on development, the regime was motivated by the need to curtail capitalist interests, on the one hand, and the need to "bribe" society to excuse its dictatorial methods, on the other. The costly commitments imposed on the bureaucracy and public sector included employment of all university graduates, the provision of cheap housing and free health care and education, and so on. In the sixties, for instance, public-sector companies were forced to increase wages by 40 percent to absorb the quadrupling of university students without a corresponding increase in productivity or profit. In the bureaucracy alone, Egypt

---

* It is true that the economy grew during the first Five-Year Plan (1960–1965) at 6.9 percent, and industry in particular grew by 11 percent, but still this fell short of Nasser's official goals of 9 percent growth and 15 percent industrial growth during the 1960s. There was also the soaring budget deficit of £E417 million in 1967, which brought state-led growth to a grinding halt (Sherif Yunis, *Al-Zahf al-muqadas: Muzaharat al-tanahi wa tashkil 'ebadet Abd al-Nasser* (The Sacred March: The Resignation Demonstrations and the Shaping of the Cult of Abd al-Nasser), Cairo: Dar Merit, 2005: 64).

had one million civil servants on the payroll by 1967.[52] The price was administrative chaos and corruption, but now there were millions of white-collar employees ready to root for the ASU. Clearly, Nasser perceived state institutions more or less as political power structures, as incubators for a new class of citizens whose interests were tied to his ruling party.

To empower a stratum of conservative village notables and civil servants appeared much more expedient to Nasser's security coterie than to mobilize urban activists or unruly peasants. Egypt's long experience with elections (dating back to 1866) had laid down certain political practices in the countryside, such as having village notables register peasants to vote for their landlords or mobilize them to show support for a particular candidate. All Nasser's faction needed to do was to utilize this preexisting setup for its own purposes; that is, all it had to do was to lock into existing authority structures instead of creating new ones. In that sense, the emasculation of the upper class in the village was symbolic; its political influence was simply passed on to those next in line.

With peasant support channeled by rural notables, and employees and workers' support channeled by their supervisors in the bureaucracy and public-sector companies, the ASU had a considerable social base. These notables and managers, in turn, dominated the apparatuses of the ruling party and got themselves elected to the various representative bodies. That is not to say that this stratum constituted a new "ruling class," because its role was rather one of sustaining those in power. Its influence was mostly local, and its aspirations were limited to increasing its wealth and status. In Gaetano Mosca's terms, it represented the "second stratum of the ruling class," one that mediates power between regime and society without actually holding the keys to political authority.[53] According to another political scientist, Timothy Mitchell, Nasser's experiment provides a good case study of the complex set of relations that constitute the state: "These no longer appear primarily in the form of a central power intervening to initiate change, but as local practices of regulation, policing, and coercion that sustain a certain level of inequality ... The center did not initiate change, but tried to channel local forces into activities that would extend ... regime influence."[54]

The fingerprints of Nasser's security elite appear all over this power-building process. The president himself aimed for a wider popular base. For example, in a speech delivered on October 16, 1961, he criticized the National Union for including fewer than 2,000 urban activists among its 29,520 committee members, with the rest representing the forces of reaction in the countryside, and pledged that the new ASU would come up with preventive measures against the infiltration of these elements, the most important of which was that its membership would include 50 percent workers and peasants. The presidential initiative was quickly frustrated when Sabri and the rest of the security crew agreed to include those who owned 50 feddans in the peasant category, and to consider those who sat on the boards of public-sector companies as workers.[55] Nasser then delegated to his security men the task of filtering out conservative elements during the transition from the NU to the ASU. The result was that only 1.5 percent of NU members who applied to join the ASU were disqualified, and a striking 78 percent of those in charge of NU village units, and 60 percent of those heading NU secretariat positions in the cities, continued to occupy the same posts under the new organization.[56] Not only that, but while village notables occupied 11.7 percent under the NU watch in the 1957 parliament, their share more than doubled (to 30 percent) in the ASU-supervised parliamentary elections in 1964.[57] It was the typical "the devil we know" mentality that governs security thinking that assured the continued predominance of the rural middle class and its urban offshoots. As the senior intelligence official Abd al-Fattah Abu al-Fadl concluded after his five-year tenure at the ASU, the new party was not only formed of the same social material as that of the old, but of the exact same people.[58]

It is this group of middle-class opportunists that would run and benefit from the ruling party for the next five decades—although it would have to share the spoils with more affluent businessmen after the seventies. Instead of undermining the new class of security officers, the ASU provided this mostly urban class with a bridge to the countryside, thus tightening relations between security and politics more than ever. Eventually, this security-political alliance would succeed in marginalizing the military, but at the price of fortifying the dictatorship. An early demonstration of the fatal consequences of this emerging alliance was there for all to see in 1966 in a small village on the Nile Delta known as Kamshish.

THE KAMSHISH AFFAIR

The Kamshish Affair brought into sharp focus the alignment of forces in place during the final days leading up to the climactic 1967 war. This small village of perhaps 10,000 inhabitants and 2,120 feddans in al-Munufiya province on the Nile Delta in northern Egypt (the home province of Sadat and Mubarak) became an international cause célèbre in 1966, receiving extensive coverage from Egyptian and world media, and attracting visits from no less than Che Guevara, Jean-Paul Sartre, and Simone De Beauvoir, as well as honorable mention in one of Fidel Castro's fiery speeches. It was celebrated as the only instance of peasant revolt in postcoup Egypt, though the reality was much more humble.

Its true significance was that it accurately reflected the political configuration and power balances of the time. Lutfi al-Kholi, editor of
the regime's mouthpiece, *Al-Tali'ah*, thought it was "a political and
economic thermometer" of the state of the country.[59] In fact, the GIS
director, Salah Nasr, described it as the "apex of the power struggle"
that consumed the country during the 1960s.[60]

The whole affair began with peasant activists leading a campaign
against the large landowning family of al-Feqi, which retained 650
feddans above the limit prescribed by the land-reform laws. Complaints
against the formerly dominant landlords also incriminated ASU and
security officials, who—together with village notables—facilitated the
family's fraudulent behavior. The campaign, which centered on petitions to the president and the ASU leadership in Cairo, was led by two
Communists, Salah al-Din Hussein and his wife, Shahendah Maqlad.
But Nasser's security lieutenants kept a lid on it, making sure he never
saw any of the letters addressed to him. But it all came into the open
during the president's tour of the countryside in March 1966, when he
heard demonstrators chanting: "The Kamshish Revolution Salutes the
Mother Revolution!" followed by Maqlad rushing toward his motor-
cade to hand him a memo detailing the whole story—how Kamshish
peasants were among the first to back up the land-reform laws in 1952;
how appalled they were when the "feudal" al-Feqis became the representatives of Nasser's first popular organization (the Liberation Rally),
and afterward made sure that NU and ASU dignitaries in the province
were their junior allies; how al-Feqis regularly consorted with security
officials to make sure peasant petitions were intercepted and their draft-
ers detained; and finally, how this whole charade made it seem as if the
revolution's political organizations were "born dead."[61] Upon returning
to Cairo, Nasser demanded a full investigation. Party and police officials claimed it was a minor affair stirred by Communist troublemakers,
and decided to shelve the case. Weeks later, Hussein was shot dead by
a police-hired peasant, sparking massive peasant riots that soon made
local and international headlines. The press coverage highlighted how
little the power structure had shifted in the countryside after a decade
and a half of land reform.

In his dual capacity as intelligence operative and ASU functionary,
Abu al-Fadl was asked to investigate the murder. A few weeks later,
he reported that Hussein had in fact been submitting one complaint
after another to ASU officials and the PBI concerning violations by al-
Feqis. The complaints were ignored, and the Interior Ministry detained
Hussein twice, once (between November 1954 and February 1956)
for being a Communist, and the other (during the second week of
September 1965) for being an Islamist.[62] Hussein's widow also provided
investigators with a security memo written weeks before the murder (on

March 3, 1966), accusing her husband of rabble-rousing and warning of his subversive activities, thus further implicating the security apparatus in his assassination.[63] The investigation also revealed that the Speaker of Parliament, Anwar al-Sadat, intervened in al-Feqis' favor, and that even after the murder he tried to shore them up by claiming that his own investigations (carried out by Mahmoud Game', a confidant who also happened to be a member of the Muslim Brotherhood) confirmed their innocence of all charges—whether land-reform violations or incitement to murder. Sadat further claimed that Hussein and his wife were Soviet agents, who received regular visits and funding from the Russian embassy.[64] Sadat was not the only actor in this unfolding drama who would later assume a high public position (that of president), but others who were also involved in the cover-up would rise to power and fame—rather than suffer for their complacency. Prominent examples included, on the political side, Kamal al-Shazly, future minister of parliamentary affairs and deputy secretary-general of the ruling party, who was back then the ASU representative in Munufiya, and on the security side, the future interior minister Abd al-Halim Musa, and the future director of state security Hassan Tal'at.[65] And without getting too much ahead, it is worth mentioning that in September 1998 al-Feqi family and their hirelings spearheaded the repression of Kamshish peasants who resisted President Hosni Mubarak's reversal of the state protection guaranteed to tenant farmers in the 1950s. Al-Feqis still owned land above the limit prescribed by law and were hungry for more, and Shahendah Maqlad, Hussein's widow, was still there to lift the peasants' spirits. Little had changed in three decades.*

The complacency of political and security cadres alarmed Nasser, who pointed to the "tragedy of Kamshish" during his May Day speech of 1967, as an indicator that opportunists had hijacked the ASU, and that even after he sequestered the lands of large landlords, "they remained emperors just as they were before, even more so."[66] A few days before, the daily *Al-Akhbar* came out with a dramatic headline that read: "Nasser Warns of Counter-Revolutionary Forces."† But it was Amer who was truly disturbed by the intimate relations that were forming behind his back between the president's ASU and security men (at the PBI and the Interior Ministry) and the rural elite, and saw this as a potential threat to the political influence of the army. Determined to liquidate this last bastion of social reaction, Nasser and Amer, each for his own reasons, agreed to form the Committee for the Liquidation of Feudalism. Infighting over who should be included, however, produced a catchall twenty-two-member committee with all the usual suspects

---

* Fatemah Farag, "Kamshish: Take Two," *Al-Ahram Weekly* 397: 3. Cairo (10/1/1998).

† *Al-Akhbar* 4893: 1. Cairo (3/4/1968).

from both security factions: Sabri, Sharaf, Gomaa, and others associated with Nasser, alongside Amer, Badran, Nasr, and their allies.[67]

In a matter of weeks, the committee received complaints from hundreds of villages against the still dominant power of large landowners. Investigations revealed that more than 45 percent of the peasants were still landless, that 95 percent of the landed peasants held less than 5 feddans, and that only 5 percent of landowners controlled 43 percent of all arable land. Petitions also highlighted how the rising agricultural bourgeoisie was gaining political control over the countryside. Soon the committee issued its final report: "After eight months of continued work ... the Agricultural Reform [Agency] sequestered or placed under state guardianship about 200,000 feddans ... banished 220 feudalists from the countryside ... expelled hundreds of mayors, clerics, and officials who were dominated by feudalists, and dissolved dozens of ASU village committees ... This was an 'agricultural revolution.'"[68] It was excellent propaganda for Amer and his associates.

In reality, the results had been much more modest. Probably under pressure from ASU-connected security officials, the committee examined only 330 cases out of Egypt's five thousand villages before hastily concluding that there were no systematic violations, only a handful of pockets of illegality. It did not matter that some of these "irregularities" were as blatant as the six families that each held between 1,275 and 4,500 feddans, although the law allowed for only 300 feddans per family.[69] Nor did it matter that, as the report confessed, there was as much as 200,000 feddans concealed from legal authorities. The problem was reduced to the survival of individual feudalists associated with the old regime, rather than an indicator of the emergence of a new landowning class nurtured by the new regime.[70] The civilian and military security elite had no need to investigate how this happened—they were the ones who allowed it. Committee members also had no real stake in changing the situation. Nasser's faction (probably without his consent) was determined not to alter the power structure it had developed in the countryside, and Amer decided—after flirting a bit with the possibility of sabotaging this arrangement—that this was perhaps too distracting, that his efforts should be entirely focused on military rather than social affairs. And it was this latter decision that set the stage for the final and painfully spectacular showdown of 1967.

THE MILITARY NEEDS A WAR

For such a brief encounter, the Arab-Israeli war in 1967 remains one of history's most consequential confrontations. In Egypt, the defeat was "so unexpected in its totality, stunning in its proportion, and soul-destroying in its impact that it will be remembered as the greatest defeat of the Arabs in the twentieth century."[71] How can we explain the astonishing sequence of events that led up to this defeat? How can we solve the central puzzle of the war, which is how a politically astute leader like Nasser held firm on the path of escalation against Israel, even though he knew how little he controlled his own military. The standard interpretation underlines the incompetence of Egypt's political and military institutions at the time. Another common interpretation in Egypt points to a mischievous plot hatched between Washington and Tel Aviv to destroy Nasser's regime. Israeli analysts and diplomats claim that Nasser thought be could actually defeat Israel, or at least snatch a substantial political concession from it through a grand military bluff. Western scholars highlight psychological pressures by other Arab states on Egypt to carry the banner of resistance against Israel and to protect neighboring Syria and Jordan, adding that it was Nasser's virtuoso politics and impulsiveness that made him rush headlong onto the perilous path of war.* Doubtlessly, there is a kernel of truth in all these claims. But if we move away from trying to explain what brought about the defeat, to considering the more perplexing question of why the military drove the country to the brink of war in June 1967, we can see that none of these interpretations hold. If regime institutions were so incompetent, and Amer knew it (as discussed below), then why rush to war? And if the United States and Israel were out to get Egypt, and both Nasser and Amer were quite aware of this (again as discussed below), then why fall into their trap? And if we blame the escalation on Nasser, then why was he desperately trying to defuse the situation until the last moment? Perhaps the "true" motivation behind this unwarranted escalation will remain forever hidden, but the logic of the intraregime power struggle provides an explanation that best incorporates the available historical

---

* For Egyptian interpretations see Wagih Abu Zikri, *Mazbahat al-abriya' fei 5 yunyu 1967* (Massacre of the Innocent on June 5, 1967), Cairo: Al-Maktab al-Masry al-Hadith, 1988, and Mohamed Hassaneim Heikal, *1967: Al-Infegar* (1967: The Explosion), Cairo: Markaz Al-Ahram lel-Targama wa-Nashr, 1990; for Israeli ones see Abba Eban, *Personal Witness: Israel through My Eyes*, New York: Jonathan Cape, 1992; Michael B. Oren, *Six Days of War: June 1967 and the Making of the Modern Middle East*, New York: Presidio Press, 2002; and Tom Segev, *1967: Israel, the War, and the Year That Transformed the Middle East*. New York: Metropolitan Books, 2007; and for Western analysis see Malcolm H. Kerr, *The Arab Cold War: Gamal Abd al-Nasir and His Rivals, 1958–1970*, New York: Oxford University Press, 1969; Anthony Nutting, *Nasser*, London: E. P. Dutton, 1972; Michael Brecher, *Decisions in Israel's Foreign Policy*, New York: Oxford University Press, 1974; Richard B. Parker, *The Politics of Miscalculation in the Middle East*, Bloomington: Indiana University Press, 1993; Walter J. Boyne, *The Two o'Clock War: The 1973 Yom Kippur Conflict and the Airlift That Saved Israel*, New York: St. Martin's Press, 2002; and Risa A. Brooks, *Shaping Strategy: The Civil-Military Politics of Strategic Assessment*, Princeton, NJ: Princeton University Press, 2008.

evidence. This logic points in only one direction: that the effectiveness of Nasser's counterbalancing strategy convinced Amer and his associates that if the military did not accomplish something spectacular soon, it would be gradually displaced from the center of power. In other words, the escalation was an attempt to salvage the image and influence of the military.

Let us first underscore how Amer knew beyond the shadow of a doubt that the army was not equipped for war, even as he pretended he was preparing for one. On December 16, 1966, the field marshal received a report by the military's high command advising against any military confrontation with Israel in the foreseeable future. The report was based on the disastrous effects that the Yemen War had had on the armed forces. The Egyptian army had sent military instructors to support Yemeni left-leaning nationalists in 1962—an opportunity Amer had embraced to boost the military's public image in what he believed would be a short and effortless campaign against pro-monarchy bandits. According to Chief of Staff Muhammad Fawzy, Amer's strategy in Yemen was theatrical, a mere show of force. He encouraged firing excessively into Yemeni mountains for no other purpose than to demonstrate lethal strength back home; he gave out field promotions and military decorations to officers who barely saw combat; and his aides fabricated press releases about the army's heroic exploits.[72] Sadat, who was responsible for the political side of the war, also complained how Amer treated the war as "a new theater to strengthen his position and extend his influence."[73] Amer's plan almost worked, in light of the fact that the United States under John F. Kennedy had initially recognized the republicans in Yemen. Soon, however, Saudi Arabia and the United Kingdom, which both supported the Yemeni monarchy, persuaded Lyndon B. Johnson to change sides. Saudis could not live with a Communist regime on their southern borders; the British could not stand losing the strategic port of Aden to Communists; and Johnson was much more hawkish than his predecessor in fighting communism.[74] Now the army was trapped in an unconventional war against Western-funded guerrillas and European mercenaries. What started out as a simple operation requiring no more than a few hundred officers turned into a quagmire that drew no fewer than 70,000 men by 1965.[75]

The report submitted by the general command at the end of 1966 assessed the impact of this new reality. It emphasized how military discipline had suffered from the exigencies of guerrilla warfare and policing in Yemen; how soldiers had unlearned all the rules of modern warfare in this unconventional operation; how combat pilots had forgotten the basics of strategic bombing and dogfighting after five years of aimless strikes against a country that had neither an air force nor air defense capabilities; how self-esteem had deteriorated as the army felt outmaneuvered at every turn; and how equipment and ammunition were being thoughtlessly expended by the frustrated troops. Subsequent reports pointed to the fact that budget constraints imposed by the Yemen War forced the military to discharge thousands of reservists in March 1967 and issue a three-month freeze on conscription, and that as a result of these constraints, in May 1967 (the month Amer decided to escalate) the army had been suffering a shortage of 37 percent in manpower, 30 percent in small arms, 24 percent in artillery, 45 percent in tanks, and 70 percent in armored vehicles; trained pilots were fewer than the available aircraft (while the Israeli ratio was 3 pilots to every plane, in Egypt it was 0.8), and not a single fortified hangar had been built in the last five years. Another report on military training described 1966–1967 as the worst training year in the history of the Egyptian army: not a single brigade-level maneuver had been conducted, and only 5.2 percent of the training fuel was used. In terms of munitions, the infantry consumed only 26 percent of its allocated share for military exercises; the armory only 15 percent; and the artillery 18 percent. Still more startling figures revealed that on average each tank fired only 1 shot during that entire training period, each howitzer only 1.5 shots, and each bazooka only 15 shots. Finally, because security considerations advised against the hiring of educated soldiers, only 19 percent of the infantry, 18 percent of the marines, and 21 percent of the air force were literate, which reduced the overall quality of the fighting force. Added to the fact that the last major divisional exercise conducted by the army had been in 1954, the picture was unmistakably bleak.[76]

Of course, Nasser was painfully aware of the sorry state of the armed forces. Even before the Yemen War, he understood that the policy of rewarding loyalty over merit, taken to an extreme by Amer's security associates, had transformed military command posts into salaried sinecures. He also knew that the army was losing in Yemen, which he used to refer to as "my Vietnam."[77] In fact, Chief of Staff Fawzy asserted that on the eve of the 1967 war, the president had virtually no control over the army, and tried to avert war at all costs.[78] But there was even more. Nasser conveyed to Amer in no uncertain terms that there was an American-Israeli plot to destroy the military and overthrow the entire regime.

U.S.-Egyptian relations had soured after 1957 because of Nasser's refusal to join U.S.-endorsed regional defense alliances. The Americans decided that Egypt's version of Arab nationalism was as subversive as communism, and began from that point on to groom Saudi Arabia to take over the leadership of the Arab world and undermine Egyptian hegemony. A telegram from the State Department to the U.S. embassy in Cairo, on September 27, 1957, stated: "Egypt seemed determined to attempt to deny other states freedom of choice which it demands for itself. It insists all its neighbors adopt a policy of 'positive neutrality' despite the fact that some of them have freely concluded that their independence can be better assured by association with collective security arrangements against Communism ... Nationalism which is used as coverall for efforts by one nation to dominate other nations and to oblige other countries to follow blindly its policies will inevitably be opposed by the U.S."[79] Keen on salvaging bilateral relations, Nasser responded warmly to a circular sent by Kennedy to Arab leaders in August 1961, triggering a two-year personal correspondence during which seventy-five letters were exchanged between the two. What kept relations from deteriorating during Kennedy's time was his belief that Nasser was more dangerous when cornered.[80] This all changed when Johnson came to office. The new president developed particularly intimate relations with Israel during his tenure as House majority leader. He resented America's role in forcing an Israeli withdrawal from Sinai after the 1956 war, and believed that force was the only language Nasser understood. Being a long-time Texan representative, Johnson was also tied to oil conglomerates that felt threatened by the spread of Nasser's left-leaning nationalism to the Gulf countries.

Johnson first charged Robert Komer, a CIA operative who later served on the National Security Council (NSC), to develop a strategy to draw the Egyptian military into a grueling struggle intended to weaken and discredit it. The Yemen War was a good starting point, and Komer played it so well that his NSC colleagues began to refer to it as "Komer's war." Next, Johnson suspended American wheat shipments to Cairo (subsidized via U.S. Public Law 480) to strain the Egyptian economy further. But an even more lethal operation was under way. Toward the end of 1966, the former World Bank president Eugene Black warned Nasser, whom he now considered a personal friend, that officials in Washington were discussing plans to "unleash Israel" against Egypt sometime next year. Nasser's closest adviser, Mohamed Hassanein Heikal, learned that an American-Israeli coordination committee composed of Walt Rostow and Robert Komer (from the NSC), Richard Helms and James Angleton (from the CIA), and Moshe Dayan, Meir Amit, and Ephraim Evron (representing Israel) was formed in 1967 to plan a war aimed at installing a friendly regime in Egypt—the operation was codenamed Turkey Hunt.[81] In fact, on the first day of the war Walt Rostow submitted a memo to Johnson that began, "Herewith the account ... of the first day's turkey shoot."[82] The timing was considered perfect because the new Soviet troika was focused on domestic affairs, and was under pressure from the Eastern Bloc and China not to support non-Communist countries militarily. Also, the United States needed to distract attention from its escalation in Vietnam.

Now, if Amer had a clear picture of the dismal state of the army, and if he had been forewarned about the American-Israeli intentions, why did he feel compelled to undertake such an incredible gamble in the summer of 1967? The answer lies in the success of Nasser's counter-balancing strategy against the military. The president and his security team decided in 1962 that it was impossible to either depose Amer and his group or lure them away from the army, and that they therefore had to ignore the army for the time being and work around it in order to increase their power. Restated in strategic terms, they decided to shift from frontal assault to siege warfare. If access to the military was blocked, there was still the prospect of enhancing political power through build-ing new organizations and controlling the executive. Thus, the ASU was created in 1962, followed by the VO in 1963, and Nasser security loyalists led the cabinet—Sabri between 1962 and 1965, and Zakaria between 1965 and 1967. Moreover, there was a progressive decline in the ratio of officers in the cabinet, from 51.5 percent in August 1961 to 47 percent in September 1962, to 36.3 percent in March 1964.[83]

The president's faction also augmented its economic influence through the socialist laws of July 1961 and other subsequent laws that expanded state control over the economy. Even ideologically, it managed to increase its hold through the wholesale adoption of an Arab nationalist and socialist discourse, which legitimated both the new political organizations and economic laws. Taken together, these strate-gies were gradually shifting the power balance within the regime away from the military and its security partners to the political apparatus and its assemblage of security organs. So while the army successfully defended itself against all attempts to impose political control, Amer believed that these new changes not only reduced the relative power of the military vis-à-vis the political apparatus, but they also threatened military autonomy in the years to come.

Driven by insecurity, Amer began with a few preventive measures. To tighten his control over the officer corps at this time of adversity, he asked his top security lieutenant, Shams Badran, to carry out a thorough reshuffling of military commands from the general staff down to bat-talion leaders. With three hundred officers reallocated in the summer of 1966, this was the most extensive wave of reassignments since 1952. For the first time loyalists were given field commands (a quite burden-some assignment) in order to keep the troops on a tight leash, while suspect officers were recalled to GHQ, where they would remain under the watchful eye of Badran and the OCC.[84] Afterward, Amer insisted that Badran be appointed war minister, a cabinet position he had never cared about before. As soon as Nasser granted him that request, in September 1966, Amer issued Vice Supreme Commander Decree 367 of 1966, which expanded the jurisdiction of the war minister to cover all administrative and budgetary affairs concerning the military, in addition to control over military intelligence, military courts, and a host of other military-related bodies. In parallel, Amer issued Vice Supreme Commander Decree 118 of 1966, reducing the responsibilities of Nasser's ally Chief of Staff Fawzy to minor administrative duties and prohibiting him from any direct contact with combat units. The field marshal and his war minister then streamlined the whole military structure to where the heads of services and administrative units would report directly to them rather than the chief of staff or the president.[85]

After defending his primary domain—the armed forces—Amer moved onto the offensive by trying to undercut competing institutions. In September 1965, Badran claimed that his men at Military Intelligence had uncovered a Muslim Brotherhood plot to overthrow the regime, and that in light of the demonstrable inefficiency of the Interior Ministry he decided to put the Military Intelligence Department in charge of the investigations. Recognizing this for what it was—a stab at the Interior Ministry—the ministry's General Investigations Directorate struggled to prove that these reports were fabricated. Hostility between the army and the GID ran so high that at one point Fouad Allam, then a junior GID officer and later its deputy director, was detained at a military prison when he exchanged words with Badran over a certain suspect. As Allam later recounted, if Zakaria had not learned about what happened and asked Nasser to interfere personally, he might have never been released.[86] To produce evidence to support Badran's allegations, the military police detained perhaps 30,000 Islamists in July 1965. The MID succeeded in putting a case together, at the cost of 250 Brotherhood lives lost under torture in various military prisons.[87] Taking the inefficiency of civilian security as a pretext, Badran not only demanded the dismantling of the GID, but he also issued Military Service Law 25 of 1966, which declared that legal disputes between civilians and officers would fall under the jurisdiction of military courts.[88] Officers were now officially above the law.

Still, Amer and his cohort did not feel safe. In November 1966, Murad Ghaleb, Egypt's longtime ambassador to Moscow and future foreign minister, overheard a conversation between the civilian intelligence director Salah Nasr and some of Amer's lieutenants in which they complained that as long as Nasser controlled the executive, their position would remain vulnerable.[89] Accordingly, Amer asked that he or Badran assume the premiership, which Nasser flatly rejected. Tensions began rising again before a compromise was reached at the end of 1966 to replace Zakaria as prime minister with Sedqi Suleiman, a reputably apolitical officer. The field marshal then reversed the decline in the military component in the cabinet, pushing it from less than 36 percent under Zakaria to 55.2 percent under Suleiman.[90] However, Amer's group lost a chip because part of the compromise was to appoint Muhammad Sadeq, Egypt's military attaché to Bonn, as MID chief.[91] Having spent many years abroad, both sides perceived him as neutral; but considering that Nasser's strategy had shifted from confronting to containing the military, this new appointment was certainly added to his column of the balance sheet, and (as the future revealed) subtracted a lot from Amer's.

All the above maneuvers notwithstanding, Amer's faction realized that if the military did not pull off a dramatic feat sometime soon, its relative weight within the regime's overall power formula would continue to deteriorate. It was not enough to handle domestic issues such as investigating land-reform violations or rounding up Islamist activists; these were tasks that could be better dealt with by civilian authorities. After its miserable performance in Yemen had wrecked its image, the army had to prove its worth in the arena that no one else could claim, that is, on the battlefield—for, as Thomas Hobbes once proclaimed, "there is no honour Military but by warre."[92] Thus, the path was set for a war that proved to be not only disastrous for the region, but also Amer's undoing.

"AT DAWN WE SLEPT"

It all started in December 1966, when Amer telegrammed Nasser from Pakistan demanding the deployment of Egyptian troops in Sinai to silence Arab critics who accused the army of hiding behind the United Nations Emergency Forces (UNEF) positioned there since 1956. The president ignored Amer's plea. But upon receiving unconfirmed reports from Russian sources that Israel was mobilizing against Syria, the field marshal immediately ordered a general mobilization into Sinai (on May 14, 1967), later justifying his decision to Nasser by citing the Egyptian-Syrian mutual defense pact, which had been concluded a year before in an attempt to rebuild the lost trust between the two countries since their breakup five years earlier. The president was infuriated. He had met with Amer the night before and agreed to double-check the Soviet report before taking any action. Nonetheless, Amer convened his high command the next morning and ordered the mobilization.[93] A suspicious Nasser then dispatched the only high-ranking officer he trusted, Chief of Staff Fawzy, to Damascus to confirm the news of an imminent Israeli attack. The latter reported back to Amer on May 15 that there were no Israeli soldiers on the Syrian border, and that the Soviet report was baseless. However, as Fawzy recalls: "The field marshal made no reaction ... I began to suspect that the alleged [Israeli] troop concentrations was not the principle reason for his mobilization order."[94]

Nasser then warned Amer that an advisory committee (under Nasser's confidant Mohamed Hassanein Heikal) recommended against escalation because of the fragile geopolitical situation and the tense relations with the United States. Moreover, the Jordanian king warned Lieutenant General Abd al-Mon'em Riyad, commander of the Joint Arab Forces and soon-to-be Egyptian chief of staff, during a meeting in Amman on May 2, that his sources in Washington and London assured him that Israel was plotting with the United States to drag Egypt into a devastating war (the king was justifiably worried about the fate of the West Bank, still under his guardianship).* Upon his return to Cairo, Riyad submitted a full report to Amer. But when the war rhetoric intensified despite his warnings, he asked Heikal on May 13 if the president had seen the report. As soon as Nasser learned of the report's existence, he demanded a copy, which Amer sent only on May 14 after the army had already crossed into Sinai, and requested a pullout of all UN troops.[95]

In a desperate attempt at damage control, Nasser asked Amer for a copy of the letter he was planning to deliver to the head of the UNEF. The field marshal sent him Arabic and English versions. Nasser amended the Arabic version so that instead of demanding a withdrawal of all UN troops, it spoke only of a partial redeployment. Nasser then told Amer to make sure both versions required nothing more than a partial real-location of forces, which Amer promised he would do. But on May 16, he called the president to apologize: due to a supposed mix-up, the English version of the letter he submitted to the UN still demanded a full withdrawal. Nasser quickly contacted UN headquarters in New York to retract the order, but the UN undersecretary-general Ralph Bunche, possibly under American pressure, refused.[96]

Now that the army was fully deployed in the peninsula, Amer raised the stakes once more. On May 21, he demanded the closing of the Strait of Tiran to Israeli navigation. When Nasser alerted him that Israel might consider this blockade a casus belli, Amer retorted that his troops in Sinai could not sit on their hands as Israeli flags flashed before them, and that if his wish was not granted, they might act recklessly, i.e., shoot Israeli vessels. When Nasser asked him if he was ready for war,

---

* New, groundbreaking work by the Israeli historian Ilan Pappé (2012) reveals, through the examination of recently declassified documents, that the Israeli government had devised a comprehensive legal and administrative plan to govern the West Bank and Gaza by a military regime as early as the summer of 1963, four years before Egypt's escalation—another triumph for foreign policy explanation based on power politics rather than contingencies. It is also acknowledged that the Israeli air strike, codenamed Operation Moked, was the result of twelve years of planning and several months of concerted practice and maneuvers (Simon Dunstan, *The Six Day War 1967: Sinai*, London: Osprey Publishing, 2009: 15).

Amer famously responded: "My neck is at stake. Everything is ready." In reality, Amer and his associates had taken the decision to close the strait—regardless of Nasser's view—five days earlier, on May 16. Again, he succeeded in stacking the deck against deescalation.[97] To further reassure the president, Badran claimed that during his recent visit to Moscow, Defense Minister Andrei Grechko pledged to defend Egypt should the Americans come to Israel's aid—a claim the Soviets vehemently denied after the war. Egypt's ambassador to Moscow, Murad Ghaleb, who had attended the meeting between Badran and the Soviet leaders, corroborated the Soviet account, confirming that the war minister made it all up, and that the Russians had explicitly said they could not intervene on Egypt's side.[98] Amer, of course, knew the truth about what happened in Moscow, but he deliberately hid Soviet misgivings and exaggerated Marshal Grechko's departing words to Badran to instill in Nasser a false sense of confidence.

Nasser, on the other hand, was not only clueless, he also had no way to verify Amer's claims regarding military readiness. He became particularly concerned when an Israeli cabinet reshuffle on June 1 brought in the hawkish Moshe Dayan, member of the U.S.-Israel committee on Operation Turkey Hunt, as defense minister. The only thing the president could do was to ask his intelligence sources to explore Israel's intentions. Based on their estimations, Nasser rounded up the general staff for one last time on June 2 and informed them that Israel was planning to attack from the air in seventy-two hours, and that they must either remove or fortify Egypt's air force squadrons in Sinai to prevent a repeat of the Suez War, when the planes were all destroyed on the ground. The president also cautioned the army not to strike first, or else he would not be able to garner international support. The commander of the air force seemed reluctant to receive the first blow, but he assured Nasser that if Israel attacked, his losses would not exceed 20 percent—of course, actual losses in the air force turned out to be 85 percent.[99] On June 3, Nasser gave an interview to the British journalist Anthony Nutting, in which he clearly stated that Egypt "planned no further escalation."[100] In a final effort to avert war, he arranged with Washington to receive Zakaria on June 5 to negotiate a way out. It was too late. June 5 was the day the war actually started.

A couple of hours after dawn, an Israeli armada of 196 fighter-bombers (approximately 95 percent of the air force) headed toward Egypt. Many of them were tracked by the Egyptian-run radar system in Jordan, but when the duty officer radioed the code word (Enab) to warn GHQ of the impending strike, the message was indecipherable because the radio codes had been changed the night before without anyone informing that advance radar outpost. Between 8:00 and 11:30 a.m., Israel destroyed 85 percent of the Egyptian air force (304 planes) on the ground, together with the seventeen airfields they were stationed at and the air defense installations protecting them. Over the next six days, Egypt lost 700 tanks, 450 field guns, 17,500 soldiers (11,500 killed and the rest injured or captured), and out of its 300,000 men in arms, only half remained in formation. But the "volume of the losses," as the future war minister Abd al-Ghany al-Gamasy bitterly noted, "betrays the immensity of the disaster."[*101]

Now, did Amer really seek war, or did he believe that a show of force in Sinai was all that it would take to restore the military's credibility and prove that it was still the most formidable institution in the country? A close examination of the events leading up to the war makes it clear that Amer and his group never imagined that their escalation would actually trigger a war; they were plainly bluffing. For one thing, when Amer's frantic chief of operations reminded him of the series of general staff reports and the recent report submitted by senior officers in May 1967, warning that the army was in no condition to engage Israel, Amer responded lightly: "There is no need to worry. This is nothing but a military demonstration."[102] The GIS director, Salah Nasr, also admitted in an interview after the war that the field marshal "mobilized the troops for a political purpose, which was to demonstrate military strength [at home]."[103] The "demonstration" aspect of the whole episode was clear enough when Amer insisted—quite imprudently—on marching his troops through the streets of Cairo, parading new Soviet weapons and chanting patriotic slogans. In reality, he knew that 80 percent of the force assembled in Sinai was untrained reservists, hastily marshaled to the front in their civilian garments and randomly assigned to units they had never served in—in fact, the mobilization plan was two years old, and these reservists had never been drilled before. Although on paper the size of the fully mobilized army was estimated at 250,000, and although in truth its size on the eve of war did not exceed 130,000, Amer claimed he commanded 2 million men, a number he fabricated

---

* Furthermore, the war crippled the Egyptian economy: military equipment worth more than $1.5 billion was lost; countless millions were spent on settling the internally displaced population of the Suez Canal cities; and billions of dollars of expected revenue from the Suez Canal ($250 million annually), the Sinai oilfields ($100 million annually), and tourism (another $100 million) were no longer available. Preparations for the upcoming battle to liberate Sinai further strained the economy, pushing the state and its citizens to the limit. The annual rate of economic growth was almost cut in half, falling from 6 percent during the 1962–1967 period to 3.6 percent in 1970, and declining further to 1.7 percent during the period 1971–1974 (O'Brien Browne, "Six Days of War Spark Forty Years of Strife," *The Quarterly Journal of Military History* 22 (1): 70–79 (2009): 75; Latif Wahid, *Military Expenditure and Economic Growth in the Middle East*. New York: Palgrave Macmillan, 2009: 131). Israel, on the other hand, lost 338 men and 122 tanks (Dunstan, *The Six Day War 1967*, 88).

to exaggerate his force. Also, a whole squadron of Soviet planes, as well as dozens of tanks and hundreds of boxes of small arms and ammunition, remained locked in military warehouses in the capital until the end of the war.[104]

In addition, the army leadership did not come up with a concrete strategy for positioning the troops, let alone commencing hostilities. Chief of Staff Fawzy remembers how the field marshal's orders were always changing and inconsistent, thus causing units to circle aimlessly around Sinai during the two weeks that preceded the war.[105] The future war minister Kamal Hassan Aly describes the chaotic preparations as follows: "As a brigade leader in the 4th Armored Division, I was handed fourteen contradictory assignments from May 25 to June 5, leading my brigade back and forth in purposeless maneuvers for ten days until my men became completely exhausted and disillusioned with their hesitant leadership."[106] Another brigade traveled 1,200 kilometers up and down Sinai, as Amer introduced four major—and contradictory —revisions to the deployment plan between May 15 and June 4. In fact, the field marshal replaced twelve divisional commanders, and a few more further down the ladder, eighteen days before Israel struck; some of them did not make it to their new commands before the war broke out. On the first day of the mobilization into Sinai, he sent shock waves throughout the high command by appointing Major General Abd al-Muhsen Murtagi—a man who, by his own admission, had been in Yemen for years and "knew little of the detailed operational plans for Sinai"—as front commander.[107] Moreover, despite Amer's threats to attack, the only plan that existed—Plan Qaher—was a defensive plan, which was formulated in December 1966 and never updated. It was, in fact, too simple to merit the label "plan," relying essentially on luring Israeli units into the peninsula and entrapping them in defensive "killing zones." Amer himself visited Sinai only three times between 1962 and 1967 to follow the erection of these defensive strongpoints.[108]

The actions of the general staff between their June 2 meeting with Nasser and the beginning of the war (three days later) provides further evidence as to how dismissive it was of the possibility of war. For starters, the military leadership ignored the president's warning of an imminent Israeli air strike on the morning of June 5. The soon-to-be-war-minister Amin Huwaidi testifies: "our fighter jets remained exposed on the front, even though inexpensive concrete shelters could have been built in a couple of days."[109] The commander of the air force in Sinai (Abd al-Hamid al-Deghidi) learned of Nasser's warning only after the defeat.[110] Not only that, but hours after the meeting, Military Intelligence circulated a report among the troops gathered in Sinai, assuring them that Arab steadfastness would certainly deter Israel from contemplating an attack. The report naturally encouraged units to relax even further. In one amusing instance, a lieutenant crossed the entire peninsula to deliver antitank ammunition to the forward outpost of Kuntilla on June 4. Once he got there, the field commander asked him to turn his convoy around, adding, "We don't need any ammunition. There isn't going to be a war. Take it back."[111]

Then came the inexplicable decision to fly Amer and his staff to the front in an unarmed transport on June 5, the very day Nasser predicted Israel would attack. As a result, when Israel struck, Egypt's entire high command (twenty-eight officers between the ranks of brigadier and lieutenant general) was divided between those suspended in midair with Amer and those who were either seeing him off at Almaza Airport in Cairo or waiting for him at Beer Tamada Airport in Sinai. To make matters worse, air defense units were ordered—hours before the strike—to hold their fire until the field marshal's plane landed safely, and Amer could not revoke these orders once the attack began, because he feared that if he broke radio silence he might be detected and shot down. Accordingly, Egypt's air defense was totally paralyzed during the first waves of this devastating attack. Gamasy, who was at the advance command center in Sinai when the war began, lamented: "I pitied the troops [who had no] commanding officers at a time like this."[112]

Next came the ultimate testimony to Amer's unpreparedness for battle: his demand for a Soviet-endorsed cease-fire one hour after the commencement of hostilities, followed by his tragic order of a general retreat from Sinai.[113] Fawzy described how he was summoned by Amer on the morning of June 6 and given twenty minutes to draft a plan to pull out the troops. "I was astounded by the request ... The field marshal was psychologically worn out and seemed on the verge of a nervous breakdown ... The land forces ... were holding out steadily, and there seemed to be no reason whatsoever to consider a withdrawal."[114] "By the end of the day, we can be said to have performed acceptably," Gamasy recalled. "Fighting was continuing ... the army reserves had suffered no losses."[115] The military historian Simon Dunstan confirmed in his exhaustive day-to-day analysis of the war that more than half of the Egyptian ground units remained intact and offered considerable resistance to the Israeli ground campaign during the first couple of days. Egyptian troops were at their best when entrenched in defensive strongpoints; this was the tactic that required the least training or skills—only bravery. In addition, the Egyptian plan in Sinai—to the extent that there was one—was purely defensive. The soldiers successfully delayed the initial Israel Defense Force advance, forcing IDF brigades into time-consuming flanking maneuvers. And time was of the essence in allowing the Egyptian high command to absorb the initial shock, revise its plans, and issue specific directives to the units scattered along the front.

The sensible thing to do was to fall back to Sinai's second line of defense, order the troops to entrench themselves in the naturally fortified Mitla and Gidi passes, block the Israeli ground invasion, and then counterattack. Fawzy, who was in charge of formulating the plan to defend Sinai a year before, believed that as long as the Sinai passes were still in hand, the peninsula could not be conquered.[116] This was also Nasser's advice to Amer when he dropped by GHQ in the early afternoon of June 5: to dig in around the passes.[117] Nonetheless, Fawzy set to work immediately in case Amer decided to ignore all that and pull out anyway. In twenty minutes he presented Amer with a rough draft of a four-day pullout plan with enough delaying tactics to keep the troops intact. After staring at him blankly for a few seconds, Amer told him he had already issued an order to withdraw in twenty-four hours.[118] Amer, who probably thought he could repeat Nasser's 1956 rapid-withdrawal tactic, apparently forgot that the number of troops this time around was enormous, and that an orderly pullout was impossible without a well-defined plan. The result was catastrophic: tens of thousands of soldiers abandoned their equipment and withdrew in chaos only to find themselves stranded in the scorching desert under the mercy of marauding Israeli firepower. In fact, less than 6 percent of the soldiers came back with their weapons. And while only 294 soldiers were lost on the first day of fighting, the general retreat of June 7 led to the killing, injuring, and capturing of 17,500 men.[119] Amer's unilateral decision to withdraw was doubtlessly the single most important reason for the defeat. Gamasy summed up those painful memories from his time at the front:

> I watched a heavy flow of troops move westward [away from Sinai]. It was completely disorganized … Could a retreat take place in this manner, when it normally required extreme discipline and precision and, according to the doctrine of war, should take place while the fighting still continued … The [field] command had given up control of its forces at the most critical time … the situation can neither be explained nor excused … troops withdraw[ing] in the most pathetic way … under continuous enemy air attacks … an enormous graveyard of scattered corpses, burning equipment, and exploding ammunition.[120]

Abandonment by senior commanders doomed the resistance at the front. A case in point was Egypt's most heavily fortified strongpoint, at Abu Ugeila, manned by the 16,000-strong 2nd Infantry Division and composed of a forest of natural defenses, barbed wires, minefields, trenches, antitank guns, and other artillery pieces, all reinforced with some ninety tanks reserved in concrete bunkers for counterattacks. There was only one weakness, however: the division commander (Major General Sa'di Naguib) was absent. Considering he owed his post to the fact that he was Amer's drinking partner, he was understandably reluctant to leave his side. And the field commander "did not have the authority to act on his own initiative." The result was that Brigadier General Ariel Sharon overran this formidable defensive complex in a few hours.[121] This abandonment was also emotionally bruising for the lower ranks. A driver with the 6th Mechanized Infantry Division by the name of Mahmoud al-Suwarqa remembered bitterly, "We were waiting to carry out our orders ... when suddenly on June 7 both the company and battalion commanders disappeared. Later I found out that they fled over the canal ... They [Israelis] fired shells and machine guns at us and after that I felt nothing. I awoke in an Israeli vehicle soaked in my own blood."[122]

A final—and quite conclusive—piece of evidence of how the mobilization into Sinai that fateful summer was no more than a bluff was Badran's confession during his trial in February 1968: "We were 100 percent sure that Israel would not dare to attack."[123] That is why the future war minister Abd al-Ghany al-Gamasy, drawing on his experience in the war, concluded that Amer must have thought that he could wipe out the effects of the Suez War (by removing UN observers and reestablishing Egypt's sovereignty over its territorial waters) without actually going to war, that he could simply intimidate Israel by rushing a sizable force into Sinai and making empty threats to attack.[124] In that sense, all the military needed to do—in Amer's view—was to look formidable. And that it did. On the Sinai front, Egypt's 100,000 soldiers, 930 tanks (mostly T-34, T-54, and T-55), and 430 fighters and fighter-bombers (MiG-17, MiG-19, MiG-21, Su-7, An-12, and Tu-16) were lined up against 70,000 Israeli troops with 800 tanks (Centurion, M-48 Patton, M-51 Sherman) and 280 fighter-bombers (Mirage and Mystère).[125] The balance seemed to be in Egypt's favor. Now that all eyes were again fixed on the armed forces and their gallant march into Sinai, Amer felt satisfied. Finally, he could "return to the center stage of ... politics after he thought he was so close to the exit."[126] Little did he know that at this point the exit had just opened wide. The defeat provided Nasser with the long-awaited opportunity to purge the field marshal and his men, and bring the military back under his control.

THE FINAL SHOWDOWN

After the destruction of the army in Sinai and the occupation of the peninsula, Nasser visited Amer on June 8, 1967, at GHQ and told him that he would deliver a speech the next day to announce his and Amer's resignation. Amer agreed on condition that his faithful lieutenant Shams Badran would be appointed president, to which Nasser conceded. But

on June 9, Nasser's primetime speech mentioned only his own resignation and named Zakaria as his successor.[127] Immediately following the
speech, hundreds of thousands flooded the streets, protesting Nasser's
decision and pledging to fight under his banner to liberate Sinai. The
spontaneity of the demonstrations was widely contested. We know that
the ASU had the organizational capacity to spark mass riots with great
speed. In February 1967, Aly Sabri tested the ASU's "political recall"
mechanism for the first time, and succeeded—relying only on word of
mouth—to mobilize 100,000 people in ten hours to welcome the Iraqi
president. The experiment was later repeated on a smaller scale, mobilizing 40,000 demonstrators in three hours.[128] The fact that these drills
took place barely three months before the June 9 demonstrations makes
it clear that regardless of the spontaneity of some demonstrations, ASU
elements must have played a role in directing them. Also, it helped
that the Interior Ministry did nothing to repress the riots. Interior
Minister Sha'rawi Gomaa called Heikal—whom Nasser delegated to
answer his phone calls right after the speech—warning that his men
would not control the street, and that the president must revoke his
decision.[129]

There are similar question marks regarding Nasser's decision to
substitute Zakaria for Badran, and to relegate Amer's resignation to
the late-night news. Heikal, who wrote the resignation speech, says it
was he who convinced the president to do so.[130] While one can never
verify an actor's true intentions, the fact that the Ministry of National
Guidance delayed the announcement of Amer's resignation until the
11:00 p.m. news bulletin, when the masses had already poured into
the streets and very few were at home watching the news, guaranteed that the people would only demand Nasser's return; Amer was
thus certainly upstaged. This was confirmed the next morning, when
daily newspapers, such as *Akhbar al-Youm*, covered Nasser's resignation
speech and the people's refusal in great detail on its front page, with
only a small report at the corner of the page mentioning that Amer
had stepped down, without further elaboration.* In addition, the choice
of Zakaria as successor seems to have been carefully calculated. Heikal
says he suggested Zakaria because he was the most capable of Nasser's
associates[131]—which he certainly was. But as Amer rightly noted, "A
fetus in his mother's womb was bound to reject Zakaria," the feared
security baron.[132]

Amer's military associates realized what was happening that night
and sounded air raid sirens to scare people away. It did not work. Then a
close ally of Amer, the GIS chief, Salah Nasr, visited Nasser (in Heikal's
presence) to dissuade him from making any changes in the general staff
or else the military might overreact and trigger a crisis. Nasser rejected

* *Akhbar al-Youm* 1179: 1. Cairo (6/10/1967).

this veiled threat and told Nasr that he would hold him personally responsible if the officers did anything foolish.[133] On June 11, Nasser retracted his resignation and put Fawzy in charge of the military. The headlines reported: "Nasser Responds to the Will of Millions: I Will Stay as the People Commanded."[*]

Upon Heikal's request, the president finally agreed to meet his discharged field marshal on June 15. Amer demanded to be reinstated, but Nasser adamantly refused.[134] The confrontation that followed "came close to being a civil war," a challenge infinitely graver than any Nasser had faced.[135] Apparently, even if Nasser and Amer were ready to call it quits, their associates refused to go down without a fight.

The first bullet in this confrontation was the fierce defamation campaign that Amer's men launched against the president, basically holding him responsible not only for the 1967 crisis, but also for all the previous setbacks, from the Syrian secession to the Yemen debacle. Nasser was presented as a psychologically disturbed would-be political virtuoso who always failed to measure up to his image of himself. And it was the president's personal grandiosity that brought about the May 1967 escalation against Israel and the subsequent defeat. The argument went as follows: sensitive to criticism from other Arab leaders, Nasser embarked on a dangerous game of brinkmanship to maintain his prestige, failing to recognize that he was unwittingly playing into Israel's hands. The defeat was therefore presented to Egyptians as the result of a reckless adventure intended to raise Nasser's standing.[136]

Second, Amer's commanders claimed that they had warned Nasser that the army was not prepared for another episode of his rash foreign-policy conquests. The chief of operations, Lieutenant General Anwar al-Qadi, pointed out that although Nasser had warned the high command in 1966 that President Johnson was trying to set him up, he still walked into the trap with his eyes wide open despite repeated warnings from the military that he should not let his pride jeopardize the country's future. The front commander Colonel General Abd al-Muhsen Murtagi equated what Nasser did with someone "throwing an army that cannot swim into the sea, and then blaming it for drowning."[137] The former president Muhammad Naguib's longtime ally, constitutional lawyer Abd al-Razeq al-Sanhouri, went so far as to claim that Nasser diabolically engineered his own army's defeat so that he could rein it in—like a merchant who burns down his store in hopes of a fresh start.[138] This latter view—as malicious as it sounds—found a receptive audience among Egypt's diplomats; having been long immersed in power politics and international conspiracies, it was easy for them to accept that their president believed that a resounding military defeat was imperative to dismiss Amer and his cronies.[139]

---

[*] *Al-Akhbar* 4664: 1. Cairo (6/11/1967).

Third, the military leadership argued that if Nasser had let them have their way and strike Israel first, victory would have been guaranteed. But instead the president turned down their plans for a first strike, and gave Israel the initiative in order to appease the Americans. Commander Sedqi Mahmoud of the air force supposedly begged Nasser during their last meeting on June 2 to allow him to launch a preemptive air strike, but the president yelled at him: "As long as you have no means to win a war against America, then shut up and follow your orders." Air Defense Commander Ismail Labib said that Mahmoud returned that day to GHQ with teary eyes, knowing quite well that taking the first strike, as Nasser insisted, would devastate the army. In addition, Labib continued, it was Nasser's cabinet that had refused his repeated requests for funding to build concrete shelters for aircraft and radar installations.

Fourth, the black propaganda campaign accused the president of encouraging Amer to issue the order to evacuate Sinai on June 6. As Commander Murtagi alleged, Field Marshal Amer confessed to him that it was Nasser who pushed for an early retreat, and Abd al-Sattar Amin, Amer's secretary, said he overheard Amer and the president agreeing on the decision.[140]

Fifth, security officials supervised the distribution en masse of Amer's 1962 resignation letter, in which the field marshal implored Nasser to adopt democracy and dismantle the dictatorship he had created before it brought about disaster.[141]

Finally, even the few remaining professional officers, who loathed Amer and his clique, still blamed the president for politicizing the military. In their view, it was Nasser's obsession with security that created competing intelligence services and gave them free rein over the corps, allowing them to promote officers based on allegiance rather than merit. In 1967 alone, 173 fine officers were purged because their loyalty was suspect. Moreover, the various agencies' focus on coup-proofing the military and spying on the political leadership distracted them from their original tasks: counterintelligence and foreign espionage. Their most fateful blunder was the failure to discover that Israel's new fighter-bombers could fly at low altitudes undetectable by Egyptian radar. The future war minister Gamasy blamed Nasser for not carrying out a total overhaul of the military command after its dismal performance in 1956.[142] Considering that many apolitical officers supported Nasser's coup because of the humiliating defeat of 1948, the thought that Israel and the West had once more ambushed their institution was unbearable.

In comparison to the well-executed pro-Amer offensive, Nasser's associates seemed at a loss. For one thing, the president committed a major misstep by failing to arrest the field marshal and his allies immediately after the defeat. By allowing them to remain free, he not only gave them enough maneuvering space to conspire against him, but he also implicitly relieved them from their responsibility for the defeat—or else why were they not behind bars? Moreover, upon learning from his intelligence sources that Amer's propaganda campaign was turning not only the officers but also the common soldiers against him, an irresolute Nasser proposed to forgive Amer, Badran, and Nasr, "the unholy trio who ran a government within the government in Egypt without his knowledge or approval," if they agreed to accept less influential posts—in Amer's case, the vice presidency.[143]

The president's hesitance encouraged Amer's faction to go further, moving from slander to action. The field marshal's security associates urged him to reject any attempt at reconciliation with Nasser—including the latter's offer of a general amnesty—and began to work out a plot to seize power. Amer's security trio (Shams Badran, Salah Nasr, and Abbas Radwan) spearheaded the conspirators, as expected. On June 10, Nasr transferred Amer to an intelligence safe house in the heart of Cairo. He was allowed back to his villa only after Badran and Radwan had turned it into a fortress guarded by two commando platoons with a handful of heavy artillery pieces, in addition to three hundred militiamen from Amer's hometown in Upper Egypt armed with machine guns and grenades. Amer's entourage then beseeched him to carry out a coup against Nasser. Their request was summarized in the words of the paratroops commander, Major General Osman Nassar: "We implore you not to give this man power over us … he will not shrink from humiliating and destroying us."[144] On June 11, six hundred officers (among whom were fifty brigadiers and generals) drove twelve military police armored vehicles into GHQ, threatening to oust Fawzy and chanting, "There is no leader but the field marshal!" before turning to Amer's house to pledge their allegiance. Upon learning about the incident, Nasser dismissed thirty senior officers, including the military's twelve-member Supreme Council of the Armed Forces.[145] Clearly, this was not enough.

An undeterred Nasr tried to curry U.S. support for Nasser's overthrow. On June 26, he contacted the CIA via an Italian intelligence back channel. He claimed that unlike Nasser, the military and intelligence community in Egypt was ready to recognize Israel and open up the economy. In return, they needed help in getting rid of the president and his acolytes. Despite American hostility toward Nasser, the State Department's Bureau of Intelligence and Research (INR) counseled that Nasr's proposal should be received with caution in case this was an Egyptian attempt to humiliate the United States in response to its complacent role in the 1967 war.[146] The field marshal's men therefore decided to go ahead without American backing.

The coup plan—a brainchild of Nasr and Badran—was for commando units to escort Amer to their headquarters near Anshas Airbase (on the outskirts of Cairo), and fly him from there to the Eastern Command, on the west bank of the Suez Canal, where the army was mostly concentrated. There, in the words of the Anshas Airbase commander, Major General Tahsin Zaki, the army would protect Amer while paratroopers, under Major General Galal Haridi, neutralized the Republican Guard back in the capital, and assisted GIS operatives in rounding up Nasser and his loyalists. At this point, Amer would address the nation, detailing Nasser's responsibility for the defeat and declaring a holy war under his command to liberate Sinai.[147] Amer's associates then prepared the public address, which began by promising "to expose the hidden truths [behind the defeat] and to rescue the citizens from this nightmare ... [because] no one has the right to deceive the nation at this stage." It then recounted how Nasser ordered the May 14 mobilization to ease the pressure on Syria, but then rejected Amer's plan for a preemptive strike against Israel, and instead "startled the entire high command," on June 2, by ordering the impracticable repositioning of the troops in Sinai from an offensive to a defensive stance in three days, and requiring the air force to passively absorb an Israeli strike. The speech also pointed out how Egypt was double-crossed by the superpowers: the Soviets recanted their pledge to fight alongside Egypt, and the United States deceived Nasser by claiming it would resolve the conflict peacefully if the military did not attack first. This is how the "geopolitical plot against us was sealed," the speech concluded, before calling Egyptians to arms to reconquer their lost territory.[148]

The plan was sound; but it was Amer's hesitancy to act against Nasser that delayed its execution. Why did the field marshal stall? One explanation is sheer ineptitude: "The same military that could not organize itself to fight a war could not organize now either."[149] The dozens of officers who "milled around [Amer's] house aimlessly" for days said he seemed unprepared "psychologically" to seize power, despite pledges of support from at least six hundred serving officers. It was only under extreme pressure from Nasr and Badran that he gathered himself and agreed to set a date for action: August 27.[150] A more likely explanation, considering the history of his relationship with Nasser, is that the field marshal expected the president to give in as he had always done, from 1956 onward. That is probably why Amer accepted Nasser's invitation to meet in order to settle their dispute peacefully. Despite the vehement objection of his security advisers—who smelled treachery, especially because the invitation was delivered by Sadat only two days before the planned coup—Amer believed that Nasser was finally ready to patch things up and reappoint him general commander.[151] After missing his chance to act, it was now Nasser's turn.

Days before the plot was to be executed, Nasser's security men got wind of Amer's intentions and began to move. The president's Bureau of Information was tipped off by well-placed informants, who included a GIS operative and four officers in the air force and artillery, in addition to Amer's own cook. Upon learning of the conspiracy, they advised Nasser to immediately ascertain the loyalty of a few officials: his handpicked commander of the Republican Guard, Lieutenant General Al-Lethy Nassef; his recently appointed MID director, Muhammad Sadeq; the new head of Military Police, Major General Sa'd Abd al-Karim; and the Interior Ministry's GID chief, Hassan Tal'at. The next step was to form a special task force to plan a counterattack. The committee included the security czar, Zakaria Muhi al-Din, the minister of state for intelligence and former GIS and PBI operative Amin Huwaidi, Interior Minister Sha'rawi Gomaa, the new commander-in-chief, Muhammad Fawzy, and the PBI director, Samy Sharaf. Meetings were held after midnight at a sporting club to avoid GIS surveillance, and after the first couple of meetings they presented Nasser with what they called Operation Johnson. The plan—as outlined in Sharaf's memoirs—was simple: (1) knowing that Amer was acting under the spell of his security lieutenants, and knowing that his faction could not act without the immensely popular field marshal, Amer had to be lured out of his stronghold and detained at a remote location; (2) relying on Amer's sentimental nature and his belief that Nasser would eventually back down, the field marshal would likely accept an invitation to clear the air with his estranged friend, especially if the invitation was delivered by someone he trusted (like his friend Sadat) and insinuated that the president felt cornered and was ready to compromise; (3) once Amer was taken into custody by military police, his heavily guarded villa would be stormed by a force of Republican Guards, under Fawzy's supervision; (4) Military Intelligence and Interior Ministry officers would then swiftly arrest the conspirators before they knew the fate of their commander; (5) with Amer and his supporters removed from the scene the army would lose its rallying point for another plot; (6) Huwaidi would be appointed war minister, and through his men at the GIS (the agency he had helped establish and which he served as its deputy director in 1957), he would also take over the agency; and (7) Fawzy and Huwaidi would finally purge the military and intelligence services of Amer loyalists, and issue laws to restructure both the armed forces and the security community. The end goal would be to depoliticize the military and redirect intelligence from domestic to external espionage.[152]

The plan was implemented successfully. Amer arrived at the president's house at 7:00 p.m. on August 24, 1967. After a stormy meeting, which lasted over ten hours, Zakaria and his aides transferred Amer to an undisclosed location guarded by military police. Fawzy and his troops took over the villa after a four-hour siege and a short skirmish. They arrested Amer's followers (including Badran and Radwan), and confiscated thirteen truckloads of weapons and ammunition. Hours after dawn, Huwaidi took charge of the GIS, and immediately issued orders to place 148 military officers and 18 intelligence operatives (including the agency's chief, Nasr) in custody. On September 13, Amer was removed to a GIS safe house near the Pyramids, whereupon he (supposedly) committed suicide through swallowing a poison pill with which Nasr had provided him in case their plot failed—or at least this is what the forensic team that examined his body reported.[153] Six days after his death, another 181 officers and civilians were arrested for allegedly planning to avenge his "murder."[154]

One might ask why the rest of the military did nothing to save its beloved leader and his men, and thus open the door for a more explicit military dictatorship. Amer certainly had supporters in the military despite the defeat. Colonel Muhammad Selim, who fought in 1967 and later in 1973, was furious to see him go.

> Under Amer, the military had its own independent character; it was stronger than the president; it was the strongest component in the regime. Nasser used the 1967 defeat as a pretext to get rid of Amer; he poisoned him and placed his archenemy [Muhammad Fawzy] in charge of the military with the explicit mandate of repressing the armed forces and forcing it into submission. But Fawzy went even further than that; he not only made the army obedient, but he purged any officer who had pride or dignity, and humiliated those who remained.[155]

So what held the soldiers back? Colonel Abd al-Aziz al-Beteshty, who served at the front in 1967, captured the general mode within the ranks in the following truism: "Soldiers abandon their leaders [in peace], if their leaders abandon them in war."[156] Brigade commander in 1967 and future war minister Kamal Hassan Aly described how he and his comrades regarded Amer's men less as fellow officers than as "security agents similar to the political commissars of the Soviet army ... a new ruling class within the army," and recalled how they habitually intimidated their comrades by threatening to report them as security risks.[157] So even though Amer and his security elite had bought off the loyalty of a considerable number of officers, a critical mass within the armed forces saw clearly how the politicization (and straightforward corruption) of the military had hurled their institution into the abyss. "Never again!" many of them thought.

Now it was Nasser's chance to sweep in before the armed forces regained their balance. His triumph in 1967 thus triggered the process of transforming Egypt from a military to a police state. Egypt's political and security leaders realized that relying on an all-powerful military was a double-edged sword. It could render the regime literally invincible to change from below, but it could also hold it hostage. Nasser's bitter experience with the officer corps during his confrontations with Naguib and Amer made that clear. Never again would the armed forces be allowed to accumulate such political leverage. The politicization trend, which began in 1952, was therefore reversed after 1967. The army's disastrous performance at war, as painful as it was, provided Nasser with a golden opportunity to purge Amer's network and subsequently minimize the political role of the military.

Acting in his dual capacity as war minister and GIS director, Huwaidi created a fact-finding committee to investigate the causes of the defeat. The committee attributed it to "the political leadership's loss of control over the military and security agencies, which behaved as autonomous, unsupervised, and self-sufficient institutions."[158] Between November 1967 and February 1968, the political leadership moved decisively to remedy this shortcoming: Nasser formed a twelve-member committee headed by Zakaria to purge Amer's followers: more than a thousand officers and three hundred GIS operatives were discharged, and ninety conspirators, including Badran, Nasr, Radwan, and members of Amer's Supreme Council of the Armed Forces were charged with treason and handed hefty prison sentences.[159] Huwaidi then submitted a long memo, "Reorganizing Work in the Higher Organs of the War Ministry," to Nasser in October 1967. Article 5 emphasized ways of empowering the president and war minister through control over the defense budget, arms procurement, and all expenditures and personnel issues within the armed forces; while Article 9 proposed dividing power over the military between the supreme commander (the president), the chief of staff, and the war minister. On January 25, Law 4 of 1968, "Control of State Defense Matters and the Armed Forces," adopted these suggestions, in addition to giving the president control over all military appointments down to the level of colonel. Nasser canceled the rank of field marshal and reduced the number of colonel generals and lieutenant generals by more than half. More important than streamlining Egypt's top-heavy rank structure, the Office of the Commander-in-Chief for Political Guidance—the nerve center of Amer's power—was dissolved, and the general command was restructured so that the service heads and major military bodies reported directly to the president. Now the war minister became the president's representative to the armed forces and not vice versa. Nasser also dissolved the military's Criminal Investigations Department, which Amer had formed to involve the army in civilian criminal investigations. He then formed the National Defense Council in 1969, to be chaired by the president and composed of the ministers

of war, foreign affairs, and interior, intelligence chiefs, and other strategic posts, and assigned it the duty of drawing up Egypt's geopolitical
strategy—thus diluting the power of the Supreme Council of the
Armed Forces.[160]

To strengthen the president's grip even further, Huwaidi created
a special section within the GIS to take over the now-dissolved
OCC role of monitoring political trends within the armed forces.*
Huwaidi then turned to intelligence. During his three-year tenure
at the GIS, he managed to "overhaul and realign" the intelligence
community, redirecting it from spying on Egyptians to foreign
espionage, delegating the job of domestic control to the Interior
Ministry and its investigative organ, the GID. Nasser was thus able to
deliver a speech on March 3 celebrating the "fall of the *mukhabarat*
state."[161] Finally, the ASU wrested control over the 367 public-sector
companies from Amer's military appointees.

The president followed these dramatic steps with issuing the March
30 Manifesto, which blamed the 1967 defeat on the military-intelligence complex, and vowed to demilitarize and open up the political
system through the new Permanent Constitution, which was drafted at
the end of 1970, though not ratified until months later. Several indicators attest to Nasser's seriousness about fulfilling these promises. For
one thing, the percentage of officers in the cabinet decreased from 66
percent in 1967 to 21 percent in 1970, and those in ASU secretariats
from 75 percent in 1962 to 43 percent in 1970.[162] Another sign was
that his new appointees to the high command were reputably professional soldiers who had long resented the clientelism of Amer's faction.
Notable examples include Ahmed Ismail, who was appointed chief of
staff in March 1969; Abd al-Ghany al-Gamasy, appointed chief of staff
of the canal front; and Sa'ad al-Din al-Shazly, placed in charge of the
paratroops. These were the three men who led the October War in
1973. Also, Hafez Ismail, Amer's neglected military secretary, who had
asked to be transferred to the Foreign Ministry in 1960 away from the
hornet's nest at the OCC, was named director of the GIS in April 1970.
That being said, Nasser also rewarded two of his loyalists in 1970: his
longtime ally Muhammad Fawzy became war minister, and the loyal
MID director Muhammad Sadeq became chief of staff. If anything,
these latter appointments reflect the fact that no matter how sincere
he was about professionalizing the army, Nasser still could not trust it
enough to turn his back on it—or at least he was dissuaded from doing
so by his top security lieutenants.

This halfhearted attitude also marked his approach to opening up

---

* The section's first success was exposing Soviet attempts to spread communism in
the air force, in a report submitted to Nasser on May 21, 1970 (Huwaidi, *Khamsin
'am min al-'awasif: ma ra'ituh qultuh*, 305–6).

the political system. With the military set on the path of political marginalization, the regime had two options: to democratize or to find
another guarantor of regime stability. Nasser signaled his determination to pursue the first path in the March 30 Manifesto. But with good
intentions aside, this option was practically ruled out by the institutional
setup that had governed Egypt for almost two decades. As military-
based security organs were either dissolved (the OCC) or redirected
toward their original duties (gathering intelligence on foreign armies in
the case of the MID, and policing members of the armed forces in the
case of the military police), and as the activities of the civilian intelligence agency (the GIS) were now restricted to counterintelligence and
foreign espionage, the only security institutions left standing were the
Interior Ministry with its dreaded General Investigations Directorate
(GID), the president's homegrown PBI, and the security-oriented
ASU, with its secret Vanguard Organization. After a brief soul-
searching journey, Nasser was swayed by his advisers toward maintaining the authoritarian regime, and only substituting military protection
for that of a devastatingly effective civilian security system. The president took a huge step in that direction by creating the Central Security
Forces (CSF) at the beginning of 1969. These antiriot shock units (num-
bering 100,000 in 1970) were composed of military conscripts placed
under the control of the Interior Ministry—a most unusual arrangement. If the GID and PBI were now solely responsible for surveillance
and investigations, neither of them had the capacity to quell street riots,
a task previously handled by the military police. Now that Nasser no
longer wanted to rely on the military, he had to create a paramilitary
police force to do the job. The CSF was therefore created to "obviate
military involvement in riot control."[163]

RISE OF THE CENTERS OF POWER

With the military reined in and the civilian security out in force, Nasser
could now devote himself entirely to the coming war of liberation.
Egypt began a fierce war of attrition against Israeli forces in Sinai on
July 1, 1967—barely three weeks after the defeat—and continued until
a cease-fire was signed in August 1970 to allow both sides a brief respite.
The first item on Nasser's agenda was a major reorientation of Egyptian
foreign policy from nonalignment with either of the two superpowers
to a close alignment with the Soviet Union—a reorientation that
would have a great effect on the domestic power balance. Why did the
president abandon the balancing act that he had always considered the
cornerstone of his foreign policy to side with the Russians? President
Charles De Gaulle of France said it best when he described the 1967
war as "an Israeli execution of an American war."[164] Throughout the

sixties, Nasser felt he went above and beyond to garner U.S. sympathy. His extended and cordial correspondence with John F. Kennedy was only one example. Another conciliatory gesture was his replacement of Sabri, whom the Americans believed to be Moscow's strongman in Cairo, with the reputably pro-American Zakaria as prime minister in 1965. Nasser explicitly informed the U.S. ambassador a few days after the cabinet reshuffle that he hoped relations would run more smoothly after this change.[165]

Nonetheless, President Johnson continued his strong-arm tactics against Egyptian troops in Yemen. Furthermore, under the influence of foreign-policy hawks such as the Rostow brothers (Walt, the national security adviser, and his brother Eugene, who served as undersecretary of state), Johnson decided that Nasser was a Soviet puppet who must be removed. Following the Egyptian mobilization of troops into Sinai in May 1967, the CIA chief, Richard Helms, highlighted to Johnson how an Israeli victory would destroy Nasser, or at least curtail his ability to project regional power. A crucial meeting then took place at the Pentagon on May 26 between Abba Eban, Israel's foreign minister, and the U.S. defense secretary, the chairman of the Joint Chiefs of Staff, and the CIA director, to discuss the upcoming battle. The strategists agreed that a swift Israeli victory depended on that country's ability to strike first. The next day, the United States telegrammed Nasser, promising to help negotiate a peaceful settlement so long as Egypt refrained from attacking first. On May 30, the Mossad chief, Meir Amit, traveled secretly to Washington to get a clear green light from Robert McNamara and Helms to begin operations.[166] The veteran U.S. negotiator William Quandt offers a diluted version of what happened during that meeting, claiming that Johnson initially tried to dissuade the Israelis from launching a first strike, but that toward the end of May the U.S. president realized that

> The only realistic means of convincing Israel not to act on its own would have entailed unilateral US military action to reopen the Strait of Tiran. This, Johnson was not prepared to undertake, in large measure because of Congress. As a result, the president acquiesced in Israel's decision to launch a preemptive war and made sure that the Israelis knew in advance that, while he was in office, there would be no repeat of the US pressure on Israel similar to that imposed during the Suez crisis in 1956. In brief, in the crucial days before Israel undertook the decision to go to war, the light from Washington shifted from red to yellow.[167]

On June 3, the United States dispatched two separate envoys (Ambassador Charles Post from the State Department, and Robert Anderson, Johnson's personal adviser) to Cairo to reassure Egypt that

Israel would not initiate armed aggression, and to invite Zakaria to meet with Johnson on June 5 to reach a compromise. The night before the war, Eugene Rostow asked Egypt's ambassador to Washington to assure Nasser that "Israel would never begin hostilities."[168] No wonder Nasser felt that the United States not only betrayed him, but also tried to make a fool out of him.

But diplomatic deception was not the only thing that enraged Nasser. Nor did active American support for Israel during the battle, by providing reconnaissance and jamming Egyptian communications, come as a surprise to him. What really disturbed the president was the U.S. reaction toward Israeli excesses in the war. He had learned that the American administration explicitly asked Israel to stay away from the West Bank, which was under the control of the close U.S. ally King Hussein of Jordan, and the Golan Heights, whose occupation would push Syria into the arms of the Soviets. The Israelis not only ignored these demands, but to preempt any American effort to stop them they bombed and torpedoed the spy ship USS *Liberty* on June 8, killing 34 sailors and injuring 171 others.[169] As far as Nasser was concerned, this incident indicated that the United States had no leverage with Israel whatsoever, and that if he wanted Sinai back he had to fight for it using all the aid he could get. At this point, only the Russians offered help.

The Soviets not only provided new offensive weapons (such as T-62 tanks, Tu-16 bombers, and the modified MiG-21 fighter-bombers), and promised Nasser, during his visit to Moscow in January 1970, an integrated air defense system (centered on SAM-6 missiles) without which Egypt could not have entered another war, they also decided—in "an unequivocal military gesture"—to send their own pilots, technicians, and instructors to help rebuild the Egyptian army and operate its air defense.[170] A few dozen instructors had accompanied the first batch of Soviet weapons to Egypt back in 1957. But with the new shipments, this number jumped to 3,000 in 1967, then to 15,000 in 1970, and 20,000 by 1972.[171] In return, of course, Nasser had to offer a few facilities to the Soviet Mediterranean fleet in the ports of Alexandria and Port Said, in addition to five air bases distributed throughout the country.[172]

But Nasser's preoccupation with war preparations forced him to entrust domestic affairs to his security and political subordinates. That and his dismantling of the military and GIS power structure cleared the path for the now unrivaled security trio of Samy Sharaf, Sha'rawi Gomaa, and Aly Sabri. The rapprochement with the Soviet Union promoted their rise even further, first by sidelining the pro-American Zakaria (the most influential security official and Nasser's closest security confidant), and second because the Russians maintained strong links with each of them (as will be discussed in the following chapter).

Ordinary citizens referred to this new triumvirate as Egypt's "hidden government."[173] The label that stuck, however, was the one Heikal carved for them: the "centers of power." Once again the very people Nasser had relied on to defend his regime began to develop their own agendas.

The question one must confront at this point is how come the defeat did not spur a popular revolt, perhaps supplemented by a few mutinous regiments, as happened in Russia and Prussia following the Great War? The part concerning the military is relatively easy to answer. For one thing, the army was in a total state of shock; after all, the defeat, as humiliating as it was, occurred in six swift days rather than four years of drawn-out battles. Also, unlike the war-hardened and emotionally worn-out soldiers of Europe's two great land powers, Egyptian soldiers scarcely saw combat during these days. Finally, the influence of a decade of politicization and security control—something without parallel in the armies of the tsar or the kaiser—needed years to wear off. But if all that explains inaction within the ranks, what accounts for popular submission? In truth, the people did rise in protest. There were massive student and worker uprisings in February and November 1968—the first of their kind since 1954. Steelworkers in Helwan set off the initial wave on February 21, against what they perceived as lenient measures against military negligence during the war. This spark ignited protests in factories and universities throughout the country. Notably, however, student demands were harsher and more comprehensive, amounting basically to a wholesale denunciation of the regime; they chanted the slogans "Down with the Military State!" and "Down with the Police State!" simultaneously, as if indicating they would not settle for a simple change in the administrators of repression. Military tanks surrounded the protestors and helicopters hovered over their heads—the military still had one foot in the door—but this was only for intimidation and to make sure things did not get out of control. It was the Interior Ministry that was now expected to restore order, and it did so with a vengeance: the February and November demonstrations, each lasting for barely a week, were finally dispersed after the police used live ammunition, killing 21 people, injuring 772, and detaining 1,100.[174] The containment of the 1968 demonstrations (a crucial year for workers and students in Egypt and around the world) could be attributed to the quick shift from military to police repression before protestors had a chance to organize their lot and articulate truly radical demands. Police brutality on those specific occasions, however, was only a symptom of the deep-seated and carefully administered repression of revolutionary alternatives in Egypt since 1952, whether by military or civilian security agencies. The real reason the demonstrations that followed the defeat did not lead to an overall change was that the regime's tight security grip scarcely allowed activists to develop the organizational resources to carry out a full-scale revolt—a phenomenon replicated in the 2011 revolt.

But as ineffective as the 1968 demonstrators were, they provided the rising centers of power with an excuse to dissuade the president from seriously contemplating a transition to democracy. Society, they argued, was still under the spell of foreign-backed agents provocateurs, and in time of war such opposition activities were intolerable. Once more, the opportunity to open up the political system had come and gone. The first time, in 1954, it was demanded by a majority within the officer corps who were concerned about the negative effects of immersing the military in politics. In 1967 these fears were vindicated, and the demand for democracy should have been even more resounding. In both cases, nonetheless, the security coterie made sure that opposition was silenced and that any such demand remained a distant hope. This time, however, the symbol of leadership and steadfastness was broken. Nasser was about to bow out of the scene.

Eradicating the Centers of Power:
The Corrective Revolution of May 1971

Gamal Abd al-Nasser's premature death of a heart attack, on September 28, 1970, could not have come at a worse time. It sent shock waves across the country, bringing out seven million mourners to his ten-kilometer funeral procession—possibly the largest in history—and forcing the funeral organizers to transfer his body from one part of the city to another via helicopter to avoid the flood of sobbing and screaming citizens. Besides the psychological attachment to the charismatic father figure, the top political spot seemed disturbingly vacant, as the late president did not groom anyone for his succession. The existing vice president, Anwar al-Sadat, was perceived as weak and unpopular within and outside the ranks. Before the 1952 coup, Sadat had been part of one of the least significant army services, the signal corps, which handled communications. And unlike most Free Officers, he had never seen war. During the 1948 war in Palestine, Sadat was a runaway from prison, where he had landed after trying to facilitate a Nazi invasion of Egypt with the hope of ejecting British occupation. He then received royal amnesty and was reincorporated into the corps after joining the Iron Guards, a secret organization devoted to assassinating King Farouk's political enemies. After the coup, his comrades tried him for working for the palace and not reporting to his position on the night of the coup. That night Sadat took his wife to the movies and picked a fight with one of the viewers and ended up at the police station. It was widely suspected among officers that if the coup had failed he was planning to use the movie tickets and the police report as alibis proving he was not there, and if it had succeeded he would claim not to have received the orders in time—which he indeed claimed. Nasser intervened on his behalf and the charges were dropped. A grateful Sadat announced in one of the first meetings of the Revolutionary Command Council that he had transferred his voting rights to Nasser, giving the latter carte blanche to take any decisions he saw fit. It was because of this meek attitude that Sadat was the only RCC member who remained by Nasser's side until the very end; and it was because of the insecure president's insistence on rotating the vice presidency among nonthreatening candidates that Sadat—barely a few months in office—found himself the legal successor to Nasser's throne.

Popular misgivings aside, it was officers who harbored grave concerns about Sadat's presidency. The military had been counting down to war after Nasser promised to liberate Sinai from Israeli occupation in a few months time. Now they worried that Sadat's feeble personality and total lack of war experience would drive him to abandon the military option and sue for peace with Israel, and that his conspiratorial nature—obvious from his intrigues with the Nazis and the palace before the coup—would tempt him toward backdoor deals with the Americans, the only country that could pressure Israel. The officer corps thus hoped for a firmer hand at the helm in these trying times. Yet it was not Sadat's position as vice president that favored his candidacy, but rather the balance of forces between the centers of power that Nasser left behind. In the fall of 1970, three security magnates were in the process of consolidating their influence over the country: the longtime intelligence official Aly Sabri dominated the ruling Arab Socialist Union; Sha'rawi Gomaa was interior minister and head of the ASU's secret Vanguard Organization; and Samy Sharaf led the President's Bureau of Information. Though the organizations controlled by the former two were considerably larger that that controlled by Sharaf, the latter supplemented his organizational might with valuable allies: his relative Muhammad Fawzy was war minister, and his PBI protégé Ahmed Kamel directed the General Intelligence Service.

Nasser's unexpected death cut short the time these magnates had to negotiate a new power arrangement. They were still divided over whether they ought to seize the top executive position, or whether it would be wiser to install a ceremonial president and run the country in his name (as they did during the last days of Nasser) without bearing any of the responsibilities that come with office; and if they decided to pursue the first alternative, which of them should be nominated president. Held back by these divisions, they agreed on a temporary and—as they believed—easily reversible decision, which was to elect Sadat to the presidency, and rule through him until they organized their ranks. To make sure the new president remained under their control, they decided to surround him from all directions, with Sabri promoted to vice president, and Sharaf to minister of presidential affairs. Sadat seemed like a safe bet; he had no following in the military or security establishment, he held no executive position between 1956 and 1969, and he was one of the least popular politicians within the ASU. Also, he was widely regarded by the public as a parasitic character.

This estimation was not theirs alone. The Americans believed Sadat would not last for more than a few weeks, and Henry Kissinger described him as a political clown.[1] Mohamed Hassanein Heikal, chief editor of Egypt's leading daily, *Al-Ahram*, and Nasser's closest adviser, who was involved in the succession deliberations and ran Sadat's election campaign, later admitted that he knew how weak Sadat was but had hoped that the "responsibilities of office would strengthen the positive elements in his character and enable him to overcome the weak ones. The example of Truman was in my mind."[2] Last but not least, Sadat himself indicated in his memoirs that he was nominated to the presidency only because of his apparent weakness.[3]

Still, the new president had some assets. It is true that in terms of institutional power he commanded no personal following, but his service as secretary-general of the National Union (1957–61) and Speaker of Parliament (1961–69), in addition to his brief stint as vice president, provided him with extensive experience in the political machinations of the state. More important, perhaps, Sadat recognized the mistrust and divisions that plagued his rivals, and was determined—as he confessed in a future interview—to play his cards carefully to divide and conquer.[4] Drawing advice from the indispensable Heikal, Egypt's unrivaled *Machtpolitik* strategist, Sadat patched together a hastily assembled coalition of Republican Guards, police officers, and professional military men, and outmaneuvered the centers of power, despite their entrenchment in the military, security, and political institutions.

TRYING TO CHECKMATE A PRESIDENT

Recognizing he was meant as a temporary fill-in until his opponents put their house in order, Sadat understood that time was not on his side. He therefore set to work immediately, issuing several unilateral decisions that aimed partly at increasing his autonomy as president but were mostly intended to distract his rivals and keep them divided over how to react. Two prominent examples were his appointment of the veteran diplomat Mahmoud Fawzy (not related to the war minister) as prime minister, and his reviving of plans to create an Arab federation among Egypt, Syria, Libya, and possibly Sudan—take two in the attempt to unite the Arab world after the dissolution of the Egyptian-Syrian merger in 1961. The first decision shrewdly deprived the centers of power from appointing one of their own to the premiership, while at the same time offering a name no one dared object to; Mahmoud Fawzy had served as Egypt's foreign minister for years, was Nasser's chief adviser on international affairs, and was reputably competent and politically neutral. The centers-of-power camp, which claimed to uphold Nasser's mantle, could not dispute Fawzy's loyalty to their master's legacy, nor could they refute Sadat's argument that the country's vulnerable geopolitical situation required an expert diplomat at the helm.

Announcing the formation of the Arab Federation was another masterful stroke. After being badgered by his opponents during an ASU Higher Executive Committee meeting on March 6, 1972, to commit to launching war against Israel in June, the federation ploy pushed back the war decision because of the lengthy procedures required to establish it, while at the same time allowing Sadat to claim that he was trying to enhance Egypt's power in war rather than just stalling. More valuably, the Federation Agreement, upon the president's insistence, called for an institutional overhaul in preparation for the intended merger. This offered Sadat a precious opportunity to weed out his rivals from the new institutions without confronting them.[5]

Sadat's bold and swift action summoned his enemies to battle. They could live with the harmless Mahmoud Fawzy as prime minister, but to go ahead with the Arab Federation was fatal because they knew Sadat was planning to use it as an excuse to remove them from their institutional power bastions. Immediately after the president's announcement, on April 21, 1971, the centers of power made sure the ASU's Higher Executive Committee vetoed it. And when Sadat tried to go around this rejection by appealing to the Central Committee of the ASU, Sharaf presented him with a memo (dated April 20) claiming that the armed forces had expressed in a general survey their adamant rejection of the intended federation—a survey Sadat had not authorized but Sharaf carried out anyway, to demonstrate that officers were eager to fight right away.[6]

More decisive steps, however, were necessary to meet the president's unexpected recalcitrance. The centers of power agreed that he must be deposed, but differed over how. The first option was to carry out a replacement coup, but it seemed too far-fetched to assume that the army would allow itself to be drawn into a political battle in Cairo while Israel was still in Sinai. In addition, GIS reports made it clear that the officer corps was resolutely against reentering the political fray, especially while it was still trying to remedy the disasters brought about by the politicization of the military. One must also remember that Nasser's wholesale purge of the armed forces after 1967 left few officers with a taste for politics. Moreover, Sadat had made it his top priority to win over the army until he could liquidate the centers of power. Between October and December 1970, he visited the front lines frequently, and conducted four meetings with senior officers. During a marathon nine-hour meeting with the general staff on December 1, he pledged to wage war as soon as the army was ready, declaring that 1971 was the Year of Decision, and insinuating that it was his rivals and their petty quibbles that were holding him back. Finally, the president promised his troops a 25 percent raise.[7]

Despite all that, War Minister Muhammad Fawzy went ahead with coup plans anyway and issued a handwritten directive, on April 21, to Chief of Staff Muhammad Sadeq ordering him to prepare an emergency plan to secure the capital using military police units, the 6th Mechanized Division, and the 22nd Mechanized Infantry Brigade. The order added, suspiciously, that once this emergency plan was activated, the military should receive instructions only from him (Fawzy), Gomaa, and Sharaf. Instead of following the directive, Sadeq simply sat on it, and informed Heikal during the first week of May that in the event the president faced domestic challenges, he was willing not only to support him and swing the rest of the officers behind him, but also to bring on board the head of the two-battalion-strong Republican Guards, Al-Lethy Nassef.[8] Determined not to lose another battle to Israel, the chief of staff was infuriated by the treacherous political intrigue occurring in the capital at a time when all attention should be directed to the war effort. Sadeq, along with the rest of the armed forces, simply wanted to win the war, and believed that political bickering only postponed it. As Major General Nassef later confessed to his fellow officer Hussein Hammudah, it was Sadeq who warned him that if the guards betrayed Sadat, he would mobilize the military to rein them in even if it led to a bloodbath.[9] Sadat gave Nassef an even stronger motive to stick with him by alleging that the centers of power were conspiring to have him dislodged in favor of one of their loyalists. Accordingly, Nassef warned Sharaf that he and his allies should not allow their differences with Sadat to reach the point of violent confrontation, or else he would be obliged to abide by his constitutional duty to defend the president.[10]

As the prospects of a military coup dimmed, the conspirators now placed their bet on a political coup. Sadat was to be ousted through an ASU decision—just as the Soviet leader Nikita Khrushchev was ejected from power in 1964. But most of the Central Committee members they approached seemed reluctant to stir trouble without a clear pretext. The decision was therefore taken to provoke a political-constitutional crisis that would spur them to action.[11] According to the new plot, ministers and ASU executives would resign collectively in protest at Sadat's growing autocracy; as soon as the resignations were announced the ASU and VO would bring about a government shutdown through a series of strikes in the bureaucracy and the public sector; state radio and television would then play patriotic anthems and broadcast stirring propaganda to propel the masses into the streets and force the military to intervene to restore order.[12] A cornered Sadat would then have to either step down or share power with his strong partners.

THE PRESIDENT'S COUP DE GRACE

May Day of 1971 was a dress rehearsal. Among those who attended the annual workers' celebration was Osman Ahmed Osman, Sadat's closest friend and soon to be the richest man in Egypt. He recalls: "I noticed how the centers of power handed out Nasser's pictures to the workers and strategically distributed their loyalists around the hall to shout pro-Nasser slogans, casting doubt over Sadat's legitimacy."[13] Sadat stood his ground, concluding his speech with a resounding condemnation of the centers of power: "The people are the owners of this country, and they will be the ones who will fight for their lives along with the armed forces … No group has the right to impose its will on the people through centers of power … the people alone are the masters of their destiny."[14] The following day he removed Sabri from the ASU and the vice presidency. To cover his back, he consulted Muhammad Fawzy, and the latter did not object. The war minister probably thought that removing Sabri would provide an opportunity for his relative Sharaf to make his move.[15]

As news of the looming confrontation spread through the country, everyone was now expected to take sides. One figure returning from the shadows was Hassan al-Tuhami, Nasser's veteran intelligence official who had run afoul of Amer and was forced to stay out of the country until the field marshal's downfall. Tuhami and Sadat had been close collaborators since the 1940s, and now the former hoped that with Sharaf and his associates gone, he could become the president's top security aide—and that is indeed what he became. Another senior officer was Hafez Ismail, Field Marhsal Amer's embittered military secretary, who had to bide his time in the Foreign Ministry until Amer disappeared from the scene. Nasser appointed Ismail GIS director in 1970, and when Sharaf replaced him a few months later with his acolyte Ahmed Kamel, Sadat took him in as national security adviser—a new position that did not outlast its only occupant. Although Ismail's days at the GIS were few, the contacts he developed came in handy during the May 1971 clash.

A precious prize then fell into Sadat's lap on May 11: audiotapes detailing the conspiracy against him. The tapes not only gave the president a heads-up, but they also provided him with the material proof he needed to try his rivals for high treason. Who recorded these audiotapes, and who delivered them to Sadat? It is generally agreed upon that there were several parties doing the recording, mostly because they did not trust one another. Sharaf charged the PBI and GIS with spying on both Sadat and his own coconspirators, Gomaa and Sabri. Similarly, Gomaa had the Interior Ministry's GID tap all the conversations that went on between state officials, including his collaborators. Who turned them in, however, is more difficult to answer. Sadat claimed it was a junior police officer (Captain Taha Zaki) who was a friend of one of his in-laws, and that the tapes revealed not only a coup plot, but also an attempt on the president's life.[16] Sharaf said it was a GIS informant who worked for Tuhami or Ismail.[17] But there is also proof that it was a CIA officer in Cairo by the name of Thomas Twetten who informed Sadat of the conspiracy, relying on information from an American KGB asset (Vladimir Sakharov) and a few calls intercepted by the U.S. embassy.[18] The following day, while Sadat was meeting with the troops stationed at Suez, Sadeq informed him of the looming conspiracy and assured him that he had his back covered because this was a time for war, not political scheming.[19]

This brings us to another significant aspect of the power struggle between Sadat and the centers of power, which is the geopolitical one. Geopolitical support was indispensable to the conspirators. They were crippled by the fact that none of them could measure up to the galvanizing charisma of Nasser, and so they tried to compensate for lack of popular support by allying themselves to a superpower: the Soviet Union. Ever since he was put in charge of the ASU in 1962, Aly Sabri had fashioned himself as an ideologically committed Communist, and was often referred to as "Russia's man" in Cairo; Gomaa, though himself no staunch ideologue, was leading the Leninist-styled VO, which the Soviets regarded as the only hope to promote "true communism" in the country; Fawzy, again not a Communist by conviction, made it clear that the army desperately needed Russian support to rebuild itself after the 1967 defeat; and Sharaf, as it turned out, was probably a KGB asset.[*] In fact, on May 14, the day the centers of power tended their collective resignation, the top Russian military expert in Cairo was dinning at Sharaf's house.[20] Based on these intimate relations between the centers of power and the Russians, Sabri visited Moscow in December 1970 to warn them of Sadat's intention to deliver the country to the Americans—the only country that could help him reach a peace deal with Israel. And in mid-April 1971, two weeks before the confrontation reached its climax, Sharaf traveled to the Soviet Union to seek its help in removing Sadat from power.[21] It helped that the plotters actually had material proof of the president's double-dealing. The GIS had recorded secret meetings conducted in March 1971 between Sadat's envoys and

---

[*] In 1974, a defected KGB officer published a book revealing how he recruited Sharaf in 1958. Sadat referred to the book during a speech to Parliament on March 14, 1974, noting that Sharaf had confessed to him in a letter from prison that he had been involved in a "special relationship" with the Soviets (John Barron, *KGB: The Secret Work of Soviet Secret Agents*, New York: Reader's Digest Press, 1974; Hammad, *Al-Hukuma al-khafiya fei 'ahd Abd al-Nasser wa asrar masra' al-mushir Amer*, 58–59, 71; Sirrs, *A History of the Egyptian Intelligence Service*, 64–65).

the U.S. intelligence man in Egypt Donald Bergus, in which the president offered to cut the Soviets loose if the Americans persuaded Israel to return Sinai.[22]

Sadat was aware of all this and frequently referred to his rivals as Russian agents. Sadat also knew that the Soviets considered him a transitional man, and were getting ready to elevate one of their own allies to power. He tried to offset that by visiting Moscow secretly in March 1971 to reassure Soviet leaders of his loyalty. There he informed them that he might need to reshuffle the political leadership but that they had no cause for concern because their alliance was with Egypt, not particular individuals.[23] As a sign of goodwill, he granted the Soviet fleets in the Mediterranean and Red Sea a few extra facilities. The president then forewarned the Soviet ambassador to Cairo that he was about to remove Sabri from office, but that there was not need to worry because, as he added emphatically, "If you have a friend in Egypt, it is Anwar Sadat."[24] He also appointed a celebrated Communist intellectual (Ismail Sabri Abdallah) to the new cabinet.[25] Finally, to ease their suspicions, Sadat signed an Egyptian-Soviet Friendship Treaty on May 23, 1971—an agreement Nasser was hesitant to conclude. But in the end, it was not just Sadat's maneuvers that deprived the centers of power of active Soviet support. Murad Ghaleb, who was concluding his decade-long service as Egyptian ambassador to Moscow, said that the Soviet leaders confided in him that they could only halfheartedly support a group that had no coherent leadership or agenda, and whose interactions were as often competitive as they were collaborative.[26]

Even though Soviet support was not forthcoming, the conspirators decided to push ahead with their plans. A day after Sabri was sacked from the ASU and the vice presidency, Muhammad Fawzy convened the general staff to report to them that the president was abandoning war preparations. The war minister also raised the state of readiness of the military units stationed near the capital.[27] In response, Sadat met with senior commanders at the Anshas Airbase in Cairo to warn of lurking traitors within and outside the armed forces.[28] With incontrovertible evidence of a conspiracy at hand, Sadat raised the stakes, announcing plans to restructure the ASU, and removing Gomaa from the Interior Ministry and VO on May 13. Knowing that his phones were tapped, the president sent a personal aide to summon the governor of Alexandria, Mamduh Salem, swore him in as interior minister, and sent him over to the ministry before Gomaa received wind of his removal. Salem was a longtime security officer who began his career in the Alexandria branch of the British-controlled secret police in the 1940s, and then headed the GID's Alexandria office after the coup.[29] Not wanting to rely solely on Salem's contacts in the Interior Ministry, Sadat sent a detachment of Republican Guards to secure his control over the ministry and confiscate any surveillance tapes found there. At the same time, Sadat met with Sharaf to reassure him that he had nothing to fear from Gomaa's removal, and that he could continue in his job as normal.[30]

Sharaf, of course, had other plans. He headed straight to the military's general headquarters, where he found Gomaa waiting for the war minister to wrap up a meeting with senior commanders. Fawzy asked the general staff to remove Sadat on account of his secret dealings with the Americans to reach a peaceful settlement and call off the war. He then turned to Chief of Staff Sadeq and asked him if he was ready to implement the directive he gave him three weeks earlier. To his surprise, Sadeq lashed out, refusing to participate in staging another coup, and adding: "If you want to resign, you can, but the army is not going to move ... [There is no way] the Egyptian armed forces would get mixed up in politics at a time when we are preparing for war."[31] As it became clear that the officer corps would not be dragged into this clash, Fawzy escorted his two guests back to Gomaa's house. Sadeq immediately seized control of GHQ and ordered the troops to stay put. He then called Sadat to inform him that the army would remain neutral in this confrontation. Sadeq was promoted to war minister that very night of May 14.[32]

It was time for the centers of power to play their last card, which came in the form of a live broadcast of their resignation en masse on state media. To preempt any anti-Sadat demonstrations, the minister of industry, Aziz Sedqi, ordered public-sector workers into the streets to express their support for the president. Sedqi was appointed prime minister the next day. That evening, Ashraf Marawan, Nasser's son-in-law and Sharaf's right-hand man at the PBI, decided to side with the president and turn in Sharaf's secret archive instead of smuggling it out of the Presidential Palace as his former boss had asked. Sadat described to his longtime friend Mahmoud Game' how Marawan rushed behind one of Sharaf's assistants and fired a few rounds in the air to force him to surrender the secret documents.[33] Marawan was immediately promoted to PBI director. At midnight, Sadat dispatched Ahmed Ismail to the GIS to serve as its new chief, and ordered him to hand in any secret tape recordings pertaining to the plot. Ismail had served as chief of staff under Nasser, but was fired twice by the former President for his ineptitude, and thus reviled Nasser and his centers-of-power cronies. After securing the streets and the major institutions, Sadat had all the conspirators arrested by the Interior Ministry on May 15, 1971: in all, 91 officials, including 6 ministers (among them Sharaf, Gomaa, and Fawzy), the GIS director, 20 ASU executives, 23 VO cadres, 4 members of parliament, 6 senior bureaucrats, 2 media officials, and the rest from the military. An emergency court was assembled, with Sadat's security lieutenant Hassan al-Tuhami as member, to try the plotters for high treason, and eventually handed the ringleaders long prison sentences.[34]

The arrests heralded what Sadat referred to fondly as his "Corrective Revolution," supposedly correcting the deviation from the goals of the 1952 coup. With officers caught up on the Sinai front, the time was perfect to transfer responsibility for domestic control from the military to the police, a process that Nasser had begun after 1967. This required a reorganizing of the security community. At the president's request, Ashraf Marawan supervised the dismantling of the PBI's intelligence core and its reinvention as an information secretariat, which would simply prepare presidential briefs relying on newspapers and memos from government agencies. Even though he could have reformed it and bent it to his own purposes, Sadat resolved that it was not really wise to maintain an intelligence organ so close to the president, where it could play the role of gatekeeper and withhold essential information. The next step was to bolster the power of the Interior Ministry. The ministry expanded considerably with more than a dozen new specialized departments, each headed by a deputy minister, in order to relieve the minister and the GID of nonpolitical policing activities. He then decreed a major restructuring of the GID, which included a purge of officers whose loyalty was suspect, as well as those with a military background, and a refocusing of the agency's effort exclusively toward countering political dissidence, instead of being divided between that and combating organized crime; the all-powerful Mabaheth Amn al-Dawla (State Security Investigations Sector, SSIS) now came into existence.[35]

The new SSIS reflected the institutional experience of its illustrious ancestors, the secret police of the precoup days, and the GID. Despite the purges that accompanied the agency's first transformation from political police to GID at the hands of Zakaria Muhi al-Din, Nasser's principal security chief, the enduring influence of institutional memory forced Nasser to treat the GID with some suspicion, and therefore flank it with parallel security institutions. He worried that it was too early to assume that GID officers had severed all their ties with the ancien regime, which they served only months before. But after the GID's relative eclipse in the 1950s and 1960s, it was reborn under Sadat as Egypt's leading security agency. Also, unlike its predecessors, it had a centralized military-type command structure that subjected even its distant provincial branches to Interior Ministry supervision. Consequently, the shift in responsibility for repression from military to security coincided with a shift in power within the security community itself, from intelligence agencies (civilian and military) to the Interior Ministry and its newly enhanced secret police. From this point onward, Sadat relied mostly on police officers in major government positions, to a point where even his personal secretary (Fawzy Abd al-Hafez) was a former police officer.[36]

Finally, the president dissolved the security-oriented Vanguard Organization and appointed himself ASU secretary-general, with a longtime friend (Abd al-Salam al-Zayat) as head of the Central Committee and a few handpicked subordinates as new ASU executives. The following year, he named Sayyid Mar'ie the new ASU secretary-general and Speaker of Parliament. Mar'ie came from a large landowning family, and served under Nasser as minister of agriculture. He also happened to be Sadat's in-law and close friend.[37] By the end of May 1971, the Permanent Constitution was finally issued. Egypt now embarked on a new chapter in its tumultuous postcoup history.

That being said, Sadat's startling emasculation of his powerful rivals remains a lingering question. The most common explanation places much emphasis on the president's cunning: he projected an image of weakness to survive politically under Nasser and reassure the unwitting centers of power enough to install him in the presidency before craftily reaching out to collaborators within the military, security, and political apparatuses, and playing his opponents against one another. Still, the centers of power dominated all major state institutions, and it is difficult to believe that his scheming alone caused them to lose this battle of wills. So while personal traits and tactics are certainly relevant, a careful institutional analysis provides a sufficient cause for this unexpected failure.

To start with, the centers of power were wholly consumed between 1956 and 1967 in a power struggle with Amer's group. Only in 1968 did they begin their bid for power, after undermining Amer's prized institutions (the military and military-linked intelligence) and making sure that Nasser was too preoccupied with war preparations to check their ascendancy. Nasser's death in September 1970 barely gave them time to produce a consensual pecking order. It was almost impossible for the centers of powers to become organized hierarchically when the main players were equally powerful in institutional terms: Sabri controlled the ASU; Gomaa the VO and Interior Ministry; and Sharaf the intelligence apparatus. Because coalitions are usually formed between weak parties and stronger ones, this balance of power ruled out a smooth alliance-building process. In fact, it was this deadlock that brought Sadat to the presidency; the contenders needed a lame-duck president to hold the position while they sorted things out. By virtue of the type of power he controlled—merely political power with no capacity for coercion—Aly Sabri proved to be the weakest link in the chain. He received a strong blow in July 1969 when a report from Sharaf that Sabri was becoming too cozy with the Russians forced Nasser to demote him from ASU secretary-general to ordinary party member in the most demeaning way—justifying this downgrade by Sabri's smuggling of commercial merchandise from Moscow. When Sadat removed him from the vice presidency and the ASU on May 2, his comrades abandoned him in the hopes that now they could elect a leader more easily. Without realizing it, though, Sharaf and Gomaa had in fact shot themselves in the foot; Sabri's experience as prime minister (1962–1965) and ASU secretary-general (1962–1969), as well as his latest position as vice president (1970–1971), in addition to the respect he enjoyed among the Soviets, all meant that he was the only likely candidate for the presidency.

Samy Sharaf thought he could become the strongest man in the country. With Sadat's approval, he sidelined Egypt's two most prominent security men, Zakaria Muhi al-Din and Amin Huwaidi. The first was removed from all official positions, while the second was offered a humiliatingly minor ministerial post in 1971, forcing him to turn down the offer and retire. Sharaf also pressured a reluctant Sadat to place his PBI assistant Ahmed Kamel at the head of the GIS. Now Sharaf believed he held all the intelligence strings in the palm of his hand. In addition, the war minister was his relative and ally. Why then did he hold back? Sharaf must have realized that his allies were little more than war trophies—shiny but ineffective. Fawzy did not command the respect or loyalty of the military: he was marginalized as chief of staff under Amer, plotted with the president against the officers' beloved field marshal, and had no time or resources between 1967 and 1971 to build an extensive patronage network; Kamel, in turn, had spent merely a few months on the job as GIS director before the May 1971 confrontation and could not possibly have penetrated the agency deeply enough; both Fawzy and Kamel, one should add, were political lightweights, especially when compared with their mighty predecessors, Shams Badran and Salah Nasr. One must add that Sharaf and his camp were double-crossed by Ashraf Marawan at the PBI and Muhammad Sadeq and Al-Lethy Nassef in the military.

Finally, there was Sha'rawi Gomaa, who controlled the Interior Ministry and VO. His control of the police force made his position seemingly more secure than the other two. However, it was only a decade into Mubarak's reign (in the 1990s) that the Interior Ministry was empowered enough to believe it could secure the regime on its own. Considering Gomaa's situation in real historical time, it was inconceivable for him back in 1971 to act independently without the support of the military and intelligence. Also, the VO might have been a strong espionage organ, but it lacked the hierarchical discipline or the ideological fervor to lead a popular revolt. As Sharaf and Gomaa were still weighing their assets and measuring their relative strength, Sadat was ready to move.

It is worth mentioning that the hastily conceived plan they executed impromptu on May 14 was nothing short of disastrous. It was virtually a repeat of the March 1954 popular uprising orchestrated to undercut President Muhammad Naguib, and the one coordinated by the ASU in the wake of Nasser's resignation in June 1967 to reinstall him. The conspirators probably forgot that unlike the 1954 crisis, they had all severed their relationship with the military. They were no longer young hotheaded officers who could call upon their comrades to move around a few tanks or artillery guns, or fly over a few jets as a show of force. And even though they tried to stir the public by claiming that Sadat was betraying Nasser's revolution (just as they had accused Naguib in 1954), that revolution was no longer young and promising enough to convince Egyptians that it still needed saving. Also, no matter how influential they were, none of the centers of power enjoyed Nasser's popularity, the popularity that made it easy (and believable) for millions of people to rush onto the streets in 1967 to demand his return. Their power essentially derived from the institutional positions they occupied. To resign their posts, and thus surrender these powerful positions, in hopes of shaking Sadat's regime was an unparalleled strategic blunder. But as Karl Marx hauntingly noted: "History repeats itself twice, first as tragedy, second as farce." What the centers of power tried to accomplish in May 1971 was certainly farce.

In a sense, therefore, May 1971 was not a confrontation between two well-defined camps, but between the president and disparate individuals scrambling to consolidate their power. Sadat won. And his triumph paved the path for the rise of Egypt's police state under the rapidly evolving Interior Ministry and its chief spy organ, the SSIS. But first, of course, there was a war to be fought. Sadat's road to power had to pass through occupied Sinai.

Twilight of the Generals:
October 1973 and Its Discontents

The power struggle in 1971 between Anwar al-Sadat and the centers of power seemed little more than a sideshow, a trifling skirmish, when compared with the uphill battle he now confronted. The depoliticization of the military, which Gamal Abd al-Nasser had started in 1967, was still at an early stage. The shift from military-based to police-based political control had only just begun. To wage a successful war against Israel at this point certainly threatened to bring the army back to center stage. To fail to go to war, or to be defeated once more, meant no less than political suicide. The middle road, if in fact one existed, was narrow and thorny. It required launching a successful war without reempowering the officer corps politically. This could be achieved only if the battlefront victory was limited, and, more important, faceless. No popular war heroes could be allowed to emerge—heroes that might command loyalty within the armed forces and captivate the public imagery. Liberating Sinai had to be perceived by soldiers and citizens alike as a primarily political rather than military achievement; war had to appear secondary to politics. At this critical juncture, Sadat's scheming talents were pushed to the limit. Success required a careful and persistent strategy whereby the president would employ some of Egypt's best generals for short-term assignments in order to accomplish challenging military tasks before deposing (and preferably defaming) them so that they could not translate their war-related achievements politically. Could it be done? That is what this chapter explores.

A STORMY MEETING

It all began in May 1971 after Sadat imprisoned War Minister Muhammad Fawzy for high treason despite his efforts in rebuilding the army after 1967 and putting together a plan to cross the Suez Canal. That November, Sadat reconfigured the set procedures for military promotion through a presidential decree that gave him unlimited authority over the committee that made these decisions, the Armed

Forces Officers' Committee.[1] He then appointed a new high command led by War Minister Muhammad Sadeq and Chief of Staff Saad al-Din al-Shazly. This last appointment provoked uproar within the ranks, considering that Shazly—the audacious head of the Commando Corps—was promoted over the heads of thirty more senior generals. But Sadat recognized that he needed someone with the exceptional daring and capabilities of Shazly to lead the Egyptian troops in the coming war. Shazly would have to stay till the end, whereas the war minister and his staff were relatively dispensable once they had pushed the army to the highest level of combat readiness.

Sadeq and his men were determined to win the war. That is why as Military Intelligence director he sided with Nasser against Amer, and as chief of staff he helped Sadat get rid of the erratic centers of power. But now the war minister and his top lieutenants were not so sure that the president had the same intention. Capturing the spirit of those days, Mohamed Hassanein Heikal, a close adviser to Sadat and Nasser before him, commented: "The chasm between arms and politics widened in Egypt. It became apparent that neither politics trusted the ability of arms, nor did arms trust the competence of politics."[2] At the heart of the dispute between Sadat and the general staff was the war plan itself. Chief of Staff Shazly recalled that the Supreme Council of the Armed Forces (SCAF) was convinced that when Egypt launched its attack it had to be "forceful and unlimited: a clean, swift sweep through Sinai ... to destroy the enemy concentrations ... [and liberate] all our occupied territories."[3] At minimum, as the January 2, 1972 meeting of the council agreed, the offensive must guarantee Egypt's seizure of the Sinai passes.[4] This was also the view of the now-imprisoned former war minister, Fawzy. Egypt's first line of defense extended from its border with Israel to the Sinai passes; the second line of defense stretched from the passes to the Suez Canal; and the third line was the canal itself. Egypt's army was presently stationed along the third line of defense, and at minimum had to advance to the second line, which was the passes.[5]

Because of the centrality of the "passes controversy" in all military histories of the October War, a few words on their strategic importance are in order. The veteran Free Officer Hussein Hammudah, who participated as a junior officer in the 1948 war, describes the Mitla and Gidi passes as nature's perfect gift to Egypt to help defend Sinai.[6] These were the passes that Nasser advised Amer to dig into on the morning of June 5 so that Sinai would not be overrun. Curiously, these were also the passes that Moshe Dayan asked the Israeli forces to stop at during the 1967 attack, arguing that they provided "much better defense lines than the canal."[7] The Israeli commander (and future prime minister) Ariel Sharon remembered vividly how well they served enemy troops in 1956: "The Israeli air attack had failed to dislodge defenders cocooned in rifle pits dug along the tops of ridges and in caves cut into the steep walls of the pass. For the Egyptians it was like shooting at a fairground target ... The only way I could see to defend ourselves was to move into the pass and take up positions there, where the steep cliffs and narrow defiles would give the oncoming Egyptian tanks no room for maneuver."[8] In fact, the Israelis felt compelled to build an artificial defense line along the east bank of the canal (the famous Bar-Lev Line) because they realized that—away from the passes—no defense was possible in Sinai's open terrain. The first international group of military experts to examine the October War referred to the passes as "impassible mountains."[9] Every cadet at the Egyptian Military Academy learned that controlling the passes was one of the few long-standing strategic doctrines in defending Egypt's eastern borders—a doctrine that extended from the days of Pharaoh Thutmosis III to the British General Allenby.[10] As the renowned U.S. military expert Anthony Cordesman summarized it: with the rest of Sinai "an exposed killing ground," any battle over the peninsula is simply "a two-way race for the passes."[11]

Why were the passes so important? Lieutenant Colonel Abd al-Aziz al-Beteshty of the Commando Corps provided a comprehensive overview. Strategically speaking, Sinai is divided into three sections: the southern triangle lying between the two great Red Sea gulfs is composed of sand dunes that are impassable by armored vehicles and troop carriers, while the northern strip along the Mediterranean is mostly quicksand beds, muddy swamps, jagged ridges, and broken foothills that hinder advance by heavy armor. The middle sector with its solid and open ground is therefore the only part suited for troop and vehicle movement. This sector, however, is too broad to be defended against air strikes and blitzkrieg armored offenses—the twin specialties of the Israeli army. Fortunately, several mountainous passes lie at the very core of this middle sector: the main two are Mitla in the south and al-Gidi in the north, roughly 32 kilometers from the Suez Canal, in addition to a few smaller ones. Once an army entrenches itself in these passes, it is impossible to push it back. For one thing, they are too narrow to allow for aerial bombardment (bombs rarely make it through the mountaintops). Also, the mountain caves along the relatively long passes (Milta is 32 kilometers, al-Gidi is 29) provide ideal posts for snipers to halt an offense (which again due to the narrowness of the passes can advance only in single file). Finally, they provide safe bases for operations, allowing units to launch sudden attacks throughout Sinai and retire back to the passes before enemy forces can overwhelm them. In short, whoever controls the passes controls Sinai's middle sector, and whoever controls this sector controls the entire peninsula. That is why military strategists consider the Sinai passes among the most insurmountable topographic barriers in the world.[12]

At the beginning of his colossal, military-endorsed history of the October War, Major General Gamal Hammad (one of the leaders of the Free Officers Movement) laid out the dangers entailed in failing to seize the passes. To start with, the Sinai passes occupy a higher slope than that of the Suez Canal, which makes those who base their defense on fixed positions along the canal banks at a great disadvantage; second, establishing one's defense line in an exposed desert area (such as the canal banks) threatens its penetration, outflanking, or encirclement by enemy troops—a fact taught to novice students of desert warfare at the Egyptian Military Academy; third, unfortified bridgeheads (such as those Sadat wanted to establish along the canal) cannot be considered military objectives in themselves, but rather as springboards for advance—if the Allied forces had remained glued to their beachheads at Normandy, they would have certainly been thrown back to sea by the Nazis. In short, Hammad concluded, asking the Egyptian army to turn from offense to defense right after it crossed the Suez Canal (i.e., before reaching the passes) would amount to surrendering the initiative to the enemy in Sinai.[13]

Now, although Sadat assured the high command that he intended to seize the passes during the first wave of attack, his generals clearly saw that he did not, simply because he wanted to launch war before securing the weapons necessary for such a sweeping assault to the passes. During a general staff meeting, on January 24, 1972, the war minister criticized Sadat openly for alienating the Soviet Union, which was Egypt's only arms supplier. Although there was no love lost between Sadeq and the Russians, he understood that waging war without adequate arms risked another military defeat. Sadat's unilateral decision to evict all Soviet experts (more than 15,000 men) in July 1972—without consulting the military—further disturbed the high command. As Chief of Operations Abd al-Ghany al-Gamasy pointed out, no one was entirely sure why and how this decision was made, "We believed in general command that the decision ... was taken by the cabinet or National Defense Council, but we later discovered it was Sadat's decision alone."[14] A stunned Shazly tried to reason with the president: "You must realize how dangerous this decision is ... Surely you know that. There is no question that it will affect our capabilities. The Soviet units play such a large role in our air defense and electronic warfare.'" Even Sadeq, an ardent critique of the Soviets, did everything he could to dissuade Sadat, but to no avail.[15]

The tense situation between the president and his generals reached its zenith on the night of October 24, 1972, during an exceptionally stormy meeting of the Supreme Council of the Armed Forces. Sadat had asked Sadeq to prepare for war by mid-November, an order that the war minister duly ignored because he knew that a premature attack could only be limited to crossing the canal without seizing the passes, and was thus potentially disastrous. Sadeq asked his senior lieutenants to sound their objections frankly the next time they met the president. During that meeting, Sadat thought he was reviewing the final preparations for war, while the high command was determined to sound their almost unanimous objection to the president's plan. According to the minutes of the meeting, Sadat began by denying rumors that he was "selling the country to the Americans," and claiming it was the United States that was trying to lure him to conclude a peaceful settlement with Israel.[16] The war minister, his deputy (Abd al-Qader Hassan), and the commander of the navy (Mahmoud Fahmy) questioned the wisdom of the president's decision to "go to war with whatever weapons we had," adding that to lose face in another battle with Israel would be demoralizing to the troops and the people. Sadat yelled back that none of them had "the right or the competence" to second-guess him.[17]

The minutes then reveal how an adamant deputy war minister insisted that a limited war could not liberate Sinai; if the army did not keep Israel under pressure through a sustained offensive, the war would quickly turn into a hopelessly defensive war of a few insignificant bridgeheads on the banks of the Suez Canal, which would give Israel the advantage because of its superior air force. The president's reply was that it was the Supreme Council's job to compensate for lack of weapons with good planning and talent. When the deputy minister objected again, Sadat barked back: "This is the second time you second-guess me. I will not allow it … I am the one responsible for the independence of this country. I know what I am doing. It is none of your business. Make one more objection, and you will be asked to stay home … Shame on you! Learn your place! You are a soldier, not a politician." When the navy commander pointed out that it was inappropriate for the president to scold his generals in this degrading manner, Sadat gave him a piece of his mind too. Following the meeting, an indignant Sadeq asked Sadat why he convened the meeting if he was not willing to respect or even listen to the military's view. The president's response came two days later, when all those who objected to his plan during the meeting (including the war minister and his deputy) were dismissed, and more than a hundred high-ranking officers were purged over the weeks that followed.[18]

When Sadat later described the meeting in an interview, he pulled no punches. The president portrayed his Supreme Council of the Armed Forces as "a group of childish pupils, [composed of] a deceived leftist, an ailing psychopath, a mercenary, a traitor to Egypt, a conspirator … then it turned out that the war minister was making rounds through the units to preach against the war."[19] In his view, Sadeq and his associates were cowards with no stomach for war. The president then claimed that Sadeq was involved in an ill-conceived coup aimed at preventing the war, and that he had to be placed under house arrest.[20] Privately, however, Sadat confided to his longtime friend Mahmoud Game' that he was worried about Sadeq's popularity among the soldiers, especially after his superb effort in training and inspiring the troops.[21] Chief of Staff Shazly, who worked closely with Sadeq and attended that fateful October meeting, reached a similar conclusion: Sadeq was very successful in cultivating popularity within the ranks through material and symbolic incentives, and Sadat believed that this threatened his security as president.[22] The Free Officer and historian Ahmed Hamroush[23] and Heikal,[24] who witnessed these events firsthand, further substantiate this claim. And it is worth noting here that the president became aware of the war minister's growing popularity from none other than the director of the General Intelligence Service, Ahmed Ismail—one of the first instances of civilian intelligence spying on the military.[25]

As testimony to both Sadeq's popularity and the fact that many officers shared his views, a month after his dismissal a secret society of officers calling themselves the Save Egypt Movement plotted to overthrow the president. The group echoed the deposed war minister's argument that there was an attempt to "push us into war while we were unprepared; that this would lead to the destruction of our armed forces."[26] To the officers' great dismay, the president charged a civilian security body, the State Security Investigations Sector, with the investigations, claiming that because it was SSIS spies, rather than Military Intelligence, that uncovered the secret plot, it had earned his trust. Shazly said he heard, to his astonishment, the president and interior minister (Mamduh Salem) accusing Sadeq and his followers of being agents for the Saudi government.[27] The investigations revealed that the conspirators were no less than the commander of the Central District (Cairo), the head of Military Intelligence, along with two divisional commanders and chiefs of staff, the commander of a ranger group, and commanders of smaller units. The organization extended deep into the armed forces, and the plan was to arrest the political and security leadership, as well as military officers loyal to the president on November 9, 1972, at Shazly's daughter's wedding.[28] Before the whole affair was settled, the president took another hugely controversial decision by appointing the intelligence director Ahmed Ismail minister of war on October 26, 1972.

ON THE ROAD TO OCTOBER

Ahmed Ismail was an old general. He graduated from the Military Academy in 1938, and was now fifty-six years old. His cautious nature kept him from joining the Free Officers though he served with many of them as a brigade commander in the 1948 war in Palestine. And his performance was as undistinguished as scores of other officers in the 1956 Suez War. So what special qualifications did he have to assume the top military position at such a critical time? Though no one can penetrate Sadat's mind, what appears to have distinguished Ismail from other generals was that his history in the armed forces, along with his medical condition, made it practically impossible for him to nurture a following within the ranks. First, Ismail had been relieved of his duties twice for incompetence, as a divisional commander in August 1967 and as chief of staff in September 1969. Thus, he assumed his new post "with the humiliation" of someone who was dismissed from the service for negligence.[29] Second, although very few officers were fond of Ismail, he had made an archenemy of one particular officer during his years in service: Saad al-Din al-Shazly, the current chief of staff. The two had remained on nonspeaking terms ever since their fistfight in the Congo in 1960, when Ismail tried to flaunt his authority as Egypt's military attaché in the face of Shazly, who served in the UN force stationed there. Although Shazly was still a young captain, he refused to obey Brigadier General Ismail not just because the latter had no jurisdiction over him, but also because he believed that Ismail was blatantly inept. In fact, Shazly had resigned in March 1969 as head of the Commando Corps when Nasser appointed Ismail chief of staff, but before his resignation was considered Ismail was dismissed once more. It is not surprising that when Sadat consulted his chief of staff over who should replace Sadeq as war minister, Shazly advised that anyone other than Ismail would do. When the president appointed him anyway, Shazly says he was appalled. He pleaded: "Mr. President … I have a history of disagreement with Ahmed Ismail going back more than twelve years, ever since we met in the Congo. We have had bad relations ever since. It would be impossible to work in harmony," but all that Sadat did was flap his hand and mumble, "I know all that."[30] Finally, Ismail was fighting a losing battle with cancer. Sadat admitted that physicians had informed him of Ismail's condition, and had asserted that he could not handle a high-stress job. Sadat dismissed their views because he trusted Ismail. Sadat also confessed that by October 19 (i.e., right in the middle of the war), his war minister spent most of his time resting in a small bed outside Operation Center 10, the war command room.[31]

So why did the president make such an unpopular decision? Despite his shortcomings, Ahmed Ismail had a few valuable political assets. For one thing, he and Sadat had been friends since 1938, which meant that the president could trust his personal loyalty.[32] It also helped that Ismail felt bitter over his repeated dismissals. His resentment of Nasser's security and military appointees made him perfectly suited to serve as GIS director after the May 1971 clash. The fact that Sadat brought him back from oblivion to such a prestigious post made him even more grateful. This all meant that he could serve the president well in terms of depoliticizing the corps. During his first meeting with Sadat as war minister, Ismail was warned that "an unacceptable level of political activity was going on" in the military, and that his first priority was to liquidate all political factions within the armed forces. The president then added that he had appointed him to intelligence first in order to gain the experience he would need to carry out this crucial task.[33]

More important, Ismail had little faith in the prospects of military victory. Weeks before assuming his new job, he submitted a GIS report to Sadat arguing, "Egypt was not ready for war … any attack mounted or led by Egypt under present conditions might lead to disaster."[34] In that sense, he was the only man among Egypt's unyielding generals that would likely accept the president's still-hidden plan to wage a limited war, meant only to serve as a catalyst for political settlement. Also, in his capacity as GIS director between May 1971 and October 1972, he ran the back channel with the CIA (discussed below), and was therefore aware of what the president was trying to arrange with the Americans.[35] Chief of Staff Shazly provided the best summary of why Sadat might have appointed Ismail as war minister:

> He was a weak man, alternating between submissiveness and bullying … He shunned the responsibility for decisions, preferring to receive orders rather than give them. He was thoroughly unpopular with the troops, not surprisingly since his manner was uniformly brusque; and while caring nothing for the personal problems of those around him, he was a fairly devoted believer in nepotism when it came to his own family … Such unpopularity was another virtue in Sadat's eyes. So, of course, was the fact that he and the Chief of Staff were at loggerheads … The unforgivable point is that Ismail was also a dying man. And President Sadat knew it. Ismail had cancer … the disease was killing Ismail for at least a year before Sadat appointed him Minister of War … He confessed he knew. In a speech in 1977, Sadat said he knew of Ismail's illness before and during the October war and had been told by doctors that Ismail was a very sick man incapable of taking decisions … Ismail was unfit for his job; and his weakness had terrible consequences for his country. [But] The wickedness lies in the man who appointed and then manipulated Ismail.[36]

Still, any war was risky, whether it was limited or otherwise. Another defeat would be politically disastrous. At the same time, a stunning victory would create military heroes who could then ride a crest of popularity within and outside the ranks to challenge Sadat. The examples of Mohamed Naguib and Nasser were instructive. Even though

Egypt lost badly in 1948, the two commanders' gallant performance in combat gained them considerable support from their brothers-in-arms, and gave them enough legitimacy to defy the king. To avoid this risk altogether, Sadat decided to shoot first for the best-case scenario: liberating Sinai without a war—a purely political triumph. Was Sadat too naïve to think that Israel would simply surrender the occupied territories? Not really. He was merely hoping for a repeat of the 1956 Suez War, minus the war. On that occasion, Egypt pulled out an astonishing political victory without having to win on the battlefield. In his notorious meeting with the Supreme Council of the Armed Forces on October 24, 1972, Sadat had in fact asserted: "We should keep in mind what we did in 1956 … [when] Nasser turned military defeat into political victory."[37] To Sadat's mind, the party that delivered that victory to Egypt on a silver platter was the United States. In his reminiscences about the war, he fondly remembered "the critical role Eisenhower played in transforming military defeat into political victory." He also saw Nasser's decision in 1967 to step down in favor of the pro-American Zakaria as an admission on his part that "there was one power that ruled Egypt and the world, that is: America." This was summarized in his favorite aphorism: "America holds 99 percent of the cards" in the Middle East.[38]

Accordingly, Sadat embarked on his own little private war to win America's heart and mind. His confidant Mahmoud Game' claimed that Sadat had developed close ties with the Americans years before he came to the presidency.[39] The former U.S. intelligence analyst Owen Sirrs says there are strong indicators that Sadat's long-standing "links to U.S. intelligence helped bolster his hold on the presidency even though many in Washington suspected he would not last long."[40] Sadat's first move after he assumed the top executive post—as recorded in his own memoirs—was an appeal to Albert Richardson, U.S. health secretary and envoy to Nasser's funeral, to "try him out."[41] Sadly, when the latter returned home he reported that Sadat would not last more than six weeks. The president then sought the support of Congress members during their visit to Cairo in March 1971. In fact, he developed what would become an intimate friendship with David Rockefeller during this visit. He also tried to appease William Rogers during his visit to Cairo in May 1971—the first visit by a U.S. secretary of state since 1953—by pledging to remove his foreign minister (Mahmoud Riyad) because of his rigid positions toward America and Israel.[42] Sadat then went above and beyond and invited Premier Golda Meir of Israel, four months after Nasser passed away, to secret talks to conclude a peaceful settlement, but she turned him down.[43]

These sporadic attempts, however, proved insufficient. What Sadat needed was a regular and reliable back channel. And for that he turned to an old liaison with the Americans, who was also a member of the original Free Officers clique, with the name of Abd al-Moun'em Amin. Sadat asked Amin to secretly contact the U.S. chargé d'affaires in Cairo, Donald Bergus, and the CIA station chief, Eugene Trone. Little did Sadat know that GIS had bugged the offices and apartments of both Bergus and Trone, and that every word they exchanged with Amin was tapped and sent to his rivals (the centers of power), and through them to the Soviets. During the first meeting, on January 22, 1971, Amin asked for U.S. support for Sadat, brandishing the new president's anti-Soviet sentiments and apologizing for the unwarranted suspicions Nasser held against the United States: "[Nasser's] complex was that he was oversuspicious, suspicious of everyone and everything ... Not only that, but he also did everything for his own glory, and believed that defying America would elevate him ... He did not do it for his country, or the Arabs, or the [developing] world, but rather to enhance his personal status." When Bergus mumbled tactfully that Nasser was also a great leader, Amin retorted: "He was only great because he brought great disasters upon his country."[44] Nonetheless, the overture came to nothing, and Sadat began searching for a more effective channel.

At this point, the president realized he needed outside help. He reached out to a friend he was so intimate with that he had stood witness to his marriage back in 1955: Kamal Adham, the legendary head of Saudi intelligence. Adham advised his friend to demonstrate goodwill to the Americans by, for example, expelling the Soviet military experts from Egypt, which Sadat did in July 1972. And in the same month he ejected the Soviets, he invited the CIA to send an official representative to Cairo for the first time since 1967.[45] But although the Nixon administration had indeed signaled its readiness, through several official statements, to work for a peaceful settlement between the belligerents if the Soviet mission in Egypt was terminated, Sadat's gesture was completely ignored. As Kissinger later explained to Esmat Abd al-Magid, Egypt's representative at the UN: Americans do not "pay for anything that is offered freely."[46] In layman's terms, Sadat had thrown away his bargaining chip without first negotiating a suitable reward, thinking that the United States was bound to appreciate his spirit of generosity—a devastating tactic to which he virtually grew addicted over the next few years. The Saudi intelligence chief then approached Heikal with the following offer: "You are the only person the president really trusts, and he asked us to talk to you. We want to arrange for the installation of a hotline between my house and your house." Heikal immediately declined because he knew that "Saudi intelligence was a stepchild of the CIA," only to learn a few weeks later from War Minister Sadeq that the president had installed such a hotline in his own house.[47] The American intelligence analyst Owen Sirrs confirmed that Sadat's home-based hotline was in fact used to contact CIA operatives.[48]

Eventually, Sadat recognized that all these shadowy communications could not deliver a highly valued political prize such as Sinai. He therefore decided to redirect all his energies toward one target, toward the man he believed to hold the keys to U.S. power: Henry Kissinger. Sadat first realized that Kissinger was interested in Egypt when Donald Kendall (Pepsi-Cola chairman, and a friend of Nixon) invited Heikal on June 18, 1971, to meet privately with the U.S. national security adviser at his vacation house in Connecticut. Heikal turned down the invitation, and tried to explain to a very disappointed president that Egypt must not conduct talks with the Americans from a position of weakness. A frustrated Sadat turned to his new war minister, Ahmed Ismail, for advice in December 1972. Ismail counseled that the president should send a personal emissary to meet Kissinger instead. Thus, a meeting was held at Kendall's house in February 1973 between Kissinger and the Egyptian national security adviser, Hafez Ismail.[49] After so many desperate attempts, something finally clicked. Although the meeting was completely useless, it inaugurated the famous secret back channel that played such a vital role during the war.

But as long as Egypt could not launch a war, there was little that could be done. Kissinger believed that Sadat could open the doors of the Arab world to the United States. The Egyptian president's eagerness to join the American camp, however, encouraged the seasoned national security advisor to wait until the fruit was ripe. And of course, the American-Soviet détente suggested there was no need to rush. So what was the would-be Metternich of the Middle East waiting for? A rearrangement of regional power required, in Kissinger's view, that all parties involved acknowledge two geopolitical realities: first, "that Israel was too strong (or could be made too strong) to be defeated even by all of its neighbors combined, and that the United States would hold the ring against Soviet intervention; and second, that the "key to the Middle East, therefore, resided in Washington."[50] In his estimation, Sadat recognized the second fact, but he still needed to taste the first. So even though Hafez Ismail tried to promote his boss by pointing out "This was the first time in a quarter of a century that an Arab leader was willing to enter into a peace agreement with Israel," Kissinger was still unimpressed.[51] In remembering those days, Kissinger pondered: "What did I do in those conversations? I talked with [Sadat's envoy] about the weather and every other subject in the world … I played with him. I toyed with him. My aim was to gain time and postpone the serious stage for another month, another year."[52]

The pressure for war was thus building up domestically and internationally—albeit for very different reasons: Egyptians were eager to redeem themselves, while the Americans wanted to impress on them the fact that they could not do so through war. Throughout Egypt, tens of thousands of students took to the streets calling for war. And in a particularly alarming incident, on October 12, 1972, a mechanized battalion commander (Captain Aly Hassan) stationed outside the capital drove his tanks to Al-Hussein Mosque at the heart of Cairo to rally people against Sadat's hesitance to wage war. What was most disturbing about the incident was that none of the military checkpoints along the way tried to stop him.[53] On the other hand, Sadat's national security adviser relayed Kissinger's belief that Egyptians should not expect too much as long as they remained militarily defeated. Hafez Ismail highlighted a section in his meeting with Kissinger in France on May 20, 1973, where the latter said: "I told you last time, and I will continue to say that there is no better position for the Israelis than the one they are in right now ... As long as Israel feels it could preserve its position, we do not think, honestly, that it will pull back."[54] The message was clear: war could no longer be postponed.

"THE VICTORY EGYPT THREW AWAY"

As the United States seemed reluctant to furnish Sadat with a purely political solution, he was now forced to walk the delicate path of unleashing the military, on the one hand, and curbing its success, on the other. While his generals wanted to liberate Sinai by force of arms, the president aimed for a recipe similar to that of 1956: an act of symbolic military defiance that would pave the way for a purely political settlement. From here arose the notion of a "limited war," which Sadat believed would involve a crossing of the Suez Canal and the seizure of a narrow strip of land on the east bank to prove to Israel that Egyptians could jeopardize its security. His alibi to the soldiers and the people would be that Egypt was forced to fight a limited war because it could not secure enough weapons from the Soviets, and that the United States would not allow Israel to lose. As the strategy analyst Risa Brooks had to admit: "Sadat's war concept ... premised on the fact that Egypt's inadequate military could not prevail against its superior adversary, was far from conventional."[55] The military specialist Julian Schofield described it as an unorthodox "demilitarized [war] strategy [which] manifested itself as a diplomatic offensive pegged to a military attack."[56]

The problem was that the president's commitment to this limited-war concept clashed with the military's insistence (from the high command downward) on liberating Sinai through a long war of attrition. The armed forces understandably rejected the president's wish to attack Israel in such a way as would produce "a diplomatic rather than a battlefield victory."[57] But after several failed attempts at defying or trying to unseat the president, the military's hand was forced. Officers were partly exhausted by the passage of time, and partly hopeful that once the war started, they could see their mission through with minimal interference from the capital. Hence, they jumped into the abyss. Sadly, however, as a few senior officers predicted, Sadat's tight-leash control over operations eventually led to what was described variously as Egypt's "Lost Victory," by the *Sunday Times*;[58] "The Victory Egypt Threw Away," by the team of international experts who studied the war; Egypt's road "From Victory to Self-Defeat," by a Western military scholar;[59] and, more evocatively, as the "savage struggle that Egypt ... had little hope for winning but nonetheless came very close—perhaps within hours—to doing so," by the military historian Walter J. Boyne.[60] This outcome was expected because, as Heikal reminded us, "The fate of battles is determined before the first shot is fired."[61]

Sadat had made his intention clear from the very beginning. Although the president, as Chief of Operations Gamasy noted, insisted on working alone on setting the general war strategy and conducting field operations, he did signal his objective to wage a "symbolic" battle early on.[62] For example, during a meeting with his general command in February 1973, he expressed his belief that it was important to win only the first twenty-four hours of the war.[63] He also shared the outlines of his plan with Egypt's soon-to-be-foreign-minister Ismail Fahmy in the summer of 1973, and Fahmy was duly shocked. He tried to explain to his boss that Egypt's national security demanded that the war succeed in liberating the occupied territories, or at the very least controlling the Sinai passes. If not, then Israel would maintain the upper hand in the negotiations that would follow the war.[64] The military specialists who studied the war corroborated this view. It is true that the Egyptian army lacked Israel's blitzkrieg capacity and could scarcely fight a mobile war across the peninsula, but it could achieve a "static victory" by holding the perfectly defensible passes.[65] This had in fact been the original plan, which was finalized in September 1970 by the former war minister Fawzy under the name Plan 200. The plan laid out three stages to liberate the entire peninsula in twelve days: the first (Granite 1) covered the crossing of the Suez Canal, to be followed immediately by a second stage (Granite 2) to seize the passes, and then the general command was supposed to reassess the situation before ordering an advance to the Egyptian-Israeli border. The plan was ready to be rehearsed in March 1971, and implemented shortly afterward, but Nasser's death led to its postponement.[66] Sadat claimed that the plan, which he personally reviewed with Nasser at the beginning of September 1970, was merely defensive.[67] When Shazly became chief of staff, he was asked to update the plan and give it a more offensive edge.[68]

The new plan was quite similar. It had Egyptian infantrymen and armor crossing the Suez Canal and storming the Bar-Lev fortifications under cover of heavy artillery barrages and air raids; then, if the situation allowed, they would march quickly to the mountain passes and dig in there until the general command assessed the viability of further advance. So as Gamasy confirmed, controlling the topographically impervious Sinai passes was the primary goal of the whole operation.[69] Meanwhile, the Syrians—who had lost the Golan Heights in the 1967 war—would attack at the same time and eject the Israeli occupation there. The plan seemed perfect on paper, yet the Egyptian top brass was not entirely certain about what Sadat had up his sleeve, as evidenced by the fact that after receiving the first war directive on October 1, they asked for another one on October 5 (both directives were penned by Heikal). They wanted the president to explicitly state that the objective of the war was to "liberate the occupied territories in progressive stages according to developments." There was a lurking fear that Sadat intended to launch a limited attack, and then hold the army responsible for failing to liberate the whole peninsula.[70]

By October 1973, Egypt had mobilized an army of 1.2 million. The general staff believed it now had the capacity to offset Israeli air supremacy through a tightly integrated air defense network of fixed SA-2 and SA-3 missiles, mobile SAM-6s, and handheld SA-7 Strelas; to check Israeli armored supremacy through an abundant supply of antitank Sagger missiles and RPGs; and to deter Israeli missile threats to the Egyptian interior through Scud and FROG missiles capable of reaching deep into Israel. For the first time in years, they felt ready to take on their rival in a fair battle. Before dawn on October 6, frogmen sabotaged the underwater oil pipes that Israel had planned to set ablaze if Egyptians attempted to cross the canal. At 2:05 p.m. an armada of 222 fighter jets delivered a devastating air strike against Israeli communication centers, airfields, and Hawk missile sites in Sinai, as 2,000 howitzers and heavy mortars heralded incessant waves of artillery fire across the canal, covering the crossing of a massive stride of infantrymen in rubber dinghies and floating bridges. The troops ran over the Bar-Lev Line's thirty-five fortifications, and established five bridgeheads on the east bank of the canal. By nightfall, the Egyptians had just achieved "the largest crossing in military history," with 100,000 troops armed with shoulder-held antitank missiles, 1,000 tanks, and 13,500 armored vehicles.[71]

With a combination of innovative antiarmor and antiaircraft infantry tactics, under the protection of a dense umbrella of SAM batteries stationed along the canal, the Egyptian army managed by the end of the second day of fighting to destroy 49 Israeli planes and 500 tanks. Moreover, while the general command estimated that at least 10,000 soldiers would be killed in the crossing, only 200 were lost during the first two days. With Israel's strongest branches (its armor and air force) temporarily neutralized, Egypt dominated the battlefield and was in a position to advance to the passes before the Israelis knew what hit them.[72] The prominent Israeli historian Avi Shlaim was forced to admit: "Military history offers few parallels for strategic surprise as complete as that achieved by Egypt."[73]

The next step was to seize the passes and exhaust the Israeli army by incessant combat. It was not too far-fetched: "Simple mathematics made it certain that Israel could not sustain a prolonged defensive war."[74] In his first press conference during the war, the Israeli defense minister, Moshe Dayan, confessed, "I doubt whether there is another place in the entire world that is protected by such a dense array of modern missiles. I doubt whether there is a place in Russia or Vietnam that is equipped like ... the Egyptian front at the canal."[75] In other words, Israeli commanders understood that if Egypt kept the initiative, they would be dragged into a drawn-out war of attrition in Sinai—that no quick knockout was possible. In fact, Dayan secretly admitted to his staff: "There was not a single tank between Tel Aviv and the Israeli lines in the Sinai."[76]

The Israeli reporter Matti Golan captures the mood in Tel Aviv during those first couple of days: "[Prime Minister] Mrs. Meir, Dayan, and Chief of Staff [David] Elazar were so tired and pessimistic that they were ready to throw in the towel."[77] At the same time, the *New York Times* war correspondent Henry Tanner summarized the spirit on the Egyptian front as follows: "The Aim of Every Egyptian Soldier: To Advance Eastward."[78] The international team of experts who studied the war thus concluded: "[I]f the Egyptians chose to press on, it did not look as if Israel—even with its reserves—would be able to do other than fight a continuing rearguard action. The Israeli tank crews were becoming unnerved by the 'creeping, crawling' techniques of the Egyptian missile infantry and the seeming inability of the dashing Israeli tactics of the past to cope with their endless ambushes."[79] And indeed, by the evening of October 8, Egypt had amassed a fighting force of more than 100,000 men a few kilometers away from the passes, backed up by four divisions (two armored and two mechanized) and two armored brigades just across the canal. It was time to move forward.

But instead of advancing to the passes, Egypt decided to "hand over [its] brilliantly won initiative to the Israelis."[80] As the future war minister Kamal Hassan Aly related, despite the war command's pressing for a rapid advance to occupy the strategically indispensable passes, Sadat halted the offensive on October 9.[81] The decision was nothing short of catastrophic. Egyptian armor had not penetrated Sinai deep enough, and while the Egyptian bridgehead stretched the length of the canal, it was only sixteen kilometers deep—half the distance between the canal and the passes. This was the "first—and ultimately fatal—setback" in the war. Afterward, Egypt practically "frittered [its] gains away by waiting far too long to launch the second phase."[82]

Gamasy said he tried to warn the president that any delay, any relaxing of the pressure on Israel meant giving it the initiative, and allowing it to consolidate its defenses and launch a counterattack; that the only way to protect Egypt's gains was to continue the offensive eastward until they reached the passes, an offensive that at the moment would be carried out "under the best conditions for us and the worst for them."[83] Even the Military Advisory Board (composed of three major generals, and referred to as Operations Center II) summarized its recommendations to Sadat on October 7 in one short sentence: "Advance to the passes."[84] A cable sent by the U.S. Interests Section in Cairo to the Pentagon predicted that the Egyptian military would surely seize the passes right away.[85] A similar message came from the Soviet embassy on October 8. Ambassador Vladimir Vinogradov invited Heikal over for what he described as an urgent matter. He then told his Egyptian guest that Russian military experts were bewildered by Sadat's decision not to advance to the passes, and that he personally told the president that based on Soviet reconnaissance there were fewer than two Israeli brigades blocking his way, which meant that the passes could be seized in a couple of hours.[86] Foreign Minister Murad Ghaleb, relying on contacts he developed in Moscow during his decade-long tenure as ambassador, says the Soviets warned Sadat that spreading his troops over the 200-kilometer-long east bank without penetrating Sinai and entrenching the assault force in the passes would be nothing short of military suicide.[87] Over the next days, Soviet generals repeatedly warned Egypt that such a blunder amounted to "throw[ing] away all that had been won" so far.[88] Yet to no avail.

Sadat then received Situation Report No. 4 from his field commanders on October 9, which stressed that the Israelis had redirected their energy away from the Egyptian to the Syrian front, and that this was the best chance to develop the attack. The former prime minister, and now acting foreign minister, Mahmoud Fawzy, also called the president on October 11 to convey that many friendly states had expressed concern over Egypt's unwarranted halt, to which Sadat responded: "Rest assured, everything is in my hand." This was followed by Situation Report No. 6 on October 11 from the front, which noted that an Israeli counterattack was expected in forty-eight hours, and that they needed to advance to the passes now. On the same day, Sadat received two reports, one from the Military Affairs Department warning that the tactical halt had caused confusion within the ranks and that it had become the sole subject of discussion among officers and soldiers who no longer understood their mission. The second report came from the Interior Ministry, saying that many Egyptians (including several retired officers) were confused by the sudden halt.[89]

Even Sadat's ally War Minister Ahmed Ismail seemed puzzled. Like everyone else at general command, he believed that the bridgeheads were meant to serve as springboards for capturing the passes—especially after the Egyptians performed much better than anticipated (and Israelis much worse) during the first two days of the war.[90] Encouraged by Ismail's bewilderment, Gamasy tried to win him over so that he might persuade the president to permit an advance. The chief of operations explained to the war minister that militarily speaking, Sadat's order to halt was not only unjustified, but also potentially tragic. He then added emphatically, "I beg you to remember that ... the principle of proceeding eastward to the passes was predetermined and there was no disagreement over this." His pleas fell on deaf ears. Ismail was clearly unwilling to question the president's orders. It was a political decision, he said.[91] When interviewed by Heikal barely a month after the war, on November 14, 1973, in the Egyptian daily al-Ahram, Ismail would not open up about why he went through with this "tactical halt," offering nothing but a brisk and vague response: "I am not the adventurous type."[92] In reality, though Ismail did have some insight into the president's thinking, he knew that Sadat did not aspire to a straightforward military victory, but wanted to use the war to spark a serious-enough crisis to convince the United States that the regional situation was too dangerous to remain unresolved. To achieve this goal, there was no need to push any farther across Sinai.

With that in mind, a look at what Sadat was conducting behind the scenes might uncover the secret behind his ordering of a "tactical halt" against the advice of his entire military, as well as the experts of a few other militaries. Unknown to his high command, a mere twenty hours after his troops had crossed the canal, Sadat sent a secret cable to Henry Kissinger through the back channel run by Hafez Ismail. While the Egyptian forces were marking success after success, the president assured Kissinger that "Egypt had no intention of intensifying the engagements or widening the confrontation."[93] The U.S. national security adviser (who had just become secretary of state as well) responded instantly with a message of approval that highlighted how his intervention would have no chance if the fighting escalated. These were the first of thirty-eight secret cables transmitted between October 7 and 29 in which Sadat desperately tried to push Kissinger to intervene with Tel Aviv, to agree to evacuate Sinai through a peaceful settlement.[94] As Kissinger mentioned in his memoirs, "Not one day passed throughout the period of the war when we did not receive a message from Cairo or send one to it."[95] Sadat's war decisions, therefore, had nothing to do with battlefield developments, but rather with his campaign to enlist Kissinger's support in settling the dispute without further fighting, and thus achieve his ultimate goal of a political solution aided only partially by a modest military operation.

But instead of aiding Sadat, Kissinger summoned the Israeli ambassador to Washington, Simcha Dinitz, to his office to inform him of Sadat's pledge not to expand beyond the narrow foothold he had secured on the east bank. He told Dinitz frankly: "They say they will not deepen their bridgeheads farther than they are right now," and prompted Israel to act accordingly.[96] Kissinger also found the cable useful during his meeting with Defense Secretary James Schlesinger on October 7. Pentagon analysts had concluded that it was madness to expect the Egyptian forces to cross the canal and then just sit still and bide their time. The secretary of state, however, assured them that this was exactly what they would do, and advised the Pentagon to draw up its plans accordingly.[97] This conversation soon found its way to Israel. Chief of Staff Elazar had asked for the U.S. military's help to evaluate his options. On October 8, a Pentagon official arrived in Tel Aviv with a thick dossier of satellite images of troop positions on the Egyptian and Syrian fronts. His recommendation was to freeze one front, and concentrate all efforts on the other, before turning back to finish off the first.[98] Israeli generals concurred, knowing that they did not have the resources to engage both fronts simultaneously. The only question now was which front to freeze? The depth of the Sinai peninsula compared with the proximity of the Golan Heights to Israel's population centers made Egypt a better candidate for this freezing strategy—as long, of course, as the Egyptians were not planning on taking the passes, which, thanks to Sadat, everyone knew was the case.[99]

Major General Kamal Hassan Aly, who witnessed these developments on the battlefront, finally figured out Sadat's logic when his secret correspondence with the United States was declassified in the nineties. He describes how he learned afterward that Kissinger had promised Sadat that if he slowed the army advance, he could persuade Israel to withdraw peacefully, but the Americans then double-crossed Egypt and told the Israelis that they could safely turn their back on the Egyptian forces and focus on the Syrians, then return to the Sinai front when they were ready. And so suddenly the Syrians, who at this point were on the verge of successfully liberating the Golan, found themselves overwhelmed, at the same time that the Egyptians were forced to remain in place although Israeli resistance in Sinai was dying down.[100] Gamasy also penned a few haunting reflections regarding this back channel. His first comment was notably reserved: "It seemed unnecessary for us to reassure the United States regarding its interests at a time when it stood openly against Egypt and Syria and supported Israel entirely at every level ... I believe that political actions in this case did not help the military operations." Later in his memoirs he became more candid: the secret correspondence not only explains why the president's directions seemed constantly "out of step with the military achievements," but it was quite devastating to learn that while soldiers were dying on the battlefront, "the political leadership had divulged its military intentions" to a country that was actively assisting the enemy.[101] The war historian Walter J. Boyne agreed: "Just the knowledge that Sadat intended only to cross the canal and hold a small but symbolic strip of land ... allowed Kissinger to shuffle the diplomatic cards to the advantage of the United States while aiding Israel at exactly the right level."[102] Heikal's remarks were typically more dramatic: "This was the first time in history that a country at war disclosed its intentions to its enemies, and gave them a free hand on the political and military fronts."[103]

The U.S. contribution to the Israeli war effort increased when it became clear that Israel's heavy losses during the first days of the war had effectively crippled its offensive capabilities. Kissinger convinced Nixon during their meeting on October 9 that if the Arabs won, they would be impossible to negotiate with, and that the only way to prevent this was to compensate the Israeli losses.[104] He repeated the same argument in a meeting of the Washington Special Action Group on October 17: "Without our airlift, Israel would be dead."[105] So although some commentators resented Kissinger's unsuccessful attempt to tie the aid package to Israel to a pledge by the Jewish lobby to drop the Jackson amendment, which conditioned the U.S.-Soviet trade agreement on allowing the free emigration of Russian Jews,[106] and others blamed him for holding back the aid for tactical reasons,[107] the end result, however, was that the airlift took off in time to alter the direction of the war by replenishing all the Israeli weapons that the Egyptians had fought so hard to destroy, and providing new, more sophisticated equipment that Egypt could not counter. It is important to add, though, that Nixon had no reservations. Recalling his reaction a few months later (June 1974) in a gathering of American Jewish leaders, the U.S. president turned to his secretary of state and said: "Henry, do you remember that on that fourth day [of the war] you came and suggested that I send five planes?—and I said if it's all right to send them five, let's send them fifty."[108] It was clear that despite Kissinger's valuable intervention, it was the U.S. president who ultimately made the crucial decisions. The tipping point was Nixon's October 9 meeting with his national security team, where he made it clear "that Israel must not lose the war ... and that Israel be told that it could freely expend all of its consumables ... in the certain knowledge that these would be completely replenished by the United States without any delay."[109]

The first batch of U.S. military supplies arrived on October 10 at al-Arish Airport in Sinai. Despite the urging of his generals and the Soviets, Sadat refused to destroy Sinai's last remaining airport (al-Maliz and Beer Tamada had been already destroyed) without sharing his motives with any of them. Later Sadat recorded in his memoirs that although he learned that American "tanks landed in Arish, loaded and fueled, and joined the battle immediately," he did not want to provoke the Americans by bombing the airport.[110] Three days later, on October 13, the biggest airlift in history—Operation Nickel Grass—was in full swing. In thirty-three days (between October 13 and November 14), gigantic U.S. transport planes (C-5 Galaxies and C-141 Starlifters) carried out a total of 569 missions with equipment worth $88.5 million. In all, 90 percent of the missiles fired during the war were supplied through the airlift. Shipments included 600 tanks (M-48 and M-60) and dozens of jets (A-4 and F-4). But what really tipped the balance were three types of advanced missiles: the antitank TOW missiles, the television-guided Mavericks, and the Shrike missiles and electronic jamming devices, which suppressed SAM radar and kept the Israeli Air Force safe.[111] As Elazar gratefully noted, the Pentagon had not only prepared these weapons for immediate use, but had also sent American instructors to train Israelis on how to use them. The airlift was thus in Gamasy's estimation a "direct and open military action" by the United States against Egypt, and that without this "flagrant assistance" Israel would not have been able to turn the tide in its favor. Yet when the chief of operations complained to the president that America was tipping the balance, "he listened calmly to my exposé, showing no alarm."[112]

Rearmed and ready, Israel managed to blunt the Syrian attack between October 8 and 14, while the Egyptian force remained in place. As Syria became increasingly a spent force, a counterattack in Sinai was under way. This was when Sadat, again defying the entire high command, ordered an advance not only to the passes, but to six advance points in the heart of the peninsula beyond enemy lines. Why the sudden change of heart? His official justification was that the Syrians were under so much pressure, and he felt obliged to relieve them. This is a curious explanation considering the fact that the onslaught against the Syrian forces was possible only because of his inexplicable weeklong tactical halt. A more realistic interpretation could be derived from Kissinger's suspicious aloofness during the past few days. Sadat's domestic situation was becoming critical as Israeli fighters penetrated deep into the home front, bombing Port Said and several Nile Delta cities, and leaving behind five hundred civilian casualties. But as the tone of the president's letters to Washington became frantic, Kissinger's responses were patronizing and dismissive, claiming, for example, in a message on October 12 that the United States was "not following the Israeli operations in detail, nor does it get informed of them in advance," and so there was nothing it could do to stop them.[113] As befitting a soldier who never saw combat, Sadat believed that a resumption of the offensive would be a brilliant tactical maneuver to unnerve Washington. Little did he know that this was exactly what Israel was waiting for, now that it had contained the Syrians, rearmed its troops, and came back with a vengeance.

The military leadership went far and beyond to prevent what it saw as an incredible blunder, one no less fatal than the tactical halt, albeit in the opposite direction. The Military Advisory Board in Operations Center 11 strenuously disputed the order, explaining that at this late stage of the game its probability of success did not exceed 20 percent.[114] Shazly, Gamasy, and others highlighted the fact that early in the war Israel was on the run, now it was preparing a counteroffensive. Egypt's only option at this point was to defend the bridgeheads as best it could until a cease-fire agreement was reached; any movement would break the lines and allow the enemy to penetrate.[115] Further, the commanders of the Second and Third armies (i.e., the two field commanders) tendered their resignation—though the war minister refused to accept and said they had to follow orders.[116] It was clear that for all concerned "the plan was madness."[117]

To ease the pressure, Sadat ordered the 21st and 4th armored divisions to cross the canal to back up the offensive. Now his generals were becoming positively livid. These two divisions represented the core of Egypt's strategic reserve. If they forsook the west bank of the Suez Canal and crossed to the east, then it would be impossible to deter Israel from invading the Egyptian mainland. Again, though this was certainly another major blunder, the president would have none of it. As expected, the ill-conceived order to attack on October 14 cost the army 260 tanks (to only 10 Israeli ones) and had to be called off on the same day after the commander of the Second Army (Saad Ma'moun) suffered a heart attack and had to be replaced.[118] One of the most bizarre reactions to the whole debacle occurred at 3:00 a.m. on October 18, when fifteen middle-ranking officers made their way from GHQ to the Presidential Palace and demanded to see Sadat without delay. Anxious to discover what was behind them, the baffled president received them in his bedroom in pajamas. The officers confessed that the army was boiling with anger and frustration because of Sadat's inexplicable decisions, and that "crazy ideas" were spreading among their colleagues—clearly insinuating a coup—and so they decided to come and level with him. Sadat thanked them for their honesty and promised to get back to them—which, of course, he never did.[119]

More important, the troop movement, as the generals rightly predicted, opened a gap wide enough for Israel to slip behind Egyptian lines and cross the canal to the now exposed west bank. Again, America's role was vital. According to Kissinger's calculations, a future settlement of the dispute on U.S. terms required a spectacular Israeli accomplishment before the cease-fire. His plan was simple: to stall a cease-fire agreement, and continue feeding Israel weapons and strategic information he received from Sadat until Israel "either ousted the Egyptians from the east bank … or made their position there untenable," after which he could proceed with a "cease-fire-in-place" to dilute Egypt's military achievements.[120] On October 9, Mordechai Gur, the Israeli military attaché in Washington, asked Kissinger for aerial and satellite images, and the secretary of state instructed General Brent Scowcroft to provide them.[121] Then, as Sadat was tacitly threatening in his correspondence with Kissinger to escalate matters on the front—hoping that a veiled ultimatum would get the secretary of state moving—a curious incident happened. For the first and last time during the war, an American reconnaissance plane (SR-71A Blackbird) mapped the battlefront on October 13 and October 15, i.e., the day before Egypt ordered the advance and the morning after it had failed. The aim was to discover if the troop movement had in fact created a breach between the lines, and if so, where exactly. When the images were examined by the Israeli high command, one such gap was indeed located between the bridgeheads of the Second and Third Egyptian armies at Deversoir.[122] Immediately, as Kissinger recounted in his memoirs, he urged the Israelis to take decisive action if they wanted to finish "on top" before a cease-fire was negotiated[123]—and that they surely did. On October 15, two brigades made their way below the right flank of the Second Army across the canal; the breach widened as Israeli forces continued to pour westward, and by October 22, when Israel commanded seven armored brigades on the west bank, Kissinger called for a cease-fire.[124]

The breach offered one positive advantage for Sadat, though: a pretext to remove Shazly and destroy his legacy. Sadat really had no choice, considering that never since Amer had an officer enjoyed such charismatic authority inside and outside the ranks. On October 18, the president asked his chief of staff to travel to the front to stop the flow of Israeli troops. Shazly returned to the capital on October 20 to warn Sadat and the rest of the war command that unless four brigades fell back from the east to the west bank to counter the Israeli intrusion, then the breach would only widen. According to Chief of Operations Gamasy, this was also his opinion and that of the field commanders. Yet the president ruled it out without providing a reasonable excuse.[125] When Shazly insisted, Sadat exploded in his face: "Why do you always propose withdrawing our troops from the east bank … You ought to be court-martialed. If you persist in these proposals I will court-martial you. I do not what to hear another word."[126] At this point, Shazly realized that his trip to the front was nothing but a political setup meant to hold him responsible for failing to close the breach. Nonetheless, he did his job. War experts agreed that what Shazly advocated was "the biggest threat to an Israeli victory ... It was Israel's good fortune that ... his recommendations had been rejected."[127] No wonder Shazly later confided in his war diary, "To refuse to withdraw the four armored brigades was a combination of madness, ignorance, and treason."[128] The president's decision, according to the military historian Boyne, was "a self-inflicted Stalingrad. He gambled the Egyptian 3rd Army, exposing it to be outflanked, surrounded, and ... exterminated. In the coldest manner, Sadat calculated that ... the possible destruction of the 3rd Army was a risk worth taking in the hope that he could still pull off a diplomatic coup."[129]

Sadat in turn described his chief of staff as a coward: "He returned to me [from the front] trembling, and told me ... we have to withdraw all our troops from Sinai ... That night, I removed him and appointed Gamasy in his place."[130] Sadat repeated the same allegations to reporters after the war, that Shazly had "collapsed ... saying that the war was over, a disaster had struck, and that we had to withdraw entirely from Sinai."[131] In the president's account, Shazly was dispatched to the front on October 16 (two days earlier than he really had been), at a time when it was "very easy to liquidate the breach ... but he wasted valuable time gathering information and establishing a leadership [on the front] to compete with his rival General Ismail. In fact, the Special Forces had already advanced to Deversoir and the Israelis admitted how fierce the resistance was ... but Shazly pulled them back under the pretext of collecting more information, and the result was that the breach widened."[132] Later students of the war were taken aback by the "amazing disingenuousness" that characterized Sadat's account of this and other war incidents.[133]

Sadat's only witness was none other than his air force chief, Hosni Mubarak. Everyone else who attended that meeting refuted his story. Gamasy, who eventually took Shazly's job, asserted that Shazly neither suffered a nervous breakdown nor did he call for a total withdrawal, and that the president did not really dismiss the chief of staff until December, two months after he claimed he did.[134] Even before the witnesses to these events published their memoirs few people believed this fabricated story, least of all in the army. Shazly's long-standing reputation in both the Arab world and Israel as Egypt's "most dashing and aggressive combat officer" made it quite inconceivable for him to act in this degrading manner. A Western diplomat described Shazly in 1973 as "Egypt's Dayan," adding that although he never sought this "mythopoeic status, he was nevertheless a hero to the Egyptian public even before the October War—a model of the 'new Egyptian officer.'" Folk tales circulated about how he was almost overrun by Nazis in 1942 but refused to withdraw until his men were safely evacuated; how he performed brilliantly as an infantry platoon leader in 1948, and as a paratrooper in Yemen in the 1960s; and particularly how he managed to return all his soldiers to Cairo unscathed in 1967, an episode that had become "encrusted with legend." Despite the gulf that commonly separated army officers from their soldiers, Shazly was quite affectionate with his men. "Instead of the medals and gold braid he could affect, he wore standard beret, jump boots, and camouflage smock of a paratrooper." And with his sharp mind and organizational brilliance, his "legendary popularity" was inflated even more during the buildup to the war.[135] It was thus clear to all that Sadat schemed with "conspiratorial instinct against a soldier who commanded immense professional respect and popular following in the armed forces."[136]

In December 1973, Shazly was dispatched to London, then Portugal to serve as military attaché, before being dismissed from service in 1978 after he published his memoirs, which he began as follows: "I have written it with reluctance, with sorrow and with anger ... at the man who is currently the President of my country," a man that he held responsible for the "wholesale distortion of the achievements of the armed forces as a group."[137] Shazly then devoted a substantial part of the memoir to exposing Sadat's deceitful behavior during the war, and detailing how the political leadership undermined the country's national security "to preserve a regime of autocratic privilege, which it upheld by lying to its citizens and then spying on them to see if they believed the lies. Even if the price were the failure of our assault on the enemy, the regime was determined to keep the armed forces subservient to that real, secret end."[138] Expectedly, Shazly was tried in absentia for revealing military secrets, and had to move to Algeria, where he formed the Egypt National Liberation Front, a movement aimed at overthrowing Sadat's regime. In 1992, he returned to Egypt to be immediately seized at the airport and taken to prison. A couple of years later, he was released and subsequently retired from public life. The top brass never abandoned him, though. His family admits that Defense Minister Hussein Tantawy (1991–present) regularly checked on his health, and helped issue a court order to drop all the charges against him in 2005.[139] It was Mubarak, following in Sadat's footsteps, who considered him an enemy until the last day. Shazly lived through the January 2011 revolt, but died one night before the military forced the president to step down. A few weeks after, his so-far-banned memoirs were published in Egypt and quickly made it to the top of the best-seller chart—a symbolic gesture from the military to its cherished commander.

Going back to the October War, there was now a cease-fire agreement in hand, negotiated in Moscow between Kissinger and Leonid Brezhnev, and sanctioned via Security Council resolution 338. On his way back from Moscow, on October 22, the U.S. secretary of state stopped at Tel Aviv to reassure an anxious Golda Meir that the resolution did not appoint UN observers to supervise the cease-fire, and that it was understandable if the Israelis needed a couple more days "to complete the encirclement of the two Egyptian armies."[140] Operating almost freely on the west side of the canal, Bren Adan and Ariel Sharon's brigades tore a twenty-four-kilometer hole in the SAM air defense umbrella, which protected the Egyptian ground troops, allowing Israel to resume its lethal combination of armor and air power on both sides of the canal.[141] Refusing to admit his mistakes, Sadat dismissed the breach as a "circus show aimed at television audiences."[142] But he then quickly accepted the cease-fire.

Like all his previous decisions, accepting a cease-fire-in-place was also hotly disputed, this time by his most intimate aide, Hafez Ismail. The Egyptian national security adviser was startled by Sadat's unconditional compliance. He advised his chief to insist on an Israeli pullout from the west bank of the canal first—which was already a huge concession from Egypt's initial position that fighting would continue until Israel withdrew to the June 1967 borders. Ismail was also dismayed by Sadat's unshakable confidence in Kissinger despite all that has happened, especially now when the latter turned a blind eye to Israel's violations of the cease-fire. Moreover, a cease-fire-in-place left the encircled 45,000-strong Third Army at Israel's mercy, never mind the fact that they had cut off the main access to Sinai by the Cairo-Suez road.[143] During a meeting of Sadat, Hafez Ismail, and Heikal on October 21, both advisers additionally highlighted that the UN resolution not only demanded a cessation of hostilities, but also direct negotiations between the belligerents, which contradicted Egypt's long-standing position not to negotiate directly with Israel. In other words, accepting the resolution would represent an enormous political compromise, not just a military one. The national security adviser implored his boss to reconsider: "Mr. President, there is no need for this rush ... I honestly believe that the armed forces could still confront the situation." When his calls fell on deaf ears, Hafez Ismail took a step that would soon cost him his job. Instead of explaining the rationale behind Egypt's acceptance of the cease-fire to a group of bewildered cabinet members on October 24, he lost his nerve and confessed that the president was acting alone. Two days earlier, on October 22, Heikal heard the same message from the frustrated head of the Military Affairs Department (Lieutenant Colonel Abd al-Ra'ouf Reda), essentially that "Egypt is in danger ... the President does not listen to his advisers, and sometimes refuses even to see them ... [I] tried to explain to him the military situation ... and the rage spreading among young officers ... but he would not listen."[144]

Finally, the president called a meeting of the Supreme Council of the Armed Forces on November 21. The officers thought he was finally considering a resumption of the war to save the Third Army and the canal cities that were now besieged by Israel. It was not Egyptian gung-ho talking; the Israeli chief of staff himself had submitted an alarming memo to Golda Meir warning that a prolonged siege would give Third Army soldiers an opportunity to catch their breath while their comrades on the east bank reconstituted the SAM air defenses, "And with the Israelis so extended, the situation could abruptly reverse itself, with the Egyptians forcing the IDF into the final battle."[145] But instead of discussing plans to resume the war, Sadat thanked them all for their great service to the country, and declared that he now considered the war over and expected the armed forces at this point not to meddle in politics, adding that the upcoming disengagement talks were "a political matter. Whether they reach an agreement or not is nothing to you. You must mind your own business."[146] This, of course, did not bode well among the officers, who felt that the president had ended the war abruptly and prematurely.

To top it all, Sadat presented what he called the October Paper to Parliament in May 15, 1974, to lay out his vision for the future. The president claimed that his strategy during the October War had "finally put an end to Zionist expansionism, which had progressively secured more land ... in every generation ... [And that] with the end of its expansionist hopes ... Israel had embarked on a comprehensive soul searching journey, and a review of the basis of the Zionist doctrine itself."[147] For the officers, this was a clever twist of words which implied that the war's goal was to prevent further Zionist expansion rather than liberate the Arab land already occupied by Israel. The worst was yet to come. In this same paper, Sadat blamed military expenditure for the drop in Egypt's economic development, hinting—even before Sinai had been recovered—that the defense budget would be substantially reduced. Sadat also made explicit overtures to Egyptian investors, signaling his intention to open up the economy. Sadat was aware that this was the class that supported his war strategy most. Even before the October War, there was a plain consensus among Egyptian capitalists that a future war should not impair their scheme to join the Western camp and partner with American investors. Their preference, accordingly, was for a short and limited war to be followed immediately by a peaceful settlement, regardless of the political or military concessions involved. The Egyptian military's hope for a long war of attrition, with all the instability and economic loss associated with it, was absolutely out of the question.[148]

There was no one to challenge Sadat. The short list of officers who wielded some influence within the ranks was getting even shorter. One month before the war, the Republican Guard commander, al-Lethy Nassef, was pushed from a balcony in London. Nassef had been dismissed a few months before, presumably because he had walked into the president's office without his beret, which Sadat's interpreted as a sign of disrespect. The president then offered him an ambassadorship in Europe, but the offended general insisted on staying in Egypt. Eventually Nassef had to travel to London for medical checkups and never returned. Two months after the war, Shazly was appointed military attaché to London; the three major field commanders were assigned civilian jobs as provincial governors; and the chief of artillery was transferred to the protocol section of the presidency.[149] Ahmed Bahaa al-Din, chief editor of al-Ahram, remembered how the commanders felt betrayed for being cut off so ruthlessly from the army after all they had done.[150] It was inconceivable for Sadat, however, to act otherwise. He intended for the military to pave the road for a political settlement, not in the Clausewitzian sense, where the army accomplishes political ends, but rather by its proving incapable of achieving militarily what only the political leader could achieve through negotiations.

Equally important, Sadat wanted to conduct the war in a way that would not jeopardize his plan to win America's patronage for his regime. This last aim frequently left Sadat's commanders and diplomatic advisers perplexed. No one could figure out why Sadat was so fond of Kissinger, to the point of describing him as someone who was "sincere and carried out what he promised."[151] Sadat explained to reporters that he accepted the U.S. secretary of state's proposals without demur because he "liked Kissinger very much. I regarded him as a friend. And I don't like to haggle with my friends."[152] This is probably why upon receiving a message from Kissinger offering to visit Cairo if Egypt accepted a cease-fire-in-place, Sadat immediately obliged. The president's faith in Kissinger, however, was best demonstrated during the final two days of the war. On October 24, the Soviets threatened to intervene to prevent Egypt's total defeat after it had become obvious that Israel was not willing to faithfully implement the cease-fire agreement. Kissinger and James Schlesinger responded to Brezhnev's note by elevating the American combat alert (including the nuclear Strategic Air Command) to DEFCON 3, and reinforced the U.S. Sixth Fleet with another aircraft carrier. To stress how the United States was determined to "go to the brink" over this issue, Kissinger threatened in a television address, "We possess, each of us, nuclear arsenals capable of annihilating humanity. We, both of us, have a special duty to see to it that confrontations are kept within bounds that do not threaten civilized life."[153] But then Kissinger turned to Sadat to set the Soviets straight, and although the Egyptian president had previously asked for a joint American-Russian mission to observe the cease-fire, he shocked the Soviets, on October 26, by asking them to stay out of it.[154]

This sort of behavior astonished Kissinger more than anyone else. On several occasions he recorded how Sadat "agreed almost immediately" to Israel's requests, while only demanding as a face-saving measure that they be presented as American—not Israeli—proposals.[155] Kissinger was equally surprised that throughout the war, and after all that he had done for Israel, Sadat was still warm and cordial toward him in a most unusual sense.[156] Foreign Minister Ghaleb reasonably concluded that Israel's military breach resulted from the "political breach through which the U.S. penetrated" Egypt's political leadership.[157] In a conversation with Heikal following his first encounter with Kissinger, on November 7, 1973, Sadat relayed proudly how he began the meeting: "I told him, Henry, do not waste your time with details ... You are a man of strategy, and so am I, so let us not be held back by details ... The future hangs on one question: Can we be friends? I want us to become friends, and if Egypt becomes your friend, then the whole region will open up to you." He went on to describe the Soviets as the real enemy; how he planned to consult his friend David Rockefeller on the best way to open up the Egyptian market to foreign investors; and how he considered this war Egypt's last battle with Israel. It was only a year later, in September 1975, during a dinner at the Georgetown house of the veteran American journalist and presidential speechwriter Joseph Kraft, that Heikal learned that Sadat also asked for the United States to "secure him personally and his regime" because there were many people plotting against him "inside his own country."[158]

WHEN THE GUNS FELL SILENT

By the time the war ended, only one of its major authors was left standing. With Shazly removed from office, Ismail transferred to a London hospital before passing away in December 1974, and the field commanders transferred to the civilian sector, Abd al-Ghany al-Gamasy was appointed war minister. It was now his turn to fall from fame. Gamasy's military stature was certainly threatening. He enjoyed immense prestige as the true architect of the gallant Suez Canal crossing, and he was an ardent critic of the way the president had run the war. Moreover, he would have undoubtedly objected to Sadat's plan to redirect the army from combat toward economic and civilian projects. Gamasy attributed the 1967 defeat to this misuse of military energies: "The armed forces became involved in land reclamation, housing, the national transport system ... the growing power and presence of the army in civilian life was detrimental to its main responsibility, which was to be a fighting force, ready for battle."[159] And this was exactly what Sadat had in mind for the military in the postwar era. Letting Gamasy go at this stage was therefore dangerous; first he had to become enmeshed in the unpopular peace talks and the other postwar arrangements; he had to sign on the dotted line.

Against his will, Gamasy (while still chief of operations) was charged, on October 28, with the thankless mission of heading Egypt's delegation to the first direct Egyptian-Israeli negotiations, held in a tent on the Cairo-Suez road (101 kilometers from Cairo) with the vague goal of finding a way to disentangle the Egyptian and Israeli troops in Sinai and pave the way for a political settlement.[160] But although Gamasy was a professional soldier who always followed orders, Israeli officers could not help but notice that throughout the negotiations, he remained "demonstratively somber."[161] Gamasy was then invited to meet Kissinger in Aswan, on January 11, days after he was promoted to chief of staff, to further discuss steps toward disengagement. As soon as the meeting started, Kissinger stunned everyone by announcing that Sadat had already agreed to permanently limit the Egyptian presence in Sinai to 7,000 troops and 30 tanks, i.e., to reduce the two armies currently stationed there (a 100,000-strong and heavily equipped force) to eight lightly armed battalions. Gamasy lost control. As he recorded in his memoirs, he screamed at Kissinger:

> "You are giving Israel what would guarantee the security of its forces and denying us everything that would safeguard our forces. I do not approve of this and I cannot as Chief of Staff of the Armed Forces justify this to our forces" ... I left the meeting room angry, with tears in my eyes, and I went to the bathroom ... I had appreciated the enormous effort and the sacrifices in the war, and there seemed to be no need for this huge concession which might endanger our armed forces. I had expected President Sadat to consult General Ahmed Ismail, or me ... There was no need—politically or militarily—to accept this reduction in troops and weapons.[162]

Unknown to the chief of staff, however, there *was* a need for this reduction, which was simply the president's desire to win American patronage at all costs. The next day, Sadat scolded Gamasy and warned him that the promises to Kissinger must be fulfilled and that he did not have to consult the military before making political decisions.[163] Two months later, in March 1974, a rebellion broke out among the soldiers of the besieged Third Army in protest of the decision to reduce troops and accept an end to hostilities. There was little these soldiers could accomplish, though, considering they were cut off from the rest of the army, and the whole country for that matter.[164] In June 1975, forty-three officers from several units were arrested for planning an anti-Sadat coup. Then again between February and April 1976 a large number of officers (which remains unspecified) resigned in protest of the president's policies. Sadat also removed several high-ranking commanders in mid-1977 for supporting an attempted coup by naval officers. This was followed by the arrest of fourteen paratroopers and a major shake-up of the armed forces in July 1977, when many appeared to be sympathetic to former Chief of Staff Shazly's call for the army to rise against its dictator.[165]

Apparently, Gamasy's outrage (and that of numerous other soldiers) was not just that of a tough-minded old general. Foreign Minister Ismail Fahmy, who ran the early negotiations with the United States and Israel, noted that Sadat's concessions shocked both Kissinger and the Israelis.[166] Kissinger described to the Israeli cabinet how the Egyptian president constantly rebuked his military and diplomatic advisers: whenever Gamasy and Fahmy criticized Israeli proposals, Sadat would ask them to leave the room and then apologize to his American guest that "Gamasy and Fahmy were good men but did not understand [anything]." On the issue of troop reduction, for example, Gamasy insisted that Egypt could not protect Sinai without at least 250 tanks. Kissinger's aim was to push this figure down to 100 tanks. When he met Sadat, he started with the implausible number of 30 tanks with the hope that Egypt would then agree to 100. Shockingly, Kissinger reported, Sadat immediately agreed. The U.S. secretary of state felt tempted to try his luck once more. The Israelis had requested a withdrawal of the SAM air defense umbrella—the only cover for an Egyptian presence in Sinai—twenty kilometers from the canal. Gamasy said it was impossible to pull back more than five kilometers. Kissinger then appealed to Sadat, who instantly approved—with one request, though: that the "details of the thinning out of forces and arms restrictions be spelled out in ... private letters sent by President Nixon to him," so that the public would not know about it.[167] The concessions kept flowing: the Egyptian artillery would only have thirty-six small guns in Sinai; the border would be strictly sealed against Palestinian infiltrators; the Red Sea straits and the Suez Canal would never be closed to Israeli navigation; the Suez Canal cities would be rebuilt, expanded, and heavily populated as a guarantee against the eruption of future conflicts; Sadat would plead with the oil-rich countries to lift their embargo even before a settlement was reached; Egypt would supply Israel with two million tons of energy annually; and Nixon would be received in Cairo with cheering crowds to help improve his image in the wake of Watergate.[168]

What was Sadat trying to accomplish? In a private conversation with Bahaa al-Din, he explained: "My generals ... are wasting time over ... trivial details. They do not understand that I was not negotiating disengagement with Israel, but rather with America. When I went to war, I did not go to war against the Israeli army, I was fighting to shake the convictions of all the American institutions: the presidency, Congress, the CIA, the Pentagon ... and their businessmen as well."[169] The president's national security team saw things differently. Foreign Minster Fahmy concluded in his memoirs that Sadat single-handedly squandered all that the Egyptian military had managed to achieve during the war.[170] Murad Ghaleb, Egypt's foreign minister during the war, asserted that Sadat's conviction that the United States was the best guarantor to his regime "cost us the glory we achieved during the crossing."[171] Heikal noted that Sadat misunderstood the doctrine of limited war in which military achievement is used to increase a state's political leverage rather than sacrificed to please would-be political allies.[172] It was only normal that this attitude toward the war would hit the military leaders hardest. "Egypt's soldiers and Egypt's commanders were of a high standard and they fought well," lamented Shazly, but "they were let down by their political leaders."[173]

When the guns fell silent, the plain statistics indicated an Israeli victory: 15,700 Arab soldiers were killed compared with 4,150 Israelis; 8,031 were imprisoned compared with 241; 1,950 tanks were destroyed compared with 875; 412 planes were shot down compared with 119; and 30 naval vessels were hit compared with only 1; in terms of land, Israel ended up controlling more territory on the west bank of the canal than that seized by Egypt on the east bank. In January 1974, Egypt had to pull its Second and Third armies back to the west bank, leaving only a token force of 7,000 soldiers (down from 100,000) to protect the ten-kilometer-wide strip they controlled after the crossing, while the Israeli troops now entrenched themselves in the passes that controlled the peninsula. The following year, the Israelis agreed to reposition right behind the passes and UN troops were deployed between the two armies.[174] Little wonder then that Egypt's officers believed, as Shazly aptly described it, that "Sadat had single-handedly given away all that the Egyptian army had won with great sacrifice. Without consulting anybody, he had caved in to the Israeli request that the Egyptian military presence east of the canal be reduced to nothing."[175] Or as the Egyptian chief of staff during the war somberly remarked: "The president had thrown away the greatest army Egypt had ever assembled."[176] Yet to this day, the military historian Simon Dunstan noted, Egyptians continue to believe—against the consensus of all the studies of the October War—that they were triumphant, adding mockingly, "In the Middle East, perception is everything."[177]

With such bitterness toward the president, Defense Minister Gamasy, Chief of Staff Mohamed Aly Fahmy (air defense commander during the war), and whoever remained in the ranks among their senior comrades had to go. They had all become increasingly critical of the president's warming up toward the United States and Israel, and more

important, about his "downgrading of the military and the redirec-
tion of its mission."[178] On October 5, 1978, the entire leadership of
the October War was therefore replaced. The timing stung, however.
Gamasy recorded, "I was annoyed and dismayed at the choice of the
date 5 October to introduce changes in the military command, thereby
denying the old leadership—those who had played a major role in
October 1973—the privilege of taking part in the armed forces victory
celebration on 6 October."[179] Mahmoud Game' admitted that his friend
Sadat had deliberately chosen that day so that Gamasy and the others
would learn their place.[180]

Gamasy's successor was not any more fortunate. Just like Ahmed
Ismail before, the new defense minister, Kamal Hassan Aly, had been
appointed intelligence director for a brief period to prepare him for the
top military post. Also, similar to Ismail, his job was to keep the army in
check and away from politics. Sadat and Aly had first met at the Maadi
Military Hospital on June 20, 1967, when the latter was being treated
for battlefront wounds. Sadat was impressed by his resentment of the
politicization of the officer corps, and the half-witted arrogant army
confidants that were in charge of the military.[181] Aly's appointment thus
promised to reinforce professionalism. But his understanding of professionalism was to root out mediocre officers whose presence in the
corps subjected the army to grave danger, as was obvious in 1956 and
1967.[182] Professionalism for him was not an encoded way of saying that
the army should be diminished as a fighting force and kept away from
national security policy. Aly advocated a strong military, and his distinguished performance as commander of the elite 4th Armored Division
during the war gave him enough leverage among the troops to press
forward with this demand. The new minister lasted only a few months
in the military before being appointed foreign minister and charged
with the unpopular task of developing peaceful relations with Israel, a
task that could hardly have endeared him to the troops.[183] Aly candidly
expressed his "frustration with being ... demoted" to the new minister
of state for foreign affairs, Boutros-Ghali, yet he had little choice but to
follow orders.[184]

Aly's replacement in the Defense Ministry scarcely survived a year
in office. On March 2, 1981, Defense Minister Ahmed Badawy, another
influential officer, was killed in a helicopter crash four hundred miles
southwest of Cairo with thirteen senior commanders (nine major generals, three brigadier generals, and a colonel). The official story was that
the helicopter's tail got tangled in an electric wire, which caused it to
lose balance and crash. The pilot had a different story, though, asserting that the helicopter's engine experienced a sudden loss of power.[*]
Moreover, Badawy's secretary said that right before the crash one of the

---

[*] Reporters in *Al-Akhbar* 8965: 3. Cairo (3/6/1981).

officers (Major General Salah Qassem) cried out, "There is something wrong with this aircraft."[185] These testimonies were not the only reason the public became suspicious. There were also questions regarding why the defense minister and thirteen of his top lieutenants would all be on the same helicopter, and, more important, how the pilot responsible for such a distinguished crowd could commit such a rookie mistake, driving his helicopter into an electric wire in broad daylight. The government's response was not very convincing. An editorial in the leading daily *Al-Ahram* passionately denied the accusations, quoting Sadat's claim that these types of conspiracies occur only in shabby regimes like the Syrian and Libyan ones, but not in Egypt.[186] The weekly magazine *October* responded, in its March 8 issue, more creatively, cataloging twenty similar flying accidents from around the world to imply that these were only normal.[187]

Badawy was considered a war hero, and enjoyed considerable popularity within the officer corps. He famously defended Suez against an imminent Israeli invasion during the last days of the October War, and was responsible for checking the Israeli forces on the west bank of the canal until the disengagement agreement was signed. More significant though, was that Badawy made a few controversial remarks in Parliament weeks before his death, stating: "The transition of the Middle East from a conventional [weapons] theater to a nuclear theater is very dangerous. We hope it does not happen. But if it did happen and a regional country [i.e., Israel] came to possess nuclear weapons, then we would have no other option but to balance against it"; he also reiterated that "Egypt will always remain the credible force in the face of the dangers confronting the Arab world ... [and that] peace should not lead to any change in the nature or missions of the armed forces."* Badawy clearly insinuated his rejection of the president's attempts to sideline the army, or pledge (as discussed below) not to develop unconventional weapons to deter Israel. But there was even more to the story.

Alwy Hafez, a Free Officer who was elected to Parliament in the 1980s, was an old friend of Badawy, and he accused Sadat and Mubarak of conspiring to kill the defense minister and his colleagues because they were planning to expose the corrupt arm deals in which the political leadership was involved, as well as naked attempts to keep the military subservient. Badawy confided to Hafez two weeks before he was killed that he had confronted Sadat with what he knew, but instead of taking action, the president handed him a list of senior officers that he needed to have immediately purged. The infuriated defense minister declined, reminding his boss that these were among Egypt's best soldiers, and—according to his friend—he became convinced that the political leadership must be overthrown.[188] After incessant attempts,

---

* Reporters in *Al-Akhbar* 8963: 7. Cairo (3/4/1981).

Hafez finally succeeded in submitting a request during an official parliamentary session, on March 5, 1990, for a proper investigation of the conspiracy against Badawy and his fellows, but his request was quickly shelved. After the 2011 revolt, Ahmed Abdallah, one of the leading cadres of the ruling party and a relative of Badawy, confirmed that the latter had indeed met Sadat forty-eight hours before the accident and threatened to resign because of attempts to corrupt and control the army from the presidency.[189]

Expectedly, many within and outside the army refused to innocently believe that the crash was an accident, viewing it instead as a preemptive move by Sadat against his unruly high command. Kamal Hassan Aly acknowledged how far this "rumor" traveled around Egypt, though he personally refused to believe it.[190] However, eyebrows were raised once more when the pilot, who mysteriously survived the crash, was shot a few months later at his apartment.[191] In fact, one of the justifications cited by Sadat's assassins during their interrogations in 1981 was his implication in the Badawy affair.[192]

Besides the character (or literal) assassination and dislodging of almost all officers who carried some weight in the armed forces, Sadat dealt his military an even harsher blow in May 1979 in the form of Presidential Decree 35. According to the decree's explanatory memorandum, "officers who occupied the most senior posts in the armed forces, in operations, and as commanders of the main branches of the forces in the October 6, 1973, war shall remain in service in the armed forces for life ... They will remain military advisers for life, loyal to the armed forces. They shall not occupy military posts in the organizational structure of the armed forces so that honoring them and benefiting from their unique experience will not run counter to the principles of renewal and continuity."[193] The decree sealed the fate of the entire "October Generation." It condemned the war-seasoned leaders to a surreal existence, a state of limbo in which they could neither occupy military commands nor move on to play an influential role in politics.

Even though the Israeli military sociologist Amos Perlmutter wrote in 1974, reflecting the wisdom of his time, that Sadat's regime remained completely dependent on the military, which was now in a position to "arbitrate and, in fact, dictate Egypt's foreign and defense policies,"[194] this could not have been further from the truth. Sadat's policies during the seventies pushed the military to the point of oblivion and downgraded its political influence. A few microindicators show the diminishing ratio of officers to civilians in the cabinet: from nineteen ministers representing 65.5 percent in 1967, to eleven representing 33.3 percent in 1970, to four representing 12.5 percent in 1976, to a mere three representing 9.1 percent of the cabinet in 1977; another indicator was that while 9 percent of Nasser's ambassadors were officers, Sadat completely blocked their access to the diplomatic corps; lastly, while twenty-two of Egypt's twenty-six governors were officers in 1964, only five officers held that post in 1980.[195]

The overall view of the thorny path Sadat treaded in the 1970s reveals a much more persistent strategy to rein in the officer corps. In May 1971, the president imprisoned War Minister Muhammad Fawzy for high treason despite his efforts in rebuilding the army after 1967 and putting together a plan to cross the Suez Canal. In October 1972, his replacement, Muhammad Sadeq, and his top lieutenants were placed under house arrest and accused of defeatism despite their valiant struggle to prepare the army for the imminent battle. Then, rather than promoting the strong-willed and popular chief of staff, Saad al-Din al-Shazly, to the top military post, the president appointed the ailing Ahmed Ismail as war minister on the eve of the war, and days before the war ended Sadat replaced Shazly, for his alleged cowardice in battle, with Chief of Operations Abd al-Ghany al-Gamasy. Gamasy was then promoted to war minister as soon as Ismail lost his battle with cancer, as was expected, in 1974, but as soon as he concluded the disengagement agreements and other aspects of the political settlement, he was replaced with Kamal Hassan Aly, the single-minded advocate of military professionalism who was serving as GIS director at the time. Sadat then chose a vice president (Hosni Mubarak) from Egypt's weakest service and the one least capable of plotting a coup: the air force. In addition, a few mysterious accidents took care of the remaining military heavyweights. Al-Lethy Nassef, commander of the Republican Guards, was pushed off a balcony in London, and War Minister Ahmed Badawy and thirteen senior officers were killed in a helicopter crash. At the same time, Sadat carried out an extensive reshuffle of all major commands, and issued a presidential decree barring those who participated in the October War from either retiring from the army (and thus freeing themselves to pursue a political career) or assuming active military commands (where they might capitalize on their war reputation to cultivate a following), thus effectively banishing all of Egypt's great fighting generals to a no man's land between politics and the military, to a twilight zone from which they could never return. The president then redirected the military as a whole from a combat-oriented to an economic institution, famously declaring that October 1973 was Egypt's last war and that the army should now direct its energy toward the "war of economic development."

One must pose a question, before concluding this section, regarding the military's seeming passivity vis-à-vis its civilian leader, though his policies obviously threatened its corporate interests and Egypt's national security. What prevented the officer corps from rising against Sadat? There are two answers. The short one is that it did in fact rise against him. Sadat's decade-long tenure was rife with attempted coups plots, and senior military men challenged his decisions at every step of the way. A second answer is that despite the fact that soldiers expressed their frustration (and on many occasions, their indignation) to the president, the army was still in no shape to take on the political apparatus in the 1970s. Nasser's decapitation of the leadership of the armed forces between 1967 and 1968, and Sadat's follow-up on that front between 1971 and 1972, left the military virtually leaderless. On a wider scale, the purging of thousands of officers between 1954 and 1974, and two resounding military defeats in 1956 and 1967, followed by an inconclusive war in 1973, undermined military coherence, hurt its popular image, and made it too weary of political intervention. Moreover, the expansiveness and aggressiveness of the politically loyal security forces played a crucial role in keeping the military in check (as discussed below). With a vacuum on top, a hole in its body, and a gun pointed to its head, the military could not muster the power to overthrow its political leadership.

SEASON OF MIGRATION TO THE WEST

With the military demobilized and directed away from politics, the Egyptian regime was no longer military-based. It relied on security and political organs to control the populace, but it was still looking for a new ruling partner, an overall guarantor of regime stability. Because Nasser was so adamant about Egyptian independence, he had refused the readily available option of becoming a client of one of the world powers, as many of his contemporaries did. His aim was to build Egypt into a regional power, and manage through strategic alliances to play a major role in world politics as well—hence the need for a strong military capable of projecting power across the developing world. By the time Sadat came to power it was fairly obvious that empowering the military had its political costs, whether it supported democracy (as in early 1950s) or tried to dominate the regime (as in the 1960s). A stable authoritarianism required the political isolation and weakening of the military. Egypt had to turn back to the option that Nasser had tried to avoid for so long: to become a satellite of one of the superpowers. The only question was which one. Sadat chose the United States not just because the Russians never trusted (or respected) him, but also because by the mid-1970s it was obvious to all that the USSR was struggling to catch up with the West. A unipolar world was emerging, and Sadat wanted to end up on the winning side.

There were, of course, several military concessions involved. Demilitarizing Sinai was on top of the list. It not only provided Israel with a 37,000-square-kilometer buffer zone, but it also deprived the

Egyptian army of training or preparing installations in the most strategic part of the country. Announcing in April 1974 the end of Egypt's exclusive reliance on Soviet weapons, followed by linking Egyptian arms supply and training to the United States from 1979 (via the annual $1.3 billion military aid package), despite the latter's alliance with Israel, was a second important concession. Agreeing in November 1980 to conduct joint military exercises with U.S. troops (the annual Bright Star maneuvers) to help familiarize them with desert wars, a skill Americans were keen on acquiring for future contingencies, was a third offering of friendship. A fourth (confidential) military concession was Sadat's pledge to abandon the Nasser-instigated efforts to develop nuclear weapons.[196] There were also many cherries on top of all these concessions, sudden bouts of generosity if you will, such as Sadat's decision in 1975 to hand over a complete battery of Soviet SAM-6 antiaircraft missiles (the highly prized weapon the USSR had provided him to protect Egypt's skies) to the U.S. Army so it could explore ways of neutralizing it.[197]

There were major political concessions as well, concessions that puzzled the whole diplomatic corps and caused three foreign ministers to quit their job between 1972 and 1978 in protest of Sadat's undermining of the country's national interests, concessions that forced Sadat to reshuffle his cabinet four times between 1978 and 1980 to be able to oust his critics in government. What were some of these political concessions? The most valued concessions were naturally related to the negotiations that followed the October War. To begin with, the president had surrendered totally to the machinations of U.S. Secretary of State Henry Kissinger and his "shuttle diplomacy" between 1973 and 1975. He refused to allow his top aides to question anything Kissinger proposed, and referred to him fondly as "the man who never lied to me, or ever betrayed his promises."[198] Not only that, he suddenly began singing America's praises, commending "American chivalry, and the real America ... that stands by every country in need of assistance to help establish a better world"[199]—forgetting, of course, that the United States was single-handedly responsible for reversing Egypt's military fortunes during the October War.

Even though Kissinger's efforts came to nothing, Sadat continued to place all his eggs in the American basket and decided to unilaterally annul the Egyptian-Soviet Friendship Treaty in March 1976 and to humiliate the Soviets on every occasion in hopes of pleasing the United States, even though his current and future foreign ministers (Ismail Fahmy and Muhammad Ibrahim Kamel) explained to him that although they were personally pro-American, what the president was doing betrayed all sound diplomatic principles. The United States would always look after Israel's interests first and foremost, and without some measure of Soviet support, Egypt would place itself at Israel's mercy.[200] Moreover, by linking Egypt's political and military fortunes to Israel's chief ally, the president was not only committing the country to indefinite negotiations with Israel, but also forcing it to negotiate from a position of weakness.

For his diplomatic aides, however, the straw that broke the camel's back was his decision to travel to Jerusalem in 1977. In October of that year, Sadat received a handwritten note from President Jimmy Carter conditioning U.S. support on "a bold, statesmanlike move [by Sadat] to help overcome the hurdles" facing the peace talks.[201] Although Sadat denied that Carter's note inspired his grand Peace Initiative, Ahmed Bahaa al-Din, who was with him when he received the letter, said that Sadat showed it to him and bragged: "You see, the American president is begging me," and he could not let him down.[202] The soon-to-be-foreign-minister Muhammad Ibrahim Kamel also mentioned that Sadat confessed to him that the initiative to fly to Israel was inspired by Carter's note.[203] On November 5, a few days after receiving the note, Sadat convened his top military and diplomatic staff to share his thinking. Foreign Minister Fahmy tried to reason with him, explaining that after all the cards he had squandered, he had only one left: recognizing Israel and ending the state of war. He pleaded with him not to throw away this last card unless he had strict guarantees that at least Sinai would be returned unconditionally, let alone other occupied Arab territories. If the president insisted on going through with his plan to recognize Israel unilaterally in the hopes of shaming the world, dazzling the Americans, and exposing Israeli intransigence, then Egypt would be completely naked in any future negotiations. War Minister Gamasy was less subtle than his diplomatic counterpart. Upon hearing of Sadat's planned initiative, "Gamasy raised his hands and screamed: 'The Knesset no! There is no need.'"[204] Sadat typically ignored the advice and decided to proceed with his plan anyway. Fahmy and a handful of senior diplomats resigned. The president looked for someone outside the diplomatic corps he could count on. Days before his trip to Israel, he appointed the Cairo University professor Boutros-Ghali (future UN secretary-general) as minister of state for foreign affairs, and right after the trip, he asked his longtime friend Muhammad Ibrahim Kamel (who shared a prison cell with him in the 1940s because of their anti-British activities) to serve as foreign minister. Kamel took the job after the trip to Israel. He recalled that on the day of his appointment, Sadat told him: "I allowed myself to appoint you without consulting you first because I consider you my son, and I need someone I can completely trust."[205] On Boutros-Ghali's part, it was clear why he was asked to join the president's delegation on such a controversial trip. In his diaries, Boutros-Ghali remarked that Sadat chose him because he believed he was already stigmatized: he descended from one of the largest landowning families; several of his ancestors served the monarchy as ministers; his family's possessions were either confiscated or placed under state guardianship under Nasser; he was a Christian Egyptian married to a Jew; and he was avidly pro-Western; in short, he belonged entirely to the ancien régime.[206]

Jimmy Carter's national security adviser, Zbigniew Brzezinski, wrote that, to America's delight, Sadat's initiative fit perfectly with Israel's goal "to confine the peace process to a separate Israeli-Egyptian agreement, which would split the Arabs while letting Israel continue its occupation of the West Bank and Gaza."[207] Any student of Arab-Israeli relations knows quite well that neutralizing Egypt, the largest, most populous, and strongest Arab state from the equation of the struggle severely weakened the Arab camp and deprived other negotiators (Syria, Jordan, Palestine, Lebanon) of the power to end Israeli occupation of their territories. But as Fahmy predicted, Sadat's very visit to Tel Aviv and his vow in the Knesset to make the October War the last war between the two states offered Israel all it needed—recognition and peace—and gave it no reason to present concessions. By the end of 1978—that is, one year following the visit—negotiations were still stuck where they had been under Kissinger. Israel was occupying Sinai, and the bulk of the Egyptian army was positioned on the west bank of the canal— exactly where it had been since 1967. The United States now offered to host a marathon peace summit at Camp David. The goal, as described by the Camp David talks architect, Brzezinski, was to pressure Sadat and limit his choices to either walking out on the United States or accepting whatever the Israelis offered—and as Brzezinski duly noted, "Sadat chose the latter."[208] Little wonder that the president went without his war minister, Gamasy, or any other military representative, and that he removed Gamasy and the rest of the general staff two weeks after signing the Camp David Accords.[209]

Gamasy and his men had learned from sources close to the president that he had already agreed in principle to demilitarize the area within 150 kilometers east of the Sinai passes even before traveling to Camp David, and they warned Sadat that this would "put the forces in a weaker defensive and offensive position, which was unacceptable from a military perspective."[210] Just as they expected, however, the accords divided Sinai into three zones: in Zone A, which covered the area 50 kilometers east of the canal, Egypt was allowed to deploy one mechanized infantry division (22,000 men armed with 230 tanks), but then in Zones B and C, which varied in width from 20 to 40 kilometers west of the international border, only three lightly armed border patrol units and civil police forces were allowed. Moreover, Egypt was prohibited from using any of Sinai's airfields or building new ones.[211] It was not that the officer corps was vying for another war, but as the military strategist Anthony Cordesman explained, "Egypt's support of the peace process does not mean that it had to accept strategic inferiority or the kind of 'edge' that gives Israel offensive freedom of action."[212] And this was exactly what Sadat provided to Israel.

One has to admit, though, that the pressure on Sadat was substantial. Foreign Minister Kamel said that the president did not expect that after all his concessions and flirting with the United States, it would still adopt the Israeli position to the letter.[213] Two days before the signing of the Camp David Accords, Sadat threatened to withdraw, frustrated that despite his seemingly unbounded willingness to accommodate American interests, he was still being asked to deliver more than he could afford. At this tense moment, Carter decided to pay him a visit. And here is how the U.S. president described the scene in his own words: "Before going up I actually went and changed my clothes so that I would look more formal ... [Sadat's] whole delegation was with him on the porch. I asked him to step inside. He looked extremely drawn and nervous ... I don't think I've ever been so grave or so serious about anything that I have said in my life. I then said to him, 'I understand you're leaving ... [This] will mean first of all an end to the relationship between the United States and Egypt' ... Sadat looked absolutely shaken."[214] Of course, he decided to stay on. Not only that, but after Carter's stern warning, the Egyptian president gave him "carte blanche for his subsequent negotiations with the Israelis."[215] To justify to his aides this unwarranted submission, Sadat claimed that Carter wanted to corner the Israeli prime minister, Menachem Begin, and show the world that Israel was against peace. In reality, as William Quandt, who was part of the U.S. team at Camp David, later told Boutros-Ghali, who was also present at the talks, Sadat assured Carter that he was willing to accept the Israeli offer, but wanted his subordinates to think he had done so reluctantly.[216]

Expectedly, the Egyptian delegation, according to Boutros-Ghali, saw the settlement as "a humiliation to Egypt," and the demilitarization of Sinai in particular as a serious impediment to its capacity to defend itself against a future Israeli attack.[217] Moreover, by entering into a separate peace deal with Israel, Egypt isolated itself from the Arab world, thus undermining its geopolitical power even further. Foreign Minister Kamel resigned the day of the signing. His assessment of Sadat's negotiating strategy at Camp David was vividly captured in his memoirs: "I almost died of disgrace, disgust, and grief as I witnessed this tragedy unfold."[218]

A young diplomat by the name of Nabil al-Araby tried, in one last desperate attempt, to explain to his chief that Carter's promises concerning the Palestinians and Jerusalem were worthless. After pretending to listen to al-Araby intently, Sadat responded: "As you have seen, I have heard you out without interruption so that my critics would stop spreading rumors about how I do not listen to anyone or read anything. But what you have just said has entered my right ear and exited from the left one. You people in the Foreign Ministry believe you understand politics, but the truth is you do not understand anything. I can no longer concern myself with your advice or memos. I am a man who is following a grand strategy that none of you is capable of perceiving or comprehending. I have no more need for your sophistry and petty reports."[219] Notably, al-Araby became Egypt's first foreign minister after the 2011 revolt. At that time, however, Sadat would have none of it. After the signing ceremony, he returned to his hotel to meet with reporters. Upon being asked why Kamel had resigned, Sadat replied: "I excuse him because his weak nerves broke under pressure," then after questions regarding his disgruntled delegation kept coming, he turned to Boutros-Ghali and said: "Obviously your ministry needs a cleanup."[220] Curiously, the only two junior diplomats who seemed on board with Sadat at Camp David (Ahmed Maher and Ahmed Abu al-Gheit) were to later serve as Mubarak's last foreign ministers, whose compliant foreign policies helped fuel the 2011 revolt.

In truth, Sadat's subordinates were probably not that far out of line, considering that Brzezinski himself recorded with amazement how Sadat was "excessively deferential to American concerns and needlessly irritating to the rest of the Arab world," and that he frequently overruled members of his delegation in front of the Americans and Israelis when they tried to say so.[221] Kamel and Boutros-Ghali recounted that whenever one of them pointed out that the president's concessions threatened Egypt's interests, he would often repeat: "Let's just do this one for Carter's sake."[222] In fact, Sadat was so compliant that Carter and Brzezinski became concerned at "the possibility of something unpleasant occurring" to him at Camp David, and felt the need to take precautions. As Brzezinski recalled, "After returning to my cabin … I met with the security people to instigate tighter controls over access to Sadat's cabin."[223] On the last day of the negotiations, Brzezinski confided to his diary: "We might get a compromise agreement today, though the burden will fall on Sadat's shoulders. It will be hard for him to justify it."[224] Although Brzezinski sympathized with the desperate plight of his Egyptian counterparts, he understood that Sadat was only eager to impress the Americans. What Egypt's negotiating team failed to grasp, according to Brzezinski, was that their boss "saw the peace process as an opportunity to fashion a new American-Egyptian relationship … to becoming America's favorite statesman."[225]

Besides military and political concessions, Sadat also agreed to close security cooperation with his new partner. A key aspect of U.S. covert operations was to locate regional allies willing to fund, organize, and ultimately assume public responsibility for these operations. Because the CIA had become highly suspect during the obsessively secretive Nixon years, the Carter administration was keen on minimizing black ops, and instead getting others to do what was needed. Prepping Egypt for this role had been one of the underlying aims of Kissinger's Middle East policy in the mid-1970s. So on September 1, 1976, the heads of U.S. and French intelligence met in Cairo with four of their Middle East counterparts (Egypt, Iran, Saudi Arabia, and Morocco) to establish the Cairo-based Safari Club, a secret organization aimed at countering communism in Africa. In two years the club had carried out covert operations against Communists in Congo, Ethiopia, and Somalia.[226]

But then the toppling of the shah in 1979 promoted Egypt's position as America's foremost regional security partner. Its first task in this new capacity was to supply Iraq with Soviet arms to help its effort to overthrow Iran's new regime. The second and more spectacular task was to help fight the Soviets in Afghanistan. The Russian occupation of this neutral buffer state prompted Brzezinski to devise a plan to bury the Soviets there without direct American military intervention—just as the Soviets had done to the United States in Vietnam. His plan was simple: to unleash Islamist zealots against the Soviet occupiers. Brzezinski submitted a memo to Carter on January 9, 1980, outlining his strategy to use Egyptians, Saudis, and Pakistanis to execute this scheme.[227] By the end of month, he had sealed the deal in Cairo after Sadat agreed to recruit and train a volunteer army of young Egyptian Islamists; equip them with AK-47 rifles and ammunition, mortars, SAM-7 Strela surface-to-air missiles, and Sagger and RPG antitank missiles from Egypt's depots; and finally, ship them to Afghanistan on authorized U.S. cargo planes flying from bases in Egypt's southern cities of Qena and Aswan. The Saudis contributed money and preachers, and Pakistan agreed to handle logistics. In effect, Sadat and his men became "virtual recruiting sergeants and quartermasters to the secret army of zealots being mustered to fight the Soviets."[228] These, of course, were the militants who returned to Egypt in the 1990s to lead a violent campaign against the regime, and later took their militancy internationally through al-Qaeda.

In return, Sadat was promised U.S. protection for him and his regime. The CIA operative William Buckley put together an impressive CIA-managed program of personal security with an annual budget of $20 million for the Egyptian president. As part of that program, the CIA case officer in Cairo, James Fees, contracted U.S. antiterrorism experts to train Sadat's bodyguards. But more than a hundred bodyguard teams (each varying in size according to its mission) were clearly not enough. Sadat still felt the need to travel by helicopter—for unlike his predecessor, who traveled in an open motorcade, he knew how unpopular he had become. Three out of the five Westland helicopters Egypt had bought using U.S. funds went to the presidency. Sadat then expanded the Republican Guard from an infantry battalion to a brigade of special troops, equipped with tanks and armored cars, and a sophisticated communication system. More important, the United States helped boost Egypt's security organs, which were so vital to regime stability. American surveillance technology allowed the Interior Ministry to increase its telephone-tapping capabilities from 1,200 lines in 1971 to 16,000 in 1979. In 1980, the United States also provided street cameras to monitor major thoroughfares and public squares in Cairo, mobile listening posts, and other advanced electronic espionage devices that augmented Egypt's capacity for spying on its citizens to disrupt organized opposition.[229]

Why did Sadat make so many unnecessary concessions? This was the question that occupied Kissinger and the Israeli cabinet during the cease-fire talks; the question that provoked National Security Adviser Hafez Ismail's outburst during a cabinet meeting where he openly criticized Sadat; the question on War Minister Gamasy's lips when he rushed out of his meeting with Kissinger with teary eyes; the question that prompted the resignation of three foreign ministers in four years, and caused Sadat's falling out with his closest advisers, including Heikal and Game'; the question that puzzled Brzezinski for days at Camp David. Why did Sadat dissipate Egypt's military's achievements, undersell its geopolitical assets, deliver it solidly into the U.S. orbit, and in the process jeopardize its national interests?

Every player came up with a different answer. Kissinger told the Israeli leaders that "Sadat had fallen victim to human weakness. It was the psychology of a politician who wanted to see himself—and quickly—riding triumphantly in an open car ... with thousands of Egyptians cheering him."[230] Brzezinski was more imaginative. He noted in his Camp David diary, "My worry is that Sadat does not seem to differentiate clearly between fact and fiction," and that most of his facts were "simply untrue."[231] Heikal agreed: "Sadat the escapist became Sadat the dreamer; Sadat the dreamer became Sadat the actor. Most of his life Sadat was acting a part—or sometimes several parts at the same time."[232] Foreign Minister Fahmy had also complained of how unsettling it was to be working for someone who fabricated facts and then believed them. At the beginning of his relationship with Sadat, he judged him kindly as someone who was just "naïve and immature," but before he submitted his resignation, Fahmy had concluded that the president undermined Egypt's interests for his own glory, adding that Sadat's "fear [of war] ... and overflowing vanity were pathetic."[233] His longtime friend and foreign minister Kamel described Sadat as a "unique psychological case study," a man living in a make-believe world who constantly convinced himself that his dreams were reality, and that after becoming president, he also became unbearably narcissistic; "he fell in love with hearing the sound of his own voice and seeing his picture in the news."[234] Game', who was one of Sadat's most intimate friends, confessed that the president had become increasingly "narcissistic and arrogant" following the October War, and that his "excessive egoism" blinded him.[235] The Soviet officials who dealt with him during the war were convinced that he "suffered from megalomania."[236] Even the international experts who assessed the October War judged Sadat to be "a somewhat repressed man, prone to swoops between euphoria and depression."[237] In short, a considerable part of Sadat's entourage—friends and subordinates, military and civilian, domestic and foreign—attributed his decisions to either "arrogance [or] opportunism."[238]

These answers, however, are clearly unsatisfactory. They present Sadat as an extremely poor strategist, a delusional psychopath, or a traitor. The president's long and proud record in political survival says otherwise. It is more likely that these confounded politicians and military men were simply measuring Sadat using the wrong scale. Some of them asked in frustration how someone as shrewd as Sadat could commit all these tactical blunders, squandering Egypt's military accomplishments and diplomatic cards one after another, and receiving so little in return. Others wondered how a modern statesman could be so megalomaniac as to undermine his country's interests while continuing to think otherwise in his own fantasy world. What makes both sets of explanations misguided is that they measure Sadat's performance on the scale of national achievement, but Sadat was acting above all as a strategic actor in the intraregime power struggle that had consumed Egypt since 1952. His aim was to augment the power and stability of the political apparatus, which he represented, against the other troublesome partner in the ruling coalition: the military. On that scale, despite his numerous tactical failures, Sadat fared quite well in terms of overall strategy.

Sadat's decision to shift alliances, substituting U.S. protection for that which had been provided by the military, was a well-calculated power strategy. Reliance on the military for the past two decades had proved to be problematic (to say the least), leaving the political leadership vulnerable to the convulsions of the officer corps. Sadat had complained that under Nasser, there was a military plot uncovered every six months.[239] In contrast to the military and its mood swings, the United States offered stable support with only a few strings attached: peace with Israel, abandoning the role of Arab power builder, contributing to the global war to contain communism (and later Islamism), opening up the economy to foreign investors, and preferably signaling an opening of the political system. Sadat had no qualms about any of these demands, since none of them jeopardized his regime. Avoiding future military confrontations with Israel, as well as opting out of the chaos of Arab politics, guaranteed internal stability; combating communism abroad complemented efforts to undermine leftists at home (and the same later applied to Islamists); while economic and political liberalization could be tailored to the regime's convenience (one glance at America's allies in Latin America and Southeast Asia made it clear that democratic reforms, in particular, could remain cosmetic). Sadat himself spelled out his strategy in a private conversation with Ahmed Bahaa al-Din, a longtime acquaintance and editor of the daily newspaper *Al-Ahram*, who had just retuned from a visit to Tehran in January 1974:

> You know, for a long time I have considered the shah of Iran my role model among Third World leaders. Your nonaligned leaders whose clamor had occupied the world for years—Nehru, Nkrumah, Sukarno, even Abd al-Nasser, even Tito, who is still alive—where are they now? Some died, some were defeated, some were overthrown, and some shrank in their borders like Tito. Only one member of this generation remains on his throne, with all its power and glory, and with the whole world seeking his friendship: this is the shah of Iran. And the reason is simple. While all those other leaders believed the world has two great powers, Russia and America, and tried to deal with them on par, this could not be further from the truth; there is only one great power, which is America. Russia is not even a second great power; it is ten or twenty steps behind America ... It was the shah of Iran who realized that. So what did he do? He sat on America's lap, and clutched its gowns. And as you see, while all your friends are gone, America fulfilled the shah's needs. A revolution erupted [under Mohammad Mosaddeq in 1953], and he escaped to Italy. The Americans brought him back, and installed him again on the throne ... That is why I think he is a brilliant and extraordinary man.[240]

When Bahaa al-Din tried to remind him that the shah received this type of protection because he had vast oil reserves and his country directly bordered the Soviet Union, Sadat listened but did not comment.[241] Ironically, the shah—deposed by his people, and abandoned by the United States—was forced to spend his last days in Cairo, enjoying the hospitality of his secret admirer, Sadat. Commenting on the Egyptian president's reception of the fallen Persian monarch, one observer remarked in the *New York Times* on how amusing it was to see "the new Shah embracing the old Shah."[242]

BACK TO THE HOME FRONT

Although the umbrella of American protection was meant to substitute military protection for the political apparatus—i.e., it substituted the *function* of the military in the ruling alliance—one still has to remember that in a tripartite ruling bloc reducing the *weight* of one party (in this case the military) requires increasing that of the two other partners (i.e., the political and security apparatuses). So even as the president was reaching out to the United States, he was considering how to strengthen domestic power brokers. Empowering the Interior Ministry to handle domestic repression was a straightforward task. Less obvious, however, was what to do with the ruling party. The Nasser-built Arab Socialist Union needed rehabilitation, not just in terms of structure, but also—more fundamentally—in terms of its social base. The ASU that Sadat had inherited from his predecessor relied mostly on state functionaries (party cadres, bureaucrats, and public-sector workers) and middling landlords. These were no longer sufficient. For one thing, public functionaries—some 3.2 million in 1978—were likely to remain neutral when their employers bickered, as was proven in May 1971, when the president and his ministers fought it out and government cadres remained paralyzed, not knowing which side to support. Also, village notables (an estimated 3,600 middling landowners) had been— and would likely remain—provincial in outlook. They could garner votes in their home districts, or march out to welcome government dignitaries, but they certainly lacked the interest or the capacity to intervene in national political struggles. Hence, the support of public functionaries and village notables could only be subsidiary. The ruling party now needed an active social base that identified its interests with those of the party and would be ready to fight for them when necessary. In short, Egypt needed a new political elite.

What should this be? Reverting back to the military to staff the political apparatus, as was the case before the changes brought about by the ASU in 1962, was out of the question. The whole point behind revamping the ruling party was to counterweigh the military. Bringing in police officers to do the job would end the relative autonomy of the political apparatus, which the president represented; it would spell the end of politics. While security officers would now be exclusively responsible for rooting out domestic contenders, they could not be charged with actually running the government. Besides, even if a political order could survive for a while on naked coercion, its long-term stability required a broad social alliance. Because Sadat wanted a loyal social base that owed nothing to Nasser, and because he knew that opening up the economy was a nonnegotiable item on the American agenda, he resolved to entrust the ruling party to the hands of an emerging capitalist class. As the Middle East scholar Raymond Hinnebusch put it, "Sadat, lacking the stature to pursue Nasser's centrist balancing act between elite and mass, needed a solid support base underpinning his legal authority; since his rivals were on the left and his potential support on the right, a rightward course which would win over the power bourgeoisie made the most sense," a decision further encouraged by his "diplomatic realignment" with the United States and the need to "stimulate and reinforce American interest in Egypt, to make him a suitable client."[243] The CIA operative Miles Copeland reported that even under Nasser there were huge pressures from American investors to access the Egyptian market and set up joint enterprises with Egyptians.[244] In other words, all the signs were pointing toward the need for a business class, a solid interest group with a real stake in the regime. The president's first challenge now was to find (or create) one.

Military-backed regimes in places such as Turkey, Chile, or Indonesia were based on an alliance between generals and capitalists united by fear of an organized Communist movement. Yet the military regime in Egypt was established too early. Neither capitalists nor Communists had sufficiently developed their interests, nor had their struggle matured. Instead of having to pick a side in a clearly polarized society, the July 1952 regime nationalized the class struggle and presented itself as the custodian of the nation as a whole. Moreover, it succeeded throughout the 1950s and 1960s to preempt the development of autonomous social groups, and effectively abolished the political arena in its entirety. By the time Sadat came to power, social groups could no longer perceive themselves independently of the state; they could develop organically only within it.[245] If Sadat needed a business elite, he had to nurture one himself. This was the goal of his open-door economic policy, commonly known as *al-Infitah* (The Opening).

But where could one find the material to produce this new elite? The large landowning class had been severely damaged by the land-reform laws, the middling landowners lacked cohesion, and the capitalists refused to invest under Nasser's arbitrary laws. To the extent that there was a class that controlled the means and resources of production, it was the state bourgeoisie of the public sector and the bureaucracy, some 34,000 public-sector managers and 11,000 senior administrators. This class was badly hurt by the 1967 crisis in the balance-of-payments and budget deficits, and the subsequent economic deterioration. By the end of Nasser's reign they had become convinced that they had to look out for themselves, and thus began acting as catalysts for private capital in return for profit shares and commissions. Sadat thus found his initial base in the state bourgeoisie. "With a foot in high state office and assets in private society, this group was not only the most strategic social force, but the one most prepared to accept his leadership."[246] Hence, between 1971 and 1980, and despite all talk of economic liberalization, state employment grew by 70 percent; in the last three years of his tenure alone, employment in the civil service increased by 10 percent annually, a percentage greater than the 8.5 percent recorded average during Nasser's years.[247]

Now this unwieldy class was expected to systematically let out business to a select group of private entrepreneurs in order to transform
disparate landowners, merchants, and contractors into a coherent group
of capitalists that would remain intrinsically linked to political authority. This was relatively easy considering that the state was responsible
for issuing foreign-trade and building permits, offering tax exemptions,
pardoning tax evasion, providing loans through public banks (without
asking for collateral), allocating land at nominal prices, and so on. What
the state simply did was not reduce its role in economic life, but rather
shift its function from channeling accumulated surplus toward development, to becoming a sort of middleman between public resources
and acquisitive capitalists, both domestic and foreign. One might say
that what happened during those years was less state-fostered capitalism
than "state-fostered corruption."[248]

To breathe life into this new capitalist class and give it some character, Sadat decided to rehabilitate some of the "old money" families.
In December 1970 (barely two months after Nasser passed away), he
formed a committee under the future foreign minister Esmat Abd
al-Magid to redress past injustices by returning the sequestered agricultural and financial properties of the pre-1952 elite, some six hundred
families.[249] His aim was that yesterday's landowners would become
today's capitalists.

Even workers and peasants joined the bonanza. The increase in oil
prices that followed (and was partly caused by) the October War triggered an exponential growth in migration of the Egyptian poor to
Libya, Iraq, and the Gulf countries, an increase from 58,000 migrants
in 1970 to more than 5 million in 1980.[250] Migrants invested most of
their funds in Egypt, and returned to join the expanding business class.
Their ideological outlook had changed in the meantime from how to
secure their economic rights in the village and the factory to simply
how to make money. A 1996 survey revealed that 92.2 percent of
workers neither belonged to a political party nor held any ideological
views, and among the small percentage that did, 85.7 percent joined the
ruling party.[251]

Then came Law 43 of 1974, which officially inaugurated Infitah by
opening up the country to foreign investment and abolishing many
of the Nasser-era restrictions. Sadat enforced Infitah quite aggressively,
requiring the economic group in his cabinet to always consult with
him so that he could "facilitate" their work. Then in 1976, he replaced
the business professor Abd al-Aziz Hegazy with Interior Minister
Mamduh Salem as prime minister, justifying his decision as follows:
"When I saw tardiness and procrastination, I changed the government
… Today, Mamduh is tearing down all measures and constraints that
inhibit economic freedom."[252] As Bahaa al-Din explained, Hegazy's

crime was that he believed that economic liberalization was actually intended to rebuild the Egyptian economy, but on a new, capitalist basis. Little did he know that it was part of a political deal Sadat made with the Americans, a deal to transform Egypt from a potentially "industrial state to a service state," a perpetually dependent market on foreign products and largesse.[253]

So while Sadat claimed that Infitah encouraged industrial capitalism, the numbers say otherwise. An enormous amount of money was sucked into the real estate business and various forms of commercial activities. Between 1970 and 1980, return on investment in construction jumped from 42.1 to 62.8 percent, while wholesale commerce marked an even higher increase, from 43.6 to 75.4 percent.[254] The number of agents for foreign companies climbed from a few dozen in 1974 to 16,000 by 1981, and commercial projects consumed 42 percent of total bank loans during the same period.[255] By the end of the 1970s, "Cairo became a city of middlemen and commission agents for Europeans and Americans ... shuttling between luxury hotels and government ministries, wheeling and dealing on an ever-increasing scale." In a country that had no millionaires in 1970, more than 17,000 sprang into existence by 1980, and 7,000 of those simply became millionaires through land speculation. In the second half of the 1970s, 53.5 percent of the land owned by the state on the Mediterranean Sea was "passed into private hands without any payment being made"—this land alone was resold on the private market for £E4 billion.[256] Building construction in the second half of the seventies rose by 107 percent, more than 90 percent of which consisted of luxury apartments, villas, and vacation houses. Another indicator: between 1974 and 1979, 43 percent of the national investments, and 60 percent of the foreign aid and loans, were devoted to construction.[257]

Indeed, by 1987, nonindustrial sectors (mainly services and construction) represented 60 percent of the country's GDP and employed 53 percent of the workforce, at the same time that the industrial sector represented a humble 19 percent of GDP and employed 14 percent of the workforce, and agriculture represented 21 percent and employed 33 percent.[258] The economics professor Mahmoud Abd al-Fadeel in fact compared Egypt's deindustrialization under American tutelage in the 1970s with the deindustrialization forced upon Muhammad Ali by European powers after his 1840 defeat.[259] Sadat was thus the founder of the Egyptian dependent state, the nondeveloping, deindustrialized, and randomly liberalized state; Mubarak only followed in his footsteps.

To make maters worse, Egypt began to sink into debt. In 1971, Egypt's civilian debt amounted to $1.3 billion, but it was mostly allocated toward strategic projects and the importing of strategic goods, such as the $380 million loan provided by the Soviets to help build the High Dam and heavy industries, and the $205 million owed to the United States for wheat shipments. Military debt, on the other hand, was $1.7 billion, almost all incurred on relaxed credit terms provided by Russians. Merely a decade later (in 1981), civilian debt had jumped to $19.5 billion (mostly owed to the United States), and military debt to $5.7 billion. In other words, Sadat's ten-year tenure increased Egypt's foreign debt ten times. Worst still, three-quarters of Egypt's civilian debt went to financing consumption. Not only that, but also instead of using increased oil revenues (which grew 40 percent annually as a result of the oil boom) to pay off some of the debt, the extra cash was again directed toward consumption.[260] As for the military debt, the situation was even more unsettling. Egypt fought five wars in the twenty years between 1955 and 1975 using $2.2 billion worth of Soviet arms, of which $500 million was provided as aid. In comparison, during the short five years between 1975 and 1981 Egypt fought no wars (nor planned to fight any) yet it incurred a $6.6 billion debt to the United States, in addition to an extra $650 million per year to service this debt.[261]

The American government and private investors played a crucial part in shaping this economic reality. They were both the architects of the Sadat-era changes and its primary benefactors. By his own admission, Sadat's primary economic adviser was David Rockefeller, whose frequent visits to Egypt struck a chord with a president known for his love of celebrities and powerful men. Sadat not only bragged about how the rich and famous magnate was his "friend"—just like Kissinger and Carter were supposedly his friends—but he also gave him access to all economic data on Egypt and consulted him on every major decision. Needless to mention, Rockefeller did not always have his friend's best interests in mind, but was keen on promoting his own business and that of other American investors.[262] More worrying, however, was the fact that on the Egyptian side there were no pressures to pursue or abandon certain policies. Sadat could rule as he pleased. This was expected considering that there were no domestic pressures on the regime to open up the economy to start with, but it was rather a top-down decision, motivated in large part by American pressure. Naturally, as soon as the Egyptian market was open to foreign goods, American merchandise began pouring in. Between 1974 and 1984, Egypt imported $2.8 billion of American goods, constituting 33 percent of all Egyptian imports, at the same time that Egyptian exports to the U.S. market were a meager $33 million, representing only 8 percent of total Egyptian exports. The imbalance becomes even clearer when one considers that 85 percent of Egyptian exports to the United States represented only one item: oil.[263] This, of course, made sense considering that American investors secured 70 percent of the profits made in the petroleum business in Egypt, some $9.5 billion in a single decade (1974–1984). On a smaller scale, the imbalance in trade relations was exemplified in the case of one sector of the U.S. economy: milling. In 1983, Egypt became the largest foreign customer for American millers, importing products for $2.31 billion. In return, Egypt's strong milling industry not only suffered, but its exports to U.S. markets were met with strict protectionist barriers, allowing only $218 million to get in that year (1983). But it was U.S. banks that made the highest returns during the first years of Infitah. Between 1974 and 1980, private banks in Egypt had increased from zero to fifty-six, and many of these were American. By 1985, U.S. banks had already drawn $9.9 billion worth of foreign currency deposits. The bulk of these were then transferred abroad, thus depriving the Egyptian economy of valuable savings. In sum, it is clear that Infitah benefited U.S. investors considerably, as reflected in the phenomenal surge in exports to Egypt, and the substantial profits reaped in the petroleum and banking sectors.[264]

During the period between 1974 and 1984, the United States also offered Sadat's government $15 billion in the form of loans and aid. This was the first installment in the massive USAID program that began supplying Egypt with $2.3 billion annually after its signing of the peace treaty with Israel in 1979. Although the aid package was primarily meant to boost the Egyptian economy, the United States made substantial gains. To start with, USAID conditions required the Egyptian government to use aid funds to pay for "excessive US consultancy services ... [and the] often overpriced American goods and services," in addition to sustaining the inflated USAID bureaucracy (1,030 employees in Egypt in the 1970s compared with only 4 in Israel). Further, the United States retained the right to decide on investment priorities, thus leading some to refer to USAID as Egypt's "shadow cabinet." One example stands out: although Egypt desperately needed to develop its industries to satisfy its growing market and increase its exports (and thus remedy its chronic trade-balance deficit), the United States directed 82 percent of its aid in 1978 to the petroleum sector, which primarily served the American market, and spent less than 4 percent on industry. "On balance, therefore, it would seem fair to say that American aid to Egypt has reaped substantial American dividends in terms of investment and trade."[265]

Sadat himself lobbied directly on behalf of American investors. For example, when his cabinet turned down Rockefeller's offer to open up a branch of the Chase-Manhattan Bank in Egypt in 1973, the president not only overruled his ministers, but in order to exempt the new branch from restrictions on foreign finance, he decreed that a merger take place between Chase and one of Egypt's largest public-sector banks, the National Bank. Sadat also interfered in a Boeing deal with the Egyptian national airline. Egypt Air was about to reject the overly expensive offer when it received the following letter from Sadat's secretary: "Dear Sir, the President has given orders that the agreement with Boeing and the accompanying financial arrangements should be signed immediately."[266] Then, in 1974, against the advice of his ministers, Sadat authorized the formation of the first business lobby in the country, the Egypt-U.S. Joint Business Council—renamed the American Chamber of Commerce in Egypt (AmCham) in 1981. This interest group expectedly wielded tremendous power because of its direct links to the presidency. As a study of AmCham recommendations during its first years of operation revealed, the lobby became deeply involved in shaping national economic policy rather than just removing obstacles to U.S. investment.[267]

As the 1980s dawned, Egypt was effectively locked into the course that Sadat had set. Domestically, Infitah had made the regime dependent on an expansive bourgeoisie "unprepared to give up opportunities for commercial and speculative enrichment or to trim its new life of consumption"; reversal was made even harder by the fact that Egypt's massive dependency on the United States left it vulnerable to mounting foreign pressures to surrender the economy further into the hands of this consumption bourgeoisie,[268] a class who, in the words of the prominent Egyptian economist Ibrahim Oweiss, "devoted their activities to short-term trade, reaping high cash profits that have ... often been hoarded in the form of cash or jewelry, or spent on unnecessary luxuries, lavish consumption, or otherwise invested or saved abroad."[269] Heikal drew a stark comparison between them and the pre-July 1952 elite: "The old feudal class ... was small and exploiting, but at least its wealth and ambitions were based on land ownership. Its stake in the soil of Egypt meant that it was never wholly alienated, never devoid of fundamental patriotism, which comes from putting down roots. But the new rich had no roots."[270]

This was Nasser's greatest fear. As he one day told the director of the International Monetary Fund, Nasser was sure that a state that basically provides raw materials and services to the industrialized world, and whose economic elite are largely merchants and speculators, rather than industrialists, will shortly become the victim of "an unpatriotic, corrupted wealthy class which contributes nothing substantial to the product of the country and which is inclined to export its profits to Switzerland."[271] Ignoring Nasser's warning, Sadat infested the ruling party with the germ whose future covetousness would eventually pull the roof down in January 2011. As Heikal sardonically concluded, "Indeed, Egypt was not being transformed from a planned to a market economy, but rather to a supermarket economy ... Egyptian society was now divided between the 'fat cats' and their hangers-on, perhaps 150,000 people at most, on one side, and the rest of the population on the other."[272] World Bank statistics revealed an increase in the income of the top 5 percent on the income scale from 17 percent to 22 percent between 1970 and 1980, with an adjacent drop in the income of the lowest 20 percent on the income scale from 7 to 5 percent; all with a rate of inflation reaching a staggering 35 percent in 1979.[273]

All the above notwithstanding, Sadat finally had his new political elite, a veritable pyramid with state-nurtured capitalists on top, old ASU cadres and their rural allies in the middle, and state employees and workers (who either made gains as middlemen or lacked skills to survive outside the public sector) at the base. The new political alliance was stronger than ever. For the first time since 1952, it combined society's real economic elite with bureaucratic officials and political cadres. What was needed now was a political vessel through which Sadat could shore up their support. Hence, the National Democratic Party (NDP) was born.

Sadat had announced plans to reform the ASU back in July 1971, and again after the Permanent Constitution was approved by referendum in September 1971. But it was only after the war and Infitah that he began to reconstruct the political system. In January 1976, Sadat formed three *manabir* (platforms), representing the left, right, and center within the ASU. Prime Minister (and former interior minister and state security officer) Mamduh Salem was put in charge of the sizable centrist platform. The three platforms were then transformed into political parties via Law 40 of 1977, with the centrist platform becoming the new ruling party, first called the Egypt Socialist Party, and then renamed the National Democratic Party in July 1978. Sadat subsequently decreed that the Political Parties Committee, chaired by the NDP secretary-general, must approve any new party. The aim was to engineer a political system with a hegemonic ruling party flanked by an ensemble of loyal opposition parties from left and right.

So while the ASU was officially dissolved, in reality what happened was that its six million members simply transferred to the new party. In fact, the NDP was described as a carbon copy of the ASU: it was headed by the president; it occupied the same headquarters and regional offices; it drew funds from the state budget; it advertised freely in the state media; it received administrative support from the bureaucracy; it mobilized the same public-sector employees (both white- and blue-collar); it plugged into the same village notables' network; it employed the same corrupt opportunist cadres; and it relied on the Interior Ministry to rig elections and repress opposition. The primary difference, of course, was that after the methodical housecleaning occasioned by the transformation of the ASU to the NDP, the ruling-party elite was no longer composed of political functionaries, but rather state-nurtured businessmen. The ruling party and the parliament, which it controlled, began to cater to the needs of the rising capitalist class.

To bring these economic and political changes into focus, it might be instructive to briefly survey the career of one of the prototypes of this new political elite: the business tycoon, cabinet member, and NDP leader Osman Ahmed Osman. Osman was a contractor who opened business in the 1940s and presided over his Arab Contractors Company, which evolved into an empire in the 1960s. Through his acquaintance with General Commander Abd al-Hakim Amer and Sadat he skirted the worst effects of the nationalization wave, for although his company was officially nationalized in 1961 he retained effective control of its operations—as did 75 percent of the businessmen whose companies were nationalized. Like many, Osman's principal client was the government, whether in Egypt or in other Arab states: in 1953, he built the first Saudi military installations, including the kingdom's military academy; he established missile launch sites, concrete hangers and bunkers, and military bases in Iraq in the 1950s, in Libya in the mid-1960s, and in Abu Dhabi in 1968; he also executed civilian projects, such as the building of the Kuwaiti parliament and city councils in 1954. Osman's military-intelligence connections in Egypt then secured his grandest project: a commission to build the High Dam in the late 1950s. Amer also charged him with rebuilding Port Said after its destruction in 1956. This is the year he first met Sadat, and in his words, they became the "closest of friends."[274]

When Sadat took power, Osman was commissioned to build the longest causeway-bridge in Egypt, the October 6 Bridge; he then received a £E40 million commission to build bunkers, aircraft hangers, and missile bases in 1970; he was tasked in 1972 with creating floating tank carriers to be used in the crossing of the Suez Canal, and immediately following the crossing he was asked to build bridges connecting the east and west banks. On October 1973 he was appointed minister of construction, his task being to rebuild the Suez Canal cities and clear and expand the canal itself, relying primarily on his own company. Sadat added to his ministerial portfolio responsibility for food security in 1974, allowing him for the first time to expand his business beyond construction to fields as diverse as transportation, food production (fisheries, poultry farms, livestock rearing, and agriculture produce), and land reclamation (of more than 50,000 feddans). It was difficult to compete with a man who had official access to public resources and permits. Osman then went on to create one of the first private banks in Egypt, the Suez Canal Bank, in addition to his very own sports club. Osman was finally promoted in November 1976 to deputy prime minister for development, and head of the NDP's Development Committee.[275] During the last year of his tenure as construction minister (1981), he allocated a total of £E3.7 billion to construction projects, half of which went to his Arab Contractors. Arab Contractors also received two million square meters of army-owned land for free in Cairo (the area known as al-Jebel al-Ahmar in Cairo's Abbasiyeh neighborhood), and when an army major general opposed the deal, he was forced to resign. All in all, three-quarters of the money Osman used to establish his projects were therefore public money.[276]

Osman provided Sadat many political favors in return. He used his strong links with the Muslim Brothers to guarantee their support for Sadat and direct their vehemence against left-wing activists at universities, labor unions, and other associations. Following Sadat's dismissal of Aly Sabri on May 2, Osman "rushed to the company headquarters and loaded a hundred buses with workers and ordered them to surround the president's house to keep him out of harm's way." He then helped defame Sadat's enemies, corroborating the view that the centers of power were Soviet agents, and claiming that he had witnessed firsthand how Chief of Staff Saad al-Din al-Shazly was "hesitant, disturbed, unsettled" during the 1973 war. Osman also famously joined Sadat on his 1977 trip to Israel in a show of support. He then engineered Sadat's economic partnership with local and foreign businesses. As minister, he orchestrated USAID involvement in Egypt's economic life, and offered favorable terms to several American conglomerates, starting with Coca-Cola. He also helped set up more than eighty private firms during his years at the NDP. In his memoirs, he summarized his economic role as follows: "My policy was to open the door for the private sector to lead economic life."[277]

Osman was therefore the quintessential representative of the new ruling class: a man who expanded his capital through state commissions, and then went on to assume a leading role in government and the ruling party. It is important here to compare his fortunes under Nasser and Sadat. While Osman made a living under Nasser as a public-sector manager, he had no influence over economic, let alone political life. With Sadat in power, he not only made unfathomable financial gains, but he also became a major economic and political player. This pattern would continue with little change during Mubarak's rule.

Of course the NDP was not only an economic powerhouse, but also a small intelligence apparatus. This was mediated through the security-oriented Vanguard Organization, whose 150,000 members flocked en masse to the NDP and controlled key party and government positions.*

★ A quick survey of the careers of prominent VO members suffices to demonstrate that they constituted the core of Egypt's political elite; these included Speakers of Parliament under Sadat (Labib Shukir, Sayed Mar'ie) and Mubarak (Ref'at al-Mahgoub, Helmi Murad, Mustafa Kamal Helmi, Fathy Sourur); prime ministers under Sadat (Mustafa Khalil, Mamduh Salem) and Mubarak (Abd al-Aziz Hegazi,

But as strong as the NDP became, it could barely have operated without the blanket protection provided by the Interior Ministry. The ministry not only managed day-to-day repression, but it was also involved in every aspect of the political life of the ruling party: it screened applicants for NDP membership; it investigated rising businessmen; it intimidated and subdued anti-NDP elements at universities, factories, and villages; and it rigged parliamentary, student, and syndicate elections to guarantee NDP majority. In short, NDP authoritarianism was possible only in the shadow of what was decidedly becoming a full-fledged police state.

NEMESIS: THE MILITARY AND THE POLICE UNDER SADAT

The fact that the Interior Ministry dislodged the military from the center stage of politics and acquired many of its prerogatives naturally provoked mutual hostility. While ASU secretaries-general had always come from a military background, the new ruling party was born under the watchful eyes of a police officer: Mamduh Salem. Sadat also made sure that policemen more so than military officers were now appointed as provincial governors. More disturbing still was the amount of power accrued by interior ministers under Sadat, especially the notorious al-Nabawi Ismail, who held the position in the second half of the 1970s. Ismail was one of the few police officers that stood against Naguib and helped organize the March 1954 demonstrations that brought the pro-democracy camp down. He was rewarded by a job in the postcoup secret police and rose through the ranks of what later became the State Security Investigations Sector. He became chief aide to Salem, the first police officer to hold the post of interior minister, in 1971, then prime minister in 1976. After the ministry's failure in dealing with the January 1977 Food Riots (discussed below), Sadat brought in Ismail to toughen up the police force. Ismail proudly confessed that he became so powerful under Sadat that he was the one who "nominated" future cabinet members, including the prime minister. In a famous episode, when Sadat formed the NDP and wanted those who had joined the transitional Egypt Socialist Party to switch, Ismail walked in on one of the party meetings and ordered its members to transfer to the new party without delay.[278]

But what drove military officers through the roof was that they increasingly came under the purview of the ministry's SSIS. The

Aziz Sedqi, Fuad Muhyi al-Din, Atif Sedqi); interior ministers and intelligence directors under Sadat (Nabawi Ismail, Ahmed Kamel); foreign ministers and prominent diplomats under Sadat (Murad Ghalib) and Mubarak (Esmat Abd al-Magid, Amr Musa, Usama Baz, Mustafa al-Fiqi); in addition to several other ministers and ruling party leaders under Mubarak (Aly al-Din Hilal, Kamal al-Shazly, Hussein Kamil Baha' al-Din, Abd al-Hadi Kandil, and others) (Sharaf, *'Abd al-Nasser: Keif hakam masr?* 191–221).

former chief of staff Saad al-Din al-Shazly recalled chairing an appraisal committee composed of fifteen generals in 1972. When he submitted to the war minister the committee's recommendations for military promotions, the latter struck out a few names, citing SSIS reports as the reason. Another example was when Egypt received a shipment of T-62s (Russia's most advanced tanks at the time) and the general staff decided in a meeting on February 26, 1972, to send them immediately to the front, only to discover the next day that the tanks would have to remain in Cairo until tank brigade leaders were cleared by security. A third example occurred during a meeting between the president and his commanders on March 19, 1972, when he accused senior officers of turning the soldiers against his policies, and when the attendees denied, he produced an SSIS operative from an anteroom to elaborate on the charges.[279] A fourth example was Sadat's purging of War Minister Muhammad Sadeq and his senior aides based on security reports that he was becoming too popular within the ranks and critical of the president's policies.[280] A fifth example is Sadat's charging his security aide, the PBI director, Ashraf Marawan, to negotiate arms imports before the 1973 war, rather than sending a military delegation.[281] A final example was charging the SSIS deputy director, Fouad Allam, to investigate an alleged plot by middle-ranking officers in March 1981.[282]

As the competition between the military and the Interior Ministry intensified, the two institutions were severely tested by the January 1977 riots. Sadat's economic liberalization demanded the gradual lifting of government subsidies, something citizens had been taking for granted for almost three decades. So following a government decision to halve its subsidies (thus raising the price of flour, rice, sugar, and other basic commodities), millions took to the streets. The January 18–19, 1977, Food Riots were the largest and most violent since the 1952 coup, so violent that Sadat had to escape from Aswan to Cairo in a helicopter before the angry masses attacked his house. Knowing that the police was still ill-equipped to deal with riots as widespread and aggressive as these, Sadat was forced to call in the army. War Minister Gamasy, however, said he would not order his men in unless Sadat's government rescinded the controversial decision, which the president was propelled to do. Order was finally restored, after 160 demonstrators were killed, 800 injured, and 5,000 arrested.[283] State Security General Assem al-Genedi and his colleagues received orders from Sadat to keep track of every army vehicle and officer on the street because he suspected that the war minister was planning to carry out a coup. Not surprisingly, a bitter Sadat refused to acknowledge the role of the military in his public address following the riots, and asked all newspapers to follow suit. The lesson learned was that marginalizing the military required militarizing the police. General Al-Genedi said that the Interior Ministry immediately devised Plan 100, which determined how to control the state in the case of another popular revolt—this is the plan that failed miserably in January 2011.[284]

Aided by the ruthless al-Nabawi Ismail, the president began to augment the police force in numbers and weapons. The paramilitary Central Security Forces was rapidly inflated from 100,000 to 300,000 troops in 1977 and its arsenal was upgraded from batons and rifles to tear-gas canisters and armored vehicles.[285] In 1979 alone, the United States supplied the CSF with 153,946 tear-gas bombs, 2,419 automatic weapons, and 328,000 rubber bullets.[286] The CSF was thus set on the path to obviate the need to call on the military to restore public order; now the army would not serve as the regime's last resort. As one analyst put it, "If SSIS comprised the eyes, ears, and interrogator of the regime, the CSF was its instrument of brute force."[287] Expectedly, the degree of mistrust between Sadat and his army deteriorated to a point where he asked the Interior Ministry to handle his personal safety inside the Defense Ministry and other military bases.[288] The relationship between the soldiers and their leader was at its lowest ebb since the Nasser-Amer showdown in 1967. Colonel Muhammad Selim, who was serving his last days in the military, recalls some of the discussions he had with his colleagues back then.

> We understood that the general strategy was to weaken the army and strengthen the police force. This began with Mamduh Salem in 1971, but it picked up only after al-Nabawi Ismail took over the Interior Ministry in 1977. We lived to see the day when the interior minister became the most powerful man in Egypt. We also followed how the CFS was being propped up to take over riot control. We were quickly becoming dispensable. And there was nothing we could do about it.[289]

At this point, the Interior Ministry decided to flex its muscles in what Heikal aptly described as the "autumn of fury." Drunk with power, al-Nabawi Ismail decided on September 3 to detain three thousand of the country's leading intellectuals, journalists, clerics, priests, and members of all opposition groups—including Heikal. The aim was to lock them up until they learned their lesson and stopped criticizing Sadat's policies. Although the SSIS deputy director, Fouad Allam, had serious misgivings about this vicious campaign, he claimed he was powerless against an interior minister who believed he could take on the entire country. In fact, Allam recorded in his memoirs that his boss had originally recommended a list of 12,000 dissidents to be detained and was persuaded by more practical policemen to cut it down.[290] Two days after the mass arrests, Sadat delivered a fiery speech in Parliament, celebrating what he called the "September revolution"; gloating that one of the detainees (who happened to be a revered Islamist preacher) was "rotting in prison like a dog"; and yelling at his petrified audience: "Beware! I will no longer show mercy toward anyone!"[291]

THE CLOSING ACT

On October 6, 1981, Egyptians followed the annual victory parade celebrating the heroic crossing of the Suez Canal on the first day of the 1973 war. They knew that this one was different (though little did they realize how different). It was supposed to be the biggest parade of its kind, marking the eighth anniversary of the October War with an exhibition of Western (mostly American) weapons that Egypt had recently acquired, and it was organized a few months before Israel's final withdrawal from Sinai (in April 1982), and barely a month after Sadat's largest crackdown on domestic opposition (in September 1981). All the country's leaders and dozens of foreign dignitaries were seated in the review stand around the president in his London-tailored Prussian-style military uniform covered with ribbons and stars (that he had awarded himself) and a green shoulder-to-waist scarf (which he called the Sash of Justice) as officers and cadets marched in their shiny uniforms; as endless files of tanks and artillery guns trailed along with their crews saluting the supreme commander; and as American fighters thundered above in tight formations, twisting and diving and spewing trails of colored smoke behind them. The parade was supposed to symbolize the power and greatness of Sadat's achievements during his decade-long tenure. How the event ended was no less symbolic. At the precise moment that Sadat was gazing up at the new jets, an armored vehicle broke away from a column of twelve trailered artillery guns and made its way toward him. Four assassins launched themselves from the vehicle, throwing grenades at the reviewing stand and firing their rifles at the audience. In forty seconds, the president was gunned down with nine others, and another twenty-eight were injured. Although a record thirty-nine shots pierced Sadat's body, the medical report cited as cause of death: nervous shock.* And expectedly so: this was the first time in recorded history that Egyptians had assassinated their Pharaoh. To add insult to injury, very few people bothered to attend his funeral—forcing the American television anchor Barbara Walters to speculate that if Sadat could see from above how little Egyptians cared for him, he would die a second time, of grief.[292] As Heikal commented:

> At the time, a good many people in the West saw the assassination of Sadat as just another of those apparently senseless acts of violence which have destroyed ... so many prominent public figures ... Nothing could

---

* The medical report was printed in *Al-Akhbar* 9149: 3. Cairo (6/7/1981).

be further from the truth ... The forces that conspired against Sadat were just as much a part of the mainstream in Egyptian society as were the forces which overthrew the Shah from the mainstream in Iran ... This was tragically and graphically illustrated at his funeral, when he was taken to his grave by a most imposing galaxy of foreign statesmen, including three former Presidents of the United States and the Prime Minister of Israel, but with only a handful of his own fellow-countrymen as mourners.[293]

Sadat's assassination is one of the least-examined episodes in studies on Egypt. The assassination itself was admittedly one of the most spectacular in modern history. Rather than killing Sadat by poison, a roadside bomb, or some invisible sniper, the assassins decided to execute him in public—military-style—by a firing squad. All symbolism aside, the assassination and its aftermath shed light on the new power configuration that had crystallized by the forced end of Sadat's reign. It is therefore unfortunate that analysts have tended to dutifully ignore this momentous event, or at best treat it as a dramatic yet isolated episode of Islamist militancy, on account of the fact that those who pulled the trigger were religious zealots. The assassins' ties to the military have been regularly downplayed, and the context within which the assassination took place was inexplicably blurred. These omissions, however, cannot be sustained in light of the following facts. First, the assassins had all served in the military: the ringleader was an artillery first lieutenant (Khaled al-Islambouly of the 333rd Artillery Brigade), another was a national guard sergeant and former infantry marksman, a third was a reserve first lieutenant, and the last was a former air defense officer. Second, the assassination plot was masterminded by a renegade colonel in Military Intelligence and an October War hero who had a street in Cairo named after him (Abbud al-Zumur—who was instantly released by the military following the 2011 revolt after three decades in prison). Third, the assassination itself occurred during a military parade in a military-secured zone (with three checkpoints to ensure that no live ammunition entered the parade ground). Fourth, Interior Minister al-Nabawi Ismail revealed that the original assassination plan had an air force fighter crash into the reviewing stand—kamikaze-style—which means that the plotters had links with air force pilots,[294] and the operation's mastermind, Abbud al-Zumur, also confessed he had recruited officers in the Republican Guard.[295] Fifth, interrogations revealed that the assassins asked Defense Minister Abd al-Halim Abu Ghazala and other military leaders to step aside as they opened fire, and yelled that their targets were the president and his interior minister. Sixth, although the lead assassin was marked as an Islamist radical by Military Intelligence (he was interrogated by the MID in October 1980 for his Islamist militancy, but the investigation was shelved), and although his brother was detained a few days before the parade for the same charge, he was still allowed to participate in the parade.[296] Seventh, the assassination was supposed to serve as the opening act in a full-fledged bid for power spearheaded by a coup and supported by a popular uprising[297]—the fact that such an attempt was even thinkable points to the widespread feeling that the military has abandoned the regime, and that given the chance it would join the revolt or at least not suppress it. Eighth, as the former chief of staff Saad al-Din al-Shazly indicated in an interview with *Newsweek* days following the assassination, the officers he maintained contact with were convinced that the assassination was a step in the right direction.[298] Finally, many of the reasons the plotters gave for killing Sadat were military-related. Following his release from prison in March 2011, al-Zumur said in an interview: "We assassinated Sadat because he accepted an end to the military conflict between the Arabs and Israel … which depreciated Egypt's regional weight."[299]

In fact, al-Zumur was reportedly hesitant to authorize the assassination because he believed that in a few months he could recruit enough officers to allow him to take power effortlessly.[300] Fouad Allam, deputy director of the SSIS, said that investigations revealed that a coup by middle-ranking officers was actually planned in March 1981, but his men preempted it.[301] To top it all, Interior Minister Ismail had told the prime minister the night before the assassination that he was almost sure the president would not survive the parade because of the radicalism lurking within the ranks, and that he had warned Sadat that he would be particularly vulnerable in a military-controlled zone, but the president brushed his warning aside.[302] Major General Ahmed al-Fouli, one of Sadat's bodyguards during that fatal day, testified that Interior Minister Ismail had warned against this parade in particular.[303] Intriguingly, the SSIS got definite word regarding the assassination two hours beforehand, and quickly dispatched an envoy to evacuate Sadat, but Military Police prevented him from reaching the president or the interior minister.[304]

While none of the above indicates that the entire officer corps was implicated in the assassination, it does point toward three incontrovertible facts: that several military officers were involved in planning, executing, and covering up the assassination; that the assassins were confident that the military was at the very least indifferent toward Sadat's regime; and that, in the light of the above two facts, it was clear yet again that the military could not be trusted. This is why Robert Springborg rightly maintained that the assassination could not be explained apart from the "general dissatisfaction in the military."[305] It was not a separate incident, but rather the climactic moment in the life of a regime in crisis.

So why, then, did the attempt to seize power fail? Clearly, the plotters undermined the other coercive power in the ruling bloc, the junior partner that had come to age under Sadat: the police. Although a limited military force was dispatched to the southern provinces to preempt an Islamist uprising, the army played a minor role in restoring order. Whether negligent or complacent (or both), the military could not have been deployed fully at that stage. It was the police force that had to shoulder the burden. Hours after Sadat's death had been confirmed, the Interior Ministry was asked to implement Plan 100 to secure strategic government sites through CSF units; the SSIS then apprehended al-Zumur and the other ringleaders before they could cause any more damage; meanwhile, a specialized SSIS counterterrorist team (Intelligence Unit 75) was assigned the delicate mission of investigating the military's possible implication in the assassination.[306] The investigations lasted over two months, after which six artillery officers were court-martialed and an undisclosed number of officers were removed from service. Among those implicated were high-ranking officers such as Major General Mamduh Abu-Gabal from the artillery, and armory captain Essam al-Qamary, who reputably destroyed more Israeli tanks in 1973 than anyone else and was considered a war hero.[307] For Interior Ministry officers, this was baptism by blood. And they passed with flying colors. The CSF chief, General Abd al-Rahman al-Faramawy, who went on to become governor of Port Said under Mubarak, recalled proudly how effective and efficient the ministry was in the aftermath of the assassination.

> On the day Sadat was assassinated, I was at CSF headquarters. Without waiting to hear from the interior minister, I immediately put Plan 100 into effect. The plan arranged for CSF units to secure strategic sites, such as the television building and the major ministries, to preempt any possible coup. Over the next two days, I dispatched CSF troops to the south to deal with the threat of an Islamist insurgency down there. We were forced to rely on the military for transportation, especially since we needed helicopters. But we did not call on the army's help because it was then under SSIS investigation. Sadat was assassinated in a military-secured zone without a policeman in sight. It was widely believed during those early days that the officer corps was involved. We will never be completely sure, however, because the outcome of the investigations remains classified.[308]

By the time Mubarak began his long tenure, the course had already been set: the military had been marginalized and increasingly regarded with suspicion; the police had proven to be loyal and reliable; and the new NDP business elite had come to represent the regime's strongest social base. But there was one more challenge Mubarak had to overcome. Apparently, the army still had some fight left in it.

The Long Lull Before the Perfect Storm: Revolt in January 2011

"It was the best of times, it was the worst of times," opened Charles Dickens's haunting tale of the French Revolution. And so it was in Egypt during Muhammad Hosni Mubarak's imposing thirty-year reign—a reign longer than those of his two illustrious predecessors combined, and the longest in Egypt's modern history since Mohamed Ali (1805–1848). It was the best of times for the net beneficiaries of the July 1952 regime: a ruling class plundering with impunity, and security men who perceived themselves, in the words of one of their own, as the "masters of the country."* It was the worst of times for everyone else: the people, and the army.

BEFORE SINKING TO OBLIVION: THE MILITARY'S FINAL STAND

Egypt's fourth president was the first not to belong to the Free Officers Movement, although he graduated from the Military Academy three years before the 1952 coup. He spent the 1950s as an air force instructor, then traveled to Russia for further training, and returned to Egypt only in the mid-1960s. During the 1967 war, he famously alleged that American jets participated directly in the air strike against Egypt, aggravating the president when he failed to produce any evidence to back up his claim. After the war, Nasser removed him to an administrative job as director of the Air Force Academy. Mubarak's fortunes changed under Anwar al-Sadat, who favored low-profile and apolitical officers. He was appointed air force commander and deputy war minister in 1972, and promoted to vice president in 1975, where he—unlike many of Sadat's military and political subordinates—served his boss faithfully

---

* The security chief of one of Egypt's Nile Delta governorates (al-Behera) made this comment amid the January revolt, reminding his troops that they were the "masters of the country" and urging them to "cut the hands of those who dare to assault their masters," i.e., the demonstrators (Hassan, *Naql mudir amn al-Behera le-tatawulhu 'ala al-sha'b*, 3).

and never questioned his wisdom about realigning Egypt with the Western world. America in particular was so much on Mubarak's mind from the beginning that during one of his first interviews after taking office he bragged about how he had visited Washington so many times as vice president that he was frequently asked whether he owned a private suite in the Madison Hotel. In fact, he visited the American capital four times during the last year of Carter's administration, and met with Ronald Reagan days before Sadat's assassination in October 1981. Mubarak concluded his interview by affirming: "Without the United States it would have been difficult, if not impossible to achieve what President Sadat achieved. I am very confortable about dealing with the United States, and I will continue to do so and to enhance our relationship."*

By the time Mubarak came to power, the military had been considerably tamed. The purges of the 1950s and 1960s had removed politicized officers, while those of the 1970s retired or cashiered anyone who became either too popular or too loyal to the military (rather than to political masters). Major General Abd al-Halim Abu Ghazala (initially) seemed to be none of the above. He was only two years younger than Mubarak and began his military career around the same time. But unlike Mubarak he had joined the Free Officers, participated in the 1948 and 1956 wars, and was not involved in the 1967 debacle. Abu Ghazala also played a field role in the 1973 war as artillery commander of the Second Army in Sinai (rather than spend the war by Sadat's side in Cairo like Mubarak). Also unlike the new president, Abu Ghazala was a military scholar who had penned several books on military science (including the application of mathematics in battle) and the art of warfare, always with an eye toward improving the combat performance of the Egyptian armed forces. Yet Abu Ghazala shunned politics and did not actively cultivate popularity among the troops, and so appeared to be nonthreatening to his superiors. Furthermore, he was removed from the corps after the war and appointed military attaché to Washington (between 1977 and 1980), where his role in setting up Egypt's new alliance with the United States could not have endeared him to his wary comrades. Abu Ghazala, moreover, seemed to have good chemistry with Mubarak. They worked together on cementing relations with the Pentagon, and it was the latter—acting in his capacity as vice president—who recommended him for the position of chief of staff in 1980, and then defense minister the following year. One of Mubarak's first decisions as president was to promote his ally to the rank of field marshal, which had remained vacant since Abd al-Hakim Amer's death, in addition to naming him deputy prime minister, a step up the protocol ladder. But like everyone else who assumed the top

---

* *Al-Ahram* 34634: 5. Cairo (10/9/1981).

military post in Egypt, starting with Amer and ending with Hussein Tantawy (Mubarak's last defense minister), Abu Ghazala chose the military over political loyalty. Instead of keeping the president's back, he sought to empower the armed forces through reaching out to the soldiers and the people, and securing as much personal support as he could get from the United States.

To start with, Abu Ghazala raised his men's wages and upgraded military facilities, vehicles, and even uniforms. Soon the soldiers were referring to him in their private conversations as "the man of the hour," "that shining star," "the savior" who had rescued the army from inevitable eclipse. More dangerous, from Mubarak's viewpoint, officers were comparing him with the first field marshal (Amer) in his generosity and camaraderie.[1] And sure enough, the relationship between Mubarak and Abu Ghazala became equally strained as that of Nasser and Amer before them. The new field marshal, however, was subtler than the old. He had no taste for rows, threats, or emotional outbursts. Instead, he sidestepped rather than confronted the president, and continued to nurture his power base within and outside the army. He raised no objections, for instance, against Mubarak's reshuffling of the general command in the fall of 1983 without consulting him. Nor did he complain when the president removed him from the ruling party in 1984, invoking a constitutional article (which Sadat had blissfully ignored after tightening his grip over the armed forces) prohibiting military officers from participating in politics. Abu Ghazala simply attended whichever NDP meeting he wished to attend, under various pretenses.[2]

Also, Abu Ghazala was more successful than Amer in getting to the masses; whether out of sincerity or cunning, he took the shortest and most effective route: religion. As Robert Springborg rightly noted, "In contrast to Mubarak's unhesitating preference for secularism, Abu Ghazala has cultivated an image of devoutness."[3] A few examples suffice. In a televised interview in October 1986, the field marshal brandished his piety by stressing how faith was essential to his soldiers' well-being, and snubbing calls to secularize the army.[4] A year later, in June 1987, he explained in an interview to the daily *Al-Ahram* that Egyptian military doctrine was "inspired by the Qur'an."[5] Further, Abu Ghazala repeatedly attacked the police's draconian methods against Islamists, leading the chief Muslim Brothers' activist Muhammad Abd al-Quddus to assert that the field marshal was one of the few state officials who appreciated "the Islamic impulse in Egyptian society and politics and was willing to come to terms with it."[6] It also helped that his wife donned the veil, and that his brother-in-law (Mukhtar Noah) was a renowned Islamist figure.

The field marshal's most serious overtures, however, were reserved for the Americans. Consistent with his reputation as an "outspoken conservative" in religious matters, he was also a "fervent anti-Communist" who emphasized that a militarily strong Egypt was the surest guarantee against Soviet infiltration of the region.[7] In an interview with *Aviation Week and Space Technology*, Abu Ghazala warned that Communists threatened American oil supplies through their presence in Ethiopia, Yemen, and Libya, and that building up Egypt's military power would help contain this threat because Egypt falls at the crossroads of the Mediterranean, the Red Sea, and the Indian Ocean, and one must safeguard these three maritime routes to guarantee the uninterrupted flow of oil to the non-Communist world.[8] In another interview, this time in the summer of 1988 in the weekly magazine *Al-Musawwar*, he remarked that Cairo and Washington had a common interest in strengthening Egypt.[9] It soon dawned on Mubarak that if there were ever a showdown between him and his field marshal, the United States would probably lean toward the latter. In fact, combining Abu Ghazala's popularity within the ranks, his pious public image, and the intimate links he developed with the United States made it seem that if the president wanted to remove him, he had to "contemplate a 'corrective' revolution of at least the magnitude that Sadat launched in May 1971."[10] That is, of course, unless Abu Ghazala committed some major blunder. Unfortunately for the military, he committed two.

The first blunder was agreeing to pull back his troops after being deployed in full force to quell the Central Security Forces' mutiny in February 1986 without bargaining to increase his institution's political leverage. Aggravated by rumors of a one-year extension to their three-year service term, and infuriated by years of abusive treatment at the hands of police officers and scandalously low wages and living standards, 17,000 CSF conscripts took to the streets on February 25, 1986, burning and looting indiscriminately throughout the capital. The Interior Ministry failed to respond. The CSF chief, General Abd al-Rahman al-Faramawy, explained that although the rumor was baseless, the ministry could not risk sending in other CSF units, because they might empathize with their comrades. Regular police troops were also inadequate; they were too few and armed only with pistols. "We were in a fix," General Faramawy continued; "the CSF was the striking arm of the police force, and now that its troops were out of control, who could rein them in?"[11] The president knew the answer. To his great apprehension, he was forced to declare a three-day curfew and call in the army. The Interior Ministry did not protest. Of course, the fact that they stood helpless as some of their own spread havoc must have stung. But they did not seem too concerned about the army. In the words of the CSF chief, "We knew that there was no love lost between the army and the CSF, and so they would certainly not join in. We also knew that Abu Ghazala was a professional and patriotic officer and would not seize the opportunity to stage a coup."[12] And rightly so, instead of seizing the opportunity to stage a coup that would reestablish military dominance over the regime (like the army did in 2011) or at least preempt its further weakening by the president, the army let the opportunity slip.

Deployed on the second day of the mutiny, the military came down with a vengeance against their old foes, killing 107 conscripts and injuring 715 others in a couple of days. On the third day of the rebellion, order was restored, and Abu Ghazala ordered his men back to barracks. It was a close call, and Mubarak must have sighed in relief as he watched the tanks and armored carriers roll back to their stations. Still, Abu Ghazala's popularity soared after this critical episode. His men showed discipline and efficiency, and exited the scene in the most dignified fashion. On the contrary, public opinion resented what was revealed about police mistreatment of their conscripts, as much as by their incompetence in dealing with the mess they created.

So why did the field marshal act so graciously? This might have been a testament to the successful subordination of the military from 1967 onward. Officers no longer harbored political ambitions, nor did they envisage carrying out a new coup. But the decision almost certainly derived from Abu Ghazala's overconfidence. This overconfidence was not entirely misplaced; the field marshal commanded the loyalty of his soldiers, the confidence and admiration of his countrymen, and the support of Egypt's chief foreign patron. He did not need to stage a coup, or seize any given opportunity to have his way with the regime—or so he thought. When Abu Ghazala received the veteran editor Mohamed Hassanein Heikal in his apartment a few days after the mutiny, he complained that Mubarak was turning against him. "The presidency never crossed my mind," asserted the field marshal. "I know the country's [dire] situation and I am happy where I am. If I wanted the presidency ... then during the events [the CSF mutiny] when my tanks were stationed everywhere in the capital, taking power would not have required more than dispatching one officer, no more (even a lieutenant), to the [state] television and radio studios to deliver a communiqué on my behalf. The whole story would have been over in five minutes. And the people would have welcomed [my coming to power]."[13] As it turned out, this was the military's last chance (until 2011) to replenish its rapidly depleting power. Now, a nonsuspecting Abu Ghazala committed his second, and evidently fatal, blunder.

The blow came on September 5, 1988, when the Israeli daily *Yediot Aharonot* reported on its front page that the Egyptian defense minister might stand trial in the United States for illegally acquiring (a polite way of saying "smuggling") American missile parts and technology without the Pentagon's permission. The missile in question was a

Scud-B variant with an extended (900-kilometer) range, which Abu Ghazala was hoping to produce through a trinational project (referred to as Project-T) that involved Iraq and Argentina. To make matters worse, the newspaper exposed how Abu Ghazala was also secretly negotiating a missile deal with North Korea, and was trying to develop chemical weapons behind America's back. The president realized he had to move quickly. The news doubtlessly boosted the field marshal's status within the army. But he had lost the support of the one party Mubarak worried about: the United States.[14]

In April 1989, Abu Ghazala was demoted to presidential aide. The menial tasks a president eager to demonstrate loyalty to Washington charged him with pushed him to resign in February 1993. To preempt the possibility of him entering civilian politics, the Interior Ministry claimed he was involved in the scandalous Lucy Artin affair, an explosive case of sex, bribery, and political abuse that rocked Cairo in April 1993. Abu Ghazala was accused by *Rose al-Youssef*, a weekly magazine close to the government, of courting the famous socialite and helping her win a land dispute in court against her ex-husband. To tarnish his religious image for good, the magazine added that the police had recorded several explicitly sexual calls between the two. It is true that the field marshal's name was cleared by court two years later, but the damage had already been done. Remarkably though, when Mubarak decided to hold the first multicandidate presidential elections, in 2005 (instead of the usual referendum over the incumbent), there was a popular consensus that Abu Ghazala—more than a decade into retirement—was the only man who stood a chance against him. The reporter Muhammad al-Baz helped the old field marshal lay down the general guidelines of his presidential program, but hours before he was scheduled to announce his candidacy at the Press Syndicate, on June 29, 2005, Mubarak paid him a visit and persuaded him to back down. The former defense minister never spoke again in public. He died three years later.[15] Abu Ghazala's fall from power ended the era of eminent generals. From that point onward, as one reporter noted cleverly, "the most popular military officer on billboards in Egypt [was] Colonel Sanders of Kentucky Fried Chicken."[16]

Abu Ghazala's replacement was Youssef Sabri Abu Taleb. This was a shrewd decision on Mubarak's part for a couple of reasons. To begin with, Abu Ghazala had served under him in the Second Army through-out the 1970s, forcing the embittered Abu Taleb to resign the day his subordinate was promoted over his head to the top military post. Second, the new defense minister had been away from the corps for six years (serving in the civilian position of Cairo's governor). The grudge he openly held against Abu Ghazala ensured that even the contacts he had with former colleagues must have been circumscribed. Also, knowing that Abu Taleb's mission was to wipe out his predecessor's legacy further guaranteed that there would be no love lost between the officer corps and their new leader. By 1992, he had cut down the army's role in the economy, and terminated the controversial R&D infrastructure Abu Ghazala had laid down for missile production.[17] Mubarak's final coup de grace was to appoint Hussein Tantawy, the head of the Republican Guard, new defense minister in May 1991. Tantawy served the president faithfully for twenty years before defecting during the 2011 uprising.

THE MYTH OF MILITARY PRIVILEGES UNDER MUBARAK

The army's eventual abandonment of the regime in 2011 force us to wonder: Why did the military have anything to complain about during Mubarak's reign? Did it not control a lucrative niche of the economy? Is it not true that its members enjoyed various socioeconomic privileges? What about American patronage? Why would officers hold grievances against the regime when each year more than two hundred of them were trained by the world's only superpower, and regularly participated in joint exercises with American soldiers? What was there to rail against when their arsenal included state-of-the-art weapons (from M1A1 Abrams tanks to F-16 Falcons, Improved Hawk missiles, and all the rest)? Surely, as most scholars assumed, these perks were more than enough to stifle opposition within the ranks, to buy off the army.[18] After all, what more could soldiers ask for than a few perks to fill their pockets and boost their self-esteem? In reality, however, these ostensible privileges masked a number of troubling issues, which can be seen in the realm of economics, U.S. ties, the political constraints imposed by the regime, and the social context within which the army was forced to operate—issues that can become apparent only if one accepts the premise that those who enlist in the armed forces are occupied with war and combat readiness, i.e., that the military actually cares about acting as a military. In Clausewitz's memorable words, "The end for which a soldier is recruited, clothed, armed and trained, the whole object of his sleeping, eating, drinking and marching is simply that he should fight."[19]

(i) Military-Economic Complex

After Sadat declared the October War to be the last Arab-Israeli war, he redirected the army toward economic development projects through the National Service Projects Organization (NSPO), which was created in 1978. The military-economic complex built after Sadat is said to employ perhaps one hundred thousand people, with a diversified business portfolio that includes construction, land reclamation, agro-industries, and more than thirty factories for civilian durables and weapons (assembled helicopters, armored vehicles, mortars, howitzers, short-range missiles, and ammunition), which covered 60 percent of the military's needs and left it with enough surplus to run a billion-dollar-a-year export business to developing countries. Officers also enjoyed privileges such as discounted apartments and vacation homes, subsidized food and services, and brief stints in the bureaucracy after retirement.

In the summer of 1984, a flurry of op-ed articles penned by leftist opposition members questioned the motivation behind "reinventing the military as a primarily economic actor."[20] The military was quick to respond. After making it clear that it had nothing to do with this purely *political* decision, army spokesmen underlined the official rationale, cited in a 1979 presidential directive and reaffirmed in another one three years later, making the military responsible for attaining self-sufficiency (i.e., taking care of its own) and contributing to national economic development through the provision of cheap goods and services. Officers then elaborated on that logic through newspaper articles. For example, Major General Ibrahim Shakib reminded readers that in the absence of war the army is required to find employment for its conscripts.[21] Major General Ahmed Fakhr said that until the economy was stabilized the military could not forsake its members to the caprice of market forces; it was duty-bound to provide them at least with a decent living.[22] This was followed by a number of interviews in which Defense Minister Abu Ghazala highlighted how officers struggled with inflation, and described the subsidized services the army provided to its members as conspicuously humble in comparison with the luxurious standards enjoyed by members of the upper middle classes.[23] And verily so: it takes only a short visit to Egypt for the casual observer to note how shabby military discount stores, automobiles, housing complexes, and beach cabins are when compared with those enjoyed by an average upper-middle-class Egyptian. No wonder the military had consistently failed to recruit members of the country's educated urban elites.

Abu Ghazala then delivered a speech during the annual National Democratic Party conference in 1986, in which he complained that low defense spending subjected the army to serious financial trouble, and stressed that the current budget barely covered the modest wages and services provided to members of the armed forces.[24] Shortly afterward, Mubarak himself mentioned in a public address that critics who accused the army of amassing wealth should know that half of its earnings were "spent on soldiers' wages and the rest on their clothing and lodging and equipment maintenance."[25] A 2008 report by the Central Auditing Authority confirmed that the military's economic activity covered the necessities without really generating a noteworthy surplus.[26] At least on this account, the president was not lying. Analysts also pointed out that those who highlight officer privileges forget that the inflationary economic policies of Sadat and Mubarak eroded the value of all government wages (by at least 60 percent between 1981 and 1986, and more afterwards), but whereas civil servants could moonlight and take bribes to supplement their meager and rapidly shrinking incomes, officers were stuck with their monthly paycheck. After Mubarak was deposed, a *Financial Times* commentator confessed that the army's "reputed economic 'empire' ... is considerably more modest in volume than is commonly believed, and has probably shrunk in proportion to a national economy that has grown by more than 3 percent annually since 2003 ... [and] although a few generals are *rumored* to have become rich, the main purpose [behind the military's economic activities] ... is to ameliorate the impact of a rapidly privatizing economy on the living standards of officers."[27] Finally, in March 2012, the assistant defense minister for financial affairs and Supreme Council of the Armed Forces member Major General Mahmoud Nasr revealed in a widely attended forum in Cairo that the total size of the military's economic activities in 2011 was £E6.3 billion (roughly $1 billion), and that the profits reaped during Mubarak's reign were £E7.7 billion—a relatively modest figure.[28]

An intimately related claim is that military spending remained high under Mubarak, that the defense budget had remained untouchable by either the executive or legislative authorities. Reports by U.S., European, Israeli, and (recently) Egyptian sources have exposed the inaccuracy of this assessment. While military spending in the mid-1970s represented as much as 33 percent of the country's GDP, it fell significantly afterward, to 19.5 percent in 1980 and further down to 2.2 percent in 2010—reaching its lowest level in Egypt's recorded history. In money terms, defense expenditures oscillated between approximately $2.4 and $4.2 billion during Mubarak's three-decade term, without ever being adjusted for the erosive effects of inflation, the ever-mounting cost of technology, or the tenfold increase in Egypt's GDP from around $17.8 to $188 billon between 1980 and 2010.* Moreover, the celebrated $1.3

---

* The figures are based on Zeev Eytan and Mark A. Heller, *The Middle East Military Balance, Jaffee Center for Strategic Studies,* Jerusalem: Jerusalem Post Press, 1983: 74–90; Eytan, Heller, and Aharon Levran, *The Middle East Military Balance,* Jaffee Center for Strategic Studies, Boulder, CO: Westview Press, 1985; Eytan and Shlomo Gazit, *The Middle East Military Balance,* Jaffee Center for Strategic Studies, Boulder, CO: Westview Press, 1991: 218–31; Ephraim Kam and Yiftah Shapir, *The Middle East Strategic Balance, 2002–2003,* Jaffee Center for Strategic Studies, Tel Aviv: Kedem Printing, 2003:191–93; Zvi Shtauber and Shapir, *The Middle East Military Balance, 2004–2005,* Jaffee Center for Strategic Studies, Brighton: Sussex Academic Press,

billion provided annually by the United States had depreciated in real terms by at least 50 percent since the peace treaty was signed in 1979. Rather than basking in prosperity and privilege, the military frequently lived with the fear that to merely balance accounts it might have to "slash military salaries severely."[29] Indeed, the situation was so bad that Israeli strategists remarked: "A striking factor about the Egyptian Armed Forces' combat arsenal is that a portion of it, including aircraft, is kept in storage … [because of] budgetary constraints,"[30] and that because of these constraints "[c]ost-effective simulation training took priority over live training."[31]

The army also had serious misgivings regarding its arms industry, which had been originally instigated under Nasser in the early 1950s. Sadat convinced three Arab Gulf countries (UAE, Qatar, and Saudi Arabia) in April 1975 to contribute $260 million each to finance that industry through a new venture called the Arab Military Industries Organization (AMIO). Egypt provided its share in kind, bringing AMIO's initial assets to $1.04 billion.[32] The Arab sponsors withdrew in 1979 in protest of Egypt's unilateral peace treaty. Although Sadat took over the organization, renaming it the Arab Organization for Industrialization (AOI), its capital depreciated considerably. More injurious to military pride, one could imagine, was the fact that the end goal was no longer to liberate Egypt's strategic decision-making from foreign suppliers, as Nasser had originally intended, but rather to become a regional arms dealer.

Finally, the arms export business did not provide the military with an independent economic powerhouse, because the political leadership kept it under tight control. In March 1976, Sadat placed an intelligence man, his President's Bureau of Information chief Ashraf Marawan, in charge of military industrialization, where he stayed until October 1978. This appointment did not bode well among officers when Israel later alleged that Marawan was its primary asset in Egypt, codenamed "Top Source," though Mubarak later claimed he was working as a double agent.[33] Eyebrows were raised, too, when Sadat's former security aide moved to London, leading a lavish life as a billionaire and involved in high-profile business deals, such as the 1984 bid to acquire Chelsea Football Club. The sixty-two-year-old Marawan was eventually pushed off the balcony of the Carlton House Terrace in London in the summer

2005; Anthony H. Cordesman, *Arab-Israeli Military Forces in an Era of Asymmetric Wars*, Westport, CT: Praeger Security International, 2006; Latif Wahid, *Military Expenditure and Economic Growth in the Middle East*, New York: Palgrave Macmillan, 2009: 137–41; Roula Khalaf and Daniel Dombey, "Army Torn between Loyalty to Egyptians, President and US," *Financial Times* (2/3/2011), 3; and Wael Gamal, *Al-'Askari: mashru'atna 'araq wezarat al-defa'* (Military Council: Our Projects Are the Defense Ministry's Sweat), *Al-Shorouk* 1152: 2. Cairo (3/28/2012).

of 2007, and no one has been held responsible.[34] Under Mubarak, loyal lieutenants, such as the ex–intelligence officer Hussein Salem and the president's own brother-in-law were deeply involved in Egypt's arms trade. Even from a legal standpoint, article 108 of the 1971 Egyptian constitution gave the president authority over defense contracts and other related activities, a prerogative further expanded via Law 146 of 1981, which specifically gave him power over arms exports.[35]

(ii) Geopolitical Alliance

Though any type of foreign military assistance comes with strings attached, the reason U.S. aid was particularly problematic from day one was the specific conditions and constraints that came with it. Four years after leaving office, the former defense minister Abu Ghazala explained in an interview in June 1997 that Egyptian military men were deeply frustrated by the fact that their primary source of training and weapons was committed to keeping the military power of all Arab countries behind that of Israel.[36] This pledge was recorded in the writings of some of America's leading politicians, such as Henry Kissinger and the NSC member Robert Komer,* before being spelled out officially in a letter from President Ronald Reagan to Premier Menachem Begin in 1986, reiterating America's commitment to "guaranteeing Israeli superiority in armaments over all the Arab states combined."[37]

This general commitment was confirmed on numerous occasions. For instance, although the United States helped Egypt integrate F-16 fighter jets into its air force, their number was deliberately kept to fewer than two-thirds of those in Israel's possession. When Egypt demanded specific weapons, such as the Advanced Medium-Range Air-to-Air Missile (AMRAAM), which the Clinton administration readily provided to the UAE, the Pentagon rejected its request due to Israeli objections. Also, while the United States cooperated closely with Israel on the production of sophisticated weapons, by, for example, furnishing 70 percent of the development costs of the Arrow anti-ballistic-missile program, it refrained from helping Egypt in building an advanced missile program. So while the arsenal in both countries had many weapon types in common, Israel's lot was not only better in quantity

---

* The former CIA operative Robert Komer, who served on the Kennedy and Johnson National Security Council, noted in an internal memorandum in May 1967: "No one who has an insider's view could contest the proposition that the US is 100% behind the security and well-being of Israel. We are Israel's chief supporters, bankers, direct and indirect arms purveyors, and ultimate guarantors" (quoted in Scott, *The Attack on the Liberty*, 30). Kissinger recorded in his book *Diplomacy* that the Arab countries must be convinced that "Israel was too strong (or could be made too strong [by the US]) to be defeated even by all of its neighbors combined" (737).

and quality, but its indigenous manufacturers also had the benefit of U.S. assistance in maintaining a technology gap in its favor.[38] One needs to remember that Abu Ghazala lost his job when a reluctant United States forced him to smuggle American missile technology and deal with Communist North Korea to make sure the Egyptian army was better equipped than the United States would allow for. His dismissal for that specific reason infuriated scores of officers and soldiers.[39]

According to Israeli strategic analysts, even when the Egyptian military was driven by an "expressed dissatisfaction with the pace of weapons supplies from the U.S. and its desire to avoid excessive dependence on a single supplier" to seek the help of other countries, the United States systematically undermined its pursuits.[40] So for example, when the army asked the Russians in 1997 to upgrade its air defense system with a shipment of S-300 anti-tactical-ballistics missiles, which happened to be particularly competent in defending against the type of cruise missiles that Israel had, the Pentagon blocked the deal. After extended negotiations, Egypt was permitted only in 2003 to use American funds to upgrade some of its obsolete, low-quality SA-3 Russian missiles. Hence, U.S. missile-transfer policy to Egypt, in the view of American military experts themselves, had set "serious limitations [on Egypt's ability] in dealing with an attack by Israel."[41] A more general version of this conclusion was recorded in an early Israeli estimate of Egyptian capabilities a couple of years into Mubarak's reign: "the policy adopted by President Sadat after 1973 ... caused Egypt to fall behind Israel and other Arab states in the Middle East arms race."[42]

An even subtler analysis highlighted that U.S. assistance assigned priority to the air force and the navy (which received some 80 percent of the annual grant), and to a lesser extent the armored corps, to the detriment of the two other ground services: air defense and artillery. Air defense, which is so crucial to Egypt, as evidenced by the fact that it is organized as an independent service, continued to rely on outdated Eastern Bloc surface-to-air missiles (especially, the SAM-6), with only a handful of state-of-the-art U.S. Improved Hawks. Similarly, in the 1990s, of Egypt's 2,200 artillery pieces only 200 were American.[43] It is interesting to note the correlation between the inattention of the United States to Egypt's air defense and artillery—the two services that have repeatedly proven essential to Egypt's defense and deterrence power—and its support for the air force and navy, those technology-intensive services with which Egypt has no hope of outperforming Israel. This might explain why even Mubarak's ever-cordial defense minister Hussein Tantawy was rumored to have resisted U.S. attempts to restructure the Egyptian armed forces.[44]

What made things worse is that Egyptian officers not only felt that their patron was devoted to keeping them inferior in strength to Israel, but also updated Israel regularly concerning Egypt's weapons portfolio, strategic doctrine, and preparation.[45] This sense of discomfort was exacerbated by the fact that the army still classifies Israel as a major threat to Egypt's security. Abu Ghazala said so himself in Parliament in February 1987.[46] In addition, annual military exercises, such as Badr in 1996 and Jabal Phar'on in 1998, named Israel explicitly as the training target, and were conducted on a terrain that resembles Sinai. It is also no secret that Egypt's greatest concentration of forces lies in the area between Cairo and the Suez Canal. In short, "Almost all of Egypt's capabilities, equipment, and deployment of forces are concentrated on one front to engage one force only: the Israeli Defense Forces."[47] It was not that his men were vying for war, Abu Ghazala clarified, but relying too much on the United States made them feel exposed and defenseless against possible Israeli aggression in the future.[48] In the words of the renowned military strategist Anthony Cordesman: "In spite of Egypt's firm commitment to peace, it cannot ignore the risk of some unexpected political crisis or strategic shift that could again make Israel a threat. It must maintain a suitable deterrent and defense capability to deal with the risk of some unlikely breakdown in the peace with Israel."[49]

But even aside from Israel, Egyptian officers soon realized that they were not allowed to project regional power in any direction. As a superpower, the United States vigorously defended its interests throughout the region, from Sudan and Jordan to Yemen, Syria, and Lebanon, and of course the Gulf. Even when Egypt was summoned, along with twenty other nations, to facilitate America's liberation of Kuwait, it was not allowed to play a more active role afterward in Gulf security via the ill-fated Damascus Declaration of 1992, which hoped to create an Arab defense force under Egyptian-Syrian leadership. To add insult to injury, the performance of the two divisions it had sent to war against Iraq was assessed by American sources as "middling."[50] Colonel Norvell De Atkine, who had personally supervised the training of Egyptian officers, actually described their performance as "mediocre."[51] It was clear that after years of U.S. "modernization," the Egyptian armed forces had not advanced very far. That is probably due to the fact that, from the U.S. standpoint, war was off the table for Egypt. The Egyptian military was expected only to pose as a "deterrent force situated in the background."[52] At best, the army, which had in the past perceived itself as a vanguard of progressive forces in the postcolonial world, could be employed as a regional *gendarmerie*, deployed on the side of U.S. allies. The contrast could not have been starker when the same men who had been sent to the Congo to support Patrice Lumumba in 1960 were dispatched there again in 1977 to prop up Mobutu's pro-American autocracy.

Mubarak obviously did not share the concerns of his men. During his first meeting with the veteran editor and political adviser Mohamed Hassanein Heikal, on December 5, 1981, the recently appointed president seemed to have his mind made up regarding geopolitics and war. When Heikal criticized the ineffectiveness of the peace process and the asymmetrical alliance with the United States, the president interrupted, "Sadat was right. I do not know why Nasser befriended those impoverished Russians. Sadat [rightly] favored the lavish Americans. Nasser's biggest mistake was to defy the Americans. Besides, President Anwar [Sadat wisely] chose peace with Israel. President Nasser should have known that fighting Israel was hopeless. Jews control the whole world, as you know. Take it from me, no one can cross America."[53]

Developments on the home front were no less disheartening for officers. The army that had taken power in July 1952 in the name of the people and pursued developmental policies for the benefit of the lower middle and middle classes was now being called upon to support a regime that had identified itself with the superrich. With the rise of the president's son and his U.S.-connected business associates during the last decade of Mubarak's rule, the defense minister and chief of staff (as has been recently revealed through WikiLeaks) criticized the direction the regime was taking in general, and to the increasing role of Mubarak's son and his capitalist circle in particular. It was only natural, as the revolution theorist Jack Goldstone asserted, that the high command "fiercely resented Gamal Mubarak ... [who] preferred to build his influence through business and political cronies rather than through the military, and those connected to him gained huge profits from government monopolies and deals with foreign investors."[54] At the beginning of 2006, Defense Minister Hussein Tantawy tactfully relayed to Mubarak that it would not be wise to pit the military against the people to force them to accept an "unpopular figure" as president.[55] But ruling-party capitalists paid no heed. When the U.S. ambassador, Francis Ricciardone, confided to one of them that he heard Tantawy express concern over Gamal's candidacy, he was told that Mubarak could dismiss the defense minister whenever he wanted. "Tantawi is not stronger than Abu-Ghazala," the source added.[56]

Moreover, while politically connected capitalists were making huge profits in partnership with U.S. investors, American military aid was overly expensive. It cost Egypt only $1.7 billion worth of Russian weapons to fight the Suez War (1956), the Yemen War (1962–1967), the 1967 war, the War of Attrition (1967–1970), and the October War (1973). Compared with this two-decade relationship with the Soviet Union, the first five years of its alliance with the United States left Egypt in debt for $6.6 billion, even though it neither went to war nor planned to do so during those years.[57]

Finally, the Camp David Accords and the subsequent peace treaty of 1979, upon which U.S. military assistance was based, "sat poorly with many of Egypt's senior officers" from the very start.[58] The agreements forced a semidemilitarization of Sinai: military airfields were prohibited, and only one mechanized infantry division could be deployed along the eastern bank of the Suez Canal, while the rest of the peninsula could hold no more than three lightly armed border patrol units and policemen. These constraints made it impossible for Egypt to amass troops in Sinai, even for training purposes, without giving Israel an excuse to declare war. Not surprisingly, one of the first recommendations made by the military representatives to the National Accord Conference following the 2011 revolt was to revise Israeli constraints on the size and deployment of Egyptian troops in Sinai.

(iii) Political Constraints

Despite the military's general aversion to politicization after the 1967 defeat, the alleged professionalization that coincided with the 1973 October War was not what they had in mind. What the army yearned for was to be able to perform better in combat. It accepted depoliticization as a step toward proper professionalization after analysts unanimously assigned Egypt's battle-related shortcomings to the corruption of the corps at the hand of political appointees. But officers soon realized that authoritarianism, even without the direct politicization of the military, imposed similar constraints on their fighting capabilities. The last thing authoritarian rulers can tolerate is the ingenious war maverick who can develop an inflated ego and ride the crest of his battlefield glory to political office. Insecure regimes preempt the rise of these "born in battle" military heroes by centralizing war-making and keeping it in the hands of a few trusted generals. This politically dictated war style is too rigid to allow for the superior "war of movement" strategy, which relies on dynamic and spontaneous maneuvers and therefore requires autonomous middle-ranking officers who improvise in battle without prior orders. The effectiveness of this type of warfare has not only been proven historically (by Roman legionaries, American Union troops, the German Wehrmacht, and others), but it has also been Israel's preferred fighting strategy since 1948. The military historian Simon Dunstan noted: "Throughout the IDF, initiative was encouraged in all ranks to maintain the momentum of the offensive. This was imbued in the officer corps and junior leaders in the ethos of '*Aharai*'—'Follow me.'"[59] By contrast, the set-piece offensives and trench-style defense that characterized Egyptian warfare have repeatedly proven to be substandard. No student of the Arab-Israeli wars has failed to observe that Egypt's strength lies in its "tenacious defensive ability," while its chief weakness could be attributed to its "equally persistent inability to conduct a war of movement." With an overcentralized command-and-control structure that inhibits improvisation and unauthorized initiatives by field officers, Egyptian war conduct suffered from "the total stultification of the initiative of junior officers—precisely the cadre on whose wits mobile warfare depends."[*60] The Egyptian military was aware of this pervasive weakness. In the early 1970s, its chief military historians (led by majors general Hassan al-Badry and Gamal Hammad) reviewed the army's performance and concluded that the military "was poor at executing operations that relied on offensive maneuver, despite its inherent advantages on the battlefield."[61]

This was particularly true during the October War, where—compared with the havoc caused by the likes of Bren Adan and Ariel Sharon, who maneuvered their way behind Egyptian trenches and created the famous breach—the independence of Egypt's divisional and brigade commanders was strapped by a handful of old generals in Operation Center 10 in Cairo. When a middle-ranking Egyptian officer was asked during an interview after the war about the most vital *field* commander in his view, he simply remarked: "[War Minister] Ismail"; when a tank commander, who complained he was "half an hour from the Mitla Pass ... just half an hour," was asked why he did not seize this strategically valuable asset, he shrugged: "Ask them in Cairo"; when junior officers were asked why they had not responded to the Israeli breach of the Egyptian front lines at Deversoir fast enough, one of them explained: "To mount an operation involving both the Egyptian Second Army and Third Army, it was necessary to circulate orders bearing signatures from four different staff officers."[62] By contrast, when asked about the most important position in the State of Israel, the founder of the Israel Defense Force, David Ben-Gurion, responded without hesitation: "battalion leaders ... Those are the men who protect the future of Israel."[63] Colonel Norvell De Atkine, who accumulated years of experience in training Egyptian officers, concluded: "a sergeant first class in the U.S. Army has as much authority as a colonel in an Arab army."[64]

So while the military hoped that its seclusion from politics would render it more trustworthy in the eyes of the political apparatus, and thus allow it to enhance its war capacity without worry, it was now told that there would be no more war—even the War Ministry was renamed in 1979 and became known as the Ministry of Defense. Furthermore, the political authoritarianism that has for long prevented Egypt from adopting a "war of movement" doctrine persisted. Indeed, the sacking

---

* For a more extensive analysis of this phenomenon see Eytan, Heller, and Tamari, *The Middle East Military Balance*, 88; Norvell De Atkine, "Why Arabs Lose Wars," *Middle East* Quarterly 6 (4): 13–17; and Boyne, *The Two o'Clock War*, 185.

of great generals and the uncalled-for reshuffling of those in senior commands conveyed the sense that distinctive performance and popularity among troops continue to jeopardize an officer's career even after the regime's ostensible professionalization of the army. Like those who preceded him, Mubarak relied heavily on security organs (mostly State Security) to monitor those who "stood out" in any shape, way, or form. Security reports could send a good officer packing, usually with a decent retirement package to defuse his resentment.[65] A few years into Mubarak's reign, officers became painfully aware that "[u]ntil Arab *politics* begin to change at fundamental levels, Arab armies, whatever the courage or proficiency of individual officers and men, are unlikely to acquire the range of qualities which modern fighting forces require for success on the battlefield."[66]

(iv) Social Context

One of the most serious challenges facing the military is the pool of recruits it is allowed to draw from. Although the majority of Egypt's active forces (let alone reserves) are conscripts, this particular social group has for long been suffering from manpower quality problems because of their low educational and health standards. In preparation for the October War, a few steps were taken to remedy this problem, most important being to allow the army to recruit and retain university graduates. However, Sadat made sure that Egypt's 1.2 million war-seasoned conscripts were demobilized in the months following the war (unlike other countries that tempt experienced officers to reenlist), bringing down the size of the active forces to around 460,000 by 1980, where it had remained ever since. The fact that the army's strikingly improved performance in 1973 was attributed in large part to the inclusion of educated middle-class elements did not prevent Sadat from revising the conscription formula after the war, presumably to free this class to join the private sector. College graduates now served for nine months, and those with lower qualifications served from two to three years. Once again, the military was stuck with starved and illiterate peasants for the most part.[67]

Several complications followed. For one thing, these conscripts were perceived only to be able to handle menial duties, and so they received little or no training. When they did get trained, they received only battalion-level training (or lower) using obsolete equipment no longer deployed in active units.[68] It became therefore impossible for the Egyptian army to absorb the advanced technology and training provided by the United States. Even educated Egyptians have been handicapped by the overall deterioration in the education system, and the fact that free public education (all the way to university) dissuades many from pursing technical or vocational training. Particularly problematic was the fact that the government not only offered poor technological training, but it also regarded political and security studies with great suspicion. In a country with twenty-three universities, Egypt had only two full-fledged political science programs, and virtually no influential war study centers. Because political and national security matters under authoritarianism are best kept away from scholars, the military was deprived of the "defense intellectuals" that inform strategy and doctrine formulation in open societies. In short, the military had to suffer from the dysfunctional, underfunded, and constrained education system provided by an incompetent and corrupt regime.

When the high command asked for the right to offer special rewards for high-quality conscripts who wanted to reenlist, it was rebuffed under the pretext that there was no national security threat to justify this kind of spending.[69] Without tempting rewards, army recruiters expectedly failed to urge members of the narrow stratum of qualified and motivated elites (who without exception attend private or international schools) to consider a military career. Intriguingly, the frustrated officer corps began, in 1996, sending recruiting delegations to Egypt's expatriate communities to circumvent the fact that the local educational system did offer the kind of officers and soldiers the army needed, but to no avail.[70] As a result, as the U.S. military analyst Cordesman wrote, a "substantial part of the Egyptian army's order of battle was [now] composed of relatively low-grade and poorly-equipped units, many of which would require substantial fill-in with reservists—almost all of which would require several months of training to be effective," and because such a force could hardly be used for the rapid maneuvers and improvised tactics of modern warfare, its "structure had become increasingly static"; in effect, assuming the posture of "a garrison army."[71]

To conclude this section, it is clear that under Mubarak the military suffered from what an Egyptian scholar described as "rank disequilibrium": a psychological dissonance that spreads among members of an institution whose position becomes at odds with their original duties.[72] Egyptians officers were training for war, while knowing full well that they were never meant to fight one; they were asked to defend the nation while being deprived of the type of conscripts, arms, and funds necessary for combat; they were resolutely dependent on a country sworn to preserve their rival's superiority; they were serving a regime that had marginalized their leaders and undermined their corporate interests in the name of professional subordination; and they were promised institutional sovereignty, but were then kept under constant scrutiny by obtrusive security organs, which controlled their careers through security reports.

It did not help that the president, officially the supreme commander of the armed forces, could not prevent himself in interviews (especially with Israeli television) from asserting his conviction that "war had become outdated." The logic he so tirelessly argued was that since wars invariably end with a peaceful settlement, then why not take a short cut and get straight to negotiations—a pearl of wisdom that eluded generations of statesmen before him. What is the use of having a military, then? Deterrence, Mubarak consistently answered. It was no secret, however, that the kind of deterrence he had in mind—as he repeatedly let slip—was not to build military power, but to keep Egypt (the largest and most populous Arab country) neutral in all regional conflicts. It is difficult to imagine officers warming up to these pronouncements, especially given that their sage of a president was not so pacifist in dealing with his own countrymen. Apparently, police-led "war" against citizens was not yet outdated in Mubarak's dictionary.

PLACING THE POLICE ON A PEDESTAL

Now that the military had been successfully sidelined, the regime turned for protection and everyday control to the civilian security apparatus, led by the Interior Ministry. The ministry had proven loyal to the post-1952 political apparatus because the persistence of authoritarianism inflated its power and privileges; and by the same token, it stood to lose from a takeover by pro-democracy elements, which the military either supported or were indifferent to. It was thus natural for the regime to continually augment the power of this loyal ally. Influential military leaders, from Amer to Abu Ghazala, obstructed this trend all they could. But as the army's power declined, the security apparatus was expanded, and former police officers now manned senior political positions, such as the premiership and the general-secretariat of the ruling party.

This political-security alliance was severely tested by the CSF mutiny. The ministry realized it could no longer rely on "armed slaves" controlled from above by terror rather than rewards. On the eve of Mubarak's rise to office, the Special Force Unit had been created within the CSF as an elite corps to tackle sophisticated antiterrorist missions. But day-to-day challenges, such as riots and strikes, still had to be handled by CSF foot soldiers. These peasant conscripts suffered from the sub-human treatment they received during their three-year stints in service; they were ill fed, poorly lodged, sleep deprived, and donned wretched uniforms. After their short-lived rebellion in February 1986, General Faramawy, the CSF chief, tried his best to ameliorate their living situation. Though their pay was only modestly increased, he made sure that their nutrition, outfits, and dwellings were at least better than what they were used to back in the lowly villages they came from. He also allowed them enough breathing space to roam around the city and develop contacts for future employment.[73] To both ease their job and boost their considerably low self-esteem, a bulk of the increased police appropriations was earmarked for the purchase of CSF riot control equipment. The reformed and reinforced CSF was now better prepared to execute its duties, which Springborg summarized as follows:

> It has been called upon to subdue demonstrating students on several university campuses; to intimidate strikers at industrial centers in Delta; to confront Islamist activists at pray-ins and large gatherings in various parts of Upper Egypt; to deal with peasants demonstrating against interruption to irrigation water supplies throughout the countryside; and ... stand twelve-hour shifts at countless strategic and not-so-strategic installations around the country.[74]

General Faramawy was eventually appointed governor of the coastal city of Port Said, and the president appointed a more ruthless leadership at the Interior Ministry under Zaki Badr. Badr, the notorious executer of an unforgiving campaign against Islamists in the violence-ridden south, carried out a scrupulous housecleaning job: between March and August 1986, he retired or transferred hundreds of officers, including the director of the State Security Investigations Sector.[75]

Under Mubarak, the Interior Ministry became—as noted by one of the best studies of Egypt's public administration—"a terrifying bureaucratic empire," especially after its significant expansion via Ministerial Decree 702 of 1986, which divided it into thirty-four separate departments under the pretext of specialization. The police force swelled from 150,000 men in 1974 to more than a million in 2002, representing an increase from 9 to 21 percent of state employment. This is of course in addition to the 450,000 CSF conscripts (the numerical equivalent of twenty army divisions), who served for three years, and the 60,000 National Guards, and the 12,000 Border Patrol soldiers who reported to the ministry.[76] Overall, during the final decade of Mubarak's tenure, Egypt had approximately two million security (or security-associated) men in a population of perhaps 83 million. To grasp the enormity of this figure, one should remember that the Soviet police force under Stalin in the 1930s was a mere 142,000 men;[77] that today 142 million Russians manage with a 200,000-strong security force;[78] that the entire Chinese army in 2009 numbered only 2.3 million in a population of 1.3 billion;[79] and that Egypt's own army in 2010 was no more than 460,000. Another interesting fact: counterinsurgency experts estimate the ratio of officers to citizens needed to contain insurgencies on the scale of those raging in Iraq and Afghanistan at 20 officers per 1,000 citizens;[80] in Mubarak's Egypt—a stable country by any measure—the ratio was 25 security men to every 1,000 citizens.

At the same time, Interior Ministry expenditures increased from 3.5 percent to almost 6 percent of GDP between 1988 and 2002. In money terms, it increased from £E260 million to £E348 million during the first four years of Mubarak's tenure. Thereafter, police wages multiplied almost fourfold, from £E819 million in 1992 to £E3 billion in 2002. The real increase in police revenue, however, came from the government's tacit consent to the extortions imposed on citizens from the 1990s onward.[81]

This was not the worst of it. Beginning with the 1984 elections, repression took a new turn when the police hired petty criminals to intimidate and manhandle opponents. This was expected, considering that the president had instructed his interior minister, Hassan Abu Pasha, to make sure than the ruling party received no less than 95 percent of the vote.[82] Violence was the only means to achieve such an ambitious goal—after all, tampering with ballot boxes had its limits. Who was best placed to employ violence without implicating the government? Street thugs. This notion of "outsourcing repression" harks back to the 1970s, when Sadat's Interior Ministry supplied radical Islamists with knives, iron fists, and metal bars to bully anti-Sadat groups. The ministry also created in 1972 special student squads to attack and terrorize troublesome colleagues on campus.[83] During the last year of Sadat's reign, the police employed thugs on a limited scale to sabotage a Lawyers' Syndicate meeting criticizing the president.[84] With the waning of opposition through continued repression, first by the military in the 1950s and 1960s, then increasingly by the Interior Ministry since the 1970s, there seemed to be no more challenges to meet. The police's last sizable operation was to contain a limited Islamist insurgency between 1992 and 1997. At the cost of 2,000 killed and another 47,000 detained, the Interior Ministry brought Islamist militancy to a swift end.[85] From then on, there were no signs of trouble on the horizon, and consequently, minor repression duties and dirty jobs were delegated to seasonally hired thugs in order not to implicate the police.

Criminal investigation units would nominate petty criminals to State Security officers, who would then prep them and turn them over to the CSF to assist them on the ground. During elections, thugs would instigate brawls outside polling stations to give the police a pretext to arrest opposition representatives and suspend the voting process; they would also beat up activists during demonstrations to scare them away without implicating the government directly. The downturn, however, was that the police could scarcely prevent these thugs from bullying common citizens during their off-duty hours. "The secret business relationship between the thugs and State Security officers ... provided the former with protection on the streets, thus transforming them into unleashed and undeterred monsters."[86] During the last decade of

Mubarak's reign, police-connected thugs harassed wealthy-looking citizens for money, molested females on crowded boulevards, terrorized
shopkeepers and small business owners, and more. Not surprisingly, the
U.S. State Department's 2006 human rights report on Egypt warned
that a "culture of impunity" had spread throughout the security sector;
citizens had become practically fair game.[87]

To make matters even worse, policemen themselves had began to act
as thugs. One observer noted during a short visit to Egypt: "The average
Egyptian can be dragged into a police station and tortured simply because
a police officer doesn't like his face."[88] This has been a growing trend
since the 1970s. Between 1974 and 1976, newspapers recorded for the
first time cases of criminal—not political—suspects being tortured by
the police to confess to the crimes they had committed (or, most likely,
did not commit). Torture in criminal cases was so brutal that in several
instances suspects admitted to murder (a crime punishable by death)
only to discover afterward that their alleged "victims" were still alive.
This represented a watershed in the relationship between Egyptians
and the police: now citizens rather than activists were being tortured to
confess to crimes rather than political dissent, by criminal investigators
rather than secret police officers, in police stations rather than isolated
detention centers. Afterward, police violence became endemic. It was
no longer reserved to generating forced confessions, but also to force
citizens to pay bribes, withdraw complaints, sign business contracts, or
just to make them learn their place. Indeed, police torture transcended
the boundaries of "frequent practices" to become "standard behavior ... [something] applied automatically without effort or reflection,
something that does not require full consciousness or focus or planning;
violence had become second nature."[89] It is a known fact that as part
of their initiation rituals, young officers were asked to punch and kick
jailed suspects indiscriminately on their first day at the police station.
Those who refused became the laughingstock of their colleagues, and
were perceived as soft and incompetent by their superiors.

Not surprisingly, in a 1989 survey conducted by a research center
associated with the Interior Ministry on the popular view of the police,
one-third of the respondents expressed their dismay at the violence
being committed against common citizens in precincts. But instead of
reforming police attitudes, it was implicitly endorsed when the official police slogan was changed from "The Police Is in the Service of
the People" to "The Police and the People Are in the Service of the
State." Between 2002 and 2006, citizens filed 221 reports against police
abuse—this, of course, excludes dozens of other cases where citizens
did not complain, as well as systematic torture cases in State Security
detention centers. In 2008 alone, Egyptian human rights organizations
recorded 916 cases of police violence against nonpolitical citizens.[90]

Why were the police acting in this way? If one might expect the relationship between regimes and their contenders to be a violent one, why was there so much violence permeating the relationship between the police and "the apolitical and peaceful citizen," violence that made "common citizens afraid of merely passing by a police station ... even if they were claimants."[91] In her original and disturbing study of the Egyptian police force, Basma Abd al-Aziz concluded that because security officers had been transformed from instruments of authority to *authority itself* (i.e., from loyal servants of the regime to its main beneficiaries), the relationship between the police and the citizen had been correspondingly reformulated into that of master and slave. "The new masters could bestow their protection on whomever they chose, and they could also deprive anyone of dignity, pride, liberty, confidence, respect, or any human value."[92] This new formula required that citizens be assaulted in public, that they witness firsthand the omnipotence of the police and give up any hope of resistance. It was only natural that, by 2011, common citizens' hatred of the police had reached profound levels.

The only remaining component of the Interior Ministry that was diligent and sober was the State Security Investigations Sector. Yet the SSIS quickly developed into as "a state within the state." It dwarfed all other government institutions; scrutinized nominees for cabinet positions, parliament seats, governorships, university chairs, editorial boards, public-sector companies and banks, and, of course, the military. Everything came under its purview in a way reminiscent of fascist and Communist traditions at their worst. While the General Intelligence Service focused mostly on foreign relations, SSIS became exclusively responsible for domestic surveillance and repression, recruiting informants in every sector of society and systematically applying torture against detainees, whose number during Mubarak's thirty-year tenure exceeded 30,000. In 2010 alone, there were around 17,000 in detention centers.[93] Human rights organizations described SSIS-administered torture rituals as follows:

> When a detainee enters the prison complex, he or she is usually blindfolded and handcuffed to intimidate, disorient, or protect police identities ... Stripped down to their underwear, detainees are often subjected to insults, curses, and threatened sexual abuse directed at the prisoner and his or her family members ... Physical torture is part of the routine with detainees frequently beaten or kicked with sticks or batons. Some are hung by their wrists for extended periods ... Electric shocks to the genitals seem to be part of the torture routine.[94]

Evidence for how tightly SSIS controlled political life came from the shocking episode relating to the Muslim Brothers' success in securing 20 percent of the seats in Parliament in the 2005 elections—a historic feat considering that no opposition force had won more than a tenth of the vote during the previous six decades. Asked three years later if he expected a comparable success in the next elections, the Brotherhood's general guide said he was not sure, because last time "State Security gave us a list of districts to run in, and promised to let us win in most. They have not contacted us so far about next year." When prompted to clarify by the dumbfounded interviewer, he explained that the Bush administration was pressuring Egypt to democratize, and the SSIS wanted to scare them a little, and his organization did not mind getting a few more seats.[95] Little wonder why, when SSIS turned against the Brotherhood, their share in the following elections, held in 2010, fell from eighty-eight seats to zero. Not only did the ruling National Democratic Party control 97 percent of Parliament in that last election held under Mubarak, but also forty-nine police officers were elected for the first time.[*] Longtime Speaker of Parliament Fathy Sourur recalled his shock upon hearing the results: "I said this was political stupidity ... I telephoned Hassan Abd al-Rahman, head of State Security, and asked him what in the world was going on ... I also complained to Safwat al-Sharif [former intelligence officer and NDP secretary-general] ... I have worked with the president for 25 years, but lately I felt that the Interior Ministry was running the country."[96]

Ultimately, it was the appointment of Habib al-Adly as interior minister that gave Egypt's police state its final form. Adly graduated from the Police Academy in 1961, and served as a State Security officer from 1965 to 1993; he then served briefly as chief of security for the Sinai and Suez Canal districts, before returning to Cairo as security chief in 1995, SSIS director in 1996, and finally interior minister in 1997. As a testament to his central role in the regime, Adly occupied this post for 14 consecutive years, whereas his predecessors from 1952 onward served on average for 3.2 years. Mubarak's last interior minister expanded surveillance to include all influential figures in society, not just government and opposition figures. He systemized the use of thugs in elections and other operations, first in Cairo during the 1995 elections, and then around the country after the 2000 elections. Most important, Adly forged intimate relations with the most influential wing of the ruling party, the business-dominated Policies Committee.[97]

---

[*] The significance of the 97 percent in 2010 becomes obvious when compared with the percentage secured by the NDP in previous elections: 89 percent in 1979; 87 percent in 1984; 78 percent in 1987; 81 percent in 1990; 79 percent in 2000; and 68.5 percent in 2005 (Ghoneim, *Azmat al-dawla al-misriya al-mu'asera*, 178).

From a legal standpoint, Egypt's Emergency Law sanctioned police repression. Law 162 of 1958 had been continuously in force since 1967 (except for eighteen months between 1980 and 1981) until it became a permanent fixture of the Egyptian political system. The law allows for extended detention without trial, denies detainees habeas corpus, bans labor strikes, prohibits demonstrations without police permission, justifies press censorship, and sanctions trial of political prisoners by special courts that deliver "swift justice" and restrict defendants' right to appeal. Also, the capacity of Mubarak's security agencies was greatly enhanced by new control technologies unavailable to his predecessors. In line with Michael Mann's (1986) notion that technological advancement enables the generation of new state structures, thus allowing hitherto unavailable historical alternatives, one could argue that Egypt's tightly controlled police state was possible only because of the surveillance tools that allowed the SSIS to spy on citizens using their own cell phones, to monitor social communication networks, to trace vehicles via sophisticated satellite technologies, etc.

Finally, one should note that the consolidation of Egypt's police state was perfectly suited to the temperament of the man at the helm. As devoted as Nasser and Sadat were to regime security, Mubarak's "passion for security [was] obtrusive, possibly obsessive."[98] Mubarak adopted an unorthodox security strategy, which, rather than targeting major opposition groups, kept the entire society paralyzed with fear through a dizzying pattern of detention, release, and then redetention, striking almost randomly at various activists, common citizens, and even some of the ruling elites without explanation. Unlike his predecessors, Mubarak was also overly concerned with his personal safety. Robert Springborg recalled from his time in Cairo how "[t]he sprawling security net that spreads out from his Heliopolis villa … far exceeds any previous efforts to protect presidents. His phalanx of bodyguards is truly formidable … The conveniences and liberties of normal citizens are, in comparison to presidential security precautions, of no concern. Whole city quarters are blocked off in advance of presidential movements."[99] When Mubarak was invited to spend a night at Buckingham Palace, he sent a delegation of sixteen security experts to inspect the room he was supposed to stay in—needless to say, only a couple were admitted after frantic entreaties from Egypt's ambassador to London.[100] Little surprise then that although the trend to marginalize the military and boost the security apparatus had begun under Sadat, it was during Mubarak's time in office that Egypt had decisively evolved from a military to a police state.

STREAMLINING THE POLITICAL APPARATUS

The marginalization of the military and the empowerment of the police did not rule out the need for an entrenched ruling party. The general structure and function of this party remained fairly consistent since the 1950s, though its social composition changed drastically. The ruling party was always pyramid-shaped, with its wide base in the countryside, narrowing down as one moved upward to the cities, all the way to the Cairo-based central command. In terms of function, it continued to act as an organizer of the regime's social bases. What were these bases, and how did their relative weight shift over time? Apart from the urban professionals who were attached to the regime through employment in the bureaucracy and public factories, Nasser aspired to build a solid base of peasants and workers through the party. But although public employees, peasants, and workers did in fact become the party's foot soldiers, they remained politically insignificant. Instead of mobilizing these loyal subjects, the party preferred to buy them off through seasonal handouts to preempt their mobilization by competing political forces. It could not have acted otherwise considering the irresolvable contradiction between the interests of this (mostly lower-class) popular base and those of party elites—elites whose composition changed across time.

Under Nasser, more than a thousand military officers controlled the key political posts, and when they retired others were drawn from the same pool.[101] So, for example, the twenty-five-member general secretariat of the Arab Socialist Union in 1962 had sixteen officers.[102] By the end of the 1960s, however, it was the rural middle class and their offspring in the state bureaucracy and the public sector that pulled the strings.[103] The demands of this second stratum were minimal: like most peasants—rich or poor—the bourgeoisie in the countryside wanted to be left alone, while public employees wanted to move up the employment ladder, and maybe make a modest fortune on the side through bribes and commissions. With Sadat's economic liberalization and the oil boom, a new social group infiltrated the party: businessmen. The latter combined state-nurtured capitalists (especially in real estate, commerce, and finance) and petty businessmen (small contractors, owners of export-import and currency-exchange firms).

By the turn of the century, this last stratum gave way to monopoly capitalists, who perhaps amassed their wealth through state contacts at the beginning, but were now too big to control from above. Eventually, these billionaires assumed the top political positions, whether in the cabinet or the party leadership. While the rural middle class and state employees continued to handle routine matters, such as elections and demonstrations of support, it was these high-profile businessmen who formulated policy. For the first time since 1952, economic elites were manipulating the state rather than being manipulated by it.

Mubarak did not plan it this way. He originally hoped to preserve the structure Sadat put in place, whereby state-linked businessmen would serve as a source of support for the ruling party no more. His intention was to keep the NDP as the party of the state bureaucracy, with businessmen representing one of many interest groups. In other words, he refused to allow the party to be colonized by capitalists. Mubarak believed his years as vice president and vice chairman of the NDP had honed his domestic power-brokering skills enough to enable him to keep the party on track. When he ascended to office, three incompatible groups were running the party machine: left-wing cadres (ASU residue), capitalists (notably, the oligarch Osman Ahmed Osman), and opportunists (party functionaries and parasitic bourgeois elements, who joined the NDP for petty material gains). The president promoted the latter group because it appeared to be the most malleable, considering that opportunists have neither ideological nor economic power to draw on. Two years after he assumed office, Mubarak appointed Youssef Wali, a bureaucrat who built his career at the Ministry of Agriculture, as NDP secretary-general, assisted by Kamal al-Shazly, the experienced apparatchik who served in all post-1952 political organizations. Mubarak then replaced seven of the thirteen-member politburo, sixteen of the twenty-three-member general secretariat, and nine of the chairs of the NDP's fifteen standing committees, in a move aimed at purging prominent capitalists, the likes of Osman as well as Osman himself.[104]

Finally, the president reinforced the NDP's reliance on the state bureaucracy, which for all practical purposes functioned as an extension of the ruling party. It was no small appendage, considering that the bureaucracy had rapidly inflated from 1 million employees in 1974 to 3.5 million in 1986—the time around which these changes were taking place. But regardless of what Mubarak intended, the remaining capitalist members of the NDP "feudalized" their relationship with state bureaucrats, with the former serving as patrons and protectors, and the latter providing logistical and administrative support, and, more important, providing them with opportunities for personal enrichment. The ruling party thus gravitated slowly and surely into the orbit of big business. The economic structure Sadat erected made it difficult, if not impossible, for it to steer away from this path.

FROM OPENING UP THE ECONOMY TO DEREGULATION

Mubarak came to power seven years after the open-door economic policy (Infitah) had been implemented. And as was discussed in the previous chapter, these were seven fat years for a few, and seven lean years for everyone else. But the overall effect of this policy was so damaging to the economy that one of the president's very first decisions was to convene a national conference to explore means of averting what he saw as a looming economic crisis. Publicly, Mubarak maintained throughout his rule that Egypt's dire economic situation was the people's fault. He often identified population growth as "*the* cause" for undermining government efforts to improve socioeconomic conditions. However, the economic conference that began work in February 1982 said otherwise. Its final report, supplemented by numerous other studies during this period, exposed Infitah's bitter legacy.

Egypt's top economists agreed that opportunist capitalism had tilted the economy toward foreign trade and finance, and away from productive sectors. Foreign trade as a percentage of GDP jumped from 35 percent in 1974 to 97 percent in 1979.[105] This in itself was a troubling indicator in a country that claimed to be industrializing. But what was even more troubling was the fact that Egypt had rapidly shifted from a net exporter to a net importer of food. Egyptian exports fell in total from 38 percent in 1974 to 14 percent in 1981, while its agricultural exports, in particular, fell from 41.4 percent of total exports in 1973 to 15.5 percent in 1980.[106] At the same time, Egypt was importing 60 percent of its food requirements in the early 1980s, though perhaps half of its workforce was employed in agriculture. Strategic products suffered the most. For example, while Egypt had been exporting 40 percent of its sugar production in 1970, a decade later it had not only stopped exporting sugar, but it had also begun importing 35 percent of its sugar needs. At the same time, importing luxuries spun out of control: the import of clothes doubled; the import of cosmetics tripled; the import of cigarettes and watches increased tenfold; the import of electrical appliances increased twelve times; the import of cars increased fourteen times; and the import of luxury foods increased eighteen times. By 1979, 53 percent of Egypt's GDP went to financing imports.[107] Even within agriculture itself, there was a trend to shift to luxury produce, as expensive fruits and vegetables replaced wheat, rice, sugarcane, and other essential staples. The area devoted to such exotic produce more than doubled between 1970 and 1980, and continued to increase afterward. Economists agree that the country could no longer tolerate the speculative activities and short-term ventures of private investors and their foreign partners, nor could it afford the consumption tendencies that surfaced in the 1970s, especially those directed toward imported luxuries. In conclusion, a return to state-planned economic development was essential, even if the private sector was allowed to play a leading role in this process.[108]

The onus of the blame fell on the companies established according to Law 43 of 1974, which inaugurated Infitah. Their estimated $26 million total exports, by the end of the 1970s, was staggeringly out of step with their hefty import bill of $609 million, most of which was spent on luxury products.[109] These petty commercial capitalists helped transform Egypt not just into a consumer society, but, more dangerous, a consumer of foreign luxuries. The share of commerce in Egypt's GDP doubled during the decade Sadat spent in office from less than 10 percent to 19 percent, with the share of private companies in that sector increasing from less than 50 percent to 70 percent during the same period, and jumping to 95 percent by the mid-1990s.[110] This was translated domestically through several indicators. For instance, between 1970 and 1980, wholesale commerce expanded from 43.6 to 75.4 percent;[111] Egyptian agents for foreign merchants increased from a few dozen in 1974 to 16,000 in 1981; commercial projects consumed 42 percent of total bank loans during the same period;[112] and there was an increase in supermarkets at the rate of 22 percent annually between 1974 and 1978.[113]

The commercial capitalists of the Sadat era did not only create a broad demand for imported products that the government could not hope to satisfy, they also forged strong ties with state bureaucrats, ties that the political leadership had first encouraged, but which by the 1980s had become too entangled to be contained or disrupted. On the one hand, the "most powerful segment of the bourgeoisie derive[d] its wealth and influence from parasitic relations with the state, not through entrepreneurial activities ... [they built empires] in the shadow of the state and would wither in the direct sunlight of open economic competition."[114] They were thus fighting for their lives. On the other hand, they shared a generous portion of their profits with public employees in exchange for tailored exemptions from taxes and tariffs, illegal access to government resources (bank loans, foreign aid, land, services, etc.), trade monopolies, and so on. Indeed, in the 1970s an estimated 62 percent of public-sector activities were subcontracted to connected businessmen. Corruption, in turn, raised the standards of living of civil servants to a point where they could no longer turn back. In short, what Mubarak confronted was a vast patronage network that was untouchable by any means.[115]

Economic deformation was only one of the problems created by Infitah. A more politically urgent one was its social consequences. To start with, its nonproductive nature did not generate enough jobs; the state remained the primary employer, with bureaucrats alone increasing from 3.8 percent of the population on the eve of Infitah to 10 percent of the population in 1986—a trend that continued under Mubarak, with the bureaucracy ultimately employing close to 5.5 million Egyptians by the end of his reign. Meanwhile, public factories employed more than 600,000 workers. In comparison, private sector companies during the first decade of Infitah created a meager 28,000 new jobs.[116] What Infitah did in fact create were millionaires—thousand of millionaires in an overwhelmingly poor society. Moreover, these millionaires were no great industrialists who might eventually expand the job market, but were rather importers, moneychangers, and middlemen, as well as rehabilitated *ancien regime* landowners. Whether this band of investors constituted "a full-blown comprador bourgeoisie, or simply a mafia ... the consequence is the same."[117] They contributed neither to industry nor employment. More dangerous still was Infitah's redistributional effects. World Bank statistical findings in 1980 spelled out how the distributive effects of Sadat's economic liberalization threatened to create class tensions. While the poorest 20 percent of the population controlled 5 percent of the national income, the share of the highest 5 percent was 22 percent; the share of the richest 10 percent was 33 percent; and that of the richest 20 percent was more than 50 percent of the national income.[118]

Mubarak, like his predecessor, was granted a relatively long grace period by the oil boom of the 1970s. With the increase in oil prices, the country's revenue from oil exports, remittances of Egyptians working in oil-rich countries, and traffic in the Suez Canal increased. Over one-third of the state revenue came from these sources, as opposed to less than 50 percent from taxes. Between 1975 and 1985, remittances grew from $366 million to $3.9 billion, and petroleum exports grew from $381 million to $5 billion, while the Suez Canal administration channeled in $1 billion annually. Oil prices, however, plummeted from $36 a barrel in 1980 to $12 in 1986. The collapse was felt in Egypt in 1986 as exports were sliced in half from $2.26 billion to $1.2 billion, and Suez Canal tariffs dropped from $1 billion to less than $900 million. This immediately caused a sharp decrease in foreign currency reserves—a crippling disaster in a country with such a high import bill. By 1986, the contribution of oil exports to foreign currency reserves fell from 33 percent to 12.6 percent, while that of remittances fell from 43 to 27 percent. Inflation skyrocketed to 23 percent, and unemployment to 19 percent. What strained the economy even further was the U.S. decision that same year to suspend an aid package worth $265 million until Egypt submitted to IMF-recommended reforms.[119] The stage was set for a devastating debt crisis.

Eager to give his people a quick taste of the prosperity he promised after concluding peace with Israel, Sadat had to rely on foreign aid. His policies doubled the foreign debt from $7.5 billion in 1977 to $14.7 billion in 1980, with the associated debt service jumping from $454 million to $1.6 billion during the same period. The end of the oil boom forced the country into more debt, which by 1987 had reached the unfathomable figure of $40 billion (and projected to climb to $53 billion in 1991), with annual debt service of $2.1 billion. Debt service, which consumed 24 percent of total exports in 1980, almost doubled to 46 percent less than a decade later.[120] By the end of 1987, the Egyptian government announced it could no longer service its foreign debt, let alone be able to repay it, and in 1989 it declared bankruptcy, meaning that it was no longer eligible to receive the international loans it needed so desperately to meet its domestic obligations.

It was only through participating in the war against Iraq in 1991 that the country could start running again, since its biggest creditor, the United States, conditioned pardoning half of its debt, as well as convincing the Paris Club and Gulf countries to follow suit, on its participation. The credibility of the international coalition George Bush was trying to put together to liberate Kuwait hung on the participation of other Arab states. Egypt's involvement was, in Bush's own words, an essential "'cover' for the other Arab states who wanted to join." Mubarak initially hesitated. During his meeting with Secretary of Defense Dick Cheney on August 7, 1990, he offered overflight rights to U.S. aircraft, allowed U.S. battleships through the Suez Canal, and permitted the use of Egyptian bases for refueling, but ruled out actual participation in the war coalition. On September 1, Bush made him an offer he could not refuse: forgiving half of Egypt's foreign debt. The Egyptian president was now completely on board. Recalling his reaction during their first meeting in November 1990, Bush reported proudly: "I saw eye-to-eye with him on almost all issues ... I also asked him whether Egyptian troops would go into Iraq. He said he'd do whatever was necessary."[121]

Despite the elimination of half its foreign debt in 1991, Egypt still lost most of the workers' remittances coming from Iraq and other Gulf countries as a result of the war. Foreign assistance was also reduced as Egypt had to compete for Western aid with dozens of ex-Communist countries in Europe after the collapse of the Berlin Wall. With economic growth at barely 1 percent in 1991, and population growth at 2 percent, per capita income declined to $600 (from $750 in 1986), gravely affecting the standard of living.[122] The government was now expected by the IMF to add to its people's suffering through reducing state subsidies.

Egypt's dire finances forced Mubarak, under intense American pressure, to adopt in 1991 the IMF-tailored Economic Reform and Structural Adjustment Program, which called for reducing social welfare and selling public companies in order to bring state expenditure and debt under control. By 1995, the government had cut 75.82 percent of the subsidies it provided in the eighties, and it was no longer committed to hiring university graduates. Law 203 of 1991 restructured the public sector into 314 holding companies and affiliates to prepare for their privatization. The United States and leading capitalist

companies devoted close to $600 million to fund private-sector acqui-
sition of these companies. By 1999 the government had sold shares in
124 of its 314 enterprises.[123]

The first few years appeared to have "vindicated the principles of
neoliberalism." During its first decade (1991–2001), the program succeeded in reducing the budget deficit from 15.3 percent to 3 percent
of GDP, and achieving a 5 percent growth rate.[124] Also, as the program
intended, the share of private capital jumped from 58 percent in 1991
to 74 percent in 1996.* Indeed, between 1982 and 2002, the share of the
public sector was reduced from 54 percent of GDP and 70 percent of
total investment to 28 percent of GDP and 44 percent of investments.[125]

A closer look, however, reveals this economic boom had little to
do with the economic "reform" program. To start with, the creditors' decision to write off half of Egypt's external debt in return for
its participation in the 1991 Gulf War made available $15.5 billion in
savings on interest payments by 1996. So the greatest contributor to
Egypt's economic turnaround resulted from a political decision by the
United States and its allies. Furthermore, the state continued to derive
one-third of its revenue from rents administered by two public enterprises, the Suez Canal Company and the Egyptian General Petroleum
Corporation, rather than from taxing the expanding private sector. This
latter fact reveals how the purported economic liberalization did little
to deprive the regime of its most salient asset: its ability to tap into
various types of rents and then redistribute them in ways that allowed
it to maintain power. In addition to oil and gas fields, rents in Egypt
were derived from state control over the dispensing of foreign aid, the
revenues of the Suez Canal, and, most important, the allocation of land.
The fact that only 4 percent of the country is inhabited, with the rest
classified as public land, allows the regime to allocate land for select
property developers, hotel magnates, or realtors at whatever price and
under whatever conditions it chooses. Politically linked businessmen
dug assiduously into this gold mine: beginning from the 1990s, gated
compounds, masquerading as American-style suburbs, mushroomed
around the capital; holiday resorts spread over tens of thousands of acres
on the Mediterranean and Red Sea coasts; and real estate speculation
became the most lucrative investment in town. Indeed, by 2002, real
estate had replaced agriculture as the third-largest non-oil investment
sector, way ahead of manufacturing. Instead of generating an export
boom, economic liberalization generated a building boom. Egypt was

---

* A breakdown of the shares of private firms in the various sectors of the economy
between 1981 and 1999 reveals how their share increased from 70 to 94.4 percent
of GDP in commerce; 51.3 to 76.6 percent in construction; 26 to 32 percent in
finance; 33.6 to 73.8 percent in industry and mining; and 98 to 99.6 percent in agriculture (Abd al-Mo'ty, *Al-tabaqat al-egtema'iya wa mustaqbal misr*, 359).

paving over its arable land while its people were forced to import their food needs from the West.[126]

Another troubling aspect of this whole economic-reform episode pertains to the very rationale behind the privatization program. The conventional account emphasizes how Egypt could no longer cover the losses generated by its failed public sector. Yet on the eve of the IMF program, 260 out of the 314 state-owned companies were profitable, only 54 were suffering losses, and the rest were breaking even. Moreover, the profitable companies (making a net annual profit of $550 million) more than compensated for the losses (only $110 million every year). The real concern was the four large public-owned banks, since over 30 percent of their loans were nonperforming. The problem with these banks, however, was that they were channeling public funds through their private sector affiliates to a small group of state-connected businessmen, and it was those who were not only defaulting on their loans, but also acquiring even more loans after they had defaulted through their political links, delaying legal action against them, and arranging to flee the country before charges were pressed.[127] Public banks held 60 percent of total deposits and provided 50 percent of loans. By the late 1990s, twenty-eight politically tied clients received 13 percent of the total public credit extended to the private sector, with an average of £E1 billion each. Over 53 percent of these loans were provided without sufficient collateral. By 2002, only twelve debtors held 18 percent of nonperforming loans in the public banking sector.[128] Not surprisingly, the government used 40 percent of its proceeds from privatization ($1.5 billion by 1997) to pay off the bad debts of its business cronies, rather than provide welfare services as promised. Egypt's financial difficulties, therefore, had less to do with a failed public sector than with a situation where public funds were knotted to the projects of politically connected businessmen. That is why it is fair to conclude with the political scientist Timothy Mitchell: "The reform program did not remove the state from the market or eliminate profligate public subsidies. Its main impact was to concentrate public funds into different hands, and many fewer. The state turned resources away from agriculture and industry ... It now subsidized financiers instead of factories, cement kilns instead of bakeries, speculators instead of schools."[129]

Finally, deepening the involvement of the private sector in the economy made it more vulnerable to global capitalism, especially considering that Egyptian firms during the 1990s imported more than 70 percent of their production inputs and exported less than 44 percent of their products. The domination of the foreign component in domestic industries, which in most cases was little more than domestic reassembly of foreign-manufactured products, ruled out the possibility that a viable industrial capitalist class would emerge from the restructuring of the 1990s. In character and interests, therefore, this new class was merely an extension of the old: "the merchants of the seventies were the capitalists of the nineties."[130] The main difference, however, was that the latter group was no longer satisfied with living in the shadow of power; with so much capital accumulated, it was time to move up in the political world, they thought. For the first time since 1952, the reins of political leadership were slipping into the hands of the economic ruling class.

THE CHANGING OF THE GUARD

Who were these new capitalists? At the beginning of the new millennium, the Egyptian economy was dominated by fewer than two dozen family-owned conglomerates. The founders of these dynasties had a lot in common: most were into construction; their businesses were kicked off through state contracts; they drew funds freely from public banks; they partnered with foreign (especially American) investors; they employed a relatively small working force (3,000 on average); and their products catered to the needs of the affluent. This class fraction certainly did not represent the Egyptian bourgeoisie in its entirety, but it was the fraction off which the rest of the class members made their living, and the one none of them had any hope to compete with or dislodge. Directly below this limited group of state-nurtured superrich businessmen, another 5 percent of the population enjoyed modest affluence, while the rest of society was neatly divided between the relatively poor and the 50 percent living below the poverty line (less than $2 a day). Among the latter group, perhaps ten million dwelled in self-built shantytowns on the outskirts of the capital, described by an Egyptian sociologist as "slums with no schools, hospitals, clubs, sewage systems, public transportation or even police stations, which had become a Hobbesian world of violence and vice."[131]

This disheartening socioeconomic imbalance notwithstanding, the new megacapitalists began vying for more political power. Mubarak hesitated. He knew quite well that the stability of the 1952 regime rested on a formula that exchanged social rights for political ones. According to this unwritten social contract, the state provided employment, education, health care, and subsidized goods and services to its citizens, in return for their forgoing their right to participate in politics. But the president also realized that this arrangement required a constantly solvent state. Until 1971, sequestered land and financial assets, nationalized businesses, and cheap Soviet aid provided enough revenue for the state to carry out this role. Nasser believed that before these resources dried up, his state-led industrialization would produce sufficient returns to continue these welfare policies. However, Sadat's partnership with the United States (with its free-market price tag) replaced cheap Soviet assistance with an increasingly expensive and conditional American aid, and his open-door policy not only squandered state wealth in nonindustrial pursuits but also left the state in debt to foreign governments. More important, the wedding of business and politics, so actively encouraged by Sadat, allowed rising capitalists to entrench themselves too deeply in the bureaucracy and ruling party to be purged from above. Ultimately, Egypt's deteriorating finances and sustained pressure from the world capitalist centers propelled Mubarak to dismantle the last vestiges of state economic power (government subsidies and the public sector) and to rely more and more on private investors.

Politically speaking, however, this new stratum was the most dangerous of all the economic elite groups of the post-1952 era because it was the only one that combined alliances with global capitalist centers with alliances with state rulers and functionaries. Not only that, but they were also avid organizers. In the 1990s, they established a joint committee between the Egyptian Businessmen's Association (EBA), their formal platform since 1979, and the cabinet. The declared aim of this committee was to "advise" ministers before they issued economic policies and regulations. They then infiltrated state-run economic bodies such as the Chamber of Commerce and the Chamber of Industry, to be able to "fashion more reciprocal power relations" between these corporatist associations and the government, and use them to promote business interests.[132]

These lobbying tactics, however, soon proved to be insufficient. A more daring strategy was evidently required. They now decided to cluster around a young investment banker who had begun his career in the Bank of America and worked in London for a while before returning to Cairo in 1995. The young man had two enticing assets: he was politically ambitious, and he was the president's son. In 2000, Gamal Mubarak and his new best friends established the Future Generation Foundation (FGF), a civil association designed to promote Gamal's image as Egypt's youth leader. That same year Mubarak appointed his son to the NDP's general secretariat, as head of the Youth and Development Committee. And in 2002, Gamal created and chaired a new political body within the party: the Policies Committee (PC), which soon became the beating heart of the ruling party and the embodiment of its "New Thinking"—the NDP's 2002 convention slogan. The PC was essentially a crystallization of capitalists and self-styled neoliberal intellectuals. Gamal himself became "a symbol of what Mubarakism has wrought ... economic liberalization in the absence of political liberalization; and corrosive nepotism."[133] From the very start, the public referred to the committee sardonically as "Gamal's cabinet," not knowing, however, that its members would soon in fact form the country's first "businessmen cabinet."

On the morning of July 14, 2004, unsuspecting Egyptians woke up to the news that a computer engineer, Ahmed Nazif, was charged with forming a government stacked with Gamal's crony capitalists and neoliberals. The cabinet included six monopoly capitalists who were put in charge of ministries directly related to their business portfolios, in addition to a number of prominent neoliberal intellectuals. A few examples suffice. Ahmed al-Maghraby, owner of the tourism conglomerate Accor Hotels, was appointed minister of tourism, and a year later minister of housing and construction; Rashid Ahmed Rashid, head of the Middle East and North Africa affiliate of the multinational Unilever, became minister of industry and trade; Mohamed Mansour, chairman of Al-Mansour Motor Group, was charged with the Ministry of Transportation (he had also served as secretary-general of Gamal's Future Generation Foundation, and president of the American Chamber of Commerce in Egypt between 1999 and 2003); Youssef Boutros-Ghali, a longtime IMF executive, was entrusted with Treasury; and Mahmoud Muhi al-Din, a Cairo University professor who was later elected executive director of the World Bank, handled economics and investment. These were all, of course, members of the Policies Committee.

Seizing control of the cabinet was only the first step. What followed afterward was nothing less than a full-fledged "bourgeoisification" of the entire leadership of the ruling party. NDP businessmen more than doubled their share of Parliament seats from 37 in 1995 to 77 in 2000, i.e., from 8 to 17 percent of Parliament.[134] Their influence was further augmented by the fact that they controlled key parliamentary committees, most significantly the Planning and Budget committee, which was chaired by the iron and steel tycoon Ahmed Ezz, Gamal's mentor and closest associate. Starting from 2005, Ezz became majority leader in Parliament. In the words of Speaker of Parliament Fathy Sourur, "Whenever we vote, if Ahmed Ezz raises his hand in approval, the representatives of the majority [party] approve, if he does not raise his hand, they disapprove ... the [NDP] members believed he had the power to have them nominated [to parliamentary elections] by the party ... and he had a strong relationship with Gamal Mubarak."[135] In 2006, Gamal himself became NDP assistant secretary-general.

Controlling business lobbies, the cabinet, the ruling party, and Parliament were important steps. But there was more; there was the presidency. The new business elite now flirted with the idea of pushing Gamal to the top executive position, under the pretext of civilianizing the presidency after it had remained in the hands of former officers since 1952. And to pave the way, constitutional amendments in 2005 and

2007 placed conditions for presidential elections that fit only Gamal, and eliminated judicial supervision over the voting process. Thus began the ill-fated campaign to boost the legitimacy of the younger Mubarak, a campaign that reached the height of absurdity when Ezz introduced his friend to the last NDP conference in 2010 as "Gamal, the leader of the modernization revolution."

The NDP's old guard, of course, resisted. The regime loyalist Fathy Sourur shared his frustration with reporters after the 2011 revolt: "Their [the businessmen's] entry into the cabinet was a big mistake, especially that they were put in charge of the fields they specialized in, which caused a contradiction between public and private interests, and I said this more than once … to the party, but no one listened."[136] Many probably blamed these changes on the proud father who wanted to pass the mantle to his son (some add, under the insistence of the mother). But a number of objective conditions explain why the political apparatus became increasingly reliant on Gamal's monopoly capitalists. The most important of these were solvency and geopolitical support.

Between 1992 and 2002, domestic debt increased from 67 to 90 percent of GDP. The state was in fact running on debt. And since the ruling party lived off state finances, it too was running on debt. But who were the creditors? Half of the debt lay with public-sector banks, which had little choice but to obey the rulers, even when they went beyond regular deposits and dabbled into the pool of pensions and social security funds. A second source was treasury bills, though raising money through this route was time-consuming and cumbersome. The easiest and most readily available way to keep the political machine solvent was to count on the generosity of regime-friendly capitalists.[137] At the beginning, they channeled funds through crooked business deals, whereby the investor would secure a contract or a plot of land, and in return the politician would get a commission. Donations and philanthropy also paid part of the bill. But as monopoly capitalists began to take charge of the ruling party and government, they assumed financial responsibilities as well. They funded NDP conventions; they launched government media campaigns; they paid bribes to stifle the opposition; they bought votes and organized pro-regime demonstrations; and so on. Reliance on the generosity of friendly capitalists increased systematically. The 27 percent state budget deficit in 2011, an estimated £E140 billion, revealed that the regime was sinking deeper and deeper into debt.[138]

Also, through their business partnerships with global investors, Gamal's cronies assured the regime that despite official pressure to democratize, Western support would remain forthcoming. This was the bridging role that businessmen on the periphery of the world capitalist system traditionally played to keep their markets linked to the global investment centers. And the Egyptian capitalists performed it par excellence. They even accompanied Mubarak during his annual visits to Washington—a mobile lobby of sorts. During the first three years of the Nazif cabinet, foreign investment in Egypt tripled.[139] Then, the American decision in 2004 to allocate USAID to the private sector rather than the government further enhanced their political weight.

It was only natural afterward that Egypt's new business stratum would demand more than it used to get through shabby deals with politicians. In return for the valuable services it provided to the regime, it now wanted to restructure the economy itself through neoliberal concepts. A new tax regime, which gradually materialized between 2002 and 2010, imposed 60 percent of the tax burden on the general population via indirect taxes and tariffs (such as the sales tax) that do not discriminate between rich and poor. At the same time, taxes on business revenues were sliced in half from 40 to 20 percent. In addition, the tax-collecting authority was quite lenient on tax evasion, allowing businessmen—if caught—to pay the amount due plus a small fine without the prospect of imprisonment.[140] Then, in 2009, the government drafted the infamous real estate tax, which taxed citizens' private residences regardless of their wealth or income level—a decision so contentious that the president himself intervened against it weeks before it was supposed to come into force. Another problem was the ever-increasing price levels. In January 2003, the government floated the currency-exchange rate, causing the value of the Egyptian pound to lose 25 percent of its value vis-à-vis the U.S. dollar. The decision was justified by the need to improve Egypt's balance of trade. What happened instead was that importing activities persisted at the same level, while the price of imported goods and services (and domestic products that relied overwhelmingly on imported components) skyrocketed. For the first time in their modern history, Egyptians experienced the smoldering effects of stagflation. Mitchell, an avid student of both Egypt and neoliberalism, described why:

> Neoliberalism is a triumph of the political imagination. Its achievement is double: while narrowing the window of political debate, it promises from this window a prospect without limits. On the one hand, it frames public discussion in the elliptic language of neo-classical economics. The collective well-being of the nation is depicted only in terms of how it is adjusted in gross to the discipline of monetary and fiscal balance sheets. On the other, neglecting the actual concerns of any concrete local or collective community, neoliberalism encourages the most exuberant dreams of private accumulation.[141]

From day one, these capitalists-turned-politicians turned their back on Egypt's severe social problems: poverty, unemployment, illiteracy, deteriorating public services, urban congestion, shantytowns, pollution, and all the rest. "The rhetoric of management, financial soundness, and market forces depoliticized these complex issues ... [and] transformed questions of social inequality and powerlessness into issues of efficiency and control."[142] Unlike their rural counterparts and the small fish of the 1970s, the new capitalist elite were not only richer, but also more demanding; their business expansion required the state to deregulate the economy, privatize public enterprises, reduce subsidies for the poor and taxes for the rich, and allow them cheap access to public resources. Whatever surplus the state could use to fulfill urgent social needs was being sucked into the pockets of the ruling party's capitalist cronies. The political apparatus was strained to the limit, and the maneuvering space of traditional politicians shrank considerably.

At the same time, the level of corruption became overwhelming; and it extended from head to tail. The president and his family were rumored to have amassed as much as $70 billion, and forty of his ministers and close business associates were alleged to have made at least $1 billion each.[143] The Central Auditing Authority submitted a thousand reports between October 1999 and July 2004 detailing various violations committed by state officials and favored businessmen. The reports estimated that financial corruption cost the economy £E100 billion during those years, in addition to £E5 billion in money laundering, and £E500 million in bribes paid to public servants.[144] After the 2011 revolt, dozens of corruption cases flooded the office of the general prosecutor. It is enough to mention that in the weeks following the revolt, the president and his entire family and aides, a dozen ministers (including the prime minister), the Speakers of the upper and lower houses of Parliament, and perhaps two dozen businessmen (including Ahmed Ezz) were taken into custody or had arrest warrants issued against them for financial corruption and abuse-of-office charges. A full catalog of the charges deserves an independent study, but a few examples might illustrate the type and scale of corruption during Mubarak's final two decades.

A good place to start is the case of Hussein Salem, the president's best (perhaps only) friend. Salem started out as a security operative. He resigned his government job and turned to business on the eve of Mubarak's coming to power. His first successful enterprise was a joint venture with Mubarak's brother-in-law and two former CIA officers. The American-Egyptian Transport and Service Company (AETSCO), later known as White Wings, received (as it turned out, illegal) Pentagon commissions to transport U.S. weapons to Egypt. From then onward, Salem became one of the most notorious arms dealers, involved in such high-profile contracts as Iran-Contra in the 1980s. The whole venture was exposed in 1987, first in the American media, then the following year by a seven-hour hearing in the Egyptian parliament held by the opposition delegate Alwy Hafez. Salem then turned to tourism, building and running some of the most luxurious resorts in coastal cities such as Sharm al-Sheikh. In 2000, Salem cofounded the Egyptian Mediterranean Gas Company (EMG) with an Israeli partner, the former Mossad officer Yussi Miman. The company supplied Israel with 40 percent of its natural gas needs at a discount price, at a time when Egypt was in dire need of energy and cash. In 2008, Salem sold 12 percent of his shares to two American investors for $2.2 billion. During that time, Egypt had lost $714 million for selling its gas cheaply.[145] Salem, whose wealth was estimated at $15 billion, escaped to Dubai five days into the uprising with a bag containing $500 million in cash. The authorities refused to allow him in with all this cash and he was returned to Egypt shortly before escaping to his lavish villa in Spain, where Interpol arrested him, but refused to extradite him because—as it turns out—he had acquired Spanish citizenship and given up his Egyptian status.[146]

Another flagrant example is Ahmed Ezz, the third-richest man in Egypt (with a fortune of over $10 billion) and the self-proclaimed architect of the new political order. Ezz, who owned two small factories for steel and ceramics in 1996, monopolized the industry by 2004 after acquiring the biggest state-owned iron and steel company almost for free, and without a public auction. State largesse continued as the Trade and Industry Ministry granted Ezz licenses worth £E660 million for free to build two additional factories in the free industrial zone in Suez. Gawdat al-Malt, head of the Central Auditing Authority, submitted two 278-page reports to the Speaker of Parliament on May 29 and September 15, 2004, regarding Ezz's illegal monopolies. The reports exposed how the business tycoon controlled 55.3 percent of the domestic market and 72.3 percent of exports of reinforced iron, and 47.9 percent and 83.2 percent of exports of flat iron.[147] The Speaker of Parliament, Sourur, confessed that when the government suggested antimonopoly legislation that would seize 10 percent of the violator's profits, Ezz—the head of Parliament's Budget Committee—intervened to cap the fine at £E300 million. "I complained to the president, and told him this cannot pass, and he asked Safwat al-Sharif [NDP secretary-general] to resolve the issue. Al-Sharif came to my office and called in Ezz to relay the president's objections ... To my astonishment, Ahmed Ezz stuck to his guns ... and we were forced to compromise ... At this point, I realized that Ahmed Ezz was stronger [than the president], that he represented a dangerous power [that could] defy the president."[148]

Under Mubarak the state allocated 67,200 square kilometers (an area equivalent to the size of Palestine, Lebanon, Kuwait, Qatar, and Bahrain combined) worth £E800 billion to favored investors. In addition, the illegal diversion of 185,000 feddans of arable land to construction projects had cost the economy £E78 billion in the past decade. In the weeks following the 2011 revolt, 123 cases pertaining to violations of Law 89 of 1994, which requires allocating public land to the highest bidder, were considered by the courts. A small sample is enough to demonstrate: Ezz acquired 21 million square meters at the price of £E4 per meter in the industrial area on the Gulf of Suez, only to resell it to foreign companies for £E1,000 per meter a couple of years later; Minister of Tourism Zohair Garanah allocated plots in some of the best tourist sites at prices considerably below that of the market, thus costing the state more than £E2 billion in 2006 alone; Minister of Housing and Construction Ahmed al-Maghraby allocated between January 2006 and December 2008 over 27.2 million square meters to thirteen companies in which his family-owned Palm Hills Company controlled between 49 and 100 percent of each—in Palm Hills itself, the president's younger son's stock increased by £E16 million in 2009 alone as a result of the appreciation of the value of land acquired by the company; Minister of Agriculture Amin Abaza gave away 11,556 feddans in Sinai for free to a businessman, who then sold 8,000 of those feddans for £E350 million to foreign investors; companies owned by the president's sons and in-laws acquired vast amounts of agricultural land on the Cairo-Alexandria Desert Road for the ridiculously cheap price of £E200 per feddan to build luxurious compounds with hundreds of multi million-dollar villas; the former minister of housing and construction Ibrahim Suleiman sold 40,000 square meters of land on the Mediterranean Sea for £E300 per meter instead of its true market value of £E8,000; finally, Prime Minister Ahmed Nazif cost the country a total of £E51.2 billion by passing Ministerial Decree 2843 of 2009, which legalized the disputed acquisition of 1.5 million feddans for 2.5 percent of their market price.[149] It was only natural, then, that while Garanah's company was in debt for £E4 billion before he joined the cabinet, he was now worth perhaps £E13 billion; and al-Maghraby, who had only £E4.9 billion in 2004, quadrupled that amount after he became minister to £E17 billion, in addition to £E3 billion in the form of discounted loans from banks.[150]

Expectedly, the privatization file was reopened after the 2011 revolt. Although nationalization of the means of production took place through laws in the 1950s and 1960s, their privatization was allowed through arbitrary administrative decisions with little or no transparency. So, for example, while the government estimated the total value of the public sector at £E124 billion in 1991—though a private consultant inflated that figure to £E500 billion—by July 2000 almost half of the public sector had been sold, for a meager £E15.6 billion, leading the government to adjust its previous estimation retroactively to the absurd amount of £E28.8 billion. Soon, high-profile corruption cases were exposed. An early one that occurred in 1994 involved the selling of the public-sector affiliate of Pepsi-Cola for £E131 million divided as follows: 49 percent to the politically connected Muhammad Nusair, 49 percent to a Saudi company, and 2 percent to the global conglomerate of Pepsi-Cola. Four years later, Pepsi-Cola bought 77 percent of the shares for £E400 million, i.e., nine times the value of the entire company when it was first sold. Nusair's claim that he managed to turn the company around in such a short period did not convince anyone, especially considering that reports by the Central Auditing Authority revealed how private investors were performing so poorly in the public companies they bought. Indeed, during the period in question (1997–2002), businessmen delivered 52 percent of the promised investments in all sectors, and 26 percent of the projected investments in the industrial sector, with the state covering the rest.[151] Months after the 2011 revolt, three of the major privatized companies were returned to state ownership after the courts exposed the corrupt means by which they were passed to private hands, and dozens of other cases were being investigated.[152]

GOVERNING A TIME BOMB

Egypt's dark days were getting even darker. Between 2000 and 2009, GDP increased from $92.4 billion to $187.3 billion, and economic growth increased from 3.2 to 5 percent. But the economic growth achieved during that decade (mostly due to the doubling of oil prices after the invasion of Iraq, and the increase in foreign investments) did not translate into an improvement in the standard of living of common people. In 2006, gross national income per capita was 7 percent lower than it had been in 2000. During that same year, World Bank reports indicated that 47 percent of the population was living on less than two dollars a day.[153] In 2010, unemployment was estimated at 26.3 percent, though the government claimed it was only 10 percent.[154] More than 3 million people joined the underground economy. Education spending consumed less than 5 percent of GDP; food subsidies were reduced by 20 percent, causing the price of various food items to increase threefold; and while the rich decorated their lavish compounds with artificial lakes and swimming pools, 79 percent of Egyptians had no access to clean drinking water and a proper sewage system.[155]

During the last two decades of Mubarak's reign, almost all Egyptians suffered. The countryside was an easy and early target. Law 96 of 1992 abrogated the gains the peasantry had made through the Agricultural

Reform Law 178 of 1952. Instead of the regulated rents of the old law, the new one decreed that the 1.2 million tenant contracts in the countryside would expire by the end of 1997, allowing absentee land-owners to either negotiate new contracts or sell the land and drive the peasants out. Of course, the justification was to provide more capital for investment. But considering that 7 million peasants and their fami-lies lived on these lands, and that the government had no solution for their inevitable plight, violent protests soon erupted. Between October 1997 and the summer of 1999, land seizures and sabotage of agricul-tural equipment was so rampant that the government had to order in the Central Security Forces to subdue the angry peasants. Likewise, aggressive privatization and the government's wholesale abandonment of the public sector triggered numerous labor strikes: 161 strikes in 2001, 86 in 2003, the violent April 6 national strike of 2008, and more than 700 in 2010. In fact, between 2001 and 2011, perhaps 2 million workers participated in strikes.[156] Even within the traditional bastion of state power—the bureaucracy—things were going downhill. Only the top 0.2 percent, a little more than 8,000 officials (including ministers), were well paid (some receiving six-figure salaries), while the rest of the 5.5 million employees gradually descended to the ranks of the prole-tariat.[157] Moreover, the structure of the leading class faction—the new business elite—did not lend itself to class-based cooperation. Egyptian monopoly capitalists continued to act more like competing magnates than a consolidated class leadership, and therefore failed to absorb high-level bureaucrats, middling landowners, and agricultural capitalists into their fold. More generally, the state's deteriorating ability to provide essential services and indifference to unemployment and poverty infuriated millions.

Of course, the ultimate guarantor of the regime could not have stood by idly as billions were passing from hand to hand under its nose; it had to be given a piece of the action. Preliminary investigations revealed that Interior Minister Habib al-Adly and his immediate family owned nine villas, seven apartments, 75 feddans of agricultural land, thirteen con-struction sites, a shopping mall in Sharm al-Sheikh, and four Mercedes automobiles. In addition to bank deposits, his wealth amounted to £E8 billion.[158] State Security laid claim to a vast plot of (military) land in the buzzing Cairo neighborhood of Nasr City to establish its new headquarters. In Alexandria, thirty-eight SSIS officers acquired 750,000 square meters of land for £E13 per meter in 2000, when the market price exceeded £E300 per meter. After the uprising, Egyptian courts froze the assets of fifty-two high-ranking police officers charged with corruption.[159] Adly received a twelve-year prison sentence and a £E23 million fine for money laundering and abusing office to amass wealth.

Needless to say, increasing government corruption pushed the regime more into the Interior Ministry's iron cage. Rather than pressure the regime to democratize, as liberal theorists would predict, Egypt's capitalists-turned-ministers realized that they were now beholden to the police forces more than ever. The social unrest resulting from the shrinking of social benefits, the steady rise in price levels, the laying off of thousands of public- and private-sector workers, and the systematic and rabid corruption inflicting economic life required constant repression. Little wonder Gamal's Policies Committee was expanded in 2005 to include the interior minister in its fold. In other words, even after the post-1952 political apparatus lent itself to neoliberal control, it still rested on coercion. This was not only a domestic deformation of global neoliberalism. In Mitchell's judgment, for the advocates of neoliberalism, "repression is an unforeseen, unfortunate, intermittent, and probably temporary side effect of the shocks that accompany the expansion of the global market," but viewed critically, "violence is a common instrument of capitalist development, in particular the penetration of capitalist relations into new territories."[160] Michael Mann held a similar view of the intertwining of authoritarianism and neoliberalism. Authoritarian regimes are particularly prone to implementing policies that produce "short-term economic misery for the sake of some dubious neo-liberal vision of the long term" because they do not have to worry about winning elections.[161] This might explain why the Fact Finding Commission appointed to investigate the attempted repression of the 2011 revolt concluded that the NDP and the Interior Ministry were equally responsible for the corruption of political life.[162] The fortunes of the political and security apparatuses remained symbiotically linked until the very last day. And their alliance tempted them to push society to the limit.

What effectively happened was that the Egyptian economy became increasingly divided into two spheres, with nothing in the middle: one servicing less than 10 percent of society with a conspicuously high purchasing power, and another for the barely surviving masses. As the overwhelming majority watched, the country's minuscule upper class sent its children to overpriced private schools, received treatment in highly equipped hospitals, resided in lavish compounds with golf courses and country clubs, vacationed in extravagant beach resorts, drove luxurious cars, and shopped at some of the most expensive malls in the Middle East. Egypt had become a failed state in the eyes of its own people. It belonged to the upper class. Laws were passed only so that a few could enrich themselves by breaking them, while the rest of society suffered the brunt. The tax burden fell on the poor in order to serve the tax-evading rich. Bribery had become the norm, and legal permits were up for sale. In short, corruption had become a way of life. As the political economist Samer Suleiman somberly concluded,

"Egypt's story in the last quarter century had been the story of regime success and state failure."[163]

But how did society become so polarized? And why would the middle class that had been long nurtured by the regime turn against it? Although the nonindustrial middle class (rural and state bourgeoisie, small businessmen, and professionals) initially provided the bulwark of the coup-installed regime, changing political contingencies splintered this middle class, since different fragments proved useful at different times. And as the new regime produced more and more fragments, it became no longer capable of satisfying them all. Nor did it need many of them any longer. The rural middle class had become dispensable because the outright rigging of elections (financed by direct handouts from ruling party capitalists and carried out by the Interior Ministry) rendered its political control function in the countryside superfluous. Now they could be pressured to sell their land to satisfy the appetite of the superrich for giant agro-industrial projects. The wells of the state bourgeoisie were also drying up because the dismantling of the public sector diminished their middlemen role between aspiring businessmen and public resources. With capitalists in direct control of government, who needs middlemen? But not only was the fox in the henhouse, market deregulation and bureaucratic streamlining deprived them of the petty extortions they imposed on citizens and small businessmen. Added to the woes of the middle-class fragments were those of the parasitic business class of the late 1970s and 1980s. Ruling-party tycoons raised market entry barriers and eliminated competitors with relative ease. Tolerance for small fish in the business world was shrinking by the moment. Finally, staggering unemployment and inflation rates made life impossible for educated middle-class youth who realized that their hard-earned diplomas no longer carried them far in Egypt's neoliberal economy. All these middle-class fragments had gradually fallen out of favor and thus became disgruntled. At the end, only the tiny fragment linked directly to the political apparatus (the uppermost crust of the bourgeoisie) remained loyal, while the majority of the middle-class fragments resented the regime for abandoning them. Revolt, in this case, seemed the only way out of their suffering. With the clock ticking away toward September 2011, the date the president was supposed to pass on the mantle to Gamal and his capitalist allies, the middle class expected nothing less than their total ruin. When a call went out to make a final stand against the regime on January 25, 2011, they had only their chains to lose.

Truth be told, however, Mubarak did little more than follow the dotted line marked by his predecessor. He simply extended and reinforced the three trends set in place when he assumed office in 1981: the marginalization of the military; the empowerment of the security force;

and the increased reliance on a state-nurtured capitalist class to run the country. It was these three powerful undercurrents that carried the regime slowly but surely to its end destination: the January 25 Revolt in 2011. This does not, of course, absolve Mubarak of responsibility for all the deterioration and misfortune that befell the country under his watch. But to understand what really happened, rather than just assign blame, one must begin by recognizing that what Mubarak essentially did was hold steady and keep the regime structure he inherited on track; he was a stabilizer, not an innovator. Admittedly, the ride down this destined pathway was rough, and the outcome far from inevitable. There were storms to be weathered, crises to be defused, and obstacles at every step of the way. The military under the charismatic and resourceful Field Marshal Abd al-Halim Abu Ghazala was far from eclipsed. The supposedly reliable Central Security Forces led an armed mutiny against the government. The insatiable business elite that infiltrated the ruling party more deeply than intended thoughtlessly squeezed the state for concessions. But after all is said and done, the sudden (and maybe temporary) collapse of the regime in 2011 was the cumulative result of the six decades of power struggles within the ruling coalition.

On the Threshold of Power:
The Military After the Revolt

Commenting on the popular revolts that beset Europe in 1989, the sociologist Charles Tilly wrote, "In a time of consumerism and powerful states ... it hardly seemed that dissidents within European countries could do much more than plant bombs, scrawl graffiti, mumble curses or give up. Reform or repression, perhaps; revolution, never ... In 1989, however, the people of Eastern Europe vigorously vitiated any analysis that implied an end to rebellion. They made their own revolutions."[1] Less than two decades after Tilly penned these memorable words, it was the Arabs' turn.

The snowball started rolling from the west. When a policewoman slapped an unemployed college graduate for working as a street vendor without a permit, the indignant young man set himself on fire, triggering a massive uprising that overthrew the country's political leadership in three weeks. This all occurred in a country with strikingly similar circumstances to Egypt: Tunisia. Unlike the monarchies of Morocco and Jordan, where the army is loyal to the sovereign, and the tribal societies of Libya and Yemen, as well as the monarchical-tribal societies of the Gulf, where the reigning tribe controls the military leadership whereas the (potentially rebellious) rank and file come from lesser tribes, the Egyptian and Tunisian armies were drawn from ethnically and religiously homogeneous populations and swore allegiance to modern republican constitutions. Also, contrary to the army-controlled regimes of Syria, Algeria, and Sudan, the two countries had metamorphosed from coup-installed military regimes into full-fledged police states. In the process, armies in both countries were gradually sidelined by a suspicious political elite in favor of an expansive security institution, and thus grew eager to alter the political formula once circumstances allowed. Finally, the lower classes in both states suffered from an exploitative and corrupt state-nurtured business elite with strong ties to global investors. Tunisia was, of course, considerably smaller that Egypt in area, population, and the size of its police and military forces, but its experience had a crucial demonstrative effect for Egyptians. It showed them that the unthinkable was in fact thinkable. Now Egyptians started moving, and a demoralized military realized that at last the external factor they hoped would shift the stagnant power balance to its favor had begun to materialize.

EIGHTEEN DAYS*

The year 2011 was the year of the purported succession. Reports circulating around the country confirmed that Hosni Mubarak was planning to pass on the mantle to his son in September. With the father and the last of the ruling party's old guard gone, there would be no court of appeal against the economic corruption and exploitation of Gamal Mubarak's capitalist cronies. The day (January 25) was Police Day—a national holiday honoring that bloody morning in 1952 when the British killed dozens of Egyptian policemen because they refused to surrender their weapons and stood tall in defense of national dignity—a day that always highlighted the dark contrast between what the police used to be and what they had become.

But on January 25, 2011, Egypt had no organized opposition to speak of. Disgruntled intellectuals and activists from all walks of life joined several united fronts. There was Kefaya (Enough), a movement founded in 2004 to prevent Mubarak (father and son) from running for presidency the following year; there was the National Association for Change, which began in 2010 to campaign for free elections and advocated the candidacy of Mohamed ElBaradei, former director of the International Atomic Energy Agency (IAEA), to the top executive position; there was a mixed lot of unassuming opposition parties representing liberals and leftists, which had rarely challenged the regime; there was the eighty-year-old Muslim Brotherhood, a highly bureaucratic reform movement, which had been invariably manipulated by the regime (to scare liberals in the early fifties; leftists in the seventies; militant Islamists in the eighties and nineties; and Americans throughout) before being caste aside (usually to prison) once it had served its purpose; and there were two Internet-based movements: the April 6 Youth Movement, whose name commemorates the failed national strike on that day in 2007, when striking workers were repressed using live ammunition; and the We Are All Khaled Said Facebook page, named after the Alexandrian boy whose head was smashed on the pavement in the summer of 2010 because he exchanged words with

---

* The information in this section is based on dozens of personal interviews with demonstrators as the revolt unfolded, as well as *Al-Shorouk* newspaper's eighteen short documentaries that recorded the daily developments of the uprising (http://www.shorouknews.com/news/view.aspx?cdate=12022012&id=2cdddca8-b9d6-4148-9a2b-944d2d75794f).

police hoodlums. The fact that the latter, which was created by the thirty-year-old Google marketing executive Wael Ghonim, drew more than half a million members in three months indicated how Egyptians identified with the murdered youth; citizens felt that no matter how politically compliant they were, no one was safe anymore. In short, the Egyptian opposition on the eve of the revolt was little more than an amalgam of loosely organized platforms with overlapping memberships representing all political affiliations and age groups. And even though they had been becoming increasingly vocal and active since 2005, politicians and security men saw no cause for concern. This relaxed attitude was brilliantly captured in Mubarak's sardonic aside during the inauguration of the 2010 parliament (a month before the revolt), "Let them [opposition forces] entertain themselves."

This is why no one thought much of the call to demonstrate on January 25. The invitation was posted on the Facebook pages of the April 6 Youth Movement and We Are All Khaled Said, and on the designated day members from both Internet groups along with mostly young activists from all ideological camps (perhaps 20,000 in all) staged a demonstration in front of the Interior Ministry, three blocks away from Cairo's Tahrir Square in the historic Downtown neighborhood, built in the nineteenth century to resemble the circular layout and architecture of central Paris. This was an impressive showing, considering that past events had attracted at most a couple of hundred participants. Demonstrators were repressed using tear gas and water hoses, thirty activists were detained, and a university student from the city of Suez was killed. Over the next two days, the marches persisted, attracting more and more participants and spreading throughout the country (from Cairo, Alexandria, the Nile Delta, and the Suez Canal cities to the independent-minded southern provinces, all the way to the isolated oases of the Western Desert). The police raised the ante, arresting four thousand demonstrators and organizers (including Wael Ghonim and Egypt's future president Mohamed Morsi); adding rubber bullets to its gas-and-water cocktail (killing four people and injuring more than a hundred); attacking the press syndicate and detaining two dozen reporters for refusing to repeat state media allegations about the "saboteurs" and "outlaws" that were supposedly looting and burning public property; and issuing a stern warning to opposition forces to immediately stop whatever they thought they were doing.

But instead of scaring activists away—as they always did—this time the regime's brutal repression and outrageous lies steeled their will to resist. A call went out through all forms of social media for a Day of Rage on Friday, January 28. The embattled activists appealed to the people to join them. Egyptians hesitated. With the possibility of Gamal's succession right around the corner, their lives promised to become considerably worse. Yet a potentially devastating clampdown unnerved many. That morning, horrified citizens woke up to discover that the security had cut off all cell phone and Internet communication services, and flooded the streets with antiriot police squads and armored vehicles. Many would have preferred to stay home that day if they were not obliged to attend Friday prayers. In the mosques, however, the euphoria of the last three days apparently inspired the country's timid preachers to denounce dictatorship and urge defiance. Fired up by religious sermons and besieged by a sea of angry demonstrators pouring out of Cairo's 300,000 mosques, common folk were carried away; their mind was finally made up. Thus began the march to Tahrir Square.

Policemen tried to resist. They used live ammunition and laser-guided sniper fire; they ran over demonstrators with armored vehicles; they blinded them with a fog of tear gas; they drove them back with high-pressure water hoses—but to no avail. Policemen were exhausted. They had been out on the street in full force for four consecutive days, and by the interior minister's own admission, they were drained and overextended. Equipped only to repress a handful of urban protestors, hotheaded students, or small groups of workers and peasants, they now confronted millions of protestors; they now confronted "the people." Former State Security officer General Assem al-Genedi witnessed first-hand how police troops were left stranded without food, water, sleep, or even fresh batteries for their walkie-talkies. He saw many of them taking off their uniforms and deserting.[2] Following heroic street battles around Cairo's Downtown neighborhoods and Nile bridges, where hundreds were killed, the security forces seemed about to throw in the towel. After a particularly fierce tug-of-war on the Qasr al-Nil Bridge, the western key to Downtown, police units pulled back and the road ahead was clear. At this critical point, the revolutionaries had a choice to make: Where should they turn to next? Leftward to the Union of Television and Radio Stations Building, the regime's central media organ, and the Foreign Ministry adjacent to it; or rightward to the seat of parliament, the cabinet headquarters, and the Interior Ministry, the nerve center of Egypt's police state; or straight ahead, as was originally intended before the sudden police collapse, to Tahrir Square. They opted for the latter, providing the regime with valuable time to fortify each of these strategic posts by nightfall, so that when a few dozen demonstrators, suspecting they might have made the wrong choice, tried to make their way to some of these sites later that night, the roads were already sealed.

Why did the protestors choose a giant public square (approximately 490,000 square feet with the capacity to host perhaps a million people) rather than sensitive state organs—a fateful decision that determined the revolt's trajectory? Everyone knew that seizing a central downtown plaza would not stifle life in a sprawling city like Cairo, nor was it likely to make traffic on its congested roads any worse than it already was. Also, unlike the narrow alleyways and crammed-up buildings in the capital's popular neighborhoods, the square was an open ground with nowhere to hide. So if the demonstrators' plan was neither to paralyze the city nor to be able to maneuver if forced into street battles, then what did they have in mind? It seems obvious that the only advantage such an expansive and exposed location offered was *visibility*. The organizers of the uprising drew inspiration neither from the revolutionaries of late nineteenth- and early twentieth-century Europe, nor from their neighbors in Libya and Syria. They did not grasp the necessity of creating a situation of dual power by occupying government buildings, entrenching themselves in crowded neighborhoods, seizing entire cities, and using all these as bases for incrementally supplanting the regime. Instead the organizers drew inspiration from Eastern Europe in 1989 (in fact many of them later admitted to studying this experiment thoroughly). The dazzling success of peaceful demonstrators in overturning their Communist regimes was enviable. And occupying plazas and wide boulevards seemed to be a viable strategy indeed. For a strategy based on galvanizing domestic and world opinion and daring the regime to shoot civilians in front of hundreds of cameras and news reporters, Tahrir Square (and other central squares throughout Egypt's provincial cities) fit perfectly. And it worked—for the moment.*

Still the police had one more card up their sleeve. The gates of eighteen prisons and dozens of police stations were opened and inmates incited to make the best of the chaotic circumstances. When the head of the prison administration (Police General Muhammad al-Butran) resisted, he was shot dead. Police officers reckoned that ransacking criminals would terrorize citizens enough to go home. Instead the demonstrators torched police stations and ruling-party headquarters throughout the state in retribution and quickly formed neighborhood

---

* Of course, the missing ingredient here was the radically different geopolitical context. With the Soviet patron of the ailing Communist regimes of Eastern Europe retrenching, and the anxious capitalist world, spearheaded by the United States and the European Union, determined not to allow the chance to slip by, the 1989 demonstrators were offered every possible form of help, including sustained media attention and Western ultimatums against their violent repression. In Egypt, by contrast, the authoritarian regime had been serving the interests of the strongest regional and world powers, and after the initial wave of international support subsided, the country's new rulers were expectedly allowed (regardless of American and European rhetoric) to slowly liquidate the revolt, or do whatever was necessary to return to business as usual. In the months following Mubarak's ousting, Tahrir Square became more like an open-air prison, where demonstrators could be sealed off and ignored as life outside continued as normal, and government troops waited for the revolutionary steam to run out, which it inevitably did.

watches to guard their families and properties. For a few valuable hours, the demonstrators controlled the streets, and the twin chants that had come to define the uprising reverberated across the country: "The People Demand to Overthrow the Regime!" and "Raise Your Head High, You're Egyptian!"

Waiting in the winds were the armed forces. As it became clear that the Interior Ministry was unable to stem the uprising, the cornered president was forced to summon his gravediggers—the military—in a final attempt to restore order. An army that had been subdued by its other two ruling partners for four decades rolled confidently into the streets. The fact that members of the general staff were doubt-lessly loyal to Mubarak (or at least indifferent to his policies) did not prevent them, under the weight of general opinion within the corps, from abandoning their old political master to his fate. Acting otherwise risked fracturing the army, which from day one was visibly supportive of the revolt—without waiting for instructions from above. On that first night, soldiers were seen on television smiling and hugging dem-onstrators. Tanks paraded scrawls that read "Down with Mubarak!" and the demonstrators chanted: "The People and the Army Are One Hand!" A group of demonstrators threw themselves over an army jeep before it reached Downtown Cairo, crying frantically: "Are you here to shoot us?" A colonel descended from the vehicle and wrapped his arm around a demonstrator's shoulders and replied: "You have nothing to fear. We would cut our hands before firing one bullet. Your demands are legitimate. Go ahead, and don't turn back." The message was unmis-takable. Even before the military knew how massive or persistent the uprising was, it was here to see it through.

At the end of this bloody day, President Barack Obama of the United States held a press conference expressing concern at the use of violence against peaceful protestors. Still, Mubarak had to try. The seasoned dic-tator mixed sticks with carrots during his first address to the nation after the revolt, close to midnight on January 28. A curfew was declared in all the major cities, but the president dismissed the "businessmen cabinet" and appointed a vice president for the first time in thirty years. The apprehensive demonstrators were soon frustrated when it turned out that the vice president was no other than the fearsome intelligence chief Omar Suleiman, and that the new cabinet was formed under Mubarak's intimate friend Ahmed Shafiq, former commander of the air force and civil aviation minister in the old cabinet. To add insult to injury, fifteen members of the just-dismissed cabinet retained their positions, and only the interior minister and a handful of monopoly capitalists were removed. Clearly, Mubarak was not prepared to go an inch beyond what he thought was absolutely necessary. Demonstrators declared a "permanent" sit-in in Tahrir and other major squares around Egypt until Mubarak stepped down. Hard-core activists camped continuously in the central squares (Tahrir Square, for example, was occupied by no fewer than 50,000 at all times), but during the day their ranks were swelled by tens of thousands of citizens. Field hospitals, open-air theaters, stages for singing and speechmaking, gigantic television screens, food vendors, a garbage collection service, and even barbershops were set up for the comfort of the demonstrators. With their flags, placards, and tents, the revolutionaries were prepared for the long haul. From this point on, it was a waiting game.

On January 30, the police cautiously deployed its forces but strayed away from hot spots, preferring to let the military handle the situation. The next day, the high command issued its first communiqué asserting that the armed forces would not use force to repress the demonstrators. Mubarak's last Speaker of Parliament admitted that during a meeting he attended with the president and his top aides, the defense minister made it clear that "the soldiers are not going to strike against demonstrators; that they are there to protect, not assault them."[3] As one member of SCAF later explained, "The armed forces took charge before the president stepped down in accordance with the communiqué that stated that the military acknowledges the legitimacy of the [demands of the] Egyptian people."[4]

So the following day, Mubarak had to try harder. In an emotional speech, he promised not to run or allow his son to run in the coming elections, and reminded citizens of his patriotic role during the October War in 1973. He also hinted at fundamental changes in the ruling party and a thorough investigation of police responsibility for the violent repression of protests. Many were swayed by his sentimental plea. Less than twenty-four hours later, however, NDP- and police-hired goons dashed into Tahrir on camels and horses, whipping protestors and chasing them around the square, and in a few hours more regime supporters appeared on the rooftops of the surrounding buildings, showering demonstrators below with Molotov cocktails. The revolutionaries fought back with hastily built barricades and stones. After a sixteen-hour battle, the attackers withdrew. The notorious "Battle of the Camel" incident on February 2 further convinced Egyptians that Mubarak had to go. But instead of stepping down, the president tried his best to appease the revolutionaries through political concessions: the vice president was directed to negotiate with the organizers of the revolt; a committee to amend the constitution was set up; the NDP secretary-general and leading cadres, including the president's son Gamal and his chief lieutenant, Ahmed Ezz, were removed from the ruling party, the infamous Policies Committee was dissolved, and a reformist figure was appointed to overhaul the entire party; the interior minister and the businessmen-ministers of the old cabinet were banned from travel, their assets were frozen, and they were interrogated by the general prosecutor; a handful of activists, including Wael Ghonim, were released (the latter gave a stirring television interview, breaking down in tears toward the end, and thus winning more public sympathy for the revolt); Internet service returned; and it was announced that Mubarak was traveling to Germany for medical checkups. But the protestors remained adamant. Beginning on February 8, daily marches and sit-ins were supplemented by strikes in public and private companies and factories. At the same time, governments all around the world, with the notable exception of Israel and Saudi Arabia, called on the regime to submit to popular demands. Then on February 10, the military legend and staunch regime opponent Saad al-Din al-Shazly, chief of staff during the 1973 war, passed away. Sobbing demonstrators marched around Tahrir yelling out his name and offering condolences to the teary-eyed officers that surrounded the square.

On that same day, the Supreme Council of the Armed Forces (SCAF) convened without its supreme commander (the president) in what was perceived as a soft coup. Later that night, state television announced that the president was going to deliver an important speech. The CIA director, Leon Panetta, said in Congress that Mubarak was going to step down. Demonstrators prepared for the party of a lifetime. Instead, the president gave a pedantic and anticlimactic address, ending it with his decision to temporarily delegate his powers to the vice president. This last part of the address was hardly heard, as the stunned demonstrators began screaming and hurling shoes at the television screens in Tahrir Square. As soon as it was over, hundreds of thousands marched to the Presidential Palace, some forty kilometers from Downtown, and were surrounding it by early dawn on February 11. This was it. Either Mubarak was going to order the army and security to liquidate the revolution using all means necessary, effectively causing a bloodbath, or he would be pushed by SCAF to resign. Later in the afternoon, a helicopter transported the president and his family to the Red Sea resort of Sharm al-Sheikh, and the vice president announced that Mubarak had surrendered authority to SCAF. The high command instantly declared its intention to withdraw from politics after a six-month transition period, which would supposedly end with the passing of power to an elected authority. After eighteen days of popular defiance and more than one thousand martyrs, a new chapter had begun.

THE MILITARY AND THE PRICE OF POLITICAL HIBERNATION

Despite the fact that perhaps twelve million Egyptians participated in the eighteen-day uprising, decades of police repression ruled out the possibility that an organized revolutionary movement could have emerged to lead the way. If the military had not sided with the people, it is doubtful that the revolt would have persisted long enough to convince the political leadership it had to step down. And if intraregime relations were not volatile due to the simmering power struggle within the ruling bloc, the military would not have turned its back on its political and security partners at this critical juncture. After having been sidelined by the security and political apparatuses for years, the military saw the revolt as an opportunity to outflank its partners and get back on top. Now that the military was (at least temporarily) back in the political saddle, how did it exploit its new position?

In the months that followed Mubarak's overthrow, the military took several bold foreign policy steps in a clear indicator of its frustration with Egypt's diminished geopolitical role, and its determination to project regional power. These steps included allowing two Iranian vessels (rumored to be carrying missiles to Lebanon) to sail through the Suez Canal in March 2011 for the first time since the Islamic Revolution, despite vehement opposition from the United States and Israel (and repeated the same move in February 2012); sending popular delegations spearheaded by Islamist figures to Tehran to mend Egyptian-Iranian relations; dispatching the new Intelligence Director Murad Muwafi to Syria and Qatar (two countries Mubarak almost considered enemy states) to explore means of resuming cooperation; opening up the border with Hamas-controlled Gaza against Israeli protests; brokering a national accord between Hamas and Fatah after the old regime's unconditional support for the latter had stalled its prospects for years; brokering a prisoners swap that freed more than a thousand Palestinian activists for one Israeli solider (the famous Gilad Shalit, who had been captured by Hamas operatives in June 2006, and whose liberation was the official pretext for Israel's devastating attack on Gaza in December 2009); encouraging public discussion of the necessity of reversing the demilitarization of Sinai and amending the Egyptian-Israeli peace accords; arresting an alleged Mossad officer (who also happened to be an American citizen by the name of Elyan Gabriel) for the first time in decades, and trading him for twenty-five Egyptian detainees in Israeli prisons; raiding foreign NGOs using military units and banning nineteen Americans from travel for receiving illegal funding (though it had to release them under U.S. pressure two months later); and other similarly controversial steps.

One remarkable incident is the military response to the killing of six Egyptian soldiers in Sinai by Israelis on August 17. The military insisted on an official Israeli apology, and received a curt and formal one. Although this does not display particular bravado, one should note that between September 2004 and August 2011, twenty-two Egyptians were killed in similar border incidents with little complaint from Mubarak's

diplomatic corps. Moreover, in an angry rejoinder published the following month in the military's mouthpiece, *Al-Nasr*, Major General
Abd al-Mon'em Kato warned that Israel could no longer act with
impunity, and attacked the United States for "offering all its support
to Israel ... as usual," adding that the Egyptian-Israeli peace agreement
granted each party the right to revise the articles governing the size of
troops in Sinai, "even though," he added indignantly, "the old regime
never utilized this right."[5] Finally, the military approved the cancella-
tion of the controversial Egyptian-Israeli natural gas exporting deal in
April 2012, and the defense minister responded to Israeli remonstrations
by asserting that the military would break the arms of anyone who
dares threaten Egypt. Even though these erratic endeavors did not add
up to much, they at least reflected the high command's desire to rock
the boat a little after the political leadership had taken the wind out of
Egypt's sail for over three decades.

On the home front, however, the military acted much more hesi-
tantly. During its first two months in power, SCAF was too timid and
cautious in isolating the powerful players in the old regime. It required
court orders to dissolve Parliament, municipal councils, and the ruling
party; it put regime leaders (including the president, his family, and
top political and security aides) on trial only for financial corruption
and criminal charges rather than political charges; it winked at demonstrators to raid State Security headquarters and branches before its
operatives could shred incriminating documents, but then quickly
directed its troops to protect police stations and the Interior Ministry,
and authorized limited security purges, which stuck to the letter of law,
and cashiered officers close to retirement age; and instead of annul-
ling the 1971 Permanent Constitution, it reissued it (after sweeping
amendments) in the form of a Constitutional Declaration approved via
popular referendum.

But it is not just that reforms were stubbornly slow and partial. More
unsettling, was the fact that the military police progressively resorted to
violence to repress popular demands for more radical changes, beginning with the forced dispersion of Tahrir Sqaure sit-ins in March 9 and
April 8. Worse still, the military soon unleashed the Interior Ministry
against demonstrators, starting from June 28 when the families of the
revolt martyrs were assaulted because they insisted on faster trials, as
well as endorsed the use of security-hired thugs (posing as SCAF supporters) to entrap and manhandle a march to the Defense Ministry
on July 23. Thereafter, military-security violence against demonstrators became systematic, occurring like clockwork once a month during
the year following Mubarak's resignation, and has followed more or
less the same pattern: police assaults on demonstrators in conjunction
with or following provocations by hired thugs; the rallying of thousands

of activists and common folk to repulse the attack; the call on the military police to intervene to protect key installations; and the inevitable dragging of the military into the fray. State brutality reached a particularly high pitch in the last two months of 2011 when nerve gas (in addition to your run-of-the-mill tear gas) and live ammunition was used against demonstrators and close to a hundred activists were killed. In a particularly shocking incident, in February 2012, pro-revolution soccer spectators (the so-called Ultras, the semianarchist activists organized as sports fans who regularly protected demonstrators against police brutality) were assaulted during a game in Port Said by thugs (killing perhaps seventy and injuring dozens) while security forces chained the stadium gates to prevent anyone from escaping. The military throughout turned a blind eye (and sometimes participated in) the detention and torture of revolutionary activists, and resorted to gray and black propaganda and character-assassination tactics to defame them (as in July 2011 when SCAF members openly accused the April 6 Youth Movement of being funded and trained in subversion by foreign agents).

In short, although SCAF decapitated the political and security institutions, it refused to carry out the revolutionary changes that its forerunners resorted to in 1952 to reconfigure the regime. Assistant Defense Minister for Legal Affairs Mamduh Shahin made it clear in an interview with the daily *Al-Masry Al-Youm* on March 17, five weeks after Mubarak stepped down, that the high command shunned politics and that—unlike the Free Officers—SCAF ruled in the name of the military as a whole, not as a revolutionary actor:

> Some believe that the armed forces took charge by virtue of revolutionary legitimacy, but what happened was that ... when the armed forces found the country collapsing, they intervened by virtue of being the only power on the ground capable of protecting the country. They managed the country's affairs in accordance with a declaration based on Article 88 of the [1971] constitution, which holds the military responsible for the security and protection of the country ... What happened in 1952 in fact had been revolutionary legitimacy, because the Free Officers ... carried out the revolution and seized power ... Now we have a different situation, where those who revolted on January 25, 2011 were not the ones who seized power.[6]

What the general did not explain was *why* the army could not pursue a course similar to that of the Free Officers Movement in July 1952. Why has the military's domestic performance been so circumscribed and confusing, with one step forward and several steps back? Is this proof of army complacency, or simply a symptom of the conservative and paternalistic "military mind," which is naturally ill-disposed to revolutionary changes?*

One the one hand, the objective interests of the officer corps are not necessarily inconsistent with the revolution's democratic ideals. Contrasting the status of armies under authoritarianism and democracy makes this much clear. Dictators such as Mubarak are typically suspicious of their militaries, and so despite the privileges they offer them, they keep officers on a tight leash through constant security surveillance, promoting loyalists regardless of merit, fostering divisiveness within the ranks, checking the influence of popular generals (such as Abu Ghazala), weeding out independent-minded figures, and ignoring military input during policy formulation—strategies that undermine professionalism and combat readiness. Many democracies, by contrast, shower their armies with privileges and social distinctions, celebrate military heroism, encourage retired generals to pursue lucrative careers in the private sector or to run for office (the examples of Dwight Eisenhower and Colin Powell come to mind here), and involve the chiefs of staff in developing national security goals and defense doctrines. It is not a coincidence that the armies of democratic states have repeatedly proved their worth on the battlefield against armies of autocracies. The truth is that armies tend to thrive in democracies and wither in the shadow of authoritarianism. Most important, democracy removes once and for all the threat of an entrenched security apparatus charged with taming the armed forces to satisfy the dictator's insatiable appetite for control—a sore impediment on the autonomy of the Egyptian armed forces.

However, striving to improve one's position within the pecking order of an authoritarian regime is one thing, and transforming society to maximize the overall interest of one's institution is another. The latter is a pioneering feat probably beyond the grasp of a military caste

---

* The paternalistic attitude of the army was evident in Field Marshal Hussein Tantawy's comment that "the revolutionaries are our sons and brothers, but maybe they lack a clear and comprehensive understanding of the situation" (quoted in Tawfik, "Al-Mushir: Al-qwat al-musalaha musamema 'ala taslim al-sulta," 1). This attitude reached comic proportions when one SCAF member tried to justify the council's harsh response to demonstrators as follows: The relationship between the military and the revolutionaries "resembles a father whose son goes to school, and he encourages him to study every once in a while, saying: 'Study, my dear, for my sake.' Then exam time draws near, and he has to yell at him: 'Attend to your studies!'" (Mamduh Shahin in Bahnasawy. "Maham 'adaa al-'ala lel-qwat al-musalaha," 7). It was also graphically represented by a picture produced by the Defense Ministry and disseminated all over the country in the summer of 2012. The picture, which was meant to symbolize the unity of the army and the people, had a a soldier gazing adoringly into the eyes of an infant he held carefully in his arms—the helpless infant here, of course, represents the people.

that could hardly imagine what free governance looks like. Yet it is not only a failure of the imagination that accounts for the officers' timidity toward democratic reform. A closer look reveals there are three reasons that might have held the military back from fully endorsing the revolution's demands or dashing confidently into politics as it had done in 1952, and all have to do with the security apparatus.

To start with, the sealing of the armed forces from all political currents from the 1970s onward, by placing officers under constant security surveillance and removing politicized elements, prevented the creation of a movement with the daring and political imagination of the Free Officers within the ranks. Hence, those who came to the helm had no alternative vision for Egypt's future, or even an adequate understanding of its political terrain and socioeconomic complications. Second, contrary to the rudimentary and malleable security infrastructure that fell into the coup makers' laps in 1952, the military now faced an overbearing and hydra-headed establishment capable of resisting a takeover from above with great ferocity. The menace represented by today's Interior Ministry was further enhanced by the fact that police officers had become too closely wedded to public officials, businessmen, and petty (and not-so-petty) criminals to go down without stirring intolerable havoc. Third, the extent of economic distortion, social inequality, and political deprivation produced by the old regime compels the military to think twice about the forces it might unleash by opening up political life, and the turmoil that might result if security organs were weakened to the point where they could not check this popular stampede. Especially relevant here is the anarchic and mind-bogglingly polarized political scene SCAF inherited, where (over a year after the uprising) no recognized leadership emerged and no concrete movement crystallized to harness popular energy and negotiate on the people's behalf—thanks to decades of security preemption and fragmentation of the opposition. Neither the uneasy alliance of ideologically opposed activists who spearheaded the revolt, nor the Muslim Brotherhood—the large opposition movement waiting in the winds to reap the gains—were up to the task of directing the uprising they helped generate. The absence of a reliable revolutionary vanguard that credibly represents the demands of the uprising and is capable of controlling the street (in cooperation with the military) has added to SCAF's fear that if the dam of autocracy is broken, a sea of angry people will flood the country. By the same token, the failure of the democratic activists to recognize the potentially revolutionary role of the army has prevented them from considering a real partnership with the officers. Liberals continued to hold dogmatically to the axiom of civilian control, and leftists saw the military only as a conservative institution in the service of the ruling class—both positions, one must add, were based mostly on theoretical clichés (and unsubstantiated news reports and hearsay) rather than on an accurate analysis of the specific situation and grievances of the military in the Egyptian ruling bloc.

SCAF therefore flinched from taking on the security organs and opted for the safer route: to side with the police, even if it meant wasting a rare opportunity to dismantle its authoritarian foe while preserving its own power and privileges within a democratic framework. Little did it realize that by cooperating with the police, the military played into the hands of the security establishment. Interior Ministry officials were well aware that the army does in fact have a choice. Both democracies and autocracies have external enemies and therefore need strong armies, but only dictatorships, with their natural obsession with "the enemy within," sanction unbridled domestic repression. If Egypt becomes a democracy it can still take pride in its military, but it will surely abolish the inflated prerogatives of the security organs. So although military interests dictated the restructuring of a security apparatus that has been employed against it for decades, and although these interests did not necessarily contradict with democratic rule, political inexperience and fear that internal instability might drag the army into protracted policing activities prevented SCAF from conquering and streamlining the security forces, preferring to delegate this thankless task to an elected civilian authority that could carry it out whenever circumstances allowed—if ever. SCAF dared not open Pandora's box.

This position has tied the military's destiny—at least temporarily—to the security organs. Those who chanted "The People and the Military Are One Hand!" began to cry furiously: "The People Demand the Execution of the Field Marshal!" Praise for the patriotism and integrity of the armed forces has turned into sour denunciation by activists of the corrupt and complacent officer corps. The international acclaim for the military's professionalism gave way to condemnation of the appalling policies of the high command, and threats to suspend American aid. Even nonassuming citizens, who have not yet warmed up to the revolt, have come to regard the military with suspicion (though they might still support it as an antidote to civil unrest). In short, the public image of the armed forces has deteriorated from an esteemed partner in the revolution to the avowed leader of the counterrevolution. With eyes wide shut, the army seemed to have crossed over to the other side of the barricade, and joined its most ruthless competitor for power: the security apparatus. Months after the revolt, the most popular chant in demonstrations became: "The Military and the Police Are One Hand!" It appeared as though the army had surrenderd to the power formula created by Sadat and maintained by Mubarak, whereby the security apparatus dominates, its political auxiliaries enjoy status and wealth, and the military watches passively from a faraway corner.

There was, of course, another unspoken option: a coup or some kind of breakdown in the chain of command. Yet officers and soldiers have remained united behind their commanders for a number of reasons: first, the absence of a revolutionary movement inside or outside the ranks; second, past frustration with the top brass had sprung from the feeling that it was too subservient to politicians, which it no longer is; third, army members do not see their leaders as devious or complacent: the revolt demanded democracy, and SCAF has indeed organized free elections—"What else do the revolutionaries want?" they keep asking. Also, violent repression of civilians has been relatively limited and carried out mostly by the military police, and so occasions for fraternization have been few. Furthermore, the army does not suffer from ethnic, tribal, sectarian, or social divisions. Its members come from a fairly homogeneous background. And although there is a clear distinction between the middle-class corps and lower-class (mostly peasant) conscripts and noncommissioned officers (NCOs), historically this has not produced class tensions. Conscripts serve for three years before returning to their respective provinces, and consider their term an unfortunate yet temporary ordeal. The only recorded conscript mutiny (in 1986) occurred in the police, not the military, and was triggered by rumors that their term of service was going to be extended. As for NCOs, joining the service is the best road to social status and mobility, or at least a safety net against poverty and humiliation. They might have financial complaints every now and then, but there is no evidence of them clustering into a coherent opposition front. It is true that the impromptu politicization that followed the revolt might precipitate a coup at some point, but even in that case, those who come to power will probably be as politically clueless as the rest of their colleagues.

THE SECURITY FORCES: "BLOODIED BUT UNBOWED"

With so much power at hand, one must wonder, what paralyzed Egypt's all-powerful security institution during the revolt? The evidence so far suggests that it was the arrogance of power that infected the security apparatus during the final years of the regime that caused it to dismiss signs of an imminent uprising. The always-sober State Security Investigations Sector was not really caught off guard. On January 18, 2011, the SSIS chief submitted a report to the interior minister warning of a repetition of the Tunisian scenario in Egypt, and proposed practical steps to avert a popular revolt, such as relieving citizens of some of the new economic burdens, halting (temporarily) illegal acquisitions of public land, and reducing the level of police violence.[7] But an overconfident interior minister ignored the report, and as a result, the ministry's striking arm, the Central Security Forces, were neither briefed regarding the anticipated uprising nor equipped to confront it. In the city of Suez, for instance, where some of the bloodiest confrontations took place during the revolt, the CSF chief complained in an official memo that his men were not prepared to meet the massive demonstrations because SSIS reports "were not taken seriously."[8]

Expectedly, the overconfident minister was in a state of shock. For years, security men had been dealing with scattered activists and ineffective opposition groups, but never expected a mass uprising, which they believed would need extensive—and easily detectable—preparations. After his arrest, Interior Minister Habib al-Adly confessed to the general prosecutor how bewildered he and his men were:

> We met at the Interior Ministry on January 24, [one day] before the first outbreak [of demonstrations], and again on January 27, one day before the Day of Rage on Friday, but none of us foresaw the size or persistence of the demonstrators, we never thought we might be outnumbered ... We had no plan to deal with such [momentous] events ... the troops did not have the know-how and training to conduct a multiple-day operation ... I decided to inform the president that we must resort to the armed forces ... Nobody expected demonstrations with this size and those numbers. This was unprecedented. Nobody could have expected what happened.[9]

Nobody indeed. In an interview with the daily *Al-Ahram* on the morning of the planned demonstrations on January 25, this same minister assured citizens that "those who plan to take to the streets have no weight ... that the security force is capable of deterring them ... [and] that those who hope for a possible repeat of the Tunisian scenario ... [are] intellectual adolescents."*[10] Thus, one of the main reasons the uprising succeeded was the fact that demonstrators had no coherent plans or an organization that could have alerted the security agencies. They coordinated on site, rather than beforehand, and made their decisions one day at a time. And after the revolt broke out, there was no well-defined revolutionary movement to be dismantled, no particular leaders to be detained, and no detailed schemes to be uncovered. In short, there was no specific object to monitor and repress.

Moreover, the quality of the riot-control forces was evidently low. The absence of effective opposition movements had made them sloppy to the point of delegating repression to hired thugs (as discussed in the previous chapter). The CSF remained until the very end "poorly trained, paid, and equipped and ... [composed of] lower-grade conscripts."[11] During the interrogations that followed the uprising, al-Adly admitted that he failed to suppress the demonstrators because "the CSF

---

* Full interview with Editor-in-Chief Osama Saraya in *Al-Ahram* 45340: 3. Cairo (1/25/2011).

became exhausted ... They were only used to dispersing limited demonstrations using batons, or at most water hoses, tear gas canisters, and rubber bullets ... They [panicked because they] were outnumbered for the first time."[12]

One month after the president was deposed, the top ministry officials (headed by al-Adly himself) were arrested for issuing orders to shoot demonstrators and abusing power to amass wealth. The list included, in addition to the interior minister, the heads of the SSIS, the CSF, and general security, as well as the chiefs of security in five governorates, and fourteen high-ranking officers. Curiously, the interior minister's top lieutenants were all members of the Class of 1971 at the Police Academy, that is, the year Sadat began his empowerment of the police force. The post-revolt interior minister issued Ministerial Decree 509 of 2011, which replaced the SSIS with a new agency: the National Security Sector. The old SSIS leadership was supposedly purged: 500 officers (out of 1,100) were dismissed, including 23 generals, while 66 brigadier generals were transferred to other police departments.[13] These purges, however, were cosmetic—mostly applied to officers in peripheral positions or eligible for retirement.

The police then made its grand comeback on June 28, 2011, when CSF units assaulted protestors in Tahrir Square, who were calling for more resolute measures against the old regime. Police violence was not just excessive, with the generous use of new and more devastating tear gas bombs (made in the USA in May 2011—America's generous contribution to democracy in post-Mubarak Egypt), but it was also accompanied by verbal abuses and threats that the police was determined to punish the people for what they had done. After an all-night street fight, however, where more than a thousand civilians were injured, the police were forced to retreat under pressure to the Interior Ministry's fortified headquarters, and military police units soon cordoned the demonstrators. The incident sparked a second uprising, the July 8 Second Day of Rage, which began with a million-man march on Friday followed by a three-week sit-in in Tahrir. SCAF responded by reshuffling the powerless civilian cabinet and authorizing the purge of 669 senior police officers, including 505 generals, 82 brigadier generals, and 82 lieutenant colonels, in addition to transferring 54 junior officers accused of killing demonstrators to administrative duties pending trial, and rotating another 4,000 officers.[14]

But the fight was far from over. This asymmetrical tug-of-war between demonstrators and police continued over the next few months, making two facts abundantly clear: first, that the embittered security apparatus, despite the purges and humiliation, still hoped to weather the revolt and regain its privileged position by creating a rift between the people and the army—the always helpful divide-and-rule strategy; and second, that the police strategy had so far succeeded because of the army's cautious attitude and apprehension over the possibility of domestic chaos. Clearly, these security-instigated episodes have managed to entrap the armed forces on a spiraling course of violence aimed at liquidating the revolutionary camp.

More important, symbolically speaking, was that no security official had been held responsible for killing demonstrators during the revolt itself. On June 2, 2012, a judge sentenced Mubarak and his last interior minister to life in prison for failing to protect the demonstrators—a political rather than a criminal charge—but was forced to release the leaders of the security establishment for lack of evidence. Despite all that has passed during and after the revolt, the security apparatus emerged miraculously unscathed.

WITHER THE POLITICAL APPARATUS?

If the January revolt and its aftermath have proven anything, it is that the security apparatus was not just the main supporter of the regime; it was the throbbing heart of the regime itself. Without the rigging of elections, the suppression of civil society, the intimidation of political contenders, the containment of mass unrest, and the close monitoring of the armed forces, the political apparatus was likely to crumble just as it had done after the Interior Ministry was temporarily defeated by the revolt. As soon as the police withdrew from the scene, the political component of Egypt's ruling bloc, with its ruling party, state agencies, established norms and regulations, and foreign alliances could hardly put up a fight. The president, his family, and top associates were arrested; the ruling party was dissolved; party leaders, cabinet ministers (including the prime minister), Speakers of the upper and lower houses of Parliament, and their business allies (starting with the steel tycoon and political mastermind Ahmed Ezz) were taken into custody and their financial assets were frozen; regime loyalists in the press, the universities, and the state bureaucracy were purged; and the existing political map was scrapped in a matter of weeks with almost no resistance. Regime cadres denounced their old masters and scrambled to join new parties; the most stubborn among them—encouraged by the partial return of their police protectors—could only hope to stir enough trouble for SCAF to leave them alone, rather than reempower them. It became clear that the political apparatus, as exploitive and despotic as it was, had no power of its own; it was wholly reliant on its security lieutenants for survival. And this is why it is only natural to expect that as long as this institution persists there remains a high probability that future elected officials will be corrupted or blackmailed into submitting to its omnipotence. Exhibit A here is how fast Interior Minister Mansour al-Essawi, appointed in March 2011 to restructure the ministry, was co-opted. His complacency, could not have been more blatant than in his interview with *Al-Masry Al-Youm*, on September 19, 2011 where he mocked the million-man marches in Tahrir Square by claiming that the square cannot hold more than 300,000 people; deprived hundreds of martyrs of their special status by arguing that those who died in confrontations with the police were simply thugs, and that only those killed by sniper fire in Tahrir Square during the first eighteen days of the revolt were true martyrs; and then ended by insisting that those snipers were foreign agents who crossed the border days before January 25, thus absolving the police of any responsibility. The supposedly "revolutionary" minister concluded by warning Egyptians that whoever dares to attack a police station or other public installation will be shot mercilessly in the heart.[15]

But now that the Mubarak political apparatus had been overthrown, the search for those who could fill the vacuum began in earnest. Out of the ruins of the old political temple emerged an incredibly chaotic political scene—thanks to decades of police repression. The leaderless character of the revolt might have contributed to its success, but it proved quite problematic once the dust began to settle down. Islamists, who claim to represent a critical mass of the population (a claim that has been substantiated by their winning 70 percent of parliamentary seats and eventually the presidential elections) were divided into two great camps: the fundamentalists (*salafis*), historically known for their political passiveness (except for a small militant fringe, whose leaders were imprisoned by Mubarak); and the Muslim Brotherhood, the prominent eight-decade-old sociopolitical movement. Fundamentalists debated whether it was appropriate for them to descend from their moral high ground into the political swamp. Those who agreed to participate in politics organized themselves into more than four different parties (the largest being al-Nur Party), and those who refused still added a political twist to their televangelist role. The Brotherhood was equally fragmented. In the weeks following the revolt, the conservative leadership jostled to keep its members in check, but reformist cadres (especially young ones) argued that since the movement was finally out of the political can, the iron rule of "obedience" was no longer necessary. Although the central leadership formed an official political wing, the Freedom and Justice Party, hundreds broke off and created three other political parties, or joined factions that had already done so a few years ago.

Despite their fragmentation, Islamists have all accepted SCAF's road map (which called for managing the transition through elections and legal reforms rather than radical measures) without reservations, and refused to endorse revolutionary marches and calls for reigniting the revolution. If they can effortlessly win elections, why risk confrontations with the military? In return, the military and security allowed Islamists to consolidate their power over parliament. The Brotherhood's Freedom and Justice Party secured 45.7 percent of the vote, and the fundamentalist al-Nur Party won 24.6 percent. This certainly had nothing to do with army and police officers' political outlook or religiosity, but rather with the potential use of Islamists in stabilizing the political situation. Islamists were not only historically used to being cast into subordinate roles despite their popularity; and not only was their understanding of politics limited to trying to make themselves useful to whoever is in authority; and not only did their "religious determinism" push them to prioritize spiritual over political struggle in the hope for divine intervention;* but they had two specific traits that rendered them particularly useful to both military officers and security men. From a military standpoint, geopolitical powers (whether regional or international) will never completely trust Islamists at the helm, and will always prefer having a prudent guardian on their side to check their excesses—and who better and more responsible than the high command. In addition, of course, Islamism's grand geopolitical designs could potentially furnish the army with the kind of rhetoric needed to expand its influence, maintain its privileges, and play a more active regional role.

Likewise, the security institution recognized that Islamists could be made repression-friendly. Years of underground operations have made them paranoid and willing to see conspiracies everywhere, and an agenda for strict moral reform demands constant policing. Hence, they might appreciate expansive monitoring and law enforcement organs and turn a blind eye to the transgressions naturally associated with them. Such is the nature of ideological movements, which allow themselves exceptional prerogatives to be able to accomplish the wholesale transformation of society they aspire toward, regardless of how pragmatic or opportunistic their members are. And the more society proves recalcitrant and unwilling to change along the lines of their imagined utopia, the more doses of despotism are justified to force society to fall into line. This is why they are not fundamentally opposed to authoritarianism, as long as they are not its victims.

---

* This attitude may be traced to their "religious determinism" thesis, a peculiar philosophy that demands piety of its members in return for political rewards. Good Muslims, in this interpretation, need not confront authority; power will fall in their lap if they exert themselves on the moral field (with some minimal effort in the worldly as well) so that they can deserve divine grace. The 2011 revolt is seen as a prime example. Nonsuspecting revolutionaries challenged political power, forcing a new leadership (the military) to hold free elections, which the Islamists—despite their minor role in the revolt—won by a landslide; divine intervention indeed.

In the year that followed the revolt, Islamists have proved they are up to the task. They have turned their backs on several opportunities to spearhead the revolt, as Islamists had done in Iran in 1979; and despite the turmoil that has embroiled the country, their strategy for change remained pretty much the same. They have believed in using political gains—such as electoral victories—as platforms for propagating and popularizing their cultural agenda and legitimizing their role as representatives of Islam, in the hopes that eventually all Egyptians will commit to their ideological project and submit to their absolute command. Only then will they grip power firmly and shove away all political competitors. In their view, patience is the key to victory; real triumph will come only when Egyptians rally under their banner out of ideological conviction, not merely as a matter of preference. Right now, they need to pass with flying colors this probation period (which tests their commitment to democracy) and pursue their campaign for cultural transformation without antagonizing the military, the security, or the people. Eventually, they will be in a position to stand on their own feet and overpower the military and security institutions. Will this strategy work? Maybe. Frictions between officers and Islamists show that their alliance is tension-ridden—Islamists are justly concerned the military will sell them out (as Nasser did in 1954), and the officers are worried Islamists might be tempted to monopolize power and push them aside. But then again, there is a chance that Islamists might be steered by the military and the police to play the role in which they have always excelled: the role of catalyst to those in power. Once again, they might find themselves on the wrong side of history.

Secular groups, who have cooperated since 2005 in several united front groups, such as Kefaya (Enough) and the National Association for Change, were no less diversified than Islamists, but their influence in the street was much weaker. This has been demonstrated by the fact that their concerted campaign against the Islamist-endorsed referendum on the Constitutional Declaration in March 2011 convinced only 23 percent of voters, and their gains in Parliament were equally humble. Secular activists drew legitimacy from their role in sparking the revolt, which Islamists joined reluctantly later; that they could provide the new regime with more modern and democratic statesmen; and that they had more international sympathy. Yet the months that followed the revolt witnessed continued friction between them and the army because of SCAF's restrained attitude toward the old regime and its insistence on referendums and elections (which secularists cannot win) as the only means to reform. Also, the fact that both liberals and leftists were openly skeptical about the value of maintaining a sizable and expensive military force certainly did not endear them to the high command. This all suggests that in the absence of another major shock—possibly the result of the amalgamation of local resistances by a now seemingly fearless citizenry—non-Islamist forces will not be able to accomplish through the ballot box what they have failed to accomplish through revolution.

One could thus conclude that in the months that followed the revolt, the political balance of forces has been a balance of weakness. The military's abandonment of the old regime, and the police's temporary defeat, exposed how weak the political component of the regime had been, and the opposition forces that dominated the scene after the revolt proved to be even weaker than the one that was overthrown. The two effective players remain the military and security establishment. And a new round of struggle is about to begin.

It remains to be seen who will win the race to the summit—will Egypt once again become military-dominated, as it started out in the 1950s, or will it continue to function as a police state, as it has been since the late 1970s? One thing is for sure: bickering between these two players has been momentarily shelved as they both found themselves driven into an alliance of necessity to stabilize the political situation through undercutting radical forces and ushering into the transfigured ruling bloc a reform-minded political partner.

A SECOND REPUBLIC?

The tensions and confusion of the transitional period came into sharp focus in the summer of 2012. As Egyptians prepared for the country's first competitive presidential elections, divisions among revolutionaries reached tragic proportions as they failed to agree on a single representative, producing instead five presidential candidates. Meanwhile, the Muslim Brotherhood presented its own candidate, professor of engineering and the leader of the Freedom and Justice Party Mohamed Morsi, and the remnants of the old regime clustered around Air Marshal Ahmed Sahfiq, former air force commander and Mubarak's last prime minister. In the first round, held during the last week of May, Egyptians voted decisively for the revolution—yet, alas, their votes were scattered among the five revolutionary nominees, thus failing to carry any of them to the second round. The runner-ups, the Islamist and old-regime candidates, now competed for the votes of Egypt's 51 million registered voters.

In mid-June, however, the military got a head start to ensure its supremacy in the new regime—what was now being referred to in the Egyptian media as the Second Republic—regardless of the winner. On June 14, the Constitutional Court dissolved parliament over a legal technicality. Three days before the second round of the presidential elections, scheduled to start on June 16, the minister of justice granted the military police and Military Intelligence the right to arrest citizens, thus legalizing their domestic security responsibilities. And an hour after the ballot stations for the presidential elections closed, the Supreme Council of the Armed Forces issued a complementary constitutional declaration reclaiming legislative power pending the election of a new parliament; securing a veto over the drafting of the new constitution; maintaining exclusive authority over all decisions pertaining to the armed forces; and requiring the elected president to seek its permission before declaring war.

The most significant development, though, was SCAF's reviving of Egypt's National Defense Council (NDC), first created by Nasser to tackle national security threats (both external and internal). The old council convened at the invitation of the president and had only two military representatives: the general commander and the war minister. Since Nasser and his successors usually took unilateral decisions without much consultation, the council rarely met and soon fell into disuse. SCAF's latest rendition, introduced on June 18 via Decree 348 of 2012, was drastically different. The council has eleven military representatives and only six civilians, including the president.* It could be convened at the wish of the majority of the members and makes decisions by absolute majority. Practically speaking, this means that the NDC can assemble and pass resolutions without the president, and—by the same token—cannot do so if officers choose to ignore the president's call.

After a fiercely competitive election, in which only half of the registered voters participated, the Muslim Brotherhood candidate, Mohamed Morsi, won by 51.7 percent of the vote, becoming the first civilian, the first Islamist, and the first popularly elected president in Egypt's history. Islamists, with military and security blessing, have finally come close to assuming the role they have aspired to for eight long decades, that of the ruling political apparatus. But with a reinvigorated military, and a security establishment kept intact despite the revolutionary turmoil, the Muslim Brotherhood has a strategic choice to make. If it decides to counterbalance the two coercive institutions in a bid to dominate the regime through a sadat-style corrective revolution, then Egypt will certainly be headed for more political turmoil, with the outcome still uncertain. If it follows in the footsteps of the old regime and allies itself with the security forces, then Egypt's former authoritarian regime will likely be reproduced, albeit with an Islamic flavor that adds to its

---

* The military representatives are the defense minister, assistant defense minister (for the topic being discussed at the NDC), chief of staff, three service chiefs, chief of operations, secretary-general of the defense ministry, chief justice of the armed forces, military intelligence director, and civilian intelligence director (usually an army officer). The civilian representatives are: the president, the prime minister, speaker of parliament, and the ministers of interior, foreign affairs, and treasury.

legitimacy. Finally, if the Brotherhood negotiates separate (yet overlapping) spheres of influence with the armed forces, whereby the latter would have the final say in military and national security affairs, while civilians would retain control over political life in general, then Egypt's nascent democracy might be gradually consolidated and expanded—as in Turkey and other cases where the military (as an institution not a political junta) maintains a decisive influence over "high politics" without necessarily undermining multiparty politics.

What one has to look forward to, therefore, is the unfolding of yet another round of struggle between the three members of the reconstituted power triangle: with the military determined to regain its long-lost dominance; the security establishment adamant it should keep its leverage; and the new political partner striving to establish its position among these mighty players. And while this outcome might not seem gratifying for those who sacrificed their lives to liberate their country from the grip of these powerful institutions, it is what we are left with in light of the existing balance of forces.

Acknowledgments

Writing is certainly a lonely job, but thinking is not. There are so many to thank, but one should always start with one's teachers. My first teacher was my father. At a very young age, he imprinted in my mind that one should never discuss a topic one has not thoroughly researched from several different angles. He is the one to blame for the length of this book's bibliography, though I must credit him for sending me on a two-decade reading journey that culminated in the work at hand. I also want to thank him and my uncles for turning every family gathering into an intellectual debate. My first academic teacher was Professor Bahgat Korany, who introduced me to the world of scholarship and challenged me to rise to his standards of dedication and hard work. Professor Emad Shahin has been both a teacher and a very good friend. Professors Farhad Kazemy and Timothy Mitchell, and later Professor William Roy, have been generous with their advice and encouragement. I am particularly indebted to Professor Rogers Brubaker for always pushing me forward with his carefully articulated critiques. His devotion to academia and to helping students achieve their fullest potential is really admirable. I also know that my current career trajectory was possible only because of the unconditional backing of Professor Jeffrey Prager, a truly noble and gracious soul.

Many young scholars complain about never having found the kind of mentorship to which they aspired. At a time when one great mentor is hard to come by, I have been blessed with two. Professors Perry Anderson and Michael Mann, two towering figures in historical sociology, have not only offered their guidance and extensive comments on this manuscript, they have also inspired me by example and attitude.

I have benefited tremendously from conversations with friends, colleagues, and students in Cairo and Los Angeles, particularly the members of the intellectual circle clustered around Khaled Mahmoud, a guiding light in my life. Professor John Thompson at Cambridge played a crucial role in helping me formulate this book for the general reader. I also want to thank Amr Kandil, Adham al-Khouli, and Amira Shahin for providing me with rare archival material.

All thanks are due to Audrea Lim, my editor at Verso, for making the best out of this work while preserving its integrity rather than ripping it apart to cater to the short attention span of the casual reader.

On the personal level, I want to thank my parents for their unshakable support. My wife, Naheed, is the only person I know that could have put up with my unreasonable working routine and my intrinsic irritation with the immediate and the practical. No words could convey my gratitude for all she has done and continues to do, but above all, for her smile, which lightens up my somber days.

My only hope is that my children, Laila and Aly, who were too young to demonstrate at Tahrir Square, will grow up in a different Egypt; that when they are old enough to read this book, they will do so with great skepticism, refusing to believe that their countrymen had to endure so much corruption, repression, and despair. To them I relay a word of advice that has meant so much to me growing up: "Not to know what happened before you were born is to remain forever a child."

Notes

INTRODUCTION

1. Macchiavelli, *The Prince* (2004), 68–69.
2. Carr quoted in Jonathan Haslam, *The Vices of Integrity*, 136.
3. Boutros Boutros Ghali, *Tariq masr ela al-Quds*, 9–10.

PRELUDE

1. See Abd al-Rahman Al-Rafe'I, *Thawrat 23 yulyu 1952: Tarikhna al-qawmi fei saba' sanawat, 1952–1959* (The Revolution of July 23, 1952: Our National History in Seven Years, 1952–1959), Cairo: Dar al-Ma'aref, 1989; Tareq Al-Bishri, *Al-haraka al-siyassiya fei masr, 1945–1953* (The Political Movement in Egypt), Cairo: Dar al-Shorouk, 2002; and Anwar Abdel-Malek, *Egypt: Military Society*, New York: Random House, 1968.
2. Ali al-Din Helal, Al-Sayed Zuhra, Diaa Rashwan, and Dina al-Khawaga, "*Al-Entekhabat al-parlamaniya fei misr men Saad Zaghloul ela Hosni Mubarak*" (Parliamentary Election in Egypt from Saad Zaghloul to Hosni Mubarak), in *Al-Tatawer al-demokraty fei misr: qadaya wa munaqashat* (Democratic Development in Egypt: Issues and Debates), ed. Ali al-Din Helal, Cairo: Maktabet Nahdet al-Sharq, 1986, 243.
3. Tareq Al-Bishri, *Al-haraka al-siyassiya fei masr, 1945–1953* (The Political Movement in Egypt), Cairo: Dar al-Shorouk, 2002, 539–41.
4. Kamal Hassan Aly, *Mashawir al-'umr: asrar wa khafaiya sab'een 'aman min 'umr masr fei al-harb wel-mukhabarat wel-siyasa* (Life Journeys: Secrets of War, Intelligence, and Politics During Seventy Years in Egypt's Life), Cairo: Dar al-Shorouk, 1994, 50.
5. Said K. Aburish, *Nasser: The Last Arab*. New York: St. Martin's Press, 2004, 18–19.
6. Muhammad Naguib, *Kunt ra'isan lei masr* (I Was President of Egypt), Cairo: Al-Maktab al-Masry al-Hadith, 1984, 66–67.
7. Mohamed Hassanein Heikal, *Seqout nizam: lemaza kanet thawarat yulyu 1952 lazema?* (Regime Fall: Why Was the July 1952 Revolution Necessary?), Cairo: Dar al-Shorouk, 2003, 407.
8. Al-Bishri, *Al-haraka al-siyassiya fei masr*, 395.
9. Ref'at Sayyed Ahmed, *Thawrat al-general: Qesat Gamal 'Abd al-Nasser kamila min al-milad ela al-mout (1918–1970): Mawsu'a fikria wa siassia* (The General's Revolution: Gamal Abd

al-Nasser's Complete Story from the Cradle to the Grave [1918–1970]—An Intellectual and Political Register), Cairo: Dar al-Huda, 1993, 73.

10. Aburish, *Nasser: The Last Arab*, 24.

11. Naguib, *Kunt ra'isan lei masr*, 72.

12. Al-Bishri, *Al-haraka al-siyassiya fei masr*. 292–95.

13. Aly, *Mashawir al-'umr: asrar wa khafaiya sab'een 'aman min 'umr masr fei al-harb wel-mukhabarat wel-siyasa*, 63.

14. Selma Botman, *The Rise of Communism in Egypt*, Syracuse, NY: Syracuse University Press, 1988, 116.

15. Naguib, *Kunt ra'isan lei masr*, 67.

CHAPTER I: THE DARK SIDE OF MILITARISM

1. Salah Nasr, *Muzakirat Salah Nasr (al-guze'al-awal): Al-Sou'd* (The Memoirs of Salah Nasr, Part One: The Rise), Cairo: Dar al-Khayal, 1999, 156, 186.

2. Abd al-Muhsin Abu al-Nur, *Al-Haqiqa 'an Thawrit 23 Yulyu* (The Truth About the July 23 Revolution), Cairo: Al-Hay'a al-Masriya al-'Ama lel-Kitab, 2001, 34.

3. Abd al-Rahman Al-Rafe'i, *Thawrat 23 yulyu 1952: Tarikhna al-qawmi fei saba' sanawat, 1952–1959* (The Revolution of July 23, 1952: Our National History in Seven Years, 1952–1959), Cairo: Dar al-Ma'aref, 1989, 53–54.

4. Gamal Abd al-Nasser, *Wathaiq thawrat yulyu* (The July Revolution Documents), Cairo: Dar al-Mustaqbal al-Araby, 1991, 5–6.

5. Salah Nasr, *Muzakirat Salah Nasr (al-guze'al-awal): Al-Sou'd* (The Memoirs of Salah Nasr, Part One: The Rise), Cairo: Dar al-Khayal, 1999, 226.

6. Laleh Khalili, and Jillian Schwedler, "Introduction," in *Policing and Prisons in the Middle East: Foundations of Coercion*, ed. Laleh Khalili and Jillian Schwedler, New York: Columbia University Press, 2010, 13.

7. Anthony Gorman. "Confining Political Dissent in Egypt Before 1952," in ibid., 158–69.

8. Mohamed Hassanein Heikal, *Seqout nizam: lemaza kanet thawarat yulyu 1952 lazema?* (Regime Fall: Why Was the July 1952 Revolution Necessary?), Cairo: Dar al-Shorouk, 2003, 507.

9. Sirrs, *A History of the Egyptian Intelligence Service*, 37.

10. Abd al-Fattah Abu al-Fadl, *Kunt na'iban le ra'is al-mukhabarat* (I Was Deputy Director of Intelligence), Cairo: Dar al-Shorouk, 2008, 87.

11. P. J. Vatikiotis, *Nasser and His Generation*. London: Croom Helm, 1978, 164–65.

12. Copeland, *The Game of Nations*, 82.

13. Sirrs, *History*, 32–34.

14. Nasr, *Muzakirat*, 158.

15. Riyad Samy, *Shahid 'ala 'asr al-ra'is Muhammad Naguib* (A Witness to the Reign of President Muhammad Naguib), Cairo: Al-Maktab al-Masry al-Hadith, 2004, 21.

16. Anthony McDermott, *Egypt from Nasser to Mubarak: A Flawed Revolution*, London: Croom Helm, 1988, 16.

17. Niccolò Machiavelli, *The Prince*, Indianapolis: Hackett Publishing, 1995 [1532]: 20.

18. Sirrs, *History*, 45.

19. Suleiman Hafez, *Thekrayati 'an al-thawra* (My Memories of the Revolution), Cairo: Dar al-Shorouk, 2010, 108–11.

20. Copeland, *Game*, 48–49.

21. Barry Turner, *Suez 1956: The Inside Story of the First Oil War*, London: Hodder & Stoughton, 2006, 96.

22. Ibid., 90.

23. Copeland, *Game*, 51–53.

24. Hussein Mohamed Ahmed Hammudah, *Asrar harakat al-zubat al-ahrar wa al-Ikhwan al-Muslimeen* (Secrets of the Free Officers Movement and the Muslim Brothers), Cairo: Al-Zahraa lel-'Ilam al-Arabi, 1985, 88–89.

25. Aburish, *Nasser*, 43.

26. Copeland, *Game*, 63.

27. Khaled Muhi al-Din, *Al'an atakalam* (Now, I Speak), Cairo: Al-Ahram lel-Targama wel-Nashr, 1992: 188.

28. Telegram photocopied in Mohamed Abd al-Wahab Sayyid Ahmed, *Al-'Alaqat al-masriya al-amrekiya men al-taqarub ela al-taba'ud, 1952–1958* (Egyptian-American Relations Between Proximity and Distance, 1952–1958), Cairo: Dar al-Shorouk, 2007, 131.

29. Copeland, *Game*, 64–65.

30. Turner, *Suez 1956*, 116.

31. Ahmed, *Al-'Alaqat*, 19–20.

32. Arthur M. Schlesinger, *A Thousand Days: John F. Kennedy in the White House*, Greenwich, CT: Fawcett Publications, 1965, 186–87.

33. Helmi Yassin interviewed in Selma Botman, *The Rise of Communism in Egypt*, Syracuse, NY: Syracuse University Press, 1988: 125–30.

34. Nasr, *Muzakirat*, 198–204.

35. Aburish, *Nasser*, 49–51.

36. Ref'at Younan, *Muhammad Naguib: Za'im thawra am wagehat haraka?* (Muhammad Naguib: A Leader of a Revolution or the Figurehead of a Movement?), Cairo: Dar al-Shorouk, 2008, 25.

37. Abd al-Muhsin Abu al-Nur, *Al-Haqiqa 'an Thawrit 23 Yulyu* (The Truth about the July 23 Revolution), Cairo: Al-Hay'a al-Masriya al-'Ama lel-Kitab, 2001, 41–43.

38. Al-Rafe'i, *Thawrat*, 130–34.

39. Memoranda photocopied in Fouad Allam, *Al-Ikhwan wa ana* (Al-Ikhwan and I), Cairo: Akhbar al-Youm, 1996, 548, 556.

40. Samy, *Muhammad Naguib*, 51.

41. Abu al-Nur, *Al-Haqiqa*, 41–43.

42. Samy, *Muhammad Naguib*, 33–35.

43. Naguib, *Kunt ra'isan lei masr*, 211.

44. Ibid., 181.

45. Nasr, *Muzakirat*, 167.

46. Muhi al-Din, *Al'an atakalam*, 222.

47. Gamal Hammad, *Asrar thawrat 23 yunyu* (Secrets of the July 23 Revolution), vols. 1 and 2. Cairo: Dar Al-'Ulum, 2010, 714.

48. Naguib, *Kunt*, 186–87.

49. Hafez, *Thekrayati*, 117.

50. Nasr, *Muzakirat*, 228–32; Abu al-Nur, *Al-Haqiqa*, 58–64.

51. Muhi al-Din, *Al'an atakalam*, 270–73.

52. Tahiya Abd al-Nasser, *Zekrayaty ma'ahu* (My Memories with Him), Cairo: Dar al-Shorouk, 2011, 80.

53. Muhi al-Din, *Al'an atakalam*, 277.

54. Ibid., 253.

55. Hammad, *Asrar thawrat 23 yunyu*, 886–88.

56. Naguib, *Kunt*, 240.

57. Muhi al-Din, *Al'an atakalam*, 277–79.

58. Hammad, *Asrar thawrat 23 yunyu*, 938–39.

59. Anwar Sadat, *Al-Bahth 'an al-zat* (In Search of Identity), Cairo: Al-Maktab al-Masry al-Hadith, 1978, 157.

60. Nasr, *Muzakirat*, 236–39.

61. Ibid., 240–43.

62. Mahmoud Game', *'Araft al-Sadat* (I Knew Sadat), Cairo: Al-Maktab al-Masry al-Hadith, 2004, 51.

63. Naguib, *Kunt*, 247–50.

64. Hammad, *Asrar thawrat 23 yunyu*, 1028.

65. Nasr, *Muzakirat*, 262.

66. Naguib, *Kunt*, 252.

67. Sadat, *Al-Bahth*, 38; Muhi al-Din, *Al'an atakalam*, 43–47.

68. Hammad, *Asrar thawrat 23 yunyu*, 524–27.

69. Naguib, *Kunt*, 167.

70. Hammudah, *Asrar*, 33–37, 74.

71. Abd al-Nasser, *Zekrayaty ma'ahu*, 24.

72. Hammad, *Asrar thawrat 23 yunyu*, 319–22.

73. Game', *'Araft al-Sadat*, 32.

74. Hafez, *Thekrayati*, 78.

75. Ref'at Sayyed Ahmed, *Thawrat al-general: Qesat Gamal 'Abd al-Nasser kamila min al-milad ela al-mout (1918–1970): Mawsu'a fikria wa siassia* (The General's Revolution: Gamal Abd al-Nasser's Complete Story from the Cradle to the Grave (1918–1970)—An Intellectual and Political Register), Cairo: Dar al-Huda, 1993, 201–3.

76. Vatikiotis, *Nasser*, 142–45.

77. Hammad, *Asrar thawrat 23 yunyu*, 1069–79, 1167.

78. Naguib, *Kunt*, 257–63.

79. Vatikiotis, *Nasser*, 142–45.

80. Ahmed Abdallah, *The Student Movement and National Politics in Egypt, 1923–1973*, London: Al Saqi Books, 1985, 122.

81. Naguib, *Kunt*, 266.

82. Vatikiotis, *Nasser*, 127.

83. Naguib, *Kunt*, 253.

84. Hafez, *Thekrayati*, 148–51.

85. Machiavelli, *The Prince* (1995), 19.

86. Muhi al-Din, *Al'an atakalam*, 215.

CHAPTER 2: TWO STATES WITHIN A STATE

1. Aburish, *Nasser*, 56.

2. Samy Sharaf. *'Abd al-Nasser: Keif hakam masr?* ('Abd al-Nasser: How Did He Rule Egypt?), Cairo: Madbouli al-Saghir, 1996, 89–93.

3. Sirrs, *A History of the Egyptian Intelligence Service*, 63–64.

4. Copeland, *The Game of Nations*, 123–33, 148.

5. Hafez Isma'il. *Amn Misr al-qawmy* (Egypt's National Security), Cairo: Maktabet Madbouli, 1983, 47.

6. Abd al-Rahman Al-Rafe'i, *Thawrat 23 yulyu 1952*, 199.

7. Paul Johnson, *The Suez War*, London: Macgibbon & Kee, 1957: 11–14.

8. Turner, *Suez 1956*, 187–93.

9. Ibid., 260–64.

10. Ibid., 1.

11. Abdallah Imam, *Nasser and Amer: Al-Sadaqa, al-hazima, al-entehar* (Nasser and Amer: The Friendship, the Defeat, and the Suicide), Cairo: Dar al-Khayal, 1996: 53.

12. Aburish, *Nasser*, 119.

13. Mohamed Abdel Ghani Al-Gamasy, *The October War: Memoirs of Field Marshall El-Gamasy of Egypt*, Cairo: American University in Cairo Press, 1993, 13.

14. Elie Kedourie, *Islam in the Modern World and Other Studies*, New York: Holt, Rinehart, and Winston, 1980, 172.

15. Turner, *Suez 1956*, 468.

16. Salah Nasr, *Muzakirat Salah Nasr*, 405.

17. Gamasy, *October War*, 13–15.

18. Wagih Abu Zikri, *Mazbahat al-abriya' fei 5 yunyu 1967* (Massacre of the Innocent on June 5, 1967), Cairo: Al-Maktab al-Masry al-Hadith, 1988, 71.

19. Sirrs, *History*, 59.

20. Gamal Hammad, *Asrar thawrat 23 yunyu*, 1330–40.

21. Interview with Colonel Muhammad Selim, 2009.

22. Al-Rafe'i, *Thawrat*, 269.

23. Sharaf, *'Abd al-Nasser*, 456.

24. Amin Huwaidi, *Khamsin 'am min al-'awasif: ma ra'ituh qultuh* (Fifty Stormy Years: I Told What I Saw), Cairo: Markaz Al-Ahram lel-Targama wa-Nashr, 2002, 195.

25. Mohamed Fawzy, *Harb al-thlath sanawat, 1967–1970: muzakirat al-fariq awal Mohamed Fawzy* (Three-Year War, 1967–1970: Memoirs of Lieutenant General Mohamed Fawzy), Cairo: Dar al-Mustaqbal al-Araby, 1990, 33.

26. Ibid.

27. Sadat, *Al-Bahth 'an al-zat*, 208.

28. Abdallah Imam, *Nasser and Amer*, 87.

29. Sadat, *Al-Bahth*, 220.

30. Fawzy, *Harb al-thlath sanawat*, 54.

31. Hamada Hosni, *Shams Badran: Al-ragul alazi hakam misr* (Shams Badran: The Man Who Ruled Egypt), Beirut: Maktabat Beirut, 2008, 8.

32. Abd al-Fattah Abu al-Fadl, *Kunt na'iban le ra'is al-mukhabarat*, 90–91.

33. Gamal Abd al-Nasser, "*Hadith Gamal Abd al-Nasser al-tanzimy fei al-mu'tamar al-awal le-'ada' al-makateb al-tanfiziya fei al-muhafazat 'an eslub al-'amal fei al-etehad el-eshteraky* (Gamal Abd al-Nasser's Organizational Talk at the First Congress of the Members of the Provincial Executive Offices Regarding the Working Methods at the Arab Socialist Union)," *Al-Tali'ah* 2 (2): 11–18, Cairo (February 1966): 14–16.

34. Sharaf, *'Abd al-Nasser*, 228–29.

35. Imam, *Nasser and Amer*, 90.

36. Abd al-Muhsin Abu al-Nur, *Al-Haqiqa 'an Thawrit 23 Yulyu*, 231–33.

37. Abu al-Fadl, *Kunt*, 223.

38. Sirrs, *History*, 88.

39. Abd al-Nasser, "*Hadith*," 13.

40. Heikal, *1967: Al-Infegar*, 401.

41. Sharaf, *'Abd al-Nasser*, 183–91.

42. Hamada Hosni, *Abd al-Nasser wa al-tanzim al-tale'i, 1963–1971* (Abd al-Nasser and the Vanguard Organization, 1963–1971), Beirut: Maktabat Beirut, 2007, 20–22.

43. Ref'at Sayyed Ahmed, *Thawrat al-general*, 764–71.

44. Ibid., 786.

45. Hosni, *Abd al-Nasser*, 12.

46. Eric A. Nordlinger, *Soldiers in Politics: Military Coups and Governments*, Englewood Cliffs, NJ: Prentice-Hall, 1977, 115–17.

47. Leonard Binder, *In a Moment of Enthusiasm: Political Power and the Second Stratum in Egypt*, Chicago: University of Chicago Press, 1978: 344; Sherif Yunis, *Al-Zahf al-muqadas: Muzaharat al-tanahi wa tashkil 'ebadet Abd al-Nasser* (The Sacred March: The Resignation Demonstrations and the Shaping of the Cult of Abd al-Nasser), Cairo: Dar Merit, 2005, 69.

48. Anwar Abdel-Malek, *Egypt: Military Society*, New York: Random House, 1968: 81, 108.

49. Ibid., 160.

50. McDermott, *Egypt from Nasser to Mubarak*, 121–22.

51. Brooks, *Shaping Strategy*, 72–73.

52. Yunis, *Al-Zahf*, 66–67.

53. Binder, *Enthusiasm*, 13.

54. Timothy Mitchell, *Rule of Experts: Egypt, Techno-Politics, Modernity*, Berkeley: University of California Press, 2002: 168–69.

55. Abd al-Baset Abd al-Mo'ty, *Al-tabaqat al-egtema'iya wa mustaqbal misr: Etegahat al-taghir wa al-tafa'ulat, 1975–2020* (Social Classes and the Future of Egypt: Trends of Change and Interaction, 1975–2020), Cairo: Merit lel-Nashr wal-Ma'lumat, 2002, 78.

56. Binder, *Enthusiasm*, 309–15.

57. Amani Abd al-Rahman Saleh, "*Usul al-nukhba al-siyasiya al-misriya fei al-sab'inat: al-nash'a wa al-tatuwer* (Origins of the Egyptian Political Elite in the Seventies: The Birth and Development)," *Al-Fekr al-Strategy al-Araby* 26: 9–50 (1988): 23.

58. Abu al-Fadl, *Kunt*, 226.

59. Lutfi Al-Kholi, "*Thermometer Kamshish* (The Kamshish Thermometer)," in *Al-Tali'ah* 2 (6): 5–9 (1966): 5.

60. Nasr, *Muzakirat*, 211.

61. Shahenda Maqlad, *Min awraq Shahenda Maqlad* (From the Papers of Shahenda Maqlad), Cairo: Dar Merit, 2006, 60–94.

62. Abu al-Fadl, *Kunt*, 244–46.

63. Maqlad, *Min awraq Shahenda Maqlad*, 108.

64. Sadat, *Al-Bahth*, 216–23; Game' 2004: 75–77.

65. Maqlad, *Min awraq Shahenda Maqlad*, 138.

66. Ibid., 142–43.

67. Imam, *Nasser and Amer*, 93.

68. *Al-Tali'ah*, March 1967, 124–28.

69. Imam, *Nasser and Amer*, 94.

70. Mitchell, *Rule of Experts*, 154–70.

71. Aburish, *Nasser*, 249.

72. Fawzy, *Harb al-thlath sanawat*, 24–26.

73. Sadat, *Al-Bahth*, 211.

74. Schlesinger, *A Thousand Days*, 523.

75. Vatikiotis, *Nasser and His Generation*, 162.

76. Gamasy, *October War*, 39–40; Dunstan, *The Six Day War 1967*, 26.

77. Sharaf, *'Abd al-Nasser*, 336.

78. Fawzy, *Harb al-thlath sanawat*, 10.

79. Mohamed Abd al-Wahab Sayyid Ahmed, *Al-'Alaqat al-masriya al-amrekiya men al-taqarub ela al-taba'ud, 1952–1958*, 151.

80. Schlesinger, *Thousand Days*, 522–23.

81. Heikal, *1967*, 361–74.

82. Dunstan, *The Six Day War 1967*, 72.

83. Richard H. Dekmejian, "Egypt and Turkey: The Military in the Background," in *Soldiers, Peasants, and Bureaucrats: Civil-Military Relations in Communist and Modernizing Societies*, ed. Roman Kolkowicz and Andrzej Korbonski, Boston: George Allen & Unwin, 1982, 31.

84. Hammad, *Asrar thawrat 23 yunyu*, 1380–83.

85. Fawzy, *Harb al-thlath sanawat*, 37–38.

86. Fouad Allam, *Al-Ikhwan wa ana*, 15.

87. Hosni, *Shams Badran*, 63, 82.

88. Fawzy, *Harb al-thlath sanawat*, 42–52.

89. Murad Ghaleb, *Ma'a Abd al-Nasser wa al-Sadat: Sanawat al-intesar wa ayam al-mehan: Muzakirat Murad Ghaleb* (With Abd al-Nasser and Sadat: The Years of Triumph and the Days of Trial—Memoirs of Murad Ghaleb), Cairo: Markaz Al-Ahram lel-Targama wel-Nashr, 2001, 101.

90. Dekmejian, "Egypt and Turkey," 33.

91. Sirrs, *History*, 95.

92. Hobbes, *Leviathan* (1968).

93. Brooks, *Shaping Strategy*, 90.

94. Fawzy, *Harb al-thlath sanawat*, 72.

95. Heikal, *1967*, 268, 439–40.

96. Brooks, *Shaping Strategy*, 91.

97. Ibid., 92.

98. Ghaleb, *Ma'a Abd al-Nasser wa al-Sadat*, 107.

99. Browne, "Six Days of War Spark Forty Years of Strife," 75.

100. Brooks, *Shaping Strategy*, 65.

101. Gamasy, *October War*, 79.

102. Ibid., 22.

103. Imam, *Nasser and Amer*, 159.

104. Huwaidi, *Khamsin*, 191.

105. Fawzy, *Harb al-thlath sanawat*, 10–11.

106. Kamal Hassan Aly, *Mashawir al-'umr*, 211–21.

107. George W. Gawrych, "The Egyptian High Command in the 1973 War," *Armed Forces & Society* 13 (4): 535–59 (1987).

108. Brooks, *Shaping Strategy*, 86.

109. Huwaidi, *Khamsin*, 191.

110. Imam, *Nasser and Amer*, 143.

111. Dunstan, *The Six Day War 1967*, 15.

112. Gamasy, *October War*, 50.

113. Sadat, *Al-Bahth*, 228.

114. Fawzy, *Harb al-thlath sanawat*, 151–52.

115. Gamasy, *October War*, 61–62.

116. Fawzy, *Harb al-thlath sanawat*, 101.

117. Sadat, *Al-Bahth*, 229.

118. Fawzy, *Harb al-thlath sanawat*, 151–52.

119. Aly, *Mashawir al-'umr*, 234.

120. Gamasy, *October War*, 64–65.

121. Dunstan, *The Six Day War 1967*, 66.

122. Ibid., 84.

123. Gamasy, *October War*, 76.

124. Ibid., 76.

125. Dunstan, *The Six Day War 1967*, 25.

126. Heikal, *1967*, 818.

127. Sadat, *Al-Bahth*, 232.

128. Sabri interviewed in Yunis, *Al-Zahf al-muqadas*, 7–8.

129. Heikal, *1967*, 851.

130. Ibid., 841–43.

131. Ibid.

132. Ahmed, *Thawrat al-general*, 913.

133. Heikal, *1967*, 875–86.

134. Ibid., 881–84.

135. Aburish, *Nasser*, 267.

136. Gamasy, *October War*, 35.

137. Abu Zikri, *Mazbahat*, 380–97.

138. Abd al-Razeq Al-Sanhouri, *Al-Sanhouri min khilal awraquh al-shakhsiya* (Al-Sanhouri Through His Personal Diaries), Cairo: Dar al-Shorouk, 2005: 314.

139. Ghaleb, *Ma'a Abd al-Nasser wa al-Sadat*, 124.

140. Abu Zikri, *Mazbahat*, 378–79, 403, 442–44.

141. Sharaf, *Abd al-Nasser*, 160–61.

142. Gamasy, *October War*, 83.

143. Aburish, *Nasser*, 267.

144. Hosni, *Shams Badran*, 155.

145. Fawzy, *Harb al-thlath sanawat*, 166–68.

146. Sirrs, *History*, 105.

147. Hammad, *Asrar thawrat 23 yunyu*, 1345.

148. Ahmed, *Thawrat al-general*, 925–33.

149. Amos Perlmutter, *Egypt: The Praetorian State*, New York: Transaction Publishers, 1974, 184.

150. Aburish, *Nasser*, 271–74.

151. Sadat, *Al-Bahth*, 250.

152. Sharaf, *Abd al-Nasser*, 160–75.

153. Fawzy, *Harb al-thlath sanawat*, 175–74; Huwaidi, *Khamsin*, 249–75.

154. Brooks, *Shaping Strategy*, 112.

155. Interview with Colonel Muhammad Selim, 2009.

156. Abd al-Aziz Al-Beteshty, *Al-Tha'abin* (The Snakes), Cairo: Al-Maktab al-Masry al-Hadith, 2006, 17.

157. Aly, *Mashawir al-'umr*, 117.

158. Huwaidi, *Khamsin*, 190–91.

159. Hosni *Shams Badran*, 143, 151.

160. Huwaidi, *Khamsin*, 438–51.

161. Sirrs, *History*, 109.

162. Magdi Hammad, "*Al-muasasa al-'askariya wa al-nizam al-siasi al-masri*," 35–36.

163. Robert Springborg, *Mubarak's Egypt: Fragmentation of the Political Order*, Boulder, CO: Westview Press, 1989, 101.

164. Heikal, *1967*, 914.

165. Ibid., 245.

166. Browne, "Six Days of War," 74; Dunstan, *The Six Day War 1967*, 19.

167. William B. Quandt, "Lyndon Johnson and the June 1967 War: What Color Was the Light?" *Middle East Journal* 46 (2): 198–228 (1992).

168. Gamasy, *October War*, 30–33.

169. James Scott, *The Attack on the Liberty: The Untold Story of Israel's Deadly 1967 Assault on a U.S. Spy Ship*, New York: Simon & Schuster, 2009.

170. Gamasy, *October War*, 117.

171. McDermott, *Egypt from Nasser to Mubarak*, 155–63.

172. Saad El-Din Shazly, *The Crossing of the Suez: The October War (1973)*, London: Third World Centre for Research and Publishing, 1980, 71.

173. Gamal Hammad, *Al-Hukuma al-khafiya fei 'ahd Abd al-Nasser wa asrar masra' al-mushir Amer* (The Invisible Government during the Reign of Nasser and the Secrets of Field

Marshal Amer's Death), Cairo: Al-Shareka Al-Mutaheda lel-Teba'a wel-Nashr wel-Tawzee', 2008, 1.

174. Ahmed Abdallah, "*Rad fe'l al-shabab iza' al-hazima* (Youth Reaction to the Defeat)," in *Harb yunyu 1967 ba'd thalatheen sana* (The June 1967 War after Thirty Years), ed. Lutfi al-Khuli, 21–46, Cairo: Markaz al-Ahram lel-Targama wal-Nashr, 1997, 27–45, 149–53.

CHAPTER 3: ERADICATING THE CENTERS OF POWER

1. Henry Kissinger, *White House Years*, New York: Little, Brown, 1979, 1276–77.

2. Mohamed Hassanein Heikal, *Autumn of Fury: The Assassination of Sadat*, London: Andre Deutsch, 1983, ix.

3. Sadat, *Al-Bahth 'an al-zat*, 163.

4. Sadat in Mansour, Anis. *Min awraq al-Sadat* (From Sadat's Papers), Cairo: Dar al-Ma'aref, 2009, 420.

5. Ahmed Hamroush, *Ghorub yulyu* (July's Sunset), Cairo: Dar al-Mustaqbal al-Arabi, 1987, 37.

6. Sadat, *Al-Bahth 'an al-zat*, 299.

7. Hamroush, *Ghorub yulyu*, 30.

8. Heikal, *Autumn of Fury*, 40–41.

9. Hussein Mohamed Ahmed Hammudah, *Asrar harakat al-zubat al-ahrar wa al-Ikhwan al-Muslimeen* (Secrets of the Free Officers Movement and the Muslim Brothers), Cairo: Al-Zahraa lel-'Ilam al-Arabi, 1985, 173.

10. Sharaf, *'Abd al-Nasser*, 408–12.

11. Ibid., 425.

12. Binder, *In a Moment of Enthusiasm*, 389.

13. Ahmed Osman Osman, *Safahat min tagrebati* (Pages from My Life Experience), Cairo: Al-Maktab al-Masry al-Hadith, 1981, 402.

14. Sadat in Mansour, *Min awraq al-Sadat*, 142.

15. Hamroush, *Ghorub yulyu*, 88.

16. Sadat, *Al-Bahth 'an al-zat*, 304.

17. Sharaf, *'Abd al-Nasser*, 457.

18. Sirrs, *A History of the Egyptian Intelligence Service*, 120.

19. Brooks, *Shaping Strategy*, 117.

20. Game', *'Araft al-Sadat*, 151.

21. Barron, *KGB*, 58–59.

22. Sharaf, *'Abd al-Nasser*, 401.

23. Sadat, *Al-Bahth 'an al-zat*, 303.

24. Heikal, *October 1973*, 224.

25. Ibid., 225.

26. Ghaleb, *Ma'a Abd al-Nasser wa al-Sadat*, 161, 176.

27. Hammad, *Al-Hukuma al-khafiya fei 'ahd Abd al-Nasser wa asrar masra' al-mushir Amer*, 153–55, 181.

28. Sadat in Mansour, *Min awraq al-Sadat*, 429–30.

29. Sirrs, *History*, 21, 53.
30. Sadat in Mansour, *Min awraq al-Sadat*, 431.
31. Heikal, *Autumn of Fury*, 41.
32. Sharaf, *'Abd al-Nasser*, 417–18.
33. Game', *'Araft al-Sadat*, 168.
34. Binder, *Enthusiasm*, 393–94.
35. Sirrs, *History*, 121.
36. Heikal, *Autumn of Fury*, 76.
37. Abdallah, *The Student Movement and National Politics in Egypt, 1923–1973*, 179.

CHAPTER 4: TWILIGHT OF THE GENERALS

1. Brooks, *Shaping Strategy*, 131.
2. Heikal, *October 1973*, 262.
3. Shazly, *The Crossing of the Suez*, 25.
4. Brooks, *Shaping Strategy*, 132.
5. Fawzy, *Harb al-thlath sanawat, 1967–1970*, 101.
6. Hammudah, *Asrar harakat al-zubat al-ahrar wa al-Ikhwan al-Muslimeen*, 137.
7. Matti Golan, *The Secret Conversations of Henry Kissinger: Step-by-Step Diplomacy in the Middle East*, New York: Quadrangle/New York Times Book Co., 1976, 147.
8. Sharon in Turner, *Suez 1956*, 317–19.
9. Insight Team, *Yom Kippur War*, 70.
10. Heikal, *Autumn of Fury*, 60.
11. Anthony H. Cordesman, *Arab-Israeli Military Forces in an Era of Asymmetric Wars*, Westport, CT: Praeger Security International, 2006, 201–2.
12. Al-Beteshty, *Al-Tha'abin*, 67–74, 84–85, 107.
13. Hammad, *Al-Ma'arek al-harbiya 'ala al-gabha al-misriya*, 52–54.
14. al-Gamasy, *The October War*, 141–45.
15. Shazly, *Crossing*, 111.
16. Minutes of meeting in Musa Sabri, *Watha'eq harb October*, 31.
17. Anwar Sadat, *Al-Bahth 'an al-zat*, 319–21.
18. Musa Sabri, *Watha'eq harb October* (October War Documents), Cairo: Akhbar al-Youm, 1979, 65–67; Shazly, *Crossing*, 122–23.
19. Sadat in Anis Mansour, *Min awraq al-Sadat*, 335–36.
20. Sadat, *Al-Bahth 'an al-zat*, 320.
21. Game', *'Araft al-Sadat*, 164.
22. Shazly, *Crossing*, 123–26.
23. Hamroush, *Ghorub yulyu*, 147.
24. Heikal, *October 1973*, 251.
25. Sirrs, *A History of the Egyptian Intelligence Service*, 127.
26. Shazly, *Crossing*, 129.
27. Ibid.
28. Ibid., 130; Brooks, *Shaping Strategy*, 121.
29. Sirrs, *History*, 121.

30. Shazly, *Crossing*, 124–25.

31. Sadat in Mansour, *Min awraq al-Sadat*, 367.

32. Ibid., 362.

33. Gamasy, *The October War*, 152–58.

34. Shazly, *Crossing*, 27.

35. Heikal, *Autumn of Fury*, 64.

36. Shazly, *Crossing*, 126–27.

37. Sabri, *Watha'eq harb October*, 54.

38. Sadat, *Al-Bahth 'an al-zat*, 194, 232, 390.

39. Game', *'Araft al-Sadat*, 140.

40. Sirrs, *History*, 117.

41. Sadat, *Al-Bahth 'an al-zat*, 296.

42. Hamroush, *Ghorub yulyu*, 17, 40–46.

43. Ghaleb, *Ma'a Abd al-Nasser wa al-Sadat*, 193.

44. Tape transcript in Heikal, *October 1973*, 758–60.

45. Sirrs, *History*, 123.

46. Esmat Abd al-Magid, *Zaman al-enkesar wa al-entesar: muzakerat diplomacy masri 'an ahdath masria wa 'arabia wa dawlia: nesf qarn men al-tahawulat al-kubra* (The Time of Defeat and Victory: Memoirs of an Egyptian Diplomat Regarding Egyptian, Arab, and International Events—Half a Century of Great Transformations), Cairo: Dar al-Shorouk, 1998, 121.

47. Heikal, *Autumn of Fury*, 44–45.

48. Sirrs, *History*, 121.

49. Heikal, *October 1973*, 235, 270–71.

50. Henry Kissinger, *Diplomacy*, New York: Simon & Schuster, 1994: 737.

51. Minutes of meeting in William Burr, *Asrar harb October fei al-watha'eq al-amrikiya* (Secrets of the October War in the American Documents), translated by Khaled Daoud, Cairo: Markaz Al-Ahram lel-Targama wel-Nashr, 2004, 41.

52. Kissinger in Golan, *Secret Conversations*, 145.

53. Shazly, *Crossing*, 117.

54. Burr, *Asrar*, 37, 47.

55. Brooks, *Shaping Strategy*, 104.

56. Julian Schofield, *Militarization and War*, New York: Palgrave Macmillan, 2007, 98.

57. Ibid., 109.

58. Ghaleb, *Ma'a Abd al-Nasser wa al-Sadat*, 213.

59. Barnet, *Confronting the Cost of War*, 128.

60. Boyne, *The Two o'Clock War*, xiv.

61. Heikal, *1967*, 24.

62. Gamasy, *The October War*, 313.

63. Sadat, *Al-Bahth 'an al-zat*, 329.

64. Isma'il Fahmy, *Al-tafawed min agl al-salam fei al-sharq al-awsat* (Negotiating for Peace in the Middle East), Cairo: Maktabet Madbouli, 1985, 30, 37–38.

65. Insight Team, *Yom Kippur War*, 86.

66. Fawzy, *Harb al-thlath sanawat*, 12, 365.

67. Sadat, *Al-Bahth 'an al-zat*, 320.

68. Shazly, *Crossing*, 18.

69. Gamasy, *The October War*, 138–39.

70. Heikal, *October 1973*, 311–12; Gamasy, *The October War*, 191.

71. Shazly, *Crossing*, 157.

72. Gamasy, *The October War*, 226, 250.

73. Avi Shlaim, "Failures in National Intelligence Estimates: The Case of the Yom Kippur War," *World Politics* 28 (3): 348–80 (1976).

74. Boyne, *Two o'Clock War*, 58.

75. Insight Team, *Yom Kippur War*, 189.

76. Boyne, *Two o'Clock War*, 58.

77. Golan, *Secret Conversations*, 66.

78. *Al-Ahram* 31718: 3. Cairo (10/13/1973).

79. Insight Team, *Yom Kippur War*, 191.

80. Ibid., 226.

81. Kamal Hassan Aly, *Mashawir al-'umr*, 319.

82. Insight Team, *Yom Kippur War*, 135, 172, 232.

83. Gamasy, *The October War*, 264.

84. Heikal, *October 1973*, 438.

85. Burr, *Asrar*, 151.

86. Heikal, *October 1973*, 392–93.

87. Ghaleb, *Ma'a Abd al-Nasser wa al-Sadat*, 213.

88. Boyne, *Two o'Clock War*, 96.

89. Heikal, *October 1973*, 396–422.

90. Insight Team, *Yom Kippur War*, 169.

91. Gamasy, *The October War*, 265–66.

92. Heikal, *October 1973*, 440.

93. Gamasy, *The October War*, 237.

94. All reproduced in Heikal, *October 1973*, 792–858.

95. Quoted in Gamasy, *The October War*, 239.

96. Minutes of meeting in Burr, *Asrar*, 126.

97. Hamroush, *Ghorub yulyu*, 184.

98. Gamasy, *The October War*, 247–48.

99. Boyne, *Two o'Clock War*, 45.

100. Aly, *Mashawir al-'umr*, 319.

101. Gamasy, *The October War*, 240, 272.

102. Boyne, *Two o'Clock War*, 66.

103. Heikal, *October 1973*, 360.

104. Henry Kissinger, *Years of Upheaval*, New York: Little, Brown, 1992, 481–82.

105. Minutes of meeting in Burr, *Asrar*, 207.

106. Golan, *Secret Conversations*, 54.

107. Boyne, *Two o'Clock War*, 119.

108. Golan, *Secret Conversations*, 49.

109. Boyne, *Two o'Clock War*, 75–79.

110. Sadat, *Al-Bahth 'an al-zat*, 347.

111. Boyne, *Two o'Clock War*, 209, 263.

112. Gamasy, *The October War*, 275–79.

113. Heikal, *October 1973*, 426.

114. Ibid., 438.

115. Shazly, *Crossing*, 166; Gamasy, *The October War*, 271.

116. Heikal, *October 1973*, 432.

117. Boyne, *Two o'Clock War*, 108.

118. Ibid., 128.

119. Heikal, *October 1973*, 487.

120. Boyne, *Two o'Clock War*, 102.

121. Heikal, *October 1973*, 401.

122. Aly, *Mashawir al-'umr*, 361.

123. Kissinger, *White House Years*, 522–23.

124. Gamasy, *The October War*, 282.

125. Ibid., 290.

126. Shazly, *Crossing*, 172.

127. Boyne, *Two o'Clock War*, 180–84.

128. Shazly, *Crossing*, 180.

129. Boyne, *Two o'Clock War*, 201.

130. Sadat, *Al-Bahth 'an al-zat*, 349.

131. Insight Team, *Yom Kippur War*, 345.

132. Sadat, *Al-Bahth 'an al-zat*, 348.

133. Boyne, *Two o'Clock War*, 200.

134. Gamasy, *The October War*, 282.

135. Insight Team, *Yom Kippur War*, 226–28.

136. McDermott, *Egypt from Nasser to Mubarak*, 168.

137. Shazly, *Crossing*, 9–10.

138. Ibid., 96.

139. al-Din, "*Harb October: Al-umniya al-akhira lel-Shazly*," 20–23.

140. Golan, *Secret Conversations*, 86–87.

141. Insight Team, *Yom Kippur War*, 343.

142. Sadat in Mansour, *Min awraq al-Sadat*, 235.

143. Gamasy, *The October War*, 295–97.

144. Heikal, *October 1973*, 524–27, 569.

145. Boyne, *Two o'Clock War*, 262.

146. Shazly, *Crossing*, 195.

147. Anwar Sadat, "*Warakat October* (The October Paper)," *Al-Tali'ah* 10 (5): 131–46 (May 1974).

148. Adel Ghoneim, *Azmat al-dawla al-misriya al-mu'asera* (The Crisis of the Contemporary Egyptian State), Cairo: Dar al-'Alam al-Thaleth, 2005, 85.

149. Shazly, *Crossing*, 202.

150. Ahmed Bahaa al-Din, *Muhawarati ma'a al-Sadat*, 93.

151. Gamasy, *The October War*, 330.

152. Insight Team, *Yom Kippur War*, 442.

153. Kissinger in Golan, *Secret Conversations*, 91.

154. Boyne, *Two o'Clock War*, 260.

155. Golan, *Secret Conversations*, 112, 161.

156. Kissinger, *White House Years*, 527.

157. Ghaleb, *Ma'a Abd al-Nasser wa al-Sadat*, 214.

158. Heikal, *October 1973*, 675–80.

159. Gamasy, *The October War*, 85.

160. Ibid., 313.

161. Golan, *Secret Conversations*, 116.

162. Gamasy, *The October War*, 335–37.

163. Ibid.

164. Brooks, *Shaping Strategy*, 121.

165. Dekmejian, "Egypt and Turkey," 38–39.

166. Fahmy, *Al-tafawed*, 117.

167. Golan, *Secret Conversations*, 160–65.

168. Heikal, *Autumn of Fury*, 73, 214.

169. Bahaa al-Din, *Muhawarati ma'a al-Sadat*, 158.

170. Fahmy, *Al-tafawed*, 118.

171. Ghaleb, *Ma'a Abd al-Nasser wa al-Sadat*, 215.

172. Heikal, *October 1973*, 453.

173. Shazly, *Crossing*, 205.

174. Insight Team, *Yom Kippur War*, 450; Richard B. Parker, *The Politics of Miscalculation in the Middle East*, 352–58.

175. Brooks, *Shaping Strategy*, 141.

176. Shazly, *Crossing*, 184.

177. Dunstan, *The Six Day War 1967*, 91.

178. Springborg, *Mubarak's Egypt*, 97.

179. Gamasy, *The October War*, 402.

180. Game', *'Araft al-Sadat*, 191.

181. Sadat, *Al-Bahth 'an al-zat*, 242.

182. Aly, *Mashawir al-'umr*, 117.

183. Ibid., 441–44.

184. Boutros Boutros Ghali, *Tariq masr ela al-Quds: Qesat al-sera' men agl al-salam fei al-sharq al-awsat* (Egypt's Road to Jerusalem: The Story of the Struggle for Peace in the Middle East), Cairo: Al-Ahram lel-Targama wel-Nashr, 1997, 315.

185. Ragab Al-Banna, and Khamis al-Bakry. "*Secertair al-mushir yarwi tafasil al-lahazat al-akhirai* (The Field Marshal's Secretary Recounts the Details of the Final Moments)," in *Al-Ahram* 34416: 3. Cairo (3/5/1981).

186. Ibrahim Nafe', "*Hal al-hadeth mudabar* (Was the Accident Fixed?)," *Al-Ahram* 34417: 1. Cairo (3/6/1981).

187. *October*, March 8, 1981: 8–9.

188. Mohamed Sha'ban, "*Man qatal Ahmed Badawi* (Who Killed Ahmed Badawi?)," *El-Shabab* 410: 54–55, Cairo (9/2011).

189. Muhammad Al-Baz, "*Eteham Mubarak bei eghtiyal al-mushir Ahmed Badawi bei sabab kashfu fasad safaqat al-selah fei al-gish* (Mubarak Accused of Assassinating Field Marshal Badawi Because He Exposed the Corruption of Arms Deals in the Military," *Al-Fajr* 318: 9. Cairo (8/22/2011).

190. Aly, *Mashawir al-'umr*, 476.

191. Baz, "*Eteham Mubarak*," 9.

192. Adel Hammudah, *Eghtiyal ra'is*, 119; Antar Abd al-Latif, "*Taftah al-malaf al-sha'ek wa takshef bei al-asma*," 5.

193. Gamasy, *The October War*, 404.

194. Perlmutter, *Egypt*, 201.

195. Springborg, *Mubarak's Egypt*, 95–96; Brooks, *Shaping Strategy*, 119.

196. Bruce Riedel, 2010. "If Israel Attacks," *National Interest* 109: 6–13 (2010): 8.

197. John K. Cooley, *Unholy Wars: Afghanistan, America, and International Terrorism*, London: Pluto Press, 2000, 35–36.

198. Sadat in Mansour, *Min awraq al-Sadat*, 240.

199. Sadat, *Al-Bahth 'an al-zat*, 366.

200. Mohamed Ibrahim Kamel, *Al-Salam al-da'ie fei Camp David* (The Lost Peace in Camp David), Cairo: Ketab al-Ahaly, 1983, 108.

201. Zbigniew Brzezinski, *Power and Principle: Memoirs of the National Security Advisor, 1977–1981*, New York: Farrar, Straus and Giroux, 1983, 110.

202. Bahaa al-Din, *Muhawarati ma'a al-Sadat*, 161.

203. Kamel, *Camp David*, 177.

204. Quoted in Fahmy, *Al-tafawed*, 386–97, 398.

205. Kamel, *Camp David*, 41.

206. Ghali, *Tariq masr ela al-Quds*, 19.

207. Brzezinski, *Power and Principle*, 235.

208. Ibid., 274.

209. Brooks, *Shaping Strategy*, 136.

210. Gamasy, *The October War*, 141.

211. Accords and annexes in Kamel, *Camp David*, 623–44.

212. Cordesman, *Arab-Israeli Military Forces*, 202.

213. Kamel, *Camp David*, 514.

214. Quoted in Brzezinski, *Power and Principle*, 271–72.

215. Ibid., 283.

216. Ghali, *Tariq masr ela al-Quds*, 150.

217. Ibid., 149, 153.

218. Kamel, *Camp David*, 515.

219. Ibid., 607–8.

220. Ghali, *Tariq masr ela al-Quds*, 156.

221. Brzezinski, *Power and Principle*, 238.

222. Kamel, *Camp David*, 603; Ghali, *Tariq masr ela al-Quds*, 149.

223. Brzezinski, *Power and Principle*, 265.

224. Ibid., 270.

225. Ibid., 236, 265, 270.

226. Cooley, *Unholy Wars*, 24–27.

227. Brzezinski, *Power and Principle*, 444–54.

228. Cooley, *Unholy Wars*, 31–32.

229. Sirrs, *History*, 137, 153.

230. Quoted in Golan, *Secret Conversations*, 152–53.

231. Brzezinski, *Power and Principle*, 93.

232. Heikal, *Autumn of Fury*, 13.

233. Fahmy, *Al-tafawed*, 13, 108, 127–29.

234. Kamel, *Camp David*, 189–91, 193.

235. Game', *'Araft al-Sadat*, 191.

236. Boyne, *Two o'Clock War*, 94.

237. Insight Team, *Yom Kippur War*, 46.

238. Brooks, *Shaping Strategy*, 111.

239. Sadat in Mansour, *Min awraq al-Sadat*, 336.

240. Bahaa al-Din, *Muhawarati ma'a al-Sadat*, 68–69.

241. Ibid., 69.

242. Youssef M Ibrahim, "U.S. Stake in Egypt Rests on One Man—Anwar el-Sadat," *New York Times* (3/30/1980), E3.

243. Raymond A Hinnebusch, "The Formation of the Contemporary Egyptian States from Nasser and Sadat to Mubarak," in *The Political Economy of Contemporary Egypt*, ed. Ibrahim M. Oweiss, 188–209, Washington, DC: Center for Contemporary Arab Studies, Georgetown University, 1990.

244. Copeland, *The Game of Nations*, 213.

245. Suleiman, *Al-Nizam al-qawi wa al-dawla al-da'ifa*, 15.

246. Hinnebusch, "The Formation of the Contemporary Egyptian States," 192–93.

247. Brooks, *Shaping Strategy*, 115.

248. Amani Abd al-Rahman Saleh, *"Usul al-nukhba al-siyasiya al-misriya fei al-sab'inat: al-nash'a wa al-tatuwer,"* 16.

249. Abd al-Magid, *Zaman al-enkesar wa al-entesar*, 111.

250. Mahmoud Abd al-Fadeel, *Ta'amulate fei al-mas'ala al-eqtesadiya al-misriya* (Reflections on the Egyptian Economic Question), Cairo: Dar al-Mustaqbal al-Arabi, 1983, 11.

251. Abd al-Baset Abd al-Mo'ty, *Al-tabaqat al-egtema'iya wa mustaqbal misr: Etegahat al-taghir wa al-tafa'ulat, 1975–2020* (Social Classes and the Future of Egypt: Trends of Change and Interaction, 1975–2020), Cairo: Merit lel-Nashr wal-Ma'lumat, 2002, 247–48.

252. Quoted in Kandil, *"Al-tatawee,"* 1986, 90.

253. Bahaa al-Din, *Muhawarati ma'a al-Sadat*, 25, 90.

254. Ahmed, *Thawrat al-general*, 1993: 474.

255. al-Mo'ty, *Al-tabaqat*, 105, 191.

256. Heikal, *Autumn of Fury*, 183–91.

257. Abd al-Fadeel, *Ta'amulate*, 90; Abd al-Mo'ty, *Al-tabaqat*, 121.

258. Ibrahim M Oweiss, "Egypt's Economy: The Pressing Issues," in *The Political Economy of Contemporary Egypt*, ed. Ibrahim M. Oweiss, 3–49, Washington, DC: Center for Contemporary Arab Studies, Georgetown University, 1990, 9.

259. al-Fadeel, *Ta'amulate*, 27.

260. Heikal, *Autumn of Fury*, 78, 211.

261. Heba Handoussa, "Fifteen Years of US Aid to Egypt—A Critical Review," in *The Political Economy of Contemporary Egypt*, ed. Ibrahim M. Oweiss, 109–24, Washington, DC: Center for Contemporary Arab Studies, Georgetown University, 1990, 114; Barnet, *Confronting the Cost of War*, 130.

262. Bahaa al-Din, *Muhawarati ma'a al-Sadat*, 114.

263. Abd al-Mone'm Al-Mashat, "*Al-'Awamel al-kharegiya wa al-tatawer al-demokraty fei misr* (External Factors and Democratic Development in Egypt), in *Al-Tatawer al-demokraty fei misr: qadaya wa munaqashat* (Democratic Development in Egypt: Issues and Debates), ed. Ali al-Din Helal, 53–78, Cairo: Maktabet Nahdet al-Sharq, 1986, 61.

264. Handoussa, "Fifteen Years of US Aid to Egypt," 122.

265. Ibid., 110–17.

266. Heikal, *Autumn of Fury*, 82–83, 185; for other examples of Sadat's intervention in favor of U.S. investors see Amani Kandil, "*Al-tatawer al-siyasi fei misr wa son' al-siyasat al-'ama*," 91.

267. Kandil, "*Al-tatawer*," 103–4.

268. Hinnebusch, "The Formation of the Contemporary Egyptian States," 192–93.

269. Oweiss, "Egypt's Economy," 34.

270. Heikal, *Autumn of Fury*, 87.

271. Copeland, *Game of Nations*, 216.

272. Heikal, *Autumn of Fury*, 86–88.

273. Ref'at Sayyed Ahmed, *Thawrat al-general*, 474–75.

274. Ahmed Osman Osman, *Safahat min tagrebati*, 164–95, 226, 389–94.

275. Ibid., 422–68, 607–47.

276. Heikal, *Autumn of Fury*, 188–89.

277. Osman, *Safahat min tagrebati*, 346–62, 404–72, 578, 643.

278. Ismail in Mahmoud Fawzy, *Al-Nabawi Ismail wa guzur manaset al-Sadat*, 49, 86–90.

279. Shazly, *Crossing*, 83–99.

280. Sirrs, *History*, 127.

281. Abdel-Rahman El-Sayed, "Shrouded in Mystery," *Al-Ahram Weekly* 852: 2. Cairo (7/5/2007).

282. Fouad Allam, *Al-Ikhwan wa ana*, 413.

283. McDermott, *Egypt from Nasser to Mubarak*, 54.

284. Assem Genedi, "*Ada' gihaz al-shurta* (The Performance of the Police Force)," in *Thawrat 25 Yanaier: Qera'a awaliya wa ru'iya mustaqbaliya* (The January 25 Revolution: A Preliminary Reading and Future Prospects), ed. Amr Hashem Rabie', Cairo: Al-Ahram Center for Political & Strategic Studies, 2011, 154.

285. Ismail in Fawzy, *Al-Nabawi Ismail*, 154–56.

286. Al-Mashat, "*Al-'Awamel*," 65.

287. Sirrs, *History*, 162.

288. Hammudah, *Eghtiyal ra'is*, 239.

289. Interview with Colonel Muhammad Selim, 2009.

290. Allam, *Al-Ikhwan wa ana*, 269.

291. Hammudah, *Eghtiyal ra'is*, 65.

292. Ibid., 18–25, 233.

293. Heikal, *Autumn of Fury*, x–5.

294. Ismail in Fawzy, *Al-Nabawi Ismail*, 119.

295. Interview in Mohamed Saad Abd al-Hafeez and Mohamed Khayal, "*Abbud al-Zumur yakshef asrar gadida*," 7.

296. Hammudah, *Eghtiyal ra'is*, 28, 78.

297. Zumur in Abd al-Hafeez and Khayal, "*Abbud al-Zumur*," 7.

298. Hammudah, *Eghtiyal ra'is*, 50–52.

299. Interview in Abd al-Hafeez and Khayal, "*Abbud al-Zumur*," 7.

300. Heikal, *Autumn of Fury*, 267; Zumur in Abd al-Hafeez and Khayal, "*Abbud al-Zumur*," 7.

301. Allam, *Al-Ikhwan wa ana*, 413.

302. Ismail in Fawzy, *Al-Nabawi Ismail*, 110–14.

303. Interviewed in Gamal al-Keshky, "*Mashahid al-mout fei rewayet eghtiyal al-Sadat*," 5.

304. Ismail in Fawzy, *Al-Nabawi Ismail*, 123; Allam, *Al-Ikhwan wa ana*, 312.

305. Springborg, *Mubarak's Egypt*, 97.

306. Sirrs, *History*, 149–51.

307. Allam, *Al-Ikhwan wa ana*, 284.

308. Interview with General Abd al-Rahman al-Faramawy, 2009.

CHAPTER 5: THE LONG LULL BEFORE THE PERFECT STORM

1. Sa'id Isma'il Aly, "*Haza al-nigm al-sati'*," 3.

2. Abd al-Mone'm al-Mashat, "*Al-'Awamel al-kharegiya wa al-tatawer al-demokraty fei misr*," 67.

3. Springborg, *Mubarak's Egypt*, 100.

4. Abd al-Quddus "*Awlad al-balad*," 3.

5. Ahmed Abdallah, *Al-Jaysh*, 27.

6. Ibid., 16.

7. Springborg, *Mubarak's Egypt*, 100.

8. McDermott, *Egypt from Nasser to Mubarak*, 175.

9. Steven A. Cook, *Ruling but Not Governing: The Military and Political Development in Egypt, Algeria, and Turkey,* Baltimore: John Hopkins University Press, 2007, 81.

10. Springborg, *Mubarak's Egypt*, 102, 124–25.

11. Interview with General Abd al-Rahman al-Faramawy, 2009.

12. Ibid.

13. Mohamed Hassanein Heikal, *Mubarak wa zamanuh*, 143.

14. Muhammad al-Baz, *A-Mushir*, 78–81.

15. Ibid., 166.

16. Adam Shatz, "Mubarak's Last Breath," *London Review of Books* 32 (10): 6–10 (2010).

17. Eytan, Gazit, and Gilbo, *The Middle East Military Balance* (1993), 140.

18. See, for example, Springborg, *Mubarak's Egypt*; Yahya M. Sadowski, *Scuds or Butter: The Political Economy of Arms Control in the Middle East*, Washington: Brookings Institution, 1993; Cassandra, "Impending Crisis in Egypt" *Middle East Journal* 49 (1): 9–27 (1995);

Alan Richards and John Waterbury, *A Political Economy of the Middle East*, Boulder, CO: Westview Press, 1996; D. Weiss and U. Wurzel, *The Economics and Politics of Transition to an Open Market Economy*, Paris: Development Center at the OECD, 1998; Hillel Frisch, "Guns and Butter in the Egyptian Army," *Middle East Review of International Affairs* 5 (2): 1–14 (2001); Cook, *Ruling but Not Governing*; Philippe Droz-Vincent, "From Political to Economic Actors: The Changing Role of Middle Eastern Armies," in *Debating Arab Authoritarianism: Dynamics and Durability in Nondemocratic Regimes*, ed. Oliver Schlumberger, 195–214, Stanford, CA: Stanford University Press, 2007; Thomas Richter, "The Political Economy of Regime Maintenance in Egypt: Linking External Resources and Domestic Legitimation," in *Debating Arab Authoritarianism: Dynamics and Durability in Nondemocratic Regimes*, ed. Oliver Schlumberger, 177–94. Stanford, CA: Stanford University Press, 2007.

19. Quoted in Michael Howard, *Clausewitz*, New York: Oxford University Press, 1983, 36.

20. Mohamed Nur Farahat, "*Hawl hukm al-mu'asasat wa tahakum al-mu'asasat*," 7.

21. Ibrahim Shakib, "*Shukran ayuha al-sada*," 5.

22. Ahmed Fakhr, "*Al-fikr al-'askari al-masri wa idarit al-sira'*," 9.

23. Quoted in Baz, *A-Mushir*, 70.

24. Ibid., 64.

25. Quoted in Abdallah, *Al-Jaysh*, 20.

26. Abd al-Khaleq Farouk, *Guzur al-fasad al-edari fei misr: be'at al-'amal wa siyasat al-ugur wa al-muratabat fei misr* (The Roots of Administrative Corruption in Egypt: The Working Environment and the Policies of Wages and Incomes in Egypt), Cairo: Dar al-Shorouk, 2008, 288.

27. Yazid Sayigh, "Egypt's Army Looks Beyond Mubarak," *Financial Times* (2/3/2011): 11, my emphasis.

28. Gamal, *Al-'Askari*, 2.

29. Frisch, "Guns and Butter," 2.

30. Eytan, Heller, and Levran, *The Middle East Military Balance* (1985), 91.

31. Eytan and Levran, *The Middle East Military Balance* (1986), 131.

32. Barnet, *Confronting the Cost of War*, 143.

33. Sirrs, *A History of the Egyptian Intelligence Service*, 130–31.

34. Abdel-Rahman El-Sayed, "Shrouded in Mystery," *Al-Ahram Weekly* 852:2. Cairo (7/5/2007)

35. Mohamed Helmi Murad, "*Al-riqaba al-gha'iba 'ala al-infaq al-'askari wa al-tafwidat al-laniha'iya le-safaqat al-silah wa mizaniyat al-qwat al-musalaha* (The Absent Oversight of Military Spending and the Limitless Authorizations Regarding Defense Contracts and Budget)," *Al-Sha'b* 15. Cairo (9/9/1986).

36. Quoted in Baz, *A-Mushir*, 206–8.

37. Letter in Mohamed Hassanein Heikal, *Autumn of Fury*, 71.

38. Frisch, "Guns and Butter," 3–5.

39. Interview with Colonel Muhammad Selim, 2009.

40. Eytan, Heller, and Levran, *Middle East Military Balance* (1985), 87.

41. Cordesman, *Arab-Israeli Military Forces in an Era of Asymmetric Wars*, 175–77.

42. Eytan, Heller, and Tamari, *Middle East Military Balance* (1983), 89.

43. Eytan, Gazit, and Gilbo, *Middle East Military Balance* (1993), 136–42.

44. Gamal Essam al-Din, "*Al-Mushir al-samet Tantawy*," 1.

45. Springborg, *Mubarak's Egypt*, 95.

46. Quoted in Musa Gendy, "*Daga fei Israel hawl tasrihat al-mushir* (A Flare in Israel Following the Field Marshal's Revelations)," *Al-Ahram* 45392: 3. Cairo (2/18/1987).

47. Frisch, "Guns and Butter," 6.

48. Quoted in Baz, *A-Mushir*, 206–8.

49. Cordesman, *Arab-Israeli Military Forces*, 200.

50. Eytan, Gazit, and Giblo, *Middle East Military Balance* (1993), 141.

51. De Atkine, "Why Arabs Lose Wars," 13.

52. Frisch, "Guns and Butter," 6.

53. Heikal, *Mubarak wa zamanuh*, 65.

54. Jack A. Goldstone, "Understanding the Revolutions of 2011: Weakness and Resilience in Middle Eastern Autocracies," *Foreign Affairs* 90 (3): 8–16 (2011).

55. Heikal, *Mubarak wa zamanuh*, 306.

56. Ibid., 305.

57. Handoussa, "Fifteen Years of US Aid to Egypt," 114.

58. Waterbury, *The Egypt of Nasser and Sadat*, 376.

59. Dunstan, *The Six Day War 1967*, 22.

60. Insight Team, *Yom Kippur War*, 164, 341.

61. Brooks, *Shaping Strategy*, 130–31.

62. Insight Team, *Yom Kippur War*, 340–41.

63. Imam, *Nasser and Amer*, 33.

64. De Atkine, "Why Arabs Lose Wars," 17.

65. Interview with Colonel Muhammad Selim, 2009.

66. De Atkine, "Why Arabs Lose Wars," 20, my emphasis.

67. Barnet, *Confronting the Cost*, 143–44.

68. Cordesman, *Arab-Israeli Military Forces*, 159.

69. Barnet, *Confronting the Cost*, 143–44.

70. Frisch, "Guns and Butter," 5–6.

71. Cordesman, *Arab-Israeli Military Forces*, 162.

72. Al-Mashat, "*Al-'Awamel*," 64.

73. Interview with General Faramawy, 2009.

74. Springborg, *Mubarak's Egypt*, 142–43.

75. Sirrs, *History*, 162.

76. Farouk, *Guzur al-fasad al-edari fei misr*, 275–81.

77. Theda Skocpol, *States and Social Revolution: A Comparative Analysis of France, Russia, and China*, New York: Cambridge University Press, 1979: 226.

78. Andrei Soldatov and Irina Borogan, "Russia's New Nobility," *Foreign Affairs* 89 (4): 78–83.

79. Piers Brendon, "China Also Rises," *The National Interest* 110: 12.

80. Michael O'Hanlon, "Staying Power," *Foreign Affairs* 89 (4): 71–77 (2010).

81. Suleiman, *Al-Nizam al-qawi wa al-dawla al-da'ifa*, 84–86; Farouk, *Guzur al-fasad al-edari fei misr*, 285.

82. Heikal, *Mubarak wa zamanuh*, 121.

83. Abdallah, *The Student Movement and National Politics in Egypt, 1923–1973*, 1980.

84. Heikal, *Autumn of Fury*, 213.

85. Gilles Kepel, *Jihad: The Trial of Political Islam*, London: I. B. Tauris, 2006, 276–99.

86. Nabil Omar, "*Habib al-Adly: Asrar rehlat al-so'ud ela 'arsh al-dakhliya* (Habib al-Adly: Secrets of the Rise to the Throne of the Interior [Ministry]," *Al-Ahram* 45388: 5.

87. Cordesman, *Arab-Israeli Military Forces*, 192–95.

88. Shatz, "Mubarak's Last Breath," 8.

89. Basma Abd al-Aziz, *Eghraa al-sulta al-mutlaqa*, 45–46.

90. Ibid., 52–59.

91. Ibid., 9–10.

92. Ibid., 61.

93. Shatz, "Mubarak's Last Breath," 6.

94. Sirrs, *History*, 165.

95. Magdi al-Galad, Charles Fouad al-Masry, and Ahmed al-Khatib, "*Mahdi 'Akef fei awal hiwar sahafi ba'd azmat al-insihab* (Mahdi 'Akef in his first newspaper interview following the withdrawal crisis)," *Al-Masry Al-Youm* 11. Cairo (10/24/2009).

96. Interview with Fathy Sourur in Mahmoud Muslim, "*Al-Masry Al-Youm wagahat Fathy Sourur bei al-etahamat fakashaf asrar khatira, al-halaqa al-ula* (Al-Masry Al-Youm Confronted Fathy Sourur with Accusations, So He Revealed Dangerous Secrets, Part One)," *Al-Masry Al-Youm* 2475: 7. Cairo (3/24/2011).

97. Omar, "*Habib al-Adly*," 5.

98. Springborg, *Mubarak's Egypt*, 27.

99. Ibid.

100. Heikal, *Mubarak wa zamanuh*, 201.

101. Perlmutter, *Egypt*, 112.

102. Hosni, *Abd al-Nasser wa al-tanzim al-tale'i, 1963–1971*, 37.

103. Hamroush, *Ghorub yulyu*, 223.

104. Springborg, *Mubarak's Egypt*, 137, 158–69.

105. Abd al-Fadeel, *Ta'amulate fei al-mas'ala al-eqtesadiya al-misriya*, 50.

106. Abd al-Mo'ty, *Al-tabaqat al-egtema'iya wa mustaqbal misr*, 145, 174.

107. Heikal, *Autumn of Fury*, 210.

108. Suleiman, *Al-Nizam al-qawi*, 40.

109. Handoussa, "Fifteen Years of US Aid," 116.

110. Abd al-Mo'ty, *Al-tabaqat*, 104.

111. Ref'at Sayyed Ahmed, *Thawrat al-general*, 474.

112. Abd al-Mo'ty, *Al-tabaqat*, 105, 191.

113. Heikal, *Autumn of Fury*, 210–11.

114. Springborg, *Mubarak's Egypt*, 87.

115. Ibid., 35, 85–87.

116. Abd al-Fadeel, *Ta'amulate fei al-mas'ala al-eqtesadiya al-misriya*, 124–25.

117. Springborg, *Mubarak's Egypt*, 22.

118. Oweiss, "Egypt's Economy," 12.

119. Suleiman, *Al-Nizam al-qawi*, 54.

120. Ibid., 190.

121. George Bush and Brent Scowcroft, *A World Transformed*, New York: Vintage Books, 1998, 339–40, 41.

122. Wahid, *Military Expenditure and Economic Growth in the Middle East*, 133.

123. Ghoneim, *Azmat al-dawla al-misriya al-mu'asera*, 86, 158.

124. Mitchell, *Rule of Experts*, 272.

125. Amr Ismail Adly, "Politically-Embedded Cronyism," 11.

126. Timothy Mitchell, "Dreamland," 29, 274–81.

127. Mitchell, *Rule of Experts*, 276–82.

128. Amr Ismail Adly, "Politically-Embedded Cronyism: The Case of Post-Liberalization Egypt," *Business and Politics* 11 (4): 11–12.

129. Mitchell, *Rule of Experts*, 276–82.

130. Abd al-Mo'ty, *Al-tabaqat*, 160–76, 195.

131. Saad Eddin Ibrahim, *Egypt, Islam, and Democracy*, Cairo: American University in Cairo Press, 1996, 39–41; Diane Singerman, "The Networked World of Islamist Social Movements," in *Islamic Activism: A Social Movement Theory Approach*, ed. Q. Wiktorowicz, 143–63. Bloomington: Indiana University Press, 2004, 161.

132. Robert Bianchi, "Interest Groups and Politics in Mubarak's Egypt," in *The Political Economy of Contemporary Egypt*, ed. Ibrahim M. Oweiss, 210–21, Washington, DC: Center for Contemporary Arab Studies, Georgetown University, 1990, 215.

133. Shatz, "Mubarak's Last Breath," 9–10.

134. Mohamed Abu Reda, "*Al-Beniya al-siyasiya wa al-egtema'iya le-magles 2000* (The Political and Social Composition of the 2000 Council)," *Al-Democratiya* 1: 81.

135. Interview with Fathy Sourur in Mahmoud Muslim "*Al-Masry Al-Youm wagahat Fathy Sourur*" (Part One), 7.

136. Interview with Sourur in Muslim, "*Al-Masry Al-Youm wagahat Fathy Sourur*" (Final Part), 9.

137. Suleiman, *Al-Nizam al-qawi*, 192–96, 218.

138. Hazem Biblawi, *Arba'at ashhur fei qafas al-hukuma* (Four Months in the Government's Cage), Cairo: Dar al-Shorouk, 2012, 16.

139. Galal Amin, *Misr wa al-misrieen fei 'ahd Mubarak, 1981–2008* (Egypt and the Egyptians during Mubarak's Reign, 1981–2008), Cairo: Dar Merit, 2009, 93.

140. Suleiman, *Al-Nizam al-qawi*, 207–17.

141. Mitchell, "Dreamland," 28.

142. Mitchell, *Rule of Experts*, 230.

143. Goldstone, "Understanding the Revolutions of 2011," 11; Philip Inman, "Mubarak Family Fortune Could Reach $70bn, Say Experts: Egyptian President Has Cash in British and Swiss Banks Plus UK and US Property," *Guardian* (2/4/2011), 1.

144. Ghoneim, *Azmat*, 93.

145. Salwa Samir, "Books Banned in the Mubarak Era," *Egyptian Gazette* 17207: 1. Cairo (4/15/2011) Youssra Zahran, "*Hussein Salem: Seqot ragul al-nizam* (Hussein Salem: The Fall of the Man of the Regime)," in *Al-Fajir* 292:6, Cairo, 2/21/2011.

146. Safiya Munir, "*Miliyarat Hussein Salem* (Hussien Salem's Billions)," *Al-Shorouk* 868: 3.

147. Al-Malt interviewed in Hamdi Hamadah, "*Uhawer Gawdat al-Malt ra'ies al-gehaz al-marzaki lel-muhasabat*," 5.

148. Interview with Sourur in Muslim, "*Al-Masry Al-Youm wagahat Fathy Sourur*" (Part Two), 10.

149. Hatem al-Gahmy and Ahmed Abd al-Qawy, "*Tahqiqat niyabat amn al-dawla fei qadaya fasad al-wuzara'* (State Security Prosecutor Investigates the Corruption of Ministers)," in *Al-Shorouk* 770: 7.

150. Fouad Allam, *Al-Ikhwan wa ana*, 3.

151. Ghoneim, *Azmat*, 93–95.

152. Mohamed Bassal, "*Thalath ahkam tarrikhiya ded fasad al-khaskhasa fei ahd Mubarak* (Three Historical Court Orders Against the Corruption of Privatization under Mubarak)," in *Al-Shorouk* 964: 1.

153. Wahid, *Military Expenditure and Economic Growth*, 134–42.

154. Shatz, "Mubarak's Last Breath," 6.

155. Basma Abd al-Aziz, *Eghraa al-sulta al-mutlaqa*, 90–91.

156. Ghoneim, *Azmat*, 113–15; Benin, "The Egyptian Intifada in Historical Perspective."

157. Ghoneim, *Azmat*, 142.

158. Kamal al-Geziry, "*Mumtalakat al-Adly* (Al-Adly Possessions)," in *Al-Shorouk* 784: 1.

159. Sabri, "*Zuwar al-fajir estawlu 'ala mumtalakat al-sha'eb*," 6.

160. Mitchell, *Rule of Experts*, 297–98.

161. Michael Mann, *Incoherent Empire*, New York: Verso, 2003, 70.

162. Report in Khalaf Aly Hassan, "*Taqasi al-haqa'eq*," 4.

163. Suleiman, *Al-Nizam al-qawi*, 271.

CHAPTER 6: ON THE THRESHOLD OF POWER

1. Charles Tilly, *European Revolutions*, Cambridge: Blackwell Publishers, 1993: 2.

2. Assem Genedi, "*Ada'gihaz al-shurta* (The Performance of the Police Force)," in *Thawrat 25 Yanaier: Qera'a awaliya wa ru'iya mustaqbaliya* (The January 25 Revolution: A Preliminary Reading and Future Prospects), ed. Amr Hashem Rabie', Cairo: Al-Ahram Center for Political & Strategic Studies, 2011, 152–53.

3. Sourur in Mahmoud Muslim, "*Al-Masry Al-Youm*" (Final Part), 9.

4. Dalia Osman, "*Musa'ed wazir al-defa' lel-sho'un al-qanuniya wa al-desturiya fei hewaruh* (Undersecretary for Defense for Legal and Constitutional Affairs in His Interview)," *Al-Masry Al-Youm* 2468: 8.

5. Abd al-Mon'em Kato "*Al-Malameh al-assasiya lei edaret al-azma wa e'adet al-amn fei rebou' Sinai* (General Guidelines for Managing the Crisis and Restoring Security Throughout Sinai)," *Al-Nasr* 867:14–15.

6. Osman, "*Musa'ed*," 8.

7. Report in Khaled Hanafy, "*Hassan Abd al-Rahman rafa' taqrir lel-Adly uhazeruhu men tekrar al-scenario al-Tunsi* (Hassan Abd al-Rahman Submitted a Report to al-Adly Warning of the Repetition of the Tunisian Scenario)," *Al-Fajr* 296: 10.

8. Report in Osama Khaled, "*Shehadet qa'ed al-amn al-markazi fei al-qana* (The Testimony of the Head of the Central Security [Forces] in the [Suez] Canal [Zone]," *Al-Masry Al-Youm* 2467: 7.

9. Interrogation transcript in Nabil al-Seginy and Mohamed Donya, "*Al-Nas al-kemel*

le-tahqiqat al-niyaba ma'a al-Adly (The Complete Text of the Prosecutor's Interrogation of al-Adly)," *Al-Ahram* 45402: 4.

10. Genedi, "*Ada' gihaz al-shurta*," 149.

11. Cordesman, *Arab-Israeli Military Forces in an Era of Asymmetric Wars*, 187.

12. Interrogation transcript in Al-Seginy and Donya, "*Al-Nas al-kemel le-tahqiqat*," 4.

13. Yousry Al-Badry, "*Wazir al-dakheliya yastab'ed* (The Interior Minister Purges)," *Al-Masry Al-Youm* 2478: 1.

14. Ayman Farouk, "*Enhaa khedmat 505 lewa'at shurta wa 164 'amidan wa 'aqidan* (Retiring 505 Police Generals and 164 Brigadiers and Lieutenant Colonels)," *Al-Ahram* 45510: 1.

15. *Al-Masry Al-Youm* 2654: 13. Cairo, (9/19/2011).

Bibliography

Abd al-Aziz, Basma. *Eghraa al-sulta al-mutlaqa: Masar al-'unf fei 'elaqat al-shurta bei al-muwaten 'abr al-tarikh* (The Temptation of Absolute Power: The Course of Violence in the Relationship between the Police and the Citizen Across History). Cairo: Sefsafa Publishing House, 2011.

Abd al-Fadeel, Mahmoud. *Ta'amulate fei al-mas'ala al-eqtesadiya al-misriya* (Reflections on the Egyptian Economic Question). Cairo: Dar al-Mustaqbal al-Arabi, 1983.

Abd al-Fattah, Essam. *Muhammad Naguib: Al-Raful alazi sana'etthu wa damaratthu aqdara* (Muhammad Naguib: The Man Made and Unmade by His Destiny). Cairo: Kenouz lel-Nashr wel-Tawzee', 2009.

Abd al-Hafeez, Mohamed Saad, and Mohamed Khayal. "*Abbud al-Zumur yakshef asrar gadida* (Abbud al-Zumur Reveals New Secrets)," in *Al-Shorouk* 774:7. Cairo (3/16/2011).

Abdallah, Ahmed. *Al-Jaysh wa al-Dimuqratiyah fi Masr* (The Military and Democracy in Egypt). Cairo: Sina lel-Nashr, 1990.

———. "*Al-qwat al-musalaha wa tatwer al-dimuqratiyah fi Masr* (The Armed Forces and the Development of Democracy in Egypt)," in *Al-Jaysh wa al-Dimuqratiyah fi Masr* (The Military and Democracy in Egypt), ed. Ahmed 'Abdallah, 9–28. Cairo: Sina lel-Nashr, 1990.

———. "*Rad fe'l al-shabab iza' al-hazima* (Youth Reaction to the Defeat)," in *Harb yunyu 1967 ba'd thalatheen sana* (The June 1967 War after Thirty Years), ed. Lutfi al-Khuli, 21–46. Cairo: Markaz al-Ahram lel-Targama wal-Nashr, 1997.

———. "*Siyasiun wa 'askariun* (Politicians and Military Men)," *Al-'Arab*, 12/21/1987.

———. *The Student Movement and National Politics in Egypt, 1923–1973.* London: Al Saqi Books, 1985.

Abd al-Latif, Antar. "*Taftah al-malaf al-sha'ek wa takshef bei al-asma'* (Opening the Thorny File and Exposing Names)," in *Sout al-Umma* 532:5. Cairo (2/19/2011).

Abd al-Magid, Esmat. *Zaman al-enkesar wa al-entesar: muzakerat diplomacy masri 'an ahdath masria wa 'arabia wa dawlia: nesf qarn men al-tahawulat al-kubra* (The Time of Defeat and Victory: Memoirs of an Egyptian Diplomat Regarding Egyptian, Arab, and International Events— Half a Century of Great Transformations). Cairo: Dar al-Shorouk, 1998.

Abd al-Mo'ty, Abd al-Baset.. *Al-tabaqat al-egtema'iya wa mustaqbal misr: Etegahat al-taghir wa al-tafa'ulat, 1975–2020* (Social Classes and the Future of Egypt: Trends of Change and Interaction, 1975–2020). Cairo: Merit lel-Nashr wal-Ma'lumat, 2002.

Abd al-Nasser, Gamal. *"Hadith Gamal Abd al-Nasser al-tanzimy fei al-mu'tamar al-awal le-'ada' al-makateb al-tanfiziya fei al-muhafazat 'an eslub al-'amal fei al-etehad al-eshteraky* (Gamal Abd al-Nasser's Organizational Talk at the First Congress of the Members of the Provincial Executive Offices Regarding the Working Methods at the Arab Socialist Union)," in *Al-Tali'ah* 2 (2): 11–18. Cairo (February 1966).

———. *Wathaiq thawrat yulyu* (The July Revolution Documents). Cairo: Dar al-Mustaqbal al-Araby, 1991.

Abd al-Nasser, Tahiya. *Zekrayaty ma'ahu* (My Memories with Him). Cairo: Dar al-Shorouk, 2011.

Abd al-Qader, Mohamed, and Hossam Sadaqa. *"Lagnat al-qwat al-musalaha bei mu'tamar al-wefaq al-watani tusi* (The Armed Forces Committee to the National Accord Conference Recommends)," in *Al-Masry al-Youm* 7. Cairo (6/1/2011).

Abd al-Quddus, Mohamed. *"Awlad al-balad, Ta'zim salam lel-mushir* (Countrymen, Salute the Field Marshal)," in *Al-Sha'b* 3. Cairo (10/4/1986).

Abdel-Malek, Anwar. *Egypt: Military Society*. New York: Random House, 1968.

Abdo, Geneive. *No God but God: Egypt and the Triumph of Islam*. New York: Oxford University Press, 2000.

Abu al-Fadl, Abd al-Fattah. *"Hawl al-etehad al-eshteraky: takwinuh wa ahdafuh* (Concerning the [Arab] Socialist Union: Its Composition and Goals)," in *Al-Tali'ah* 3 (3): 89–98. Cairo (March 1967).

———.*Kunt na'iban le ra'is al-mukhabarat* (I Was Deputy Director of Intelligence). Cairo: Dar al-Shorouk, 2008.

Abu al-Nur, Abd al-Muhsin. *Al-Haqiqa 'an Thawrit 23 Yulyu* (The Truth about the July 23 Revolution). Cairo: Al-Hay'a al-Masriya al-'Ama lel-Kitab, 2001.

Abu Reda, Mohamed. *"Al-Beniya al-siyasiya wa al-egtema'iya le-magles 2000* (The Political and Social Composition of the 2000 Council). *Al-Democratiya* 1: 72–81 (2001).

Aburish, Said K. *Nasser: The Last Arab*. New York: St. Martin's Press, 2004.

Abu Zikri, Wagih. *Mazbahat al-abriya' fei 5 yunyu 1967* (Massacre of the Innocent on June 5, 1967). Cairo: Al-Maktab al-Masry al-Hadith, 1988.

Adel, Hammoudah. *Eghtiyal ra'is: bei al-watha'iq: asrar eghtiyal Anwar al-Sadat* (The Assassination of a President: With Documents—Secrets of Anwar Sadat's Assassination). Cairo: Sina lei al-Nashr, 1987.

Adly, Amr Ismail. "Politically-Embedded Cronyism: The Case of Post-Liberalization Egypt." *Business and Politics* 11 (4): 1–26 (2009).

Ahmed, Mohamed Abd al-Wahab Sayyid. *Al-'Alaqat al-masriya al-amrekiya men al-taqarub ela al-taba'ud, 1952–1958* (Egyptian-American Relations Between Proximity and Distance, 1952–1958). Cairo: Dar al-Shorouk, 2007.

Ahmed, Ref'at Sayyed. *Thawrat al-general: Qesat Gamal 'Abd al-Nasser kamila min al-milad ela al-mout (1918–1970): Mawsu'a fikria wa siassia* (The General's Revolution: Gamal Abd al-Nasser's Complete Story from the Cradle to the Grave (1918–1970)—An Intellectual and Political Register). Cairo: Dar al-Huda, 1993.

"*Al-Akhbar tuhaqeq hadith al-ta'era* (*Al-Akhbar* Investigates the Plane Incident)," *Al-Akhbar* 8965: 3. Cairo (3/6/1981).

Albrecht, Holger. "Authoritarian Opposition and the Politics of Challenge in Egypt," in *Debating Arab Authoritarianism: Dynamics and Durability in Nondemocratic Regimes*, ed. Oliver Schlumberger, 59–74. Stanford, CA: Stanford University Press, 2007.

Allam, Fouad. *Al-Ikhwan wa ana* (Al-Ikhwan and I). Cairo: Akhbar al-Youm, 1996.

Allam, Hesham. "*Sahifat al-hizb al-watani: madieh al-ams yatahawal ela zam* (National Democratic [Party] Newspaper: Yesterday's Praise Turns into Condemnation)," in *Al-Masry Al-Youm* 2434: 3. Cairo (2/11/2011).

Allison, Graham T. *Essence of Decision: Explaining the Cuban Missile Crisis.* Boston: Little, Brown, 1971.

"*Al-Shahid al-Badawy men aqwaluh* (The Martyr al-Badawy in His Words)," *Al-Akhbar* 8963: 7. Cairo (3/4/1981).

Aly, Kamal Hassan. *Mashawir al-'umr: asrar wa khafaiya sab'een 'aman min 'umr masr fei al-harb wel-mukhabarat wel-siyasa* (Life Journeys: Secrets of War, Intelligence, and Politics During Seventy Years in Egypt's Life). Cairo: Dar al-Shorouk, 1994.

Aly, Sa'id Isma'il. "*Haza al-nigm al-sati'* (That Shining Star)," in *Al-Ahali* 13. Cairo (10/8/1986).

Amin, Galal. *Misr wa al-misrieen fei 'ahd Mubarak, 1981–2008* (Egypt and the Egyptians During Mubarak's Reign, 1981–2008). Cairo: Dar Merit, 2009.

Anderson, Lisa. "Demystifying the Arab Spring: Parsing the Differences Between Tunisia, Egypt, and Libya," *Foreign Affairs* 90 (3): 2–7 (2011).

Anderson, Perry. *Consideration on Western Marxism*. London: New Left Books, 1976.

Andreski, Stanislave. *Military Organization and Society*. Berkeley: University of California Press, 1971.

Ansari, Hamid. *Egypt: The Stalled Society*. New York: State University of New York Press, 1986.

Arendt, Hannah. *Origins of Totalitarianism*. New York: Harcourt, 1994 [1951].

Asfur, Mohamed. "*Gishna al-qawi bain al-amn al-qawmi wa al-siyasa* (Our Strong Army Between National Security and Politics)," in *Al-Wafd* 11. Cairo (5/28/1987).

Ayubi, Nazih. *Overstating the Arab State: Politics and Society in the Middle East*. London: I. B. Tauris, 1996.

Badr al-Din, Hany. "*Harb October: Al-umniya al-akhira lel-Shazly* (The October War: Al-Shazly's Last Request)," in *Al-Ahram Al-Araby* 729: 20–23. Cairo (3/12/2011).

Al-Badry, Yousry. "*Wazir al-dakheliya yastab'ed* (The Interior Minister Purges)," in *Al-Masry Al-Youm* 2478: 1. Cairo (3/27/2011).

Bahaa al-Din, Ahmed. *Muhawarati ma'a al-Sadat* (My Dialogues with Sadat). Cairo: Dar al-Helal, 1987.

Bahnasawy, Ahmed. "*Maham 'adaa al-'ala lel-qwat al-musalaha* (The Tasks of the Supreme [Council] for the Armed Forces)," in *Al-Shorouk* 895: 7. Cairo (7/15/2011).

Baker, Raymond William. *Islam Without Fear: Egypt and the New Islamist*. Cambridge, MA: Harvard University Press, 2003.

———. *Sadat and After: Struggles for Egypt's Political Soul*. Cambridge, MA: Harvard University Press, 1990.

Al-Banna, Ragab, and Khamis al-Bakry. "*Secertair al-mushir yarwi tafasil al-lahazat al-akhirai* (The Field Marshal's Secretary Recounts the Details of the Final Moments)," in *Al-Ahram* 34416: 3. Cairo (3/5/1981).

Barbera, Henry. *The Military Factor in Social Change, Vol. 1: From Provincial to Political Society*. London: Transaction Publishers, 1998.

Barnet, Michael N. *Confronting the Cost of War: Military Power, State, and Society in Egypt and Israel*. Princeton, NJ: Princeton University Press, 1992.

Barron, John. *KGB: The Secret Work of Soviet Secret Agents*. New York: Reader's Digest Press, 1974.

Bassal, Mohamed. "*Thalath ahkam tarrikhiya ded fasad al-khaskhasa fei ahd Mubarak* [Three Historical Court Orders Against the Corruption of Privatization Under Mubarak," in *Al-Shorouk* 964: 1 (2011).

Bayat, Asef. *Making Islam Democratic: Social Movements and the Post-Islamist Turn*. Stanford, CA: Stanford University Press, 2007.

Bayat, Asef, and Eric Denis. "Who Is Afraid of Ashwaiyyat? Urban Change and Politics in Egypt." *Environment and Urbanization* 12 (2): 185–99 (2000).

Al-Baz, Muhammad. *A-Mushir: qesat so'ud wa enhiar Abu Ghazala* (The Field Marshal: The Story of the Rise and Fall of Abu Ghazala). Cairo: Kenuz lel-Nashr wal-Tawzee', 2007.

———. *"Eteham Mubarak bei eghtiyal al-mushir Ahmed Badawi bei sabab kashfu fasad safaqat al-selah fei al-gish* (Mubarak Accused of Assassinating Field Marshal Badawi Because He Exposed the Corruption of Arms Deals in the Military," *Al-Fajr* 318: 9. Cairo (8/22/2011).

Benin, Joel. "The Egyptian Intifada in Historical Perspective." Lecture at UCLA Center for Near Eastern Studies, February 15, 2011.

Berger, Morroe. "The Military Elite and Social Change in Egypt," in *Garrisons and Government: Politics and the Military in New States*, ed. Wilson C. McWilliams, 203–26. San Francisco: Chandler Publishing, 1967.

Al-Beteshty, Abd al-Aziz. *Al-Tha'abin* (The Snakes). Cairo: Al-Maktab al-Masry al-Hadith, 2006.

Bianchi, Robert. "Interest Groups and Politics in Mubarak's Egypt," in *The Political Economy of Contemporary Egypt*, ed. Ibrahim M. Oweiss, 210–21. Washington, DC: Center for Contemporary Arab Studies, Georgetown University, 1990.

Biblawi, Hazem. *Arba'at ashhur fei qafas al-hukuma* (Four Months in the Government's Cage). Cairo: Dar al-Shorouk, 2012.

Binder, Leonard. *In a Moment of Enthusiasm: Political Power and the Second Stratum in Egypt*. Chicago: University of Chicago Press, 1978.

Al-Bishri, Tareq. *Al-haraka al-siyassiya fei masr, 1945–1953* (The Political Movement in Egypt). Cairo: Dar al-Shorouk, 2002.

Blaydes, Lisa. *Elections and Distributive Politics in Mubarak's Egypt*. New York: Cambridge University Press, 2011.

Botman, Selma. *The Rise of Communism in Egypt*. Syracuse, NY: Syracuse University Press, 1988.

Boyne, Walter J. *The Two o'Clock War: The 1973 Yom Kippur Conflict and the Airlift That Saved Israel*. New York: St. Martin's Press, 2002.

Bradely, Matt. "Budget for New Egypt Boosts Social Spending," *Wall Street Journal*, June 3–5, 2011.

Brecher, Michael. *Decisions in Israel's Foreign Policy*. New York: Oxford University Press, 1974.

Brendon, Piers. "China Also Rises," *National Interest* 110: 6–14 (2010).

Brooks, Risa A. *Shaping Strategy: The Civil-Military Politics of Strategic Assessment*. Princeton, NJ: Princeton University Press, 2008.

Browne, O'Brien. "Six Days of War Spark Forty Years of Strife," *Quarterly Journal of Military History* 22 (1): 70–79 (2009).

Brzezinski, Zbigniew. *Power and Principle: Memoirs of the National Security Advisor, 1977–1981*. New York: Farrar, Straus and Giroux, 1983.

Burr, William. *Asrar harb October fei al-watha'eq al-amrikiya* (Secrets of the October War in the American Documents). Translated by Khaled Daoud. Cairo: Markaz Al-Ahram lel-Targama wel-Nashr, 2004.

Bush, George, and Brent Scowcroft. *A World Transformed*. New York: Vintage Books, 1998.

Carr, E. H. *The Twenty Years' Crisis, 1919–1939: An Introduction to the Study of International Relations*. New York: Perennial Press, 2001 [1946].

Cassandra. "Impending Crisis in Egypt," *Middle East Journal* 49 (1): 9–27 (1995).

Cook, Steven A. "Part of the Machine," *New York Times*. http://www.nytimes.com/roomfordebate/2011/02/10/what-will-the-egyptian-military-do/the-egyptian-military-is-part-of-the-machine (accessed on 5/3/2011).

———. *Ruling but Not Governing: The Military and Political Development in Egypt, Algeria, and Turkey*. Baltimore: John Hopkins University Press, 2007.

Cooley, John K. *Unholy Wars: Afghanistan, America, and International Terrorism*. London: Pluto Press, 2000.

Copeland, Miles. *The Game of Nations: The Amorality of Power Politics*. London: Weidenfeld and Nicolson, 1970.

Cordesman, Anthony H. *Arab-Israeli Military Forces in an Era of Asymmetric Wars*. Westport, CT: Praeger Security International, 2006.

Al-Dahrawi, Khidr. "*Al-Darba al-oula fei al-mizan* (The First Strike in the Balance)," *Al-Majala al-Askariya lel-Quat al-Musalaha al-Masriya* 185 (3): 3–13 (1976).

Dandeker, Christopher. *Surveillance, Power, and Modernity*. New York: Polity, 1994.

De Atkine, Norvell. "Why Arabs Lose Wars," *Middle East Quarterly* 6 (4): 13–25 (1999).

Dekmejian, Richard H. "Egypt and Turkey: The Military in the Background," in *Soldiers, Peasants, and Bureaucrats: Civil-Military Relations in Communist and Modernizing Societies*, ed. Roman Kolkowicz and Andrzej Korbonski. Boston: George Allen & Unwin, 1982.

Downing, Brian M. *The Military Revolution and Political Change: Origins of Democracy and Autocracy in Early Modern Europe*. Princeton, NJ: Princeton University Press, 1992.

Droz-Vincent, Philippe. "From Political to Economic Actors: The Changing Role of Middle Eastern Armies," in *Debating Arab Authoritarianism: Dynamics and Durability in Nondemocratic Regimes*, ed. Oliver Schlumberger, 195–214. Stanford, CA: Stanford University Press, 2007.

Droz-Vincent, Philippe. "A Return of Armies to the Forefront of Arab Politics?" *Istituto Affari Internazionali Working Papers* 11, 21: 1–10 (2011).

Dunstan, Simon. *The Six Day War 1967: Sinai*. London: Osprey Publishing, 2009.

Eban, Abba. *Personal Witness: Israel Through My Eyes*. New York: Jonathan Cape, 1992.

Eid, Adil. "*Al-mahakim al-'askaria laisat mahakim wa al-quda al-'askariyun laisu quda* (Military Courts Are Not Courts, and Military Judges Are Not Judges)," *Al-Sha'b* (9/16/1986).

Eisenstadt, S. N. *Revolution and the Transformation of Societies: A Comparative Study of Civilizations*. New York: Free Press, 1978.

Essam al-Din, Gamal. "*Al-Mushir al-samet Tantawy* (The Silent Field Marshal Tantawy)," in *Al-Tahrir* 80: 1 (2011).

Eytan, Zeev, and Shlomo Gazit. *The Middle East Military Balance*. Jaffee Center for Strategic Studies. Boulder, CO: Westview Press, 1991.

Eytan, Zeev, Shlomo Gazit, and Amos Gilbo. *The Middle East Military Balance*. Jaffee Center for Strategic Studies. Boulder, CO: Westview Press, 1993.

Eytan, Zeev, and Mark A. Heller. *The Middle East Military Balance*. Jaffee Center for Strategic Studies. Jerusalem: Jerusalem Post Press, 1983.

Eytan, Zeev, Mark A. Heller, and Aharon Levran. *The Middle East Military Balance*. Jaffee Center for Strategic Studies. Boulder, CO: Westview Press, 1985.

Eytan, Zeev, Mark A. Heller, and Dov Tamari. 1984. *The Middle East Military Balance*. Jaffee Center for Strategic Studies. Jerusalem: Jerusalem Post Press.

Eytan, Zeev, and Aharon Levran. *The Middle East Military Balance*. Jaffee Center for Strategic Studies. Boulder, CO: Westview Press, 1986.

Fahmy, Isma'il. *Al-tafawed min agl al-salam fei al-sharq al-awsat* (Negotiating for Peace in the Middle East). Cairo: Maktabet Madbouli, 1985.

Fakhr, Ahmed. "*Al-fikr al-'askari al-masri wa idarit al-sira': al-ahdaf al-istratigia lel-'askariya al-masriya* (Egyptian Military Thinking and Conflict Management: The Strategic Goals of Egyptian Militarism)," in *Al-Jumhuriya* 9. Cairo (1/20/1985).

Farag, Fatemah. "Kamshish: Take Two," *Al-Ahram Weekly* 397: 3. Cairo (10/1/1998).

Farah, Nadia Ramsis. *Egypt's Political Economy: Power Relations in Development*. Cairo: American University in Cairo Press, 2009.

Farahat, Mohamed Nur. "*Hawl hukm al-mu'asasat wa tahakum al-mu'asasat* (Concerning the Rule of Institutions and the Autocracy of Institutions)," in *Al-Ahali* 7. Cairo (12/19/1984).

Al-Faramawy, Abd al-Rahman. Interview with author, Cairo, June 5, 2009.

Farouk, Abd al-Khaleq. *Guzur al-fasad al-edari fei misr: be'at al-'amal wa siyasat al-ugur wa al-muratabat fei misr* (The Roots of Administrative Corruption in Egypt: The Working Environment and the Policies of Wages and Incomes in Egypt). Cairo: Dar al-Shorouk, 2008.

Farouk, Ayman. *"Enhaa khedmat 505 lewa'at shurta wa 164 'amidan wa 'aqidan* (Retiring 505 Police Generals and 164 Brigadiers and Lieutenant Colonels)," in *Al-Ahram* 45510: 1. Cairo (7/14/2011).

Fawzy, Mahmoud. *Al-Nabawi Ismail wa guzur manaset al-Sadat* (Al-Nabawi Ismail and the Roots of Sadat's Review Stand). Cairo: International Language Home, 2008.

Fawzy, Mohamed. *Harb al-thlath sanawat, 1967–1970: muzakirat al-fariq awal Mohamed Fawzy* (Three-Year War, 1967–1970: Memoirs of Lieutenant General Mohamed Fawzy). Cairo: Dar al-Mustaqbal al-Araby, 1990.

Finer, Samuel E. *Men on Horseback: The Role of the Military in Politics.* London: Pall Mall Press, 1962.

Fleishman, Jeffrey, and Amro Hassan. "Egyptian Media Finds Escape Hatch," *Los Angeles Times,* October 23, 2010, A8.

Frankel, Benjamin. *Roots of Realism.* London: Frank Cass, 1996.

Frisch, Hillel. "Guns and Butter in the Egyptian Army," *Middle East Review of International Affairs* 5 (2): 1–14 (2001).

Al-Gahmy, Hatem, and Ahmed Abd al-Qawy. 2011. *"Tahqiqat niyabat amn al-dawla fei qadaya fasad al-wuzara'* (State Security Prosecutor Investigates the Corruption of Ministers)," in *Al-Shorouk* 770: 7. Cairo (3/12/2011).

Al-Galad, Magdi, Charles Fouad al-Masry, and Ahmed al-Khatib. *"Mahdi 'Akef fei awal hiwar sahafi ba'd azmat al-insihab* (Mahdi 'Akef in his first newspaper interview following the withdrawal crisis)," *Al-Masry Al-Youm* 11. Cairo 10/24/2009.

Al-Gamal, Hamdy. *"Al-Eqtesad bein eslahat Gamal Mubarak wa thawrat midan al-Tahrir* (The Economy Between Gamal Mubarak's Reforms and the Tahrir Square Revolt)," in *Al-Ahram Al-Araby* 729: 32–33. Cairo (3/12/2011).

Gamal, Wael. *Al-'Askari: mashru'atna 'araq wezarat al-defa'* (Military Council: Our Projects Are the Defense Ministry's Sweat), *Al-Shorouk* 1152: 2. Cairo (3/28/2012).

Al-Gamasy, Mohamed Abdel Ghani. *The October War: Memoirs of Field Marshall El-Gamasy of Egypt.* Cairo: American University in Cairo Press, 1993.

Game', Mahmoud. *'Araft al-Sadat* (I Knew Sadat). Cairo: Al-Maktab al-Masry al-Hadith, 2004.

Gawrych, George W. "The Egyptian High Command in the 1973 War," *Armed Forces & Society* 13 (4): 535–59 (1987).

Gendy, Musa. "*Daga fei Israel hawl tasrihat al-mushir* (A Flare in Israel Following the Field Marshal's Revelations)," *Al-Ahram* 45392: 3. Cairo (2/18/1987).

Genedi, Assem. "*Ada' gihaz al-shurta* (The Performance of the Police Force)," in *Thawrat 25 Yanaier: Qera'a awaliya wa ru'iya mustaqbaliya* (The January 25 Revolution: A Preliminary Reading and Future Prospects), ed. Amr Hashem Rabie'. Cairo: Al-Ahram Center for Political & Strategic Studies, 2011.

Al-Geziry, Kamal. "*Mumtalakat al-Adly* (Al-Adly Possessions)," in *Al-Shorouk* 784: 1. Cairo (3/26/ 2011).

Ghaleb, Murad. *Ma'a Abd al-Nasser wa al-Sadat: Sanawat al-intesar wa ayam al-mehan: Muzakirat Murad Ghaleb* (With Abd al-Nasser and Sadat: The Years of Triumph and the Days of Trial—Memoirs of Murad Ghaleb). Cairo: Markaz Al-Ahram lel-Targama wel-Nashr, 2001.

Ghali, Boutros Boutros. *Tariq masr ela al-Quds: Qesat al-sera' men agl al-salam fei al-sharq al-awsat* (Egypt's Road to Jerusalem: The Story of the Struggle for Peace in the Middle East). Cairo: Al-Ahram lel-Targama wel-Nashr, 1997.

Gharieb, Mohamed, Ebtesam Ta'lab, and Mohamed al-Sanhouri. "*'Udow bel-magles al-'askari youtaleb bei wad'e khas lel-geesh fei al-dostour al-gadid yahmeeh men hawa al-ra'is* (A Member of the Military Council Demands a Special Status for the Army in the New Constitution to Protect It from the President's Whims," in *Al-Masry al-Youm* 2539: 1. Cairo (5/27/2011).

Ghoneim, Adel. *Azmat al-dawla al-misriya al-mu'asera* (The Crisis of the Contemporary Egyptian State). Cairo: Dar al-'Alam al-Thaleth, 2005.

Giddens, Anthony. *The Nation-State and Violence, Volume Two of A Contemporary Critique of Historical Materialism*. Cambridge: Polity Press, 1985.

Golan, Matti. *The Secret Conversations of Henry Kissinger: Step-by-Step Diplomacy in the Middle East*. New York: Quadrangle/New York Times Book Company, 1976.

Goldstone, Jack A. "Understanding the Revolutions of 2011: Weakness and Resilience in Middle Eastern Autocracies," *Foreign Affairs* 90 (3): 8–16 (2011).

Gorman, Anthony. "Confining Political Dissent in Egypt Before 1952," in *Politics and Prisons in the Middle East: Formations of Coercion*, ed. Laleh Khalili and Jillian Schwedler, 157–73. New York: Columbia University Press, 2010.

Gramsci, Antonio. *Selections from the Prison Notebooks*. New York: International Publishers, 1971.

"*Hadath qabl zalek 'eshreen mara* (It Happened Twenty Times Before)," editorial in *October* 228: 8–9. Cairo (3/8/1981).

Hafez, Suleiman. *Thekrayati 'an al-thawra* (My Memories of the Revolution). Cairo: Dar al-Shorouk, 2010.

Hamadah, Hamdi. "*Uhawer Gawdat al-Malt ra'ies al-gehaz al-marzaki lel-muhasabat* (Interviewing Gawdat al-Malt, Head of the Central Auditing Agency)," in *Sout al-Umma* 537: 5. Cairo (3/26/2011).

Hamid, Shadi. "Viewpoint: Egypt Election 'Blunder' by Mubarak's NDP," BBC News (12/10/2010).

Hammad, Gamal. *Al-Hukuma al-khafiya fei 'ahd Abd al-Nasser wa asrar masra' al-mushir Amer* (The Invisible Government during the Reign of Nasser and the Secrets of Field Marshal Amer's Death). Cairo: Al-Shareka Al-Mutaheda lel-Teba'a wel-Nashr wel-Tawzee', 2008.

——. *Al-Ma'arek al-harbiya 'ala al-gabha al-misriya* (The Military Battles on the Egyptian Front). Cairo: Dar al-Shorouk, 2002.

——. *Asrar thawrat 23 yunyu* (Secrets of the July 23 Revolution), Vols. 1 and 2. Cairo: Dar Al-'Ulum, 2010.

Hammad, Magdi. "*Al-muasasa al-'askariya wa al-nizam al-siasi al-masri* (The Military Institution and the Egyptian Political Regime)," in *Al-Jaysh wa al-Dimuqratiyah fi Masr* (The Military and Democracy in Egypt), ed. Ahmed Abdallah, 29–50. Cairo: Sina lel-Nashr, 1990.

Hammudah, Adel. *Eghtiyal ra'is: Belwatha'eq asrar eghtiyal Anwar al-Sadat* (A President's Assassination: Documented Secrets of the Assassination of Anwar al-Sadat). Cairo: Sina lel-Nashr, 1986.

Hammudah, Hussein Mohamed Ahmed. *Asrar harakat al-zubat al-ahrar wa al-Ikhwan al-Muslimeen* (Secrets of the Free Officers Movement and the Muslim Brothers). Cairo: Al-Zahraa lel-'Ilam al-Arabi, 1985.

Hamroush, Ahmed. *Ghorub yulyu* (July's Sunset). Cairo: Dar al-Mustaqbal al-Arabi, 1987.

Hanafy, Khaled. "*Hassan Abd al-Rahman rafa' taqrir lel-Adly uhazeruhu men tekrar al-scenario al-Tunsi* (Hassan Abd al-Rahman Submitted a Report to al-Adly Warning of the Repetition of the Tunisian Scenario)," in *Al-Fajr* 296: 10. Cairo (3/21/2011).

Handoussa, Heba. "Fifteen Years of US Aid to Egypt—A Critical Review," in *The Political Economy of Contemporary Egypt*, ed. Ibrahim M. Oweiss, 109–24. Washington, DC: Center for Contemporary Arab Studies, Georgetown University, 1990.

Harb, Imad K. *Military Disengagement and the Transition to Democracy in Egypt and Turkey*. Unpublished dissertation. Department of Political Science, University of Utah, 2003.

Haslam, Jonathan. *The Vices of Integrity: E. H. Carr, 1892–1982*. New York: Verso, 2000.

Hassan, Bahie. "*Naql mudir amn al-Behera le-tatawulhu 'ala al-sha'b* (Transferring al-Behera's Security Chief for His Insulting the People)," in *Al-Shorouk* 784: 3. Cairo (3/26/2011).

Hassan, Khalaf Aly. "*Taqasi al-haqa'eq: Al-watani shakal tanziman shebh 'askari lel-baltagia* (Fact Finding [Commission]: The National [Democratic Party] Formed a Paramilitary Organization of Thugs)," in *Al-Masry Al-Youm* 2475: 4. Cairo (3/24/2011).

Heikal, Mohamed Hassanein. *1967: Al-Infegar* (1967: The Explosion). Cairo: Markaz Al-Ahram lel-Targama wa-Nashr, 1990.

———. *Autumn of Fury: The Assassination of Sadat.* London: Andre Deutsch, 1983.

———. *Mubarak wa zamanuh: min al-manasa ela al-midan* (Mubarak and His Time: From the Reviewing Stand to the Square). Cairo: Dar al-Shorouk, 2012.

———. *October 1973: Al-Selah wa al-siyasa* (October 1973: Arms and Politics). Cairo: Markaz Al-Ahram lel-Targama wa-Nashr, 1993.

———. *Seqout nizam: lemaza kanet thawarat yulyu 1952 lazema?* (Regime Fall: Why Was the July 1952 Revolution Necessary?). Cairo: Dar al-Shorouk, 2003.

Helal, Ali al-Din, Al-Sayed Zuhra, Diaa Rashwan, and Dina al-Khawaga. "*Al-Entekhabat al-parlamaniya fei misr men Saad Zaghloul ela Hosni Mubarak* (Parliamentary Election in Egypt from Saad Zaghloul to Hosni Mubarak)," in *Al-Tatawer al-demokraty fei misr: qadaya wa munaqashat* (Democratic Development in Egypt: Issues and Debates), ed. Ali al-Din Helal, 228–337. Cairo: Maktabet Nahdet al-Sharq, 1986.

Heller, Mark A. *The Middle East Strategic Balance, 2009–2010.* Tel Aviv: Institute for National Security Studies, 2010.

Hinnebusch, Raymond A. *Egyptian Politics under Sadat: The Post-Populist Development of an Authoritarian-Modernizing State.* London: Lynne Rienner, 1985.

———. "The Formation of the Contemporary Egyptian States from Nasser and Sadat to Mubarak," in *The Political Economy of Contemporary Egypt,* ed. Ibrahim M. Oweiss, 188–209. Washington, DC: Center for Contemporary Arab Studies, Georgetown University, 1990.

Hintze, Otto. *The Historical Essays of Otto Hintze.* New York: Oxford University Press, 1975.

Hobbes, Thomas. *Leviathan.* London: Penguin Classics, 1968 [1651].

Hosni, Hamada. *Abd al-Nasser wa al-tanzim al-tale'i, 1963–1971* (Abd al-Nasser and the Vanguard Organization, 1963–1971). Beirut: Maktabat Beirut, 2007.

———. *Shams Badran: Al-ragul alazi hakam misr* (Shams Badran: The Man Who Ruled Egypt). Beirut: Maktabat Beirut, 2008.

Howard, Michael. *Clausewitz.* New York: Oxford University Press, 1983.

Hudson, Michael. "After the Gulf War: Prospects for Democratization in the Arab World," *Middle East Journal* 45 (3): 407–26 (1991).

Huwaidi, Amin. *Khamsin 'am min al-'awasif: ma ra'ituh qultuh* (Fifty Stormy Years: I Told What I Saw). Cairo: Markaz Al-Ahram lel-Targama wa-Nashr, 2002.

Ibrahim, Saad Eddin. *Egypt, Islam, and Democracy.* Cairo: American University in Cairo Press, 1996.

Ibrahim, Youssef M. "U.S. Stake in Egypt Rests on One Man—Anwar el-Sadat," *New York Times* (3/30/1980), E3.

Imam, Abdallah. *Nasser and Amer: Al-Sadaqa, al-hazima, al-entehar* (Nasser and Amer: The Friendship, the Defeat, and the Suicide). Cairo: Dar al-Khayal, 1996.

Inman, Philip. "Mubarak Family Fortune Could Reach $70bn, Say Experts: Egyptian President Has Cash in British and Swiss Banks Plus UK and US Property," *The Guardian* (2/4/2011), 1.

Insight Team of the London *Sunday Times. Yom Kippur War.* New York: Doubleday, 1974.

International Institute for Strategic Studies (IISS). *The Military Balance 2009: Annual Assessment of Global Military and Defense Economics.* London: Routledge, 2009.

Isma'il, Hafez. *Amn Misr al-qawmy* (Egypt's National Security). Cairo: Maktabet Madbouli, 1983.

Johnson, Paul. *The Suez War.* London: Macgibbon & Kee, 1957.

Kam, Ephraim, and Yiftah Shapir. *The Middle East Strategic Balance, 2002–2003.* Jaffee Center for Strategic Studies. Tel Aviv: Kedem Printing, 2003.

Kamel, Mohamed Ibrahim. *Al-Salam al-da'ie fei Camp David* (The Lost Peace in Camp David). Cairo: Ketab al-Ahaly, 1983.

Kandil, Amani. "*Al-tatawer al-siyasi fei misr wa son' al-siyasat al-'ama: Derasa tatbiqiya lel-siyasa al-eqtesadiya* (Political Development in Egypt and the Making of Public Policy: An Empirical Study on Economic Policy), in *Al-Tatawer al-demokraty fei misr: qadaya wa munaqashat* (Democratic Development in Egypt: Issues and Debates), ed. Ali al-Din Helal, 87–114. Cairo: Maktabet Nahdet al-Sharq, 1986.

Kassem, Maye. *Egyptian Politics: The Dynamics of Authoritarian Rule.* London: Lynne Rienner, 2004.

Kato, Abd al-Mon'em. "*Al-Malameh al-assasiya lei edaret al-azma wa e'adet al-amn fei rebou' Sinai* (General Guidelines for Managing the Crisis and Restoring Security Throughout Sinai)," *Al-Nasr* 867: 12–15 (2011).

Kedourie, Elie. *Islam in the Modern World and Other Studies.* New York: Holt, Rinehart, and Winston, 1980.

Keohane, Robert O. *Neorealism and Its Critics.* New York: Columbia University Press, 1986.

Kepel, Gilles. *Jihad: The Trial of Political Islam.* London: I. B. Tauris, 2006.

Kerr, Malcolm H. *The Arab Cold War: Gamal Abd al-Nasir and His Rivals, 1958–1970.* New York: Oxford University Press, 1969.

Al-Keshky, Gamal. *"Mashahid al-mout fei rewayet eghtiyal al-Sadat* (Death Scenes in the Sadat Assassination Account)," in *Al-Ahram* 45402: 5. Cairo (3/28/2011).

Khalaf, Roula, and Daniel Dombey. "Army Torn Between Loyalty to Egyptians, President and US," *Financial Times* (2/3/2011), 3.

Khaled, Osama. *"Shehadet qa'ed al-amn al-markazi fei al-qana* (The Testimony of the Head of the Central Security [Forces] in the [Suez] Canal [Zone])," in *Al-Masry Al-Youm* 2467: 7. Cairo (3/16.2011).

Khalili, Laleh, and Jillian Schwedler. "Introduction," in *Policing and Prisons in the Middle East: Foundations of Coercion,* ed. Laleh Khalili and Jillian Schwedler, 1–40. New York: Columbia University Press, 2010.

Al-Kholi, Lutfi. *"Democratiyat al-manaber, Democratiyat al-ta'adud* (The Democracy of Platforms, the Democracy of Pluralism)," *Al-Tali'ah* 12 (6): 5–12. Cairo (June 1967).

——. *"Thermometer Kamshish* (The Kamshish Thermometer)," in *Al-Tali'ah* 2 (6): 5–9 (1966).

Kirk, George. "The Role of the Military in Society and Government: Egypt," in *The Military in the Middle East,* ed. Sydney Nettleton Fisher. Columbus: Ohio State University, 1963.

Kirkpatrick, David D. 2011. "Egypt Military Moves to Cement Muscular Role in Government," *New York Times* (7/16/2011), 3.

Kissinger, Henry. *Diplomacy.* New York: Simon & Schuster, 1994.

——. *White House Years.* New York: Little, Brown, 1979.

——. *Years of Upheaval.* New York: Little, Brown, 1992.

Al-Leithy, Amr. *Al-'Amil Babel: Qesat so'ud wa soqut Ashraf Marawan* (Agent Babel: The Story of the Rise and Fall of Ashraf Marawan). Cairo: Dar al-Shorouk, 2009.

Lia, Brynjar. *A Police Force Without a State: A History of the Palestinian Security Forces in the West Bank and Gaza.* London: Ithaca Press, 1999.

Linke, Uli, and Taana Smith. *Culture of Fear: A Critical Reader.* New York: Palgrave, 2010.

Machiavelli, Niccolò. *The Prince.* Indianapolis: Hackett Publishing, 1995 [1532].

——. *The Prince.* New York: Pocket Books, 2004 [1532].

Al-Magdub, Taha. *"Al-Gesh al-masri ba'd yunyu 1967* (The Egyptian Army After June 1967)," in *Harb yunyu 1967 ba'd thalatheen sana* (The June 1967 War After Thirty Years), ed. Lutfi al-Khuli, 115–42. Cairo: Markaz al-Ahram lel-Targama wal-Nashr, 1997.

Mahmood, Saba. *Politics of Piety: The Islamic Revival and the Feminist Subject.* Princeton: Princeton University Press, 2005.

Makiya, Kanan. *Cruelty and Silence: War, Tyranny, Uprising, and the Arab World*. New York: W. W. Norton, 1993.

———. *Republic of Fear: The Politics of Modern Iraq*. Berkeley: University of California Press, 1998.

Mann, Michael. *Fascism*. New York: Cambridge University Press, 2004.

———. *Incoherent Empire*. New York: Verso, 2003.

———. *The Sources of Social Power, Volume 1: A History of Power from the Beginning to A.D. 1760*. New York: Cambridge University Press, 1986.

Mansour, Anis. *Min awraq al-Sadat* (From Sadat's Papers). Cairo: Dar al-Ma'aref, 2009.

Maqlad, Shahenda. *Min awraq Shahenda Maqlad* (From the Papers of Shahenda Maqlad). Cairo: Dar Merit, 2006.

Marsot, Afaf Lutfi al-Sayyid. *A Short History of Modern Egypt*. New York: Cambridge University Press, 1985.

Marx, Karl. *The Eighteenth Brumaire of Louis Bonaparte*. New York: International Publishers, 1963 [1852].

Al-Mashat, Abd al-Mone'm. *"Al-'Awamel al-kharegiya wa al-tatawer al-demokraty fei misr* (External Factors and Democratic Development in Egypt), in *Al-Tatawer al-demokraty fei misr: qadaya wa munaqashat* (Democratic Development in Egypt: Issues and Debates), ed. Ali al-Din Helal, 53–78. Cairo: Maktabet Nahdet al-Sharq, 1986.

McDermott, Anthony. *Egypt from Nasser to Mubarak: A Flawed Revolution*. London: Croom Helm, 1988.

Mearsheimer, John J. *The Tragedy of Great Power Politics*. New York: W. W. Norton, 2003.

Menze, Ernest A. *Totalitarianism Reconsidered*. Port Washington, NY: Kennikat Press, 1981.

Mitchell, Timothy. "Dreamland: The Neoliberalism of Your Desires," *Middle East Report* 210: 28–33 (1999).

———. *Rule of Experts: Egypt, Techno-Politics, Modernity*. Berkeley: University of California Press, 2002.

Morgenthau, Hans J. *Politics Among Nations: The Struggle for Power and Peace*. New York: Alfred A Knopf, 1948.

———. *Scientific Man vs. Power Politics*. Chicago: University of Chicago Press, 1974.

Moustafa, Hala. *"Al-Dawla al-policiya* (The Police State)," *Al-Masry Al-Youm* 2467: 6. Cairo (3/16/2011).

———. *"Entekhabat 2000: mu'asherat 'ama* (The 2000 Elections: General Indicators), *Al-Democratiya* 1: 58–63 (2001).

Muhi al-Din, Khaled. *Al'an atakalam* (Now, I Speak). Cairo: Al-Ahram lel-Targama wel-Nashr, 1992.

Munir, Safiya. *"Miliyarat Hussein Salem* (Hussien Salem's Billions)," *Al-Shorouk* 868: 3. Cairo (6/18/2011).

Murad, Mohamed Helmi. *"Al-riqaba al-gha'iba 'ala al-infaq al-'askari wa al-tafwidat al-laniha'iya le-safaqat al-silah wa mizaniyat al-qwat al-musalaha* (The Absent Oversight of Military Spending and the Limitless Authorizations Regarding Defense Contracts and Budget)," *Al-Sha'b* 15. Cairo (9/9/1986).

Muslim, Mahmoud. "*Al-Masry Al-Youm wagahat Fathy Sourur bei al-etahamat fakashaf asrar khatira, al-halaqa al-ula* (*Al-Masry Al-Youm* Confronted Fathy Sourur with Accusations, So He Revealed Dangerous Secrets, Part One)," *Al-Masry Al-Youm* 2475: 7. Cairo (3/24/2011).

——. "*Al-Masry Al-Youm wagahat Fathy Sourur bei al-etahamat fakashaf asrar khatira, al-halaqa al-thaniya* (*Al-Masry Al-Youm* Confronted Fathy Sourur with Accusations, So He Revealed Dangerous Secrets, Part Two)," *Al-Masry Al-Youm* 2476: 10. Cairo (3/24/2011).

——. "*Al-Masry Al-Youm wagahat Fathy Sourur bei al-etahamat fakashaf asrar khatira, al-halaqa al-akhirah* (*Al-Masry Al-Youm* Confronted Fathy Sourur with Accusations, So He Revealed Dangerous Secrets, Final Part)," *Al-Masry Al-Youm* 2477: 9. Cairo (3/24/2011).

Al-Nabulsi, Shaker. *Se'oud al-mugtama' al-askari fei Misr wa belad al-Sham, 1948-2000* (The Rise of the Military Society in Egypt and Mesopotamia, 1948–2000). Beirut: Al-Mu'assasa al-Arabiya lel-Targama wel-Nashr, 2003.

Naf'a, Hassan. "*Mulahazat hawl entekhabat 1984* (Observations on the 1984 Elections)," in *Al-Tatawer al-demokraty fei misr: qadaya wa munaqashat* (Democratic Development in Egypt: Issues and Debates), ed. Ali al-Din Helal, 35–52. Cairo: Maktabet Nahdet al-Sharq, 1986.

Nafe', Ibrahim. "*Hal al-hadeth mudabar* (Was the Accident Fixed?)," *Al-Ahram* 34417: 1. Cairo (3/6/1981).

Naguib, Muhammad. *Kalimati lel-tarikh* (My Word for History). Cairo: Dar al-Kitab Al-Jami'i, 1997.

——. *Kunt ra'isan lei masr* (I Was President of Egypt). Cairo: Al-Maktab al-Masry al-Hadith, 1984.

Nasr, Salah. *Muzakirat Salah Nasr (al-guze'al-awal): Al-Sou'd* (The Memoirs of Salah Nasr, Part One: The Rise). Cairo: Dar al-Khayal, 1999.

——.*Muzakirat Salah Nasr (al-guze'al-thani): Al-Entilaq* (The Memoirs of Salah Nasr, Part Two: The Launch). Cairo: Dar al-Khayal, 1999.

Neumann, Franz. *Behemoth: The Structure and Practices of National Socialism*. Chicago: Ivan R. Dee, 2009 [1944].

Nordlinger, Eric A. *Soldiers in Politics: Military Coups and Governments*. Englewood Cliffs, NJ: Prentice-Hall, 1977.

Nutting, Anthony. *Nasser*. London: E. P. Dutton, 1972.

O'Hanlon, Michael. "Staying Power: The U.S. Mission in Afghanistan Beyond 2011," *Foreign Affairs* 89: 4 (2010).

Omar, Nabil. "*Habib al-Adly: Asrar rehlat al-so'ud ela 'arsh al-dakhliya*

(Habib al-Adly: Secrets of the Rise to the Throne of the Interior [Ministry]," *Al-Ahram* 45388: 5. Cairo (3/14/2011).

Oren, Michael B. *Six Days of War: June 1967 and the Making of the Modern Middle East.* New York: Presidio Press, 2002.

Osman, Ahmed Osman. *Safahat min tagrebati* (Pages from My Life Experience). Cairo: Al-Maktab al-Masry al-Hadith, 1981.

Osman, Dalia. *"Musa'ed wazir al-defa' lel-sho'un al-qanuniya wa al-desturiya fei hewaruh* (Undersecretary for Defense for Legal and Constitutional Affairs in His Interview)," *Al-Masry Al-Youm* 2468: 8. Cairo (3/17/2011).

Osman, Dalia, and Pasant Zein al-Din. *"Masdar 'askari: nabhath ta'dil mu'ahadat al-salam* [A Military Source: We Are Looking into Modifying the Peace Agreement]," *Al-Masry al-Youm* 2633: 1. Cairo (8/29/2011).

Osman, Tarek. *Egypt on the Brink: From Nasser to Mubarak.* New Haven, CT: Yale University Press, 2010.

Oweiss, Ibrahim M. "Egypt's Economy: The Pressing Issues," in *The Political Economy of Contemporary Egypt*, ed. Ibrahim M. Oweiss, 3–49. Washington, DC: Center for Contemporary Arab Studies, Georgetown University, 1990.

Pappé, Ilan. "The False Paradigm of Parity and Partition: Revisiting 1967." Lecture at the G. E. Von Grunebaum Center for Near Eastern Studies at UCLA (2/24/2012).

Parker, Richard B. *The Politics of Miscalculation in the Middle East.* Bloomington: Indiana University Press, 1993.

Pearson, Anthony. *Conspiracy of Silence: The Attack on the USS Liberty.* Cambridge, MA: Charles Rivers Books, 1979.

Perlmutter, Amos. *Egypt: The Praetorian State.* New York: Transaction Publishers, 1974.

Poggi, Gianfranco. *Forms of Power.* Cambridge: Polity Press, 2001.

Quandt, William B. "Lyndon Johnson and the June 1967 War: What Color Was the Light?" *Middle East Journal* 46 (2): 198–228 (1992).

Rabei', Amr Hashim. *Watha'eq 100 youm 'ala thawrat 25 yanaier* [Documents of 100 Days of the January 25 Revolution]. Cairo: Al-Ahram Center for Political and Strategic Studies, 2011.

Ra'fat, Wahid. *"Hawl hadith ra'is al-jumhuriya 'an qadaiya al-sa'a: al-infaq al-'askari* (Concerning the President's Remarks on Current Issues: Military Spending)," *Al-Wafd* (7/10/1986).

Al-Rafe'i, Abd al-Rahman. *Thawrat 23 yulyu 1952: Tarikhna al-qawmi fei saba' sanawat, 1952–1959* (The Revolution of July 23, 1952: Our National History in Seven Years, 1952–1959). Cairo: Dar al-Ma'aref, 1989.

Richards, Alan, and John Waterbury. *A Political Economy of the Middle East.* Boulder, CO: Westview Press, 1996.

Richter, Thomas. "The Political Economy of Regime Maintenance in Egypt: Linking External Resources and Domestic Legitimation," in *Debating Arab Authoritarianism: Dynamics and Durability in Nondemocratic Regimes*, ed. Oliver Schlumberger, 177–94. Stanford, CA: Stanford University Press, 2007.

Riedel, Bruce. 2010. "If Israel Attacks," *National Interest* 109: 6–13 (2010).

Sabri, Abd al-Rahman. "*Ta'thir al-harb 'ala al-eqtesad al-masri* (The Effects of the War on the Egyptian Economy)," in *Harb yunyu 1967 ba'd thalatheen sana* (The June 1967 War after Thirty Years), ed. Lutfi al-Khuli, 105–14. Cairo: Markaz al-Ahram lel-Targama wal-Nashr, 1997.

Sabri, Ahmed. "*Zuwar al-fajir estawlu 'ala mumtalakat al-sha'eb* (Dawn Visitors Appropriated the People's Properties)," *Sout al-Umma* 535: 6. Cairo (3/12/2011).

Sabri, Musa. *Watha'eq harb October* (October War Documents). Cairo: Akhbar al-Youm, 1979.

Sadat, Anwar. *Al-Bahth 'an al-zat* (In Search of Identity). Cairo: Al-Maktab al-Masry al-Hadith, 1978.

———. "*Warakat October* (The October Paper)," *Al-Tali'ah* 10 (5): 131–46. Cairo (May 1974).

Sadowski, Yahya M. *Scuds or Butter: The Political Economy of Arms Control in the Middle East*. Washington: Brookings Institution, 1993.

Said, Mohamed Qadri. "*Ada' al-qwat al-musalaha* (The Performance of the Armed Forces)," in *Thawrat 25 Yanaier: Qera'a awaliya wa ru'iya mustaqbaliya* (The January 25 Revolution: A Preliminary Reading and Future Prospects), ed. Amr Hashem Rabie'. Cairo: Al-Ahram Center for Political & Strategic Studies, 2011.

Said, Mohamed Sayyid. "*Hal ghayaret al-hazima al-nizam al-siyasi al-misry* (Did the Defeat Alter the Egyptian Political Regime?)," in *Harb yunyu 1967 ba'd thalatheen sana* (The June 1967 War after Thirty Years), ed. Lutfi al-Khuli, 143–58. Cairo: Markaz al-Ahram lel-Targama wal-Nashr, 1997.

Salamé, Ghassan (ed.). *Democracy without Democrats? The Renewal of Politics in the Muslim World*. London: I. B. Tauris, 1994.

Saleh, Amani Abd al-Rahman. "*Usul al-nukhba al-siyasiya al-misriya fei al-sab'inat: al-nash'a wa al-tatuwer* (Origins of the Egyptian Political Elite in the Seventies: The Birth and Development)," *Al-Fekr al-Strategy al-Araby* 26: 9–50 (1988).

Saleh, Hamdi. "Egypt's Crisis Gives Mubarak a New Image," *Los Angeles Times* (3/21/1986). http://articles.latimes.com/1986-03-21/local/me-5205_1_mubarak-government (accessed on 5/8/2010).

Samir, Salwa. "Books Banned in the Mubarak Era," *Egyptian Gazette* 17207: 1. Cairo (4/15/2011).

Samy, Riyad. *Shahid 'ala 'asr al-ra'is Muhammad Naguib* (A Witness to the Reign of President Muhammad Naguib). Cairo: Al-Maktab al-Masry al-Hadith, 2004.

Al-Sanhouri, Abd al-Razeq. *Al-Sanhouri min khilal awraquh al-shakhsiya* (Al-Sanhouri Through His Personal Diaries). Cairo: Dar al-Shorouk, 2005.

El-Sayed, Abdel-Rahman. "Shrouded in Mystery," *Al-Ahram Weekly* 852: 2. Cairo (7/5/2007).

Sayigh, Yazid. "Egypt's Army Looks Beyond Mubarak," *Financial Times* (2/3/2011), 11.

Schlesinger, Arthur M. *A Thousand Days: John F. Kennedy in the White House.* Greenwich, CT: Fawcett Publications, 1965.

Schlumberger, Oliver (ed.). *Debating Arab Authoritarianism: Dynamics and Durability in Nondemocratic Regimes.* Stanford: Stanford University Press, 2007.

Schofield, Julian. *Militarization and War.* New York: Palgrave Macmillan, 2007.

Scott, James. *The Attack on the Liberty: The Untold Story of Israel's Deadly 1967 Assault on a U.S. Spy Ship.* New York: Simon & Schuster, 2009.

Sedgwick, Mark. "Measuring Egyptian Regime Legitimacy," *Middle East Critique* 19 (3): 251–67 (2010).

Segev, Tom. *1967: Israel, the War, and the Year That Transformed the Middle East.* New York: Metropolitan Books, 2007.

Al-Seginy, Nabil, and Mohamed Donya. "*Al-Nas al-kemel le-tahqiqat al-niyaba ma'a al-Adly* (The Complete Text of the Prosecutor's Interrogation of al-Adly)," *Al-Ahram* 45402: 4. Cairo (3/28/2011).

Selim, Muhammad. Interview with author, Los Angeles, March 7, 2009.

Sha'ban, Mohamed. "*Man qatal Ahmed Badawi* (Who Killed Ahmed Badawi?)," *El-Shabab* 410: 54–55. Cairo (9/2011).

Shakib, Ibrahim. "*Shukran ayuha al-sada* (Thank You, Gentlemen)," *Al-Ahali* 5. Cairo (11/7/1984).

Sharaf, Samy. *'Abd al-Nasser: Keif hakam masr?* ('Abd al-Nasser: How Did He Rule Egypt?) Cairo: Madbouli al-Saghir, 1996.

Shatz, Adam. "Mubarak's Last Breath," *London Review of Books* 32 (10): 6–10 (2010).

Shaw, Martin. *Post-Military Society.* Cambridge: Polity Press, 1991.

Shazly, Saad El-Din. *The Crossing of the Suez: The October War (1973).* London: Third World Centre for Research and Publishing, 1980.

Shehata, Samer. 2008. "After Mubarak? Mubarak," *Current History* 107: 418–24 (2008).

Shlaim, Avi. "Failures in National Intelligence Estimates: The Case of the Yom Kippur War," *World Politics* 28 (3): 348–80 (1976).

Shtauber, Zvi, and Yiftah S. Shapir. *The Middle East Military Balance,*

2004–2005. Jaffee Center for Strategic Studies. Brighton: Sussex Academic Press, 2005.

Singerman, Diane. "The Networked World of Islamist Social Movements," in *Islamic Activism: A Social Movement Theory Approach*, ed. Q. Wiktorowicz, 143–63. Bloomington: Indiana University Press, 2004.

Sirrs, Owen L. *A History of the Egyptian Intelligence Service: A History of the Mukhabarat, 1910–2009*. New York: Routledge, 2010.

Skocpol, Theda. *States and Social Revolution: A Comparative Analysis of France, Russia, and China*. New York: Cambridge University Press, 1979.

Springborg, Robert. "Agrarian Bourgeoisie, Semiproletarians, and the Egyptian State: Lessons for Liberalization," *International Journal of Middle East Studies* 22 (4): 446–72 (1990).

———. "More Pressure Needed," *New York Times* (2/10/2011), http://www.nytimes.com/roomfordebate/2011/02/10/what-will-the-egyptian-military-do/watch-the-rank-and-file (accessed on 5/13/2011).

———. *Mubarak's Egypt: Fragmentation of the Political Order*. Boulder, CO: Westview Press, 1989.

Steinberg, John W. *All the Tsar's Men: Russia's General Staff and the Fate of the Empire, 1989–1914*. Baltimore, MD: Johns Hopkins University Press, 2010.

Suleiman, Samer. *Al-Nizam al-qawi wa al-dawla al-da'ifa: Edaret al-azma al-maliya wa al-taghir al-siyasi fei 'ahd Mubarak* (The Strong Regime and the Weak State: Managing the Financial Crisis and Political Change in Mubarak's Reign). Cairo: Dar Merit, 2005.

"*Taqrir shamel 'an lagnat tasfiyat al-eqta'* (Comprehensive Report on the Liquidation of Feudalism)," in *Al-Tali'ah* 3 (3): 124–28. Cairo (March 1967).

Tawfik, Abd al-Gawad. "*Al-Mushir: Al-qwat al-musalaha musamema 'ala taslim al-sulta* (The Field Marshal: The Armed Forces Insist on Transferring Authority)," *Al-Ahram* 45524: 1. Cairo (7/28/2011).

Tilly, Charles. *European Revolutions*. Cambridge: Blackwell Publishers, 1993.

Trimberger, Ellen Kay. *Revolution from Above: Military Bureaucrats and Development in Japan, Turkey, Egypt, and Peru*. New Brunswick, NJ: Transaction Books, 1978.

Tripp, Charles, and Roger Owen (eds.). *Egypt under Mubarak*. New York: Routledge, 1989.

Trotsky, Leon. "Bonapartism, Fascism, and War," *Fourth International* 1 (5): 128–31 (1940).

Turner, Barry. *Suez 1956: The Inside Story of the First Oil War*. London: Hodder & Stoughton, 2006.

Vagts, Alfred. *A History of Militarism: Civilian and Military*. New York: Meridian Books, 1959.

Vatikiotis, P. J. *Nasser and His Generation*. London: Croom Helm, 1978.

Wahid, Latif. *Military Expenditure and Economic Growth in the Middle East*. New York: Palgrave Macmillan, 2009.

"Waking from Its Sleep: A Special Report on the Arab World," *Economist* (7/25/2009), 1–16.

Walt, Stephen. *The Origins of Alliances*. Ithaca, NY: Cornell University, 1987.

———. *Revolution and War*. Ithaca, NY: Cornell University, 1996.

Waltz, Kenneth. *Man, the State, and War: A Theoretical Analysis*. New York: Columbia University Press, 1954.

Waterbury, John. *The Egypt of Nasser and Sadat: The Political Economy of Two Regimes*. Princeton, NJ: Princeton University Press, 1983.

Weiss, D., and U. Wurzel. *The Economics and Politics of Transition to an Open Market Economy*. Paris: Development Center at the OECD, 1998.

Wickham, Carrie Rosefsky. *Mobilizing Islam: Religion, Activism, and Political Change*. New York: Columbia University Press, 2002.

Yohannes, Okbazghi. *Political Economy of an Authoritarian Modern State and Religious Nationalism in Egypt*. London: Edwin Meller Press, 2001.

Younan, Ref'at. *Muhammad Naguib: Za'im thawra am wagehat haraka?* (Muhammad Naguib: A Leader of a Revolution or the Figurehead of a Movement?). Cairo: Dar al-Shorouk, 2008.

Yunis, Sherif. *Al-Zahf al-muqadas: Muzaharat al-tanahi wa tashkil 'ebadet Abd al-Nasser* (The Sacred March: The Resignation Demonstrations and the Shaping of the Cult of Abd al-Nasser). Cairo: Dar Merit, 2005.

Zahran, Youssra. "*Hussein Salem: Seqot ragul al-nizam* (Hussein Salem: The Fall of the Man of the Regime)," *Al-Fajir* 292:6. Cairo (2/21/2011).

Zegart, Amy B. *Flawed by Design: The Evolution of the CIA, JSC, and NSC*. Stanford, CA: Stanford University Press, 1999.

Zureik, Elia, and David Lyon. *Surveillance and Control in Israel/Palestine: Population, Territory, and Power*. Clifton, NJ: Routledge, 2010.

Index

Abaza, Amin, 215
Abd al-Aziz, Basma, 197
Abd al-Hafez, Fawzy, 109
Abd al-Khaleq, Muhsen, 31
Abdallah, Ahmed, 146
Abdallah, Ismail Sabri, 106
Abd al-Latif, Mahmoud, 40
Abd al-Magid, Esmat, 122, 160
Abd al Quddus, Muhammad, 177
Abd al-Rahman, Hassan, 198
Abu al-Fadl, Abd al-Fattah, 20–1, 56–7, 58, 66, 67
Abu al-Gheit, Ahmed, 153
Abu al-Nur, Abd al-Muhsen, 17, 18, 32, 58
Abu Dhabi, 166
Abu-Gabal, Mamduh, 174
Abu Ghazala, Abd al-Halim, 172, 176–87 passim, 220, 232
Abu Pasha, Hassan, 195
Abu-Raqiq, Saleh, 28, 37
Abu Taleb, Youssef Sabri, 180–1
Acheson, Dean, 23, 26
Adan, Bren, 137, 190
Adham, Kamal, 122
al-Adly, Habib, 198, 217, 236–7
AETSCO. See American-Egyptian Transport and Service Company (AETSCO)
Afghanistan, 154
Africa, Sub-Saharan. See Sub-Saharan Africa
agriculture, 8, 61–2, 64, 69, 202, 216–17
Alexandria, 217
Algeria, 47, 136, 221
Ali, Muhammad, 27–8, 161
Allam, Fouad, 75, 169, 170, 173
Allen, George, 45
allocation of public land. See public land allocation
Aly, Kamal Hassan, 80, 90, 130, 144, 147

Amer, Abd al-Hakim, 16, 21–2, 33, 35, 37, 41–63 passim, 109, 177; Committee for the Liquidation of Feudalism, 68–9; coup attempt, 87–91; death, 90; fiefdom of, 51; Nasser relations, 21, 43, 48, 52–5 passim, 76–8 passim, 83–5 passim; Osman relations, 166; reaction to ASU, 57; resignation, 83–5; Six-Day War, 69–83 passim; Suez War, 48, 50
American Chamber of Commerce in Egypt (AmCham), 164, 209
American-Egyptian Transport and Service Company (AETSCO), 213
Amin, Abd al-Mounem, 25, 122
Amin, Abd al-Sattar, 86
AMIO. See Arab Military Industries Organization (AMIO)
Amit, Meir, 73, 94
Anderson, Robert, 94
Angleton, James, 73
Anglo-Egyptian Treaty of 1936, 9, 12
al-Ansari, Ahmed, 33–4
al-Ansari, Farouk, 32
anticommunism, 24–7 passim, 45, 46, 50, 71–3 passim, 154, 156, 178
anti-Islamism, 156, 173, 174. See also Islamists: repression
April 6 Youth Movement, 222, 223, 231
Arab Contractors, 166–7
Arab Federation. See Federation of Arab Republics
Arab-Israeli War of 1948. See Palestine War of 1948
Arab-Israeli War of 1967. See Six-Day War
Arab-Israeli War of 1973. See October War, 1973
Arab Military Industries Organization (AMIO), 184
Arab nationalism, 53, 72–3

Arab Organization for Industrialization (AOI), 184
Arab Socialist Union (ASU), 55–69 passim, 84, 92, 93, 200; under Sadat, 102–9 passim, 158, 165. *See also* Vanguard Organization (VO)
al-Araby, Nabil, 152–3
Argentina, 180
arms industry. *See* weapons industry
arms trade. *See* weapons trade
Artin, Lucy, 180
Ashmawi, Hassan, 29, 37
assassinations, 67–8, 171–4; attempted, 40
assassination squads, 7, 11, 99
ASU. *See* Arab Socialist Union (ASU)
Aswan Dam, 46, 161, 166
Atatürk, Mostafa Kemal, 13, 23–4, 29
audiotapes, 104–5, 105–6, 107

Badawy, Ahmed, 144–5
Badr, Zaki, 194
Badran, Shams, 21, 34, 38, 44, 74; under Amer, 53, 54, 55, 59, 74, 75; appointments, 52, 69; plots to oust Nasser, 87–91 passim; Six-Day War, 78, 83, 84
al-Badry, Hassan, 190
Baghdad Pact. *See* Central Treaty Organization (CENTO)
Bahaa al-Din, Ahmed, 139, 150, 157
balance of trade, 162–3, 212
bank loans, 207, 215
bankruptcy, 205
banks and banking, 63, 160, 161, 163, 207–11 passim
Bar Lev Line, 115, 126
al-Baz, Muhammad, 180
Begin, Menachem, 152, 185
Ben-Gurion, David, 190
Bergus, Donald, 106, 122
al-Beteshky, Abd al-Aziz, 90, 115
billionaires. *See* superrich
Black, Eugene, 73
bodyguards, 154, 199
Boeing, 163–4
Border Patrol, 194
bourgeoisie. *See* middle class
Boutros-Ghali, Boutros, 4, 150, 152
Boutros-Ghali, Youssef, 210
Boyne, Walter J., 125, 131, 135
Brezhnev, Leonid, 136
bribery, 38, 211, 218

Britain. *See* Great Britain
Brooks, Risa, 124
Brzezinski, Zbigniew, 151, 153, 154, 155
Buckingham Palace, 199
Buckley, William Francis, 154
building construction. *See* construction industry
Bunche, Ralph, 77
Bush, George W., 205
al-Butran, Muhammad, 225

Caffery, Jefferson, 24
Cairo: Aly Hassan drives tanks through, 124; Amer parades, 79; "city of middlemen," 161; demonstrations of February/March 1954, 35, 38; demonstrations of 2011, 223–8 passim, 237, 239; election tampering, 198; Food Riots of 1977, 169; Mubarak security, 199; Osman development in, 166–7; Police Day 1952, 12; scandals, 180; shady land allocation, 166, 217; shah of Iran in, 157; shantytowns, 208; street surveillance, 155; U.S. agents and ambassadors in, 20, 24–6 passim, 72, 105, 121, 122, 154
Camp David Accords, 151, 152, 189
Carr, E. H., 4
Carter, Jimmy, 150, 152, 153
cell phones, 199, 224
censorship, 22, 35, 36, 199, 224
Central Intelligence Agency (CIA). *See* CIA
Central Security Forces (CSF), 93, 170, 174, 193–4, 217; January Revolt, 193, 235–6; mutiny of 1986, 178–9
Central Treaty Organization (CENTO), 45
Chase Manhattan Bank, 163
Cheney, Dick, 205
China, 21, 25, 46, 47, 73, 194
Churchill, Winston, 25
CIA, 20, 24–6 passim, 45, 73, 153, 213; January Revolt information, 228; Nasr relations, 87; Sadat relations, 105, 120–3 passim, 154; Six-Day War, 94
"City Eye" network, 19, 20
class struggle, 57
Clausewitz, Carl von, 181
Club de Paris. *See* Paris Club
Coca-Cola, 167
college graduates in the military, 191
colleges and universities. *See* universities and colleges

Committee for the Liquidation of Feudalism, 68–9
commodity prices, 169
Communists and communism, 57, 59, 67, 105, 106. *See also* anticommunism
concentration camps. *See* detention camps
Congo, 119, 154, 187
conscription, 17, 72, 191–4 passim, 235, 236
conspiracies, 85, 145–6, 169, 240. *See also* coups: attempts and plots
constitutions, 27, 35, 92, 109, 241, 243; amendments, 210–11, 227, 230
construction industry, 161, 165–7, 206–7, 208, 214, 215
consumerism, 8, 202–3
Copeland, Miles, 20, 25, 45, 159
Cordesman, Anthony, 115, 151–2, 187, 192
corruption, 145, 192, 196, 218; of Amer, 44–5, 90; under Farouk, 9, 10, 13, 24, 30, 41; under Mubarak, 211–19 passim, 230; under Nasser, 23, 36, 65; Nasser prophecy, 164; in NDP, 165, 218; of police, 196, 217; under Sadat, 160, 203; of state employees, 203
cotton, 8
coups: Amer's "silent coup," 54; coup-proofing, 21, 57, 86; dissolving UAR, 53; opportunities rejected, 179; plots and attempts, 60, 87–91, 102–8, 118, 141–2, 172–3, 174; post-January Revolt, 235; Sadat fear of, 169. *See also* Egyptian Revolution of 1952
cover-ups, 67–8
Cremeans, Charles, 20
CSF. *See* Central Security Forces (CSF)
currency, 212. *See also* money laundering

Damascus Declaration, 187
Dayan, Moshe, 73, 78, 114, 127
De Atkine, Norvell, 187, 190
debt, 161–2, 204–11 passim
defense spending. *See* military spending
de Gaulle, Charles, 93
Delah, Munir, 28, 29
demonstrations, 30, 38–9; by cavalry members, 32–3; CSF repression, 194, 195, 236–7; Farouk reaction to, 12; January Revolt (and following months), 175n, 223–31 passim, 237, 239; nerve gas use to repress, 231; "outsourced" repression, 195; by peasants, 38, 217; pro-Mubarak, 211;

pro-Naguib, 35, 38; pro-Nasser, 84; pro-Sadat, 107; pro-war, 124; by students and workers in 1968, 96–7
deregulation of rent. *See* rent deregulation
detention camps, 19, 40
detention, political. *See* political detention
deterrence, 186, 193
Dinitz, Simcha, 130
domestic surveillance. *See* surveillance
drinking water. *See* water
Dubai, 214
Dulles, Allen, 51
Dulles, John Foster, 25, 46
Dunstan, Simon, 143, 189

Eastern Europe, 57, 73, 221
East Germany, 21
Eban, Abba, 94
economic effect of war, 79n
economic growth, 79n, 205, 216; U.S. views, 26
economic policy, 62–5 passim, 74, 138, 159–69 passim, 183, 200–8 passim. *See also* military-economic complex
Economic Reform and Structural Adjustment Program, 205, 207
education system, 64, 191–2, 216
Egyptian-Anglo Treaty of 1936. *See* Anglo-Egyptian Treaty of 1936
Egyptian Businessmen's Association (EBA), 209
Egyptian General Petroleum Company, 206
Egyptian Mediterranean Gas Company (EMG), 214
Egyptian pound, 212
Egyptian Revolution of 1919, 7
Egyptian Revolution of 1952, 3, 15–27 passim, 37–8; run-up, 7–13; Sadat during, 99
Egyptian Revolution of 2011, 175n, 218, 221–44; run-up, 216–20
Egypt Socialist Party, 165, 168
Egyptian-Soviet Friendship Treaty, 106, 149
Egyptian-Yemen War. *See* Yemen War
Egypt National Liberation Front, 136
Egypt-U.S. Joint Business Council, 164
Eichelberger, James, 20, 25
Eisenhower, Dwight, 25, 50
Elazar, David, 127, 130
ElBaradei, Mohamed, 222
elections, 65, 101, 165, 180, 200, 239–43 passim; constitutional amendments

and, 211; tampering and rigging, 195, 198, 211, 219, 238
Emergency Law, 199
EMG. *See* Egyptian Mediterranean Gas Company (EMG)
emigrants and emigration, 160, 204
espionage, foreign. *See* foreign espionage
al-Essawi, Mansour, 238–9
Ethiopia, 178
Eveland, Wilbur, 45
executions, 26
exiles, 39, 52, 136, 214
exports and imports, 8, 73, 161–3 passim, 185, 202–3, 207, 212; natural gas, 214, 230
extortion, 195, 196
Ezz, Ahmed, 210, 211, 214, 215, 227, 238

Facebook, 222–3
Fahmy, Ismail, 45, 125, 142, 149, 150, 155
Fahmy, Mahmoud, 117
Fahmy, Mohamed Aly, 143–4
Fakhr, Ahmed, 182
al-Faramawy, Abd al-Rahman, 174, 178, 193–4
farming. *See* agriculture
Farouk I, 7, 10–15 passim, 27, 30, 99
Fatah, 229
Fawzy, Mahmoud, 101, 102, 128
Fawzy, Muhammad, 52; under Amer, 55, 75; appointments, 53, 85, 92; counter-coup role, 89–90; imprisonment by Sadat, 113, 147; October War run-up, 114; plots to oust Sadat, 102–3, 107; under Sadat, 104, 110, 125; Six-Day War, 76, 80, 81, 82; Soviet relations, 105; Yemen War, 71
Federation of Arab Republics, 101–2
Fees, James, 154
al-Feqi family, 67–8
food imports, 202, 207
food subsidies, 169, 216
Food Riots, January 1977, 168, 169
foreign aid, 161, 203–6 passim; from U.S., 45, 73, 163, 167, 184–91 passim, 204, 209. *See also* military aid
foreign debt. *See* debt
foreign espionage, 92, 184
foreign trade. *See* exports and imports; weapons trade
Fouad, Ahmed, 59
al-Fouli, Ahmed, 173

France, 46–50 passim, 154
Freedom and Justice Party, 239, 240, 242
free industrial zones, 214
Free Officers, 8–11 passim, 15–24 passim, 231
Free Officers' coup of 1952. *See* Egyptian Revolution of 1952
Future Generation Foundation (FGF), 209

Gabriel, Elyan, 229
al-Gamasy, Abd al-Ghany: appointments, 92, 140–4, 147; on eviction of Soviets, 116; Food Riots, 169; October War, 128–35 passim; at peace talks, 141, 142, 150, 155; purge, 143–4; on Six-Day War, 79, 81, 82, 83, 86; on Suez War, 50; on U.S. aid to Israel, 132
Garanah, Zohair, 215
Game', Mahmoud, 35, 37–8, 68, 144, 155–6
gated communities, 206
Gaza, 45, 229
al-Genedi, Assem, 169, 224
General Intelligence Service (GIS), 20, 44, 52, 92, 93, 105, 110, 122
General Investigations Directorate (GID), 19, 75, 93, 108
Gerhardt, Albert, 45
Germany, 11, 21, 22. *See also* Nazis
Ghaleb, Murad, 75, 78, 106, 128, 140, 143
Ghonim, Wael, 223, 228
Golan Heights, 95, 130
Goldstone, Jack, 188
Gomaa, Sha'rawi, 52, 69, 84, 95; appointments, 59; counter-coup role, 89; plots to oust Sadat, 103–7 passim; under Sadat, 100, 109, 110
government corruption. *See* corruption
government employment. *See* state employment
government subsidies, 205, 213. *See also* food subsidies
Great Britain, 7–19 passim, 23–5 passim, 28, 39, 45–50 passim, 199
Grechko, Andrei, 78
Ground Forces Command (GFC), 55
guerrilla warfare, 71
Gulf War, 187, 205, 206
Gur, Mordechai, 134

Hafez, Alwy, 145–6, 214
al-Hafez, Fawzy Abd. *See* Abd al-Hafez, Fawzy

Hafez, Suleiman, 23, 27, 38, 39, 41
Hamas, 229
Hammad, Gamal, 33, 116, 190
Hammudah, Hussein, 24, 37, 114
Haridi, Galal, 88
Hassan, Abd al-Qader, 117
Hassan, Aly, 124
hatred of police, 197
Hegazy, Abd al-Aziz, 160
Heikal, Mohamed Hassanein, 96, 125;
      arrest, 170; meeting with Mubarak,
      188; under Nasser, 59, 73, 77, 84, 85;
      October War, 128, 131, 137; on run-up
      to October War, 114; on Sadat, 101,
      131, 155; on Sadat's assassination,
      171–2; under Sadat, 118, 122, 123, 140,
      155, 170; on "supermarket economy,"
      164
helicopter crashes, 144–5
Helms, Richard, 73, 94
High Dam. See Aswan Dam
higher education policy, 64
Hinnebusch, Raymond, 158
historiography, 4
al-Hudaybi, Hassan, 28
Hussein, Salah al-Din, 67
Hussein I, 77, 95
Huwaidi, Amin, 52, 80, 89–92 passim, 110

IMF. See International Monetary Fund
      (IMF)
imports and exports. See exports and
      imports
income, 164–5, 205, 216
inequality, 164–5, 208, 216, 218, 233
Infitah, 159–67 passim, 201–4 passim
inflation, 165, 182, 183, 204, 219
informal economy, 216
informers, 19, 58
International Monetary Fund (IMF), 205
Internet, 222–3, 224, 228
Interpol, 214
investors and investment, 161, 162, 202–16
      passim, 221. See also real estate
      investment
Iran, 45, 154, 157, 229, 241
Iraq, 13, 45, 46, 154, 160, 166, 180. See also
      Gulf War
Iron Guards, 7, 11, 99
iron industry, 214
al-Islambouly, Khaled, 172
Islamists, 177, 222, 239–43 passim;

Afghanistan, 154; in Free Officers,
      10; fundamentalists (salafis), 239; Iran
      relations, 229; Kamshish Affair, 67;
      Naguib relations, 29; Nasser relations,
      23, 36–7; repression, 75, 76, 177, 194,
      195; Sadat assassination role, 172;
      used as thugs, 195; U.S. relations, 154,
      156. See also anti-Islamism; Muslim
      Brotherhood
Ismail, Ahmed, 92, 107, 118–20, 123, 147
Ismail, Al-Nabawi, 167n, 168, 170, 172, 173
Ismail, Hafez, 92, 104, 123, 124, 129, 135, 137,
      155; death, 140
Ismailia, 8, 12
Israel, 45, 100, 102, 149–53 passim, 185–6,
      229–30; joint ventures, 214; Kissinger
      on, 124; LBJ relations, 73, 94; natural
      gas imports, 214, 230; in Suez War,
      47–50 passim; "war of movement"
      strategy, 189, 190. See also October
      War; Palestine War of 1948; Six-Day
      War; War of Attrition

January Revolt. See Egyptian Revolution
      of 2011
job layoffs. See layoffs
joblessness. See unemployment
Johnson, Lyndon B., 71, 73, 94, 95
Jordan, 46, 70, 78, 151, 221

Kafr Abdu, 12
Kafr al-Dawar, 26
Kamel, Ahmed, 104, 110
Kamel, Muhammad Ibrahim, 149–55 passim
Kamshish Affair, 66–9
Kato, Abd al-Mon'em, 230
al-Karim, Sa'd Abd, 89
Kearn, Frank, 20
Kefayah (Enough), 222, 241
Kendall, Donald, 123
Kennedy, John F., 73, 94
KGB, 21, 105
Khaled (Khaled Muhi al-Din), 10–11, 16, 17,
      25, 33, 34, 39, 41
King Farouk. See Farouk I
King Hussein. See Hussein I
Kissinger, Henry, 122–4 passim, 129–42
      passim, 149, 154, 162, 185; on Sadat,
      100–1, 155
Komer, Robert, 73, 185
Kraft, Joseph, 140
Khrushchev, Nikita, 46, 103

Kuwait, 166, 187, 205

Labib, Ismail, 86
Labib, Mahmoud, 37
Lakeland, William, 25
Lampson, Miles, 10
land allocation. *See* public land allocation
landowners, 8–9, 27–8, 61–8 passim, 159–60,
    216–17
land reform, 25, 61–2, 67
laws, 22, 56, 62, 160, 165, 185, 202–3;
    agricultural, 25, 62, 216–17;
    conscription, 17; inequality-
    perpetuating, 218; land allocation, 25,
    215; military, 17, 75, 91; nationalizing,
    63, 74; privatizing, 205. *See also*
    Emergency Law
layoffs, 218
Lebanon, 151
Leers, Johann von, 22
Liberation Rally, 22–3, 36, 38, 56
Liberty (ship). *See* USS *Liberty*
Libya, 101, 160, 166, 178, 221
Linebarger, Paul, 22
loans. *See* bank loans; debt
Lord Killearn. *See* Lampson, Miles
lower class, 9, 217, 221, 235
luxuries, 8, 202–3, 218

Mabaheth Amn al-Dawla. *See* State Security
    Investigations Sector (SSIS)
Machiavelli, Niccolò, 2, 22, 41
al-Magraby, Ahmed, 210, 215
Maher, Ahmed, 153
Mahmoud, Sedqi, 50, 86
Makhlouf, Mahmoud, 28
al-Malt, Gawdat, 214
Ma'moun, Saad, 133
Mann, Michael, 218
Mansour, Mohamed, 210
Al-Mansour Motor Group, 210
Maqlad, Shahenda, 67, 68
Marawan, Ashraf, 108, 169, 184–5
Mar'ie, Sayyid, 109
Marx, Karl, 111
al-Masri, Ahmed, 32
McNamara, Robert, 94
Meade, Steve, 25
media, 84, 223, 224, 228; Western, 171. *See
    also* Internet
Mehanna, Rashad, 29, 30–1
Meir, Golda, 121, 127, 137, 138

middle class, 188, 219; in army, 235; under
    Farouk, 9; under Mubarak, 200,
    201, 208; as Naguib supporters, 41;
    under Nasser, 61–6 passim, 159, 200;
    Revolution of 1952, 8, 9; rural, 61,
    62, 66, 200; under Sadat, 158, 159,
    164, 191, 203. *See also* upper middle
    class
Mildenstein, Leopold von, 22
Military Academy, 52
military aid, 131–2, 134, 149, 162, 169, 185,
    186, 188
military conscription. *See* conscription
military debt, 161–2, 188
military downsizing, 191–2
military-economic complex, 181–5
Military Intelligence Department (MID),
    19–20, 43, 44, 76, 93
military police: under Amer, 44, 55, 87; in
    cavalry mutiny, 34; under Nasser,
    17, 38, 39, 41, 89, 90, 93; planned
    use in anti-Sadat coup, 103; post-
    January Revolt, 230, 231, 235, 237,
    242; repression of Islamists, 75; Sadat
    assassination role, 173
military recruiting, 192
military spending, 183
milling industry, 162–3. *See also* wheat
millionaires, 161, 204
Miman, Yussi, 214
Ministry of National Guidance, 22
missiles, 95, 126, 127, 149, 154, 179–86
    passim
Mitchell, Timothy, 65, 207, 212
Mohammed Reza Pahlavi, Shah of Iran,
    157
money laundering, 217
Morocco, 154, 221
Morsi, Mohamed, 223, 242, 243
Mossad, 47, 94, 214, 229
Mubarak, Gamal, 188, 209–11, 223, 227
Mubarak, Muhammad Hosni, 135, 161, 167,
    174–93 passim, 219–23 passim, 232;
    accused of conspiracy, 145; chosen
    as vice president, 147, 175; economic
    policy, 201–16 passim; as enemy of
    Shazly, 136; January Revolt, 226, 228;
    NDP under, 201; police under, 193–9;
    rumored wealth, 213; sentenced to life
    in prison, 238
Muhi al-Din, Khaled. *See* Khaled (Khaled
    Muhi al-Din)

Muhi al-Din, Mahmoud, 210
Muhi al-Din, Zakaria. *See* Zakaria (Zakaria Muhi al-Din)
multinational corporations, 123, 167, 210, 216
Murtagi, Abd al-Muhsen, 80, 85, 86
Musa, Abd al-Halim, 68
Muslim Brotherhood, 8, 28–31 passim, 35–9 passim, 75, 222; Abu Ghazala relations, 177; election success, 198, 242–4 passim; January Revolt, 233; Osman relations, 167
mutinies, 11, 30–5, 178–9, 220, 235
Muwafi, Mamduh, 229

Naguib, Muhammad, 10–42 passim, 111, 120–1
Naguib, Sa'di, 82–3
al-Nahlawy, Abd al-Karim, 53
Nakba. *See* Palestine War of 1948
Nasr, Mahmoud, 183
Nasr, Salah, 16, 21, 31–8 passim, 44, 54, 58, 75; appointments and demotions, 52, 53; coup attempt role, 90; on Kamshish Affair, 67; meets with Nasser, 84–5; on Six-Day War, 79
Nassar, Osman, 87
Nassef, Al-Lethy, 89, 103, 139
al-Nasser, Gamal Abd, 10–13 passim, 111, 114, 200, 241; address to weavers, 17; Abd al-Mounem Amin on, 122; Amer relations, 21, 43, 48, 52–5 passim, 76–8 passim, 83–5 passim; arms deal with USSR, 45–6; assassination attempt, 40; ASU/VO creation, 56–61; consolidation of power, 35–42 passim; correspondence with JFK, 73, 94; death, 99, 100, 109, 125; demotion of Sabri, 109–10; on economic development, 164, 208; lack of ideology, 57; Mubarak on, 188; Muslim Brotherhood relations, 36–8, 40; mutinies role, 30–5; Naguib relations, 27–41 passim; Palestine War of 1948, 11–12, 120–1; Philosophy of the Revolution, 17; removal of Mubarak, 175; repression by, 26, 38–9; resignation and retraction, 83–5; Revolution of 1952, 10, 15–27 passim; Sadat relations, 16, 34, 99; Six-Day War, 69–87 passim; Soviet relations, 93, 95; Suez War, 46–50 passim; Syria

merger role, 53; U.S. relations, 23–8 passim, 73, 94
Nasser, Tahiya, 33, 37
National Accord Conference, 2011, 189
National Association for Change, 222, 241
National Charter of 1962, 56
National Defense Council (NDC), 91–2, 243
National Democratic Party (NDP), 165–8 passim, 200, 201, 218; "bourgeoisification," 209–11; election success, 198; January Revolt, 227; Policies Committee (PC), 198, 209, 210, 218, 227
National Guard, 17, 194
nationalism, Arab. *See* Arab nationalism
nationalization, 45, 63, 166, 215. *See also* renationalization
National Security Sector, 237
National Service Projects Organization (NSPO), 181
National Union (NU), 56, 65, 101
natural gas, 206, 214, 230
Nazif, Ahmed, 210, 215
Nazis, 10, 21, 99, 100
neoliberalism, 199–216 passim
nepotism, 120, 209, 215
nerve gas, 231
news media, 84
Nixon, Richard, 123, 131
Noah, Mukhtar, 177
Nordlinger, Eric, 61
North Korea, 180, 186
nuclear weapons, 149
al-Nur Party, 239, 240
Nusair, Muhammad, 216

Obama, Barack, 226
October War, 1973, 92, 113–49 passim, 190, 191
Office of Strategic Services (OSS), 20, 24
Office of the Commander-in-Chief for Political Guidance (OCC), 21–2, 92
oil industry, 160, 162, 163, 178, 204, 216; Iran, 157; LBJ connection, 73; as state income provider, 79n, 162, 204, 206; Suez Canal role, 46
Osman, Osman Ahmed, 104, 166–7, 201
Oweiss, Ibrahim, 164

Pahlavi, Mohammed Reza. *See* Mohammed Reza Pahlavi, Shah of Iran

Pakistan, 45, 76, 154
Palestine War of 1948, 11–12, 13, 21, 37, 45, 99, 119, 120–1
Palestinians, 151, 229
Palm Hills Company, 215
Panetta, Leon, 228
Paris Club, 205
parties. *See* political parties
paternalism, 232n
patronage networks, 22, 50, 51, 60, 62, 203
peace talks, 141, 142, 149–56 passim; rejected, 121
peasants, 9, 24, 25, 65, 200, 216–17; categorization, 66; as conscripts, 193–4; land distribution to, 62; "management" of, 58; used to people antidemocracy demonstrations, 38. *See also* Kamshish Affair
Pepsi-Cola, 123, 216
Peres, Shimon, 47
Perlmutter, Amos, 146
Persian Gulf War. *See* Gulf War
petroleum industry. *See* oil industry
Philosophy of the Revolution (Nasser), 17
phone taps, 52, 106, 122, 155
police, 39; corruption, 196, 217; extortion by, 195; January Revolt, 225, 227, 234, 237–8; under Mubarak, 193–9, 218; repression by, 96, 169, 177, 179, 227, 239; under Sadat, 108–9, 168–70 passim, 174; Tunisia, 221; violence by, 196–7, 222, 230, 235, 237; Zakaria purge of, 19. *See also* Interpol; military police; secret police
Police Day, 12, 222
police officers' strikes, 12, 38
Policies Committee (PC). *See* National Democratic Party (NDP): Policies Committee (PC)
political detention, 12, 18–19, 59, 75, 170, 197, 199, 223, 231
political parties, 239–42 passim; dissolved by law, 22. *See also* al-Wafd Party; Egypt Socialist Party; National Democratic Party (NDP)
political purges. *See* purges
population growth, 202
Port Said, 49, 132, 166, 174, 194, 231
Post, Charles, 94
pound. *See* Egyptian pound
poverty, 208, 213, 216, 217
Presidential Council, 53–4

President's Bureau of Information (PBI), 20, 43, 44, 52, 67, 93, 108
prisons and prisoners, 31, 34, 39, 40, 44, 59, 75, 91; January Revolt, 225; prisoners swaps, 229. *See also* detention camps; political detention
privatization, 205–7 passim, 213, 215–16
proletariat. *See* lower class; peasants
propaganda, 22, 58, 69, 231
protests. *See* demonstrations
public employment. *See* state employment
public land allocation, 206, 211, 214–16, 235
purges: of GID, 108; by Mubarak, 201; by Nasser, 16–17, 39, 83–4, 86, 91; by Sadat, 110, 117, 135, 136, 143–8 passim, 169; of SCAF, 237; by Zaki Badr, 194

al-Qadi, Anwar, 85
al-Qaeda, 154
al-Qamary, Essam, 174
Qassem, Salah, 145
Qatar, 184, 229
Quandt, William, 94, 152

Radwan, Abbas, 21, 34, 38, 44, 52, 53; plots to oust Nasser, 87, 90, 91
Ramadan War. *See* October War
Rashid, Rashid Ahmed, 210
Reagan, Ronald, 176, 185
real estate investment, 62–3, 161, 206
Reda, Abd al-Ra'ouf, 137
Ref', Fathallah, 31
Regency Council, 30
remittances, 204, 205
renationalization, 216
rent deregulation, 216–17
Republican Guard, 17, 18, 103, 106, 154–5
resorts, 206, 214, 218
Revolutionary Command Council (RCC), 15–18 passim, 22, 24, 25, 39; dissolution, 40; mutinies, 31–6 passim; Sadat role, 99
Revolution of 1919. *See* Egyptian Revolution of 1919
Revolution of 1952. *See* Egyptian Revolution of 1952
Revolution of 2011. *See* Egyptian Revolution of 2011
revolutions, Eastern European, 221
Ricciardone, Francis, 188
Richardson, Albert, 121
rich people. *See* millionaires; superrich

rigging of elections. *See* elections: tampering and rigging
riots, 1, 67, 84, 168, 169, 178, 193, 194
Riyad, Abd al-Mon'em, 77
Riyad, Mahmoud, 121
Riyad, Muhammad, 28, 29, 39
Rockefeller, David, 121, 140, 162, 163
Rogers, William, 121
Roosevelt, Franklin D., 24
Roosevelt, Kermit, 20–5 passim, 45, 51
Rostow, Eugene, 94, 95
Rostow, Walt, 73, 94
Russia, 9

Sabri, Aly, 24, 34, 52, 60, 66, 95; appointments, demotions, etc., 54, 59, 69, 74, 94, 109–10, 167; under Sadat, 100
al-Sadat, Anwar: bodyguards, 154; "corrective revolution" of, 99–111; economic policy, 138, 159–67 passim, 183, 200–1; fear of coups, 169; "friendship" with Kissinger, 100–1, 130–40 passim, 149, 162; Kamshish Affair role, 68; Mubarak on, 188; Mubarak promotion, 147, 175; Muslim Brotherhood relations, 37; Nasser relations, 16, 34, 99; October War, 113–49 passim; peace talks, 149–56 passim; psychological profile, 155–6; repression by, 169, 195; self-important uniform of, 171; shah of Iran as role model, 157; Soviet relations, 116, 122, 156; U.S. relations, 100–1, 105–6, 117–24 passim, 129, 142–3, 149–53 passim, 157–9, 164, 209; World War II, 11; Yemen War, 71
Sadeq, Muhammad, 76, 89, 116–19 passim, 122; appointments, 92, 114; purge, 147, 169; during Sadat's "corrective revolution," 103, 105, 107
Safari Club, 154
Sahfiq, Ahmed, 242
Said, Khaled, 222
Sakharov, Vladimir, 105
Salem, Hussein, 213–14
Salem, Mamduh, 106, 118, 160, 165, 167n, 168, 170
Salem, Salah, 10, 22, 35
Samy, Riyad, 21, 28, 29
al-Sanhouri, Abd al-Razeq, 26–7, 39, 85, 85
Saudi Arabia, 71, 118, 154, 166, 184

Save Egypt Movement, 118
Sawi, Sawi Ahmed, 38
SCAF. *See* Supreme Council of the Armed Forces (SCAF)
Schlesinger, Arthur, 26
Schlesinger, James, 130, 139
Schofield, Julian, 124
Scowcroft, Brent, 134
secret police, 18, 106, 108, 168, 196
Sediq, Youssef, 16
Sedqi, Aziz, 107
Selim, Muhammad, 51, 90, 170
sex scandals, 180
Shafiq, Ahmed, 226
Shahin, Mamduh, 231
Shah of Iran Mohammed Reza Pahlavi. *See* Mohammed Reza Pahlavi, Shah of Iran
Shakib, Ibrahim, 182
shantytowns, 208, 213
Sharaf, Samy, 31, 44, 52, 55, 57, 69, 95; counter-coup role, 89; as KGB asset, 105; plots to oust Sadat, 103–7 passim; under Sadat, 100, 109, 110; in VO, 59
al-Sharif, Safwat, 198, 214
Sharm al-Sheikh, 50, 214, 217, 228
Sharon, Ariel, 83, 114–15, 137, 190
Shawk, Ahmed, 39
al-Shazly, Kamal, 68, 168n, 201
al-Shazly, Sa'ad al-Din, 92, 116–20 passim, 147, 168; appointments, 114; October War, 125, 133–6; Osman on, 167; relations with Ahmed Ismail, 119, 120; on Sadat assassination, 173
Shlaim, Avi, 127
Shubra al-Khima, 38
Sinai, 114–17 passim, 132, 148–9, 189, 229–30; Camp David Accords division, 151; Six-Day War, 76–83
Sinai passes, 82, 114–17 passim, 125–32 passim, 143
Sirrs, Owen, 122–3
sit-ins, 226, 228, 237
Six-Day War, 76–86 passim, 91–6 passim; run-up, 69–76, 85
slums, 208
smuggling, 110, 179–80, 186
soccer, 231
Socialist Party of Egypt. *See* Egypt Socialist Party
Sourur, Fathy, 198, 210, 211, 214
Soviet Union, 73, 103–6 passim, 208;

Abu Ghazala sentiment, 178; in
Afghanistan, 154; Iran relations, 157;
loans, 161–2; model for Nasser, 57;
Nasser relations, 93, 95; October War
involvement, 136, 139–40; October
War opinions, 128; police force
compared to Egypt (in size), 194;
Sabri relations, 105, 109–10; Sadat
relations, 116, 122, 156; Six-Day War,
78, 88; Suez War, 49; U.S. relations,
122, 123, 131; as weapons-provider,
45–6, 80, 95, 149, 162, 169, 186, 188.
See also Egyptian-Soviet Friendship
Treaty; KGB
Spain, 214
Springborg, Robert, 173, 177, 194, 199
spying. See foreign espionage; surveillance
Stalin, Joseph, 46
standard of living, 205, 216
Stasi, 21
state employment, 63–5 passim, 158, 159,
200; corruption in, 203; police as
percentage of, 194; statistics, 203
State Security Investigations Sector (SSIS),
108, 111, 118, 168–70 passim, 191,
197–9, 235–7 passim; January Revolt,
230; land grabs, 217
steel industry, 214
Straits of Tiran, 77–8
strikes, 12, 26, 38–9, 193, 217, 228; banned by
Emergency Law, 199
student/worker uprisings, 1968. See worker/
student uprisings, 1968
Sub-Saharan Africa, 154. See also Congo
subsidies. See government subsidies
Sudan, 101, 221
Suez, 145, 214, 223, 236
Suez Canal, 46–7, 79n, 166, 204, 206, 229;
October War, 114, 117, 126
Suez Canal Zone, 9, 12
Suez War, 40–1, 45–51, 78, 121, 188
Suleiman, Ibrahim, 215
Suleiman, Omar, 226
Suleiman, Samer, 218
Suleiman, Sedqi, 75
superrich, 184, 188, 200, 208, 214, 219
Supreme Council of the Armed Forces
(SCAF), 92, 114–18 passim, 138;
January Revolt, 227–43 passim
surveillance, 18–20 passim, 44, 58–60 passim,
136, 155, 197–9 passim; of armed
forces, 233. See also phone taps; spying

al-Suwarqa, Mahmoud, 83
Syria, 13, 70, 95, 101, 151, 187, 221, 229;
October War, 130, 132; in UAR, 53

al-Tahawi, Ibrahim, 23, 38
Tahrir Square, Cairo, 223–8 passim, 237,
239
Tal'at, Hassan, 68, 89
Al-Tali'ah, 59
Tantawy, Hussein, 136, 177, 181, 186, 188,
232
tapes. See audiotapes
taxation, 206, 212, 213, 218
tax exemptions, 63, 203
tear gas, 170, 223, 224, 231, 237
telephones. See cell phones; phone taps
thugs and thuggery, 195–8 passim, 227, 230,
231
Tilly, Charles, 221
torture, 44, 75, 196, 197, 231
tourism, 79n, 210, 214, 215
trade balance. See balance of trade
treasury bills, 211
Tripartite Attack on Egypt, 1956. See Suez
War
Trone, Eugene, 122
al-Tuhami, Hassan, 20, 33, 34, 45, 52, 108
Tunisia, 221–2, 235
Turkey, 41, 45, 244
Twetten, Thomas, 105

Ultras, 231
unemployment, 204, 213, 216, 217, 219
Unilever, 210
United Arab Emirates (UAE), 184, 185
United Arab Republic (UAR), 53, 101
United Kingdom. See Great Britain
United Nations, 136–7
United Nations Emergency Forces
(UNEF), 76, 77, 143
United States: Abu Ghazala relations, 177–8;
aid to Egypt, 45, 73, 163, 167, 184–91
passim, 204, 209; Amer coup attempt
thumbs-down, 87; as creditor, 163,
188, 205, 206; Egyptian Revolution
of 1952, 15; exports, 73, 161, 162;
Israel relations, 130–4 passim, 185,
186–7; January Revolt, 226, 229; joint
ventures, 213; Mubarak relations,
5, 176, 205; Nasser relations, 23–8
passim, 39, 45, 46, 50–1, 94–5; Osman

relations, 167; propaganda role, 22;
Sadat relations, 100–1, 105–6, 117–24
passim, 129, 142–3, 149–53 passim,
157–9, 164, 209; Six-Day War role,
70–3 passim, 77, 93–5; source of
surveillance technology, tear gas,
rubber bullets, etc., 20, 170, 237;
Soviet relations, 122, 123, 131; Suez
War, 49. *See also* CIA
universities and colleges, 39–40, 63–4, 191,
195
upper middle class, 63, 182
Uprising of January 2011. *See* Egyptian
Revolution of 2011
uprisings of 1968. *See* worker/student
uprisings, 1968
USAID, 163, 167, 212
U.S. Army, 190
USS Liberty, 95
USSR. *See* Soviet Union

Vanguard Organization (VO), 58–61, 105,
109, 110, 167
Vietnam War, 72, 73, 154
Vinogradov, Vladimir, 128

al-Wafd Party, 7, 10, 13, 29, 36
Wali, Youssef, 201
Walters, Barbara, 171
war, economic effect. *See* economic affect
of war
War of Attrition, 93–5 passim, 188

"war of movement" strategy, 189–90
wars. *See* Gulf War; October War, 1973;
Palestine War of 1948; Six-Day War;
Suez War; War of Attrition; Yemen
War
water, 216
weapons industry, 184
weapons trade, 45–6, 145, 169, 180, 185,
213–14. *See also* military aid
We Are All Khaled Said (Facebook page),
222–3
wheat, 73, 161, 202
White Wings, 213
worker/student uprisings, 1968, 96–7
World War II, 10–11

Yemen, 178, 221
Yemen War, 71–2, 73, 94, 188
Yom Kippur War. *See* October War, 1973

Zakaria (Zakaria Muhi al-Din), 16,
19–21 passim, 31, 39, 44, 63, 75;
appointments, 53, 74, 94; counter-
coup role, 89–90; president briefly,
84, 121; removal under Sadat, 110;
Six-Day War, 78, 95; Suez War, 49;
supervision of civilian security
agencies, 52
Zaki, Taha, 105
Zaki, Tahsin, 88
al-Zayat, Abd al-Salam, 109
al-Zumur, Abbud, 172, 173, 174